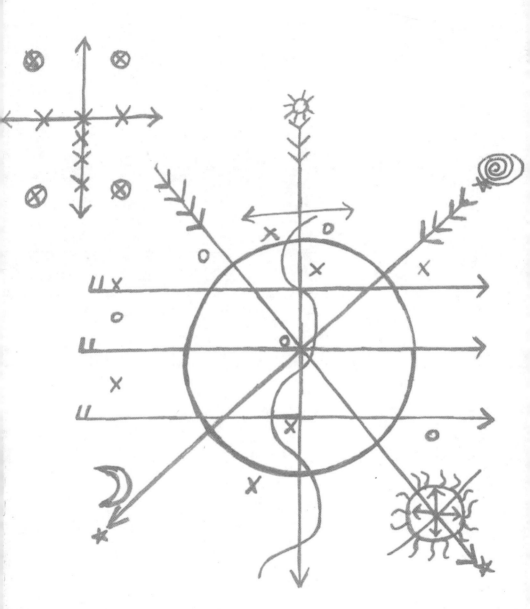

Excited Delirium

Aisha M. Beliso-De Jesús

Excited Delirium

RACE, POLICE VIOLENCE, AND THE INVENTION OF A DISEASE

Duke University Press   Durham and London   2024

publication supported by a grant from
The Community Foundation for Greater New Haven
as part of the **Urban Haven Project**

Printed in the United States of America on acid-free paper ∞
Project Editor: Ihsan Taylor | Designed by Aimee C. Harrison
Typeset in Garamond Premier Pro, Helvetica Neue, and Canela
by Westchester Publishing Services

Library of Congress Cataloging-in-Publication Data
Names: Beliso-De Jesús, Aisha M., author.
Title: Excited delirium : race, police violence, and the invention of a
disease / Aisha M. Beliso-De Jesús.
Description: Durham : Duke University Press, 2024. | Includes
bibliographical references and index.
Identifiers: LCCN 2023042653 (print)
LCCN 2023042654 (ebook)
ISBN 9781478030553 (paperback)
ISBN 9781478026327 (hardcover)
ISBN 9781478059561 (ebook)
Subjects: LCSH: Wetli, Charles V. | Beliso-De Jesús, Aisha M. | Excited
delirium syndrome—United States. | Discrimination in law enforcement—
United States. | Police brutality—United States. | Black people—Latin
America—Religion. | Hispanic Americans—Religion. | Afro-Caribbean cults. |
BISAC: SOCIAL SCIENCE / Anthropology / Cultural & Social | SOCIAL
SCIENCE / Ethnic Studies / American / Hispanic American Studies
Classification: LCC HV8141 .B38 2024 (print) | LCC HV8141 (ebook) |
DDC 363.20973—dc23/eng/20240403
LC record available at https://lccn.loc.gov/2023042653
LC ebook record available at https://lccn.loc.gov/2023042654

Cover photograph by Carlos Javier Ortiz. Courtesy of the photographer.

"Lucero Mundo" and "Brazo Fuerte" symbols courtesy of the author.

For Sito and Jeremy Ellis,
and for all those inaccurately labeled
as excited delirium

Contents

Author's Note
In Warning . . .

This book tells troubling stories of death, rape, murder, and racial violence. I am aware that the constant circulation of Black people's deaths tends to desensitize some and tantalize others. Although as scholars it is somewhat impossible to completely avoid complicity in racialized suffering, I deliberately try not to sensationalize these accounts. Yet, to examine the full scope of this problem in our society, I cannot ignore the pertinent details that have led to the emergence of the death classification I discuss in these pages. I warn you to never lose sight of the goal, which is always a collective undoing. In telling these difficult stories, I have chosen not to reproduce photographs of people's dead bodies. Afro-Latiné teachings tell us that photographs conjure their own energies. I take up the call of social justice historians who, while acknowledging that most criminal narratives are written from law enforcement perspectives, utilize their work to uncover hidden injustices. I offer this book as a prayer to undo the pandemic of police violence and death that impacts us all.

Introduction: Haunted

Our nation—on the cusp of becoming a collection
of all the words we fear; all the little truths we whitewashed and blacked out are coming back to haunt us.
—Khalisa Rae, "Epilogue for Banned Books"
(excerpt from *Ghost in a Black Girl's Throat*, 2021)

EVERYONE HAD WRITTEN JEREMY ELLIS OFF. Maybe that is why he began to haunt me.

It started about two weeks before I was scheduled to interview Jeremy's daughter, Jade Ellis. I could not sleep at night.[1] Intrusive thoughts seemed to take over my research and writing. I had strange dreams of people dying; the police were involved. I wondered if I was being triggered by studying police violence. I grew up in the 1980s and 1990s in San Francisco's Mission District. At that time, the Latiné community I came from in "the Mission" lived in fear, stemming both from street gang beefs that made it difficult to walk from one block to the next and from the police, who were known for their abuse and violence. Coming from a family of Puerto Ricans who practiced Afro-Caribbean religions made my childhood especially anxious: I had the additional concern that we would be seen as an evil "cult." I learned the hard way that the police were also a real danger.

One summer evening in 1994, I walked out of my apartment on Twenty-Fourth Street to see that René, my partner at the time, was being arrested. The cops had hopped out of their car to harass him and his friends for being young Brown men, as they regularly did. I was a teenager, nine months pregnant with my first child, and I made the mistake of asking the officer why he was arresting my partner. The officer came around the car, told me to "shut up," and with no concern for my swollen belly, roughly put my hands behind my back and handcuffed me. He then shoved my shoulders down painfully and forced me to sit on the sidewalk. I was humiliated and scared. *What would happen to our unborn child if René and I were both arrested?*

A few weeks later, I would give birth to a beautiful, brown-skinned boy, Neto. Like most mothers of Black and Brown children, and especially of Black and Brown boys, I have worried about him every day since.

That feeling of powerlessness never leaves you. It does not matter that I was not arrested and that I went on to complete a doctorate in anthropology and to become a tenured professor at two Ivy League schools. The force of racialized state power lingers.[2] It creates a nervous tension that builds up in Black and Brown people's guts when we encounter police, who are always able to wield violence with impunity.

Twenty years later, when I began to conduct research on the policing and criminalization of Afro-Caribbean religions in the United States, I was aware that research can impact the scholar. People do not usually speak much about the toll that the research of traumatic phenomena can take on the mental health of researchers themselves. I chalked up the difficulty I was having in writing this book to the subject itself—it certainly evoked strong emotions in me. Still, I could not shake the feeling that there was more to this research that was haunting me.[3]

The haunting started when I was researching the policing of Afro-Latiné religions and came across a little-known cause-of-death classification called *excited delirium syndrome*. Medical examiners have used the syndrome when assigning cause to the unexplained deaths of mostly Black and Latiné men killed during police interactions. To me, it sounded made-up. The term itself was troubling, but as I looked into the scientific explanations of the syndrome, it seemed even more problematic. I found that excited delirium syndrome was a controversial diagnosis for people who are said to have exhibited "superhuman strength"; are considered impervious to pain; are said to have become aggressive, excited, sweaty, and agitated; and who then suddenly "up and died," as police officers have been known to say. In this context, police officers are seen as innocent bystanders who just happen to witness the unexplainable deaths of so-called criminals, who are subsequently written off as having caused their own deaths. However, almost all these deaths occur during police interactions, and they almost always involve police use of force, such as hog-tying people, applying carotid choke holds, kneeling on people's bodies, stunning them with Tasers, injecting them with sedatives, or imposing other forms of forceful restraint.

After my discovery of excited delirium syndrome, I could not get it out of my head. It was as if I saw excited delirium syndrome everywhere. For example, in 2020, my eldest son, Neto, now a grown man with a family of his own, had purchased his first home. His family chose Antioch, California, whose rolling hills, warmer climate, and suburban houses promised relief from the everyday violence of city living. And he was not alone. Thousands of Black and Brown families were relocating to Antioch from San Francisco and Oakland. That same year in Antioch, on December 23, just two days before Christmas, a brown-skinned, thirty-year old Filipino man named Angelo Quinto was killed during a police interaction.

I found Quinto's story—one of the many stories of excited delirium that kept appearing to me as if by coincidence—through a newspaper archive I had accessed for my research. Medical examiners claimed Quinto's death was caused by "excited delirium syndrome." Multiple officers at the scene had knelt on Quinto's body until he ceased to struggle. When paramedics arrived, Quinto was purple and unresponsive, and he had blood coming out of his nose and mouth.[4] Just seven months earlier, the world was rocked by videos of the death of George Perry Floyd, who, like Quinto, had also been knelt on by multiple officers before dying in police custody. Amid worldwide protests and demands for police accountability during the peak of the COVID-19 pandemic, the justice system took a serious look into Floyd's death, leading to the officers' being charged. A little-known fact is that police and attorneys described both Quinto and Floyd as having allegedly exhibited excited delirium syndrome.

Although in many other cases, attributing the deaths of people in police custody to excited delirium syndrome has worked to exonerate police from culpability, the video of police treatment of George Floyd would not allow his death to be so easily dismissed. The world saw Officer Derek Chauvin kneeling on Floyd's neck for more than nine minutes. Even though Chauvin's defense team relied on excited delirium syndrome at the trial, the diagnosis seemed to evaporate from the narrative of Floyd's death. A year later, on April 20, 2021, Chauvin was found guilty on all three counts: unintentional second-degree murder, third-degree murder, and second-degree manslaughter.

I became obsessed with excited delirium syndrome. As I looked into death after death, the syndrome took over the early months of my fellowship at Stanford University, where I was on leave from teaching while writing this book. I did not realize then that it was possible I was being haunted.[5] What felt like an unexpected rabbit hole in my research had become so much more.

* * *

With excited delirium syndrome in my head, I made my way from Stanford University to the East Bay on September 17, 2021, to my son Neto's house in Antioch, where I planned to interview, at his suggestion, Jade Ellis. Neto told me that Jade had an important story.

In my research for this book, I was exploring how practitioners in the United States have been drawing on the ancestral tools of Afro-Latiné religions such as Santeria and Palo Monte to combat police violence. I wanted to see how they used *spiritual activism* to heal generational trauma and transform the world.[6] My son Neto and his partner, Naomi, are at the forefront of this work. They have created an *ile* (house-temple) in the Bay Area made up of a collective of Black and Brown queer, trans, undocumented, and formerly incarcerated young people, educators, and artists who are actively changing their world through Afro-Latiné ritual teachings. Jade, an Afro-Latiné trans woman from Los Angeles, practices spirituality as a form of activism against police violence.

A poet, liberation artist, and advocate, Jade was about to undergo initiation to become a priestess of Afro-Cuban Santeria. This religious practice, passed down from enslaved African peoples in Cuba, has continued to serve as a healing strategy for generations of Black Latiné people in the Americas.[7] My family are longtime practitioners of Santeria.

Once I arrived at my son's house, Jade's soft six-foot-tall presence hovered over my own loud five-foot-one body. Jade was dressed all in white and wore a head wrap; her sparkling eyes, caramel-colored skin, and luxurious eyelashes outlined a deep knowing. Jade's gaze revealed a person who has lived through too much pain, too much trauma, but who refuses to succumb. Her quiet assuredness made her seem fearless. I immediately admired her.

Our first interview was in my granddaughter Nayari's nursery. White-and-blue polka-dot wallpaper framed a window that looked out on the cul-de-sac of the suburban neighborhood. A wicker giraffe bookshelf with children's books accompanied a world map featuring cartoon animals. The zebra-striped blanket in the crib rounded out the gender-neutral animal theme I had helped create. We sat at a white desk, slightly facing each other. My laptop was open, and I recorded our conversation and took some notes. I was upbeat, happy to finally start the interview. Jade is a busy person, and she was in the Bay Area that weekend to undergo some of her ceremonies. I was so grateful that she had stayed an extra day so we could speak.

"I walk into a room, and I've already fucked up so many people's perceptions of what the world is, you know," Jade tells me of the violent reactions encountered by Black trans women. Jade's mother, Carmen, was born in Los Angeles to Mexican and Salvadoran parents, and Jade's father, Jeremy, was African American and raised among Mexican and Central American cholos. Jeremy spoke Spanish, ate spicy foods, and dated Latina women; he was what scholars might consider latinized as a result of the commingling of urban life in a place where Latiné tastes, customs, and cultures thrived.[8]

Jade, a Black American Latina who practices Afro-Cuban religions, identifies as Afro-Latiné, one of the myriad terms used to acknowledge the "crossings" of Blackness and Latinidad.[9] Such "ethnoracial intimacies" allow for creative and expressive blends that include "children of African American and Latino mixed heritage," like Jade, as well as Black Latiné or Afro-Latiné communities "with Afro-diasporic ancestry outside the U.S. national boundaries."[10]

I knew that Jade had become an activist against police violence because of her father's death, but I did not know much else about her when we sat down for our first interview. Within the first five minutes, Jade told me that her father, Jeremy Ellis, had been killed on June 11, 2011, during a police interaction. Jade was thirteen when she wrote her first poem, where she first put the pain of her father's death to paper, which she described as baring "her soul" on his grave and becoming her father's "shadow."

Even ten years later, Jade was still upset with her father about the timing of his death. To her, it seemed so selfish of him. Jade and her sister, Eva, had not seen Jeremy for a while, and they had made plans to celebrate Father's Day together. "Because he was either locked up or on drugs or making another family and all that shit, you know. And then literally he died the day before Father's Day. And, after a handful of years of not seeing each other, we were going to see each other, and then he died the day before Father's Day. So, I went craaaaazy." She let herself smile.

Jade felt like kin to me—someone who pushes aside pain with humor to survive. She had a knack for placing her trauma into structural perspectives, and as a result, Jade has developed a profound outlook on life in her twenty-three years. Affirming my perception of her, Jade told me that she had "always been the parent" in her household. After her father's death, she had to mobilize; at thirteen, she became an activist against police violence.

Jade told me how her father's spirit had attached to her after he died. She "kind of became him for a while." Struggling with gender and people telling her how to be, she needed an out. "And then my dad died, and I was like, 'Oh well, I know how to do that.' So, I went through this whole spiral where I was like, I have to basically become my dad to preserve him. And so, I started dressing like him." Laughing, she told me, "Yeah. I went crazy for years and started doing him."

The circumstances surrounding Jeremy Ellis's death perplexed his friends and family. With an ironic chuckle, Jade tells me, "It's on brand for him." Jade did not really know what actually happened to her dad. She knew that he was killed during a police car chase. She knew that police considered Jeremy to be responsible for his own death. "It was unexplainable," she told me. "He just up and died."

A chill ran through my body when Jade said those words. It felt as though the temperature in the room had suddenly dropped. I stopped typing on my laptop and looked up at her, stunned.

"What did you just say?" I asked, thinking I might have misheard her.

"What?" she asked me, confused at my reaction. "That he up and died?"

Hesitantly, I asked her, "Do you know if the cause of death was excited delirium syndrome?"

She slowly nodded her head up and down. "How did you know?"

I could not believe that my strange obsession with excited delirium deaths might somehow connect to Jade Ellis's father. Nervously, I responded, "I think your dad's spirit might be trying to contact me."

Then Jade surprised me. She smiled, showing a slight dimple, and said, "He's so annoying."

I was freaked out.

* * *

When I started to write this book in September 2021, I had been researching the policing and criminalization of Afro-Latiné religions in the United States for nine years. Black Latiné people in the United States have cultivated the religious interconnections of Afro-Latinidad since at least the 1800s.[11] Afro-Cubans, Afro–Puerto Ricans, Afro-Dominicans, and other Black Latiné communities in the 1920s gathered in collective solidarity struggles and religious association across the country.[12] In the United States, such ethnic and racial "crossings" are "color lines" that emerge where Blackness, Brownness, dark-Brownness, and other racial formations are brought in relation to one another through various forms of White supremacy.[13] Afro-Latiné religions historically arose from survival mobilizations of enslaved Africans; today, these religions are treasured tools that continue to be wielded in the liberatory strategies of differently racialized peoples.

Practices such as Afro-Cuban Santeria and Palo Monte, Haitian Vodou, Espiritismo Africano, and other Afro-Latiné inspirations have a history of being repressed, from the island countries from which they emerged to the transnational locations where they now live. In New York, Florida, California, and across the United States, a diverse group of people from different countries come together—an array of color lines, shades of Brown and Black Latiné people forming new communities. Still, we Black, Brown, dark Brown, and light Brown peoples find ourselves under siege, our religions depicted as "un-American," "evil," "dangerous," and "criminal."[14] We encounter the *layering* of White hegemonies, forcing us to contend with both the Anglo White supremacy in the United States and also the Latino White supremacy that attempts to conflate Latinidad with Whiteness.[15] Because Afro-Latiné religions challenge the Whiteness of Latinidad, they are met with anti-Blackness and anti-Africanness in addition to anti-immigrant xenophobia.

I began conducting ethnographic research with practitioners of Afro-Latiné religions and police officers across the country on the policing and criminalizing of Afro-Latiné religions in 2013. Now I had a fellowship at Stanford's Center for Advanced Studies in the Behavioral Sciences (CASBS) to be able to write a book on this topic. I was thankful to be getting started. But then Jeremy Ellis found me, and excited delirium syndrome haunted me.

I picked up my laptop and waved it in front of Jade, telling her, "You're not going to believe this, but I have been researching excited delirium syndrome for the past few weeks!"—as if shaking my laptop in the air would somehow demonstrate to her that this could not be a simple coincidence. But I did not need to convince Jade that her dad was haunting me. With the assuredness of her spiritual understanding, Jade accepted Jeremy's presence as truth. She explained to me that she had come to Santeria to heal her family's generational traumas.

I knew from my own understanding, gleaned from growing up within and studying Afro-Cuban religions that spirits communicate in a number of ways. Practitioners elevate and uplift deceased family members' spirits and transform the power and potentiality of what I have previously termed their *copresences*.[16]

These copresences account for the embodied ways that Afro-Latiné religious practitioners navigate the world, interacting with a range of spiritual presences that include deceased family members as well as the Yorùbá orisha or Congo spirits, among other entities. I thought out loud, suggesting to Jade that she had probably activated Jeremy's spirit. She agreed. Jade told me that her poetry was a form of spiritual recitation—that she had started creating poetry because of her dad's death. It was her form of spiritual activism.

"I started organizing, and I started getting politically educated, and I needed something that I [could] reference . . . , kind of like sort out all my shit," she told me. "That's how I started writing poetry. My first poem was about my dad dying when I was super young."

Jade's poetic spiritual activism to uplift and heal generational trauma echoes my own path from Latina teen mom to full professor. Something in my story, in my background, also has to do with this journey. Jade related to me how she used spiritual activism to relieve the pain and anger of the trauma she had experienced.

"I also knew that I needed something constructive," she told me. "So that was most of my fight. Because I also think when you first get politically educated, you're so angry about so much shit—you know what I mean—because it's like, you're being dropped from the matrix for the first time. So, it's like grief from dad and grieving. Like, everything shattering."

For me, the interview with Jade shattered everything. Two fundamental aspects of my self—the academic and the spiritual—suddenly collided. The experience opened something up in me. Jade made me realize that I had been in a struggle with myself. I had not allowed myself to see the larger impact of my work and who I was as someone born and raised in Afro-Latiné religions. Although I had dedicated my life to trying to heal generational trauma and combat structural oppression, I had tried to keep my spiritual life separate from my academic life.

While writing this book, I started keeping a journal. I hoped it would help me work through my struggle to maintain a separation between the academic and spiritual parts of myself. Instead, the journal helped me grapple with the troubling reality that medical examiners had produced an industry that effectively whitewashed police violence. This research led me to discover that the criminalization of Afro-Latiné religions and the policing of Black Americans are central to the emergence of excited delirium syndrome. These stories coincided with that of a medical examiner from Miami, Charles Victor

Wetli, the man who coined the term *excited delirium syndrome* and who also, strangely, was a so-called expert on Afro-Caribbean "cults."

Excited delirium syndrome was created to cover up the role of police violence in deaths from Tasers, choke holds, beatings, shootings, and other abuse. This fake syndrome produced a circular industry of expertise—a lucrative arrangement wherein police officers, paramedics, medical examiners, lawyers, and researchers not only hide the deaths of Black and Brown people at the hands of police but also become "experts" who are paid to medicalize this violence. Companies such as Taser International contract with this industry of experts to hide the lethality of the Taser electroshock weapon with stories of excited delirium syndrome.

I decided to share my journal entries as ethnographic data to reveal my process of discovering excited delirium syndrome. The journals also illustrate how my Afro-Latiné cultural traditions are part of my own healing process— of being a scholar traumatized by what my research uncovered, of needing to find a way through this material. All scholars are rooted in their cultural practices and social structures, and yet we are trained not to disclose the ways we can be deeply impacted by our work. As I found my way through these troubling accounts, the spirits made themselves available. This could have been because I am a social scientist also accompanied by spirits, orisha, and other copresences who have provided me with a unique attunement to the world, one that allows me to perceive the guidance of these energies. However, Afro-Latiné traditions teach me that these copresences are persistently there, engaging with people, even when individuals are unwilling to recognize their existence. The copresences have worked to make this book happen. It was Jeremy Ellis's spirit who first showed me that there was more to the story of excited delirium.

Monday, September 20, 2021
Emerald Hills, California

I keep waking up anxious. I was dreaming about excited delirium syndrome deaths again. Nameless people keep appearing to me. Even though society blames them, they're telling me that their deaths were not their fault. Jeremy Ellis showed up again. This time he was standing off at a distance. His caramel-skinned bald head and face were covered with tattoos. He stared at me with his chin held high. He was a Los Angeles cholo through and through. Jeremy wore a black-and-gray striped Charlie Brown shirt, his hands stuffed in the pockets of stiff gray Dickies pants. Jeremy looked at me with sad eyes—eyes that reminded me of Jade's.

I could sense that Jade's father, Jeremy, was urging me on, giving me clues. His clues reminded me of my own father, who's always telling me to write dreams down. That's one of the reasons I started keeping this journal.

But Jeremy is not just reaching out to me in my dreams. When I'm awake, I sense him trying to communicate. Today, I had images and thoughts in my head that I knew were not my own. After waking up from the fitful dream, I had the name "Charles Wetli" stuck in my head. It was like a skipping record.

A few days ago, I read that the Miami-Dade County medical examiner, a man named Charles Wetli, had coined the term excited delirium syndrome *in the 1980s. This morning, I kept thinking about how Wetli had "discovered" excited delirium syndrome. What led him to the conclusions that Black people had a "syndrome" that he claimed caused them to spontaneously die from small amounts of cocaine use? Why did these deaths seem to occur only with police involvement? Who was this man?*

So, today, I conducted a search in the newspaper archives to see whether anything turned up related to Charles Wetli and Santeria. I do not know why I thought to do this search. It seemed silly at first, but the thought was so persistent. I did not think anything important would turn up, but I decided to do the search to appease the urge. I had assumed that a medical examiner in Miami-Dade County would have run into Afro-Cuban religions at least a few times over the course of his career, so I figured I might find something.

I stared at my computer screen, overwhelmed by the results.

Nightmares

THE ARCHIVE HAD TURNED UP several images from different early 1980s newspapers. A young Charles Wetli, with a comb-over and dressed in a light suit and black tie, sits at a table surrounded by human skulls, "voodoo dolls," and other items pertaining to Afro-Caribbean religions. Below the image, the words "Voodoo Collection" appear in boldface type. Wetli's thin face, pointed nose, and vacant eyes stare at me. His mouth is slightly ajar, and the stark white tablecloth and contrasting lighting made the scene appear macabre. I can tell that the photographer purposefully used eerie lighting to give the image a sinister quality. As a result, Wetli's profile forms a dark shadow. The image is hair-raising, a murky figure appears like a ghost sitting beside Wetli.

The accompanying article described Dade County's young medical examiner as posing with his "ghoulish collection of Santerían [sic] memorabilia in the Miami, Fla. office." The article named the items on display: "two human skulls, one coated with chicken blood and feathers and candle wax," among other religious artifacts. I could not believe what I was seeing. Why did Dr. Charles Wetli, a forensic pathologist, have a collection of Santeria memorabilia? I thought about what these sacred items meant in our spiritual tradition. They are considered activated with specific spirits.[1] For practitioners, these religious items are extensions of themselves. They create forces of protection that stabilize one's health and well-being. These items not only contain the energies of the copresences themselves, but their spirits can also wreak havoc on unsuspecting people who encounter and mishandle these items.

The hair stood up on my arms. A few more online searches yielded more images of Wetli with his grisly collection of sacred religious items that he had turned into a Halloween sideshow. I learned that Wetli was not just a hobbyist collector of Afro-Cuban artifacts; he had also fashioned himself as a makeshift scholar. He had written several articles on Afro-Caribbean religions, specifically Afro-Cuban Santeria and Palo Monte.

To my astonishment, one of Wetli's coauthors was named Raphael Martinez. I recognized the name immediately. Eight years earlier, when I had first begun my research on the policing of Afro-Cuban religions, I had interviewed a man named Dr. Rafael Martinez, who had conducted Santeria trainings for Florida law enforcement. At first I assumed that Wetli's coauthor was the same person I had interviewed so many years ago. But then I thought, perhaps it wasn't. Rafael Martinez is a relatively common Cuban name. Besides, the person I interviewed spelled his first name differently—with an *f* instead of a *ph*.

Nevertheless, I started reading Wetli and Martinez's articles on Afro-Cuban "cults" and found that they had also coauthored several law enforcement case studies and reports. These reports criminalized Afro-Cuban refugees who had arrived in the 1980s during the Mariel boatlift. The reports framed Santeria and Palo Monte as inherently evil and dangerous, leading to criminal behavior. Why would Martinez help write reports like these? When I met him, he had been an advocate for better understanding between law enforcement and Santeria practitioners. I was perplexed by the thought that he might have participated in this troubling research.

Even though it had been many years since I had last spoken with Martinez, I sent him an email. He quickly responded. As I remembered him, he was welcoming and generous. I was eager to find out whether he was the same person who had cowritten those articles with Charles Wetli. We were well into the COVID-19 global pandemic, so we met over Zoom. My stomach was in knots before our interview.

"I came upon an article that I think that you might have cowritten," I blurted out after a short hello and update. "It's with a man named Charles Wetli." I felt so awkward.

Martinez nodded his head, confirming. "No, that was me."

I could not believe it! How was this possible? Had Jeremy Ellis led me to this? It was too coincidental. Why had Rafael's name been anglicized?

"I feel bad," Martinez told me, referring to how Santeria and Palo Monte were demonized as a result of this early work. "I tried to bring some sanity in." It was "during Mariel, you know," he told me, referring to the political turmoil of the time, the 1980 humanitarian crisis that brought more than 125,000 Cubans to the United States. Indeed, Mariel had been a social and political nightmare, especially for Afro-Cubans, who paid the highest price.

* * *

During the summer of 1980, Wetli had been in his job for only a couple of years as second-in-command of the Dade County coroner's office when unusual items started popping up around Miami: candles, coins, and fruits had been left at a riverbed or at the beach; cauldrons with iron tools and machetes had been discarded at the train tracks; dead chicken remains or torn clothing was found in wooded areas. Then, among these discarded items, rare human remains appeared—such as a skull that would have been an integral part of the Afro-Cuban Palo Monte religious spirit home (*nganga*)—and Wetli was brought in to identify whether any foul play had been involved. He homed in on the recent Cuban migrants who were arriving in Miami as the result of the international crisis known as the Mariel boatlift.

The crisis began on April 1, 1980. Animosity between the United States and Cuba, caught up in a Cold War feud, was at a peak amid the Cuban economic downturn that had been fueled by a US embargo. That day in April, six Cubans rammed their bus into the fence of the Peruvian Embassy in Havana, requesting asylum.[2] Cuban officers fired on the bus, trying to halt the fleeing dissidents, and a ricocheting bullet killed a Cuban police officer, Pedro Ortiz Cabrera. When the Cuban government asked for the Cubans from the bus, now sheltering at the Peruvian Embassy, to be handed over so they could be tried for the death of Officer Cabrera, embassy officials refused and instead granted them asylum.[3] Cuban president Fidel Castro then withdrew Cuba's police force from around the Peruvian Embassy, and more than ten thousand Cubans crowded the embassy, seeking asylum.

On May 1, President Castro announced that for the next six months, any Cuban who wanted to leave the island could do so if they secured transportation. He opened the Port of Mariel, the nearest location to the United States. Castro also ordered the release of a small number of people who had been hospitalized or incarcerated to be sent to Mariel and taken off the island. Only a few days later, on May 5, 1980, US president Jimmy Carter gave a speech stating that the United States would welcome Marielitos, as they became known, "with open arms."[4]

Cuban Americans (though, mostly White Cubans) flocked to Key West. Luxury yachts and fishing and shrimp boats were hurriedly mobilized to cross the ninety-mile stretch of water between the peninsula of Florida and the island of Cuba, with the goal of rescuing relatives. A 1,700-boat flotilla packed full of people created a surreal international scene. Amid water-skiing tourists during the height of vacation season in the Florida Keys were throngs of boats loaded with newly arriving Cubans. Hundreds of Cuban Americans looking for family members stood on the docks screaming out names of loved ones. Some boats sank. There were at least twenty-five deaths. Thousands of people were forced to stay in cramped temporary camps in Key West. By the end of the summer, more than 125,000 Cuban refugees had arrived in the United States from Cuba's Mariel Harbor.

The "Mariel boatlift" landed right on Charles Wetli's doorstep. Before becoming the Miami-Dade County medical examiner, Wetli had already accrued some experience with international crises. He had recently returned to the United States after having been stationed in Japan, where he had served as chief of pathology for the US Army Medical Laboratory Pacific.[5] Five years before that, in 1975, he had been sent on a special mission to South Korea: seven South Korean soldiers had been found dead in a tunnel, and South Korea accused North Korea of having killed them. For two days, Wetli had worked with little sleep to make the determination that the soldiers had been poisoned by carbon monoxide emanating from the cement used to build the tunnel. One reporter, Katharine Q. Seelye, claimed that Wetli's findings may have averted an international incident.[6] His teeth sharpened with this militarized medical training, Wetli would now take on the diverse immigrant community in Miami. As a medical examiner he focused on the dead— particularly on the remnants of bodies.

* * *

In August 2013, I walked through the concrete columns of the breezeway at the Carlos Albizu University in Doral, a suburb of Miami. I was conducting research on the policing of Afro-Latiné religions, and it was my first meeting with Dr. Rafael Martinez. The concrete-slabbed roof of the flat one-story building had an imposing 1970s rectangular modern design. Even though it was surrounded by swaying palms and decorated with a few pink accent walls, the Soviet-style building gave the impression of a Brutalist clinic rather than an educational institution.

Prominently displayed in the university's courtyard was the bust of its namesake, Dr. Carlos Albizu Miranda. A Puerto Rican psychologist, Dr. Albizu was committed to providing culturally relevant psychological treatment and training. The Miami campus of the private university opened in 1980, the same year as the Mariel boatlift. The main campus remains in San Juan, Puerto Rico; each campus includes a mental health clinic for Spanish speakers that is based in the university's cultural sensitivity ethos. In addition to undergraduate and graduate degree programs in psychology, education, language, and speech, the Miami campus of Carlos Albizu University offers English for speakers of other languages (ESOL). There is also a human services and criminal justice component to the curriculum. Back then, Dr. Rafael Martinez was the director of the education, criminal justice, and undergraduate psychology programs at the university.

I was just starting my research on the policing and criminalization of Afro-Cuban religions as an assistant professor at Harvard University. I had recently completed my first book, which tracked the circulation of Santeria religious practitioners between the United States and Cuba. [7] A few police officers who secretly practiced Afro-Cuban religions had reached out to me to ask if I might be able to help restart the "Santeria 101" trainings for law enforcement that began in the late 1990s. They had noticed an upsurge in racist policing that was once again targeting Afro-Caribbean religions. The officers suggested that I meet with Martinez, who had been a key figure in the previous trainings.

Martinez was warm and friendly. He was very knowledgeable about Afro-Cuban religions and law enforcement in the area. We sat for hours discussing law enforcement responses to Santeria and Palo Monte. He discussed his work training law enforcement personnel on Afro-Cuban religions and his efforts to help dispel the stigma and cultural misunderstandings that led to the criminalization of these practices. We talked about how he had thought it was an issue of expertise and training, and at the time I agreed.

Years later, I asked him about how he had started working with Charles Wetli.

"I had just finished my master's thesis in anthropology," Martinez told me. "My thesis was not on the criminal aspects of Santeria." It was titled "Afro-Cuban Santería among the Cuban-Americans in Dade County Florida: A

Psycho-Cultural Approach." It examines how Cuban practitioners draw on the religion "as a psychotherapeutic healing" technique. Martinez took a position at the Center for Drug Abuse. A mutual colleague, whom Martinez was helping with cocaine research, connected Wetli to Martinez, describing him as a "local expert" on Afro-Cuban religions.

In those early days, Martinez would go over to the medical examiner's office, and Wetli would bring him human remains to analyze forensically. Martinez would explain to Wetli and the police officers present what the religions were about. He recalled that Wetli "was all excited" when Martinez was able to explain to him that these were discarded remnants of rituals left by practitioners of Santeria and Palo Monte.[8]

Sometimes, people abandon sacred receptacles, known as *prendas*, Martinez said, on the railroad tracks. In Cuban Palo practices, *prendas*, also called *ngangas*, are precious spirit homes or sacred vessels that take the form of a clay pot or cauldron.[9] *Prendas* are crucial elements of ancestral interactivity with the living and in some cases contain human bones. Traditionally, the bones belong to deceased family members and allow the spirits to continue to impact the lives of their loved ones; today, the bones are mostly bought online through medical supply companies. The trade in human bones is legal. However, it has long been rumored that some Palo bones are sourced from grave robbing. In Cuba, graves are above ground, in tombs, making this practice easier, if it does occur. In the United States, if the *prendas* that police encounter contains human bones, the local police department's homicide team is notified, and they then call the medical examiner.

"But they had so many inaccuracies" and "so many misconceptions," Martinez recalled. "It was not just about the bones, you know, the medical examiner only looks at the bones." Martinez would tell Wetli, "Look what's on the bones. There's wax, there's feathers, there's a cauldron."

Martinez told me that he tried to bring an anthropological approach to law enforcement's handling and interpretation of Afro-Cuban religions. He had attempted to educate police that Afro-Latiné religions are complex cultural systems that should be respected and understood in the context of the long history of slavery, persecution, and discrimination out of which they arose. But Martinez would watch as police officers' eyes glazed over. He felt that his opinions often fell on deaf ears.

"I attempted to bring some sanity into this. Always saying, you know it's not everyone, there's a criminal sector that practices this. Same as there is a criminal sector in the Mafia that goes to mass, baptizes their kids. And you know, I tried to bring in that perspective. I tried to bring that in," Martinez insisted.

Charles Wetli, as medical examiner, had accumulated several dead Marielito bodies. These bodies had bullet holes, stab wounds, and tattoos. Whereas Wetli wanted to classify and categorize the tattooed bodies for law enforcement's criminal profiling of Afro-Cubans, Martinez told me that he was interested in a "social services perspective." Martinez had hoped to understand the symbolic and cultural elements of tattoos. So, in 1982, when immigration officers requested Martinez's assistance in questioning and assessing detained Marielitos at the United States Penitentiary in Atlanta, Georgia, he asked if he could also interview them about their tattoos.

Martinez took advantage of the opportunity to interview detained Marielitos in the federal prison to expand on his research with Wetli's collection of dead Cuban bodies.

"Why interview detainees in the prison?" I asked him.

"The dead bodies couldn't talk," he told me.

* * *

"They thought that we were social workers that were there to release them," Martinez told me of the Marielito detainees he interviewed in 1982 in Atlanta, at the federal penitentiary.

To deal with the influx of Cuban Marielitos, the government had opened a makeshift processing facility at the Miami Orange Bowl stadium in 1980. Those who were identified as "potentially dangerous" were sent on to detention camps in Fort Indiantown Gap, Pennsylvania; Fort Chaffee, Arkansas; and Fort McCoy, Wisconsin. They were also sent to the federal prison camp in Pensacola, Florida; to the prison in Lompoc, California; and to the federal penitentiary in Atlanta.[10] Even though they had committed no crimes, many Marielitos were held in indefinite detention in these facilities.

The US government claimed that Marielitos were initially detained because they had no family members to claim and sponsor them. The expectation of sponsorship, however, favored White Cubans whose families had fled in the early years of the Cuban Revolution and who had established ties in the United States. The need for sponsorship made it exceptionally difficult for Black Cubans, whose families had mostly remained on the island, to be released from detention. Rather than the "open arms" they had been promised by President Jimmy Carter, dark-skinned Marielitos who lacked sponsors were greeted with prison sentences. Without a judge, a jury, or even a criminal charge to justify holding them captive, many Marielitos were detained without cause. If they were suspected of having been one of the few people released from Cuban prisons, they were incarcerated and told that they needed to be observed so that the authorities could decide whether they should be released in the United States.[11]

It was heartbreaking to think that this group of unjustly incarcerated people, who had no idea why they were being detained, might have seen hope in Martinez's tattoo research.

"Yes," Martinez acknowledged. "In fact, when the authorities told them that we have someone who wants to talk to you, they started fighting to be interviewed, you know, 'I want to be first,'" Martinez told me. "But I made it clear to them, 'I'm studying tattoos.'" He told me that the detained Marielitos were confused and distraught when he first spoke to them.

Part of Martinez's task at the prison was to assess whether the person he was interviewing was actually Cuban. He would ask the detainees questions about Cuban geography and pay close attention to their Spanish accents.

Initially, detained Marielitos were told that their release would depend on good behavior.[12] They were to be monitored for a few months. However, a good number of Marielitos were detained indefinitely and never released, despite exemplary behavior. In the Atlanta federal penitentiary, for example, the Marielitos were held for twenty-three hours a day, without air-conditioning in the hot southern summers, confined "to a cramped cell with seven other Mariel Cubans"; the cell contained "four bunk beds, a sink, and an open toilet."[13]

In the US Penitentiary in Lompoc, California, Marielitos were kept in tiny two-person cells called H-Units.[14] They could not eat at the mess hall, take prison jobs, leave their cells without shackles or handcuffs, or mix with the other prisoners, even though they faced no criminal charges. Simply because they were Cuban, the Marielitos were "without the same constitutional protection as American prisoners."[15] Many lost their minds.

"We didn't know who many of them were," Martinez told me. "They were giving false names." Martinez had been working in a pretrial release program in Miami at the time; it was called the CHIC (Cuban-Haitian Intake and Case-Management) Program. This program provided social services, psychological assessments, vocational training, and English classes to "reeducate" Marielitos and Haitian immigrants while they were awaiting immigration trials. And so, as a thirty-three-year-old Cuban American with a recent master's degree in anthropology, Martinez ended up in Atlanta, working with immigration officers to assess, fingerprint, survey, and interview Marielito detainees. The detainees had to "raise their right hand" and swear that they were providing Martinez and the immigration officers with true and correct information. Martinez said he found that some of the incarcerated people were Caribbean and Latin American migrants "pretending to be Cuban."

"In order to not be deported?" I asked him.

"Yeah."

Martinez himself was a "Peter Pan kid." Between 1960 and 1962, as part of the US effort to undermine Cuban communism, fourteen thousand unaccompanied minors, also known as "Pedro Pan's," were flown off the island.[16] At age thirteen, Martinez left his parents in Havana to fly alone to Miami, where his aunt was waiting for him. It was January 1962.

"Was it scary to come to the US alone as a kid?" I asked him.

"A little bit. But I was all excited about the new life, the new bicycle they had for me. Eating American sandwiches. You know, it was fun." Martinez's parents arrived a few months later, resuming their cigar-rolling business in Miami. His father would go on to establish the RaMar Cigar Company, a fusion of the first and last names he and his son both shared.

Martinez was eager to acculturate. He had a new bike and wanted to do "regular American boy things," such as delivering newspapers. But his parents quickly dashed these hopes. They did not want him distracted from his education. In 1980, when the Marielitos arrived, he recalls wanting to provide this new group of compatriots with the same experience that he had. He wanted them to be able to have their American dream.

Martinez told me he wanted to give Marielitos a helping hand. He had hoped they would be able to access the same adjustment services that had assisted him and his family in their successful integration into the United States. He told me that the approach to Marielitos should have consisted of "acculturation" programs rather than incarceration.[17] Marielitos, however, were not welcomed. They had neither the same generational wealth nor the connections that previous Whiter and wealthier Cubans had enjoyed.

Until 1980, Cuban exiles had been seen as hardworking refugees who had fled communism and were successfully acclimating to life in the United States. They were considered a "privileged minority" and "celebrated for their heroism and patriotism."[18] Anthropologist Alyssa Garcia describes Cubans as "the most well received of any U.S. immigrant group in recent history," with their ascendancy in the United States referred to as a model of White Cuban "exile/exceptionalism."[19] The White Latiné "model minority" status had afforded Cubans a special relationship to US empire—that is, until the Mariel boatlift. As Alejandro Portes and Alex Stepick have shown, the arrival of Marielitos would forever change Cuban American émigré politics, transforming the city of Miami into a racial, economic, and cultural "experiment."[20]

Not provided the same reception or resources as previous Cuban émigrés, Black, Brown, and dark Brown Marielitos were instead seen as suspected criminals.[21] Like Afro-Cubans from previous generations, Marielitos negotiated racial identity in the United States in ways similar to the experiences of other racialized Latiné and Black diaspora communities such as Puerto Ricans, Mexicans, Central Americans, Haitians, and African Americans.[22] By 1987, 3,800 Mariel detainees were held in US prisons and in lockdown across the country, stuck in a horrific limbo between the US prison system and immigration control.[23]

By labeling both Haitians and Marielitos "boat people," the Reagan administration changed a policy for Cubans that had been in place since the 1960s. Rather than simply being granted asylum as they had been under the 1966 Cuban Adjustment Act (CAA) or the 1980 Refugee Act, which automatically provided Cubans with permanent legal status and resources to adjust to life in the United States,[24] Mariel Cubans were now designated "boat people," and a temporary "Cuban/Haitian Entrant" legal status was created for them.[25] However, unlike the Haitians, Marielitos could not automatically be deported because of the US government's fraught political relationship with Cuba's communist government as a result of the ongoing Cold War. In a paradoxical situation, then, Cubans who arrived in the United States were provided with "near automatic" asylum from the CAA,[26] but since they were also criminalized, Marielitos without sponsorship were unduly incarcerated.

Since Marielitos were associated with Afro-Cuban religions and prisons, news media and law enforcement labeled them "evil." Former Drug Enforcement Administration (DEA) agent Jim Shedd justified the indefinite detention of Marielitos by calling them "street urchins with bad intent."[27] President Reagan's treatment of Marielitos was so different from the treatment of previous Cuban asylum seekers that people were shocked when Reagan went so far as try to deport the Marielitos back to Cuba. On November 10, 1987, the Reagan administration announced that it had negotiated a deal between the United States, Mexico, and Cuba to "repatriate" imprisoned Marielitos.[28] News of the repatriation deal quickly spread among detained Marielitos, who by that point had been unjustly imprisoned for seven years. The idea that Reagan would deport them, even though they were not supposed to be deportable, infuriated the detainees.

On November 23, 1987, Cuban detainees took over the Federal Detention Center at Oakdale, Louisiana, and the federal penitentiary in Atlanta. The detainees set fire to both facilities and held them by force, demanding a fair review of their cases and their release from indefinite incarceration. The Mariel detainees' "prison riot," the longest in US history, went on for eleven days.[29] More than three thousand detainees held both sites independently in a state of siege.

Even though the detainees held 130 hostages, only one death and few injuries resulted.[30] During the siege, the Cuban detainees created a police force to manage any violence that might break out, and at both facilities they were able to provide three meals a day and to care for themselves and the hostages.[31] Detainees who played music and were uplifted described the siege as joyful; some even felt free for the first time.[32]

The siege ended when the Justice Department eventually agreed to provide each of the 3,800 Marielitos imprisoned at that time with a special hearing to review each detainee's case. However, most of these hearings never materialized.[33] Instead, the treatment of Marielitos and Haitians produced the incarceration infrastructure that would begin a policy of long-term detention for Latiné refugees who crossed the US-Mexico border, and would launch a pattern of criminalizing immigration.[34]

* * *

The nightmarish treatment of Black, Brown, and dark Brown migrants reveals how US policies blur different national bodies. Despite being a country that prides itself on welcoming immigrants, the objectionable treatment of non-White groups is the standard in the United States. Through the everyday state practices of policing, surveillance, incarceration, and deportation of racialized immigrant communities, different groups of people are made into *colors*.

In the mid-nineteenth century, diverse groups of Asian immigrants were collapsed into one another, turned into a "yellow peril," and colonial tropes were used to label them "inassimilable aliens who brought economic competition, disease, and immorality."[35] In the twentieth century, Latin American groups were seen as "Brown" because European Whiteness was thought to be dirtied by mixing with Indigenous and African bloodlines. Conflated with "dangerous waters" in the United States, Latiné immigrants were described by politicians as surges of "Brown tides," as uncontrollable floods of people who threatened to wash away Anglo-American cultural dominance and turn America Brown.[36]

The long and complicated colonial and imperial histories between the United States and the Caribbean have also provided for unique formulations of migrant Blackening, Browning, and Whitening through US immigration policy. This is especially apparent in the US immigration label "boat people," a political category that, as Martinez must have witnessed, conjoined Marielito Cubans with Haitians. Whereas Cubans in the United States had previously been afforded a Whitened status through the notion of White Cuban exceptionalism, when dark-skinned Marielitos arrived they encountered instead a different type of Anglo-American coloring. The "boat people" label served to effectively remove Marielitos from the privilege of Cuban nationalism. Marielitos were Blackened through the category "boat people," tethered to Haitians, and treated like other Black refugees.[37]

The most important example of a Blackening by the United States immigration policy can be seen in the complete exclusion of Haitian refugees, who have consistently been met with forceable repatriations and inhumane detention.[38] Even in the 1990s, the Clinton administration that had promised to change Reagan-era immigration policies admitted that its "main goal" was "to keep Haitians in Haiti."[39] Black legal scholar Malissia Lennox describes US immigration policy as racially discriminatory against Black refugees. Lennox argues that based on the United States' "debilitating" and "imperialist" role in Haiti that contributed to the catastrophic state of the Haitian economy, Haitian refugees should be granted a protected status. Importantly, Lennox ties this discriminatory treatment back to the transatlantic slave trade, stating: "The United States' role in enslaving and oppressing Haitians constitutes grounds for reparations."[40]

The Blackened immigration experience of Haitians reflects the longer history of US colonial aggression and military occupation of the Caribbean.[41] Given that Haiti's 1804 revolution was the only successful slave rebellion in the Americas, it is important to understand how Black independence has always been considered the most dangerous threat to the world system that arose through European colonial dominance.[42] Since the formerly enslaved rebels overthrew White rule and declared Haiti a Black liberated nation, Haiti and Haitians have since been punished globally.[43] Subjected to US-forced coups, economic destabilization, and military occupation, Haitians have sought refuge in the United States and neighboring Caribbean states to much peril.[44] From the 2013 stripping of the citizenship of Haitians born in the Dominican Republic,[45] to similar exclusions of Haitian Bahamians,[46] it is apparent that Black migrants and their children encounter what anthropologist Amarilys Estrella describes as a "civil death" in which Black freedom is hindered through their condition of "statelessness."[47]

Indeed, these state categories operate with a kind of innocence that obscures the destructive racist and ethnic blurrings that occur via immigration policies and practices. This concealment can be seen in how the history of transatlantic slavery is invoked alongside the notion of perpetual foreigner in such a seamless manner that the term "boat people" almost appears neutral, as illuminated by Afro–Puerto Rican poet Mayra Santos-Febres.[48] "Boat people" conjures the nonhuman status of enslaved Africans who were forcefully transported on ships and treated as property in the making of the Americas. Indeed, both Haitians and Marielitos are the descendants of these ancestors and are similarly punished for their survival. Still, the "boat people" label resurrects the stale trope of Latiné migrants as tied to dangerous water crossings, entering without government permission, and considered threats to the purity of White America.

The conflation of Marielito and Haitian identities is a form of ethnic and racial blurring that conceals the links between the United States', the Caribbean's, and Latin America's forms of White supremacy, and the American project of classifying groups of people as colors. Through immigration laws, policies, and practices, racialized migrants are transformed into Black, Brown, and dark Brown people, reinforcing the invisible norm of American Whiteness.[49]

As I dived deeper into my research, I saw this process in action in law enforcement laboratories, medical examiners' offices, and academic research, where immigrants were typecast through the making of criminological profiles. This occurs in the everyday dissections of non-White people's bodies. Indeed, dead immigrants are opened up, autopsied, and then stitched back together to build larger arguments about who they inherently are.

Saturday, September 25, 2021
San Francisco, California

Today, I took my husband, Laurence, and our two young children, Amina, 4, and Langston, 1, to the place where I was born and raised. My adult sons, Pilli, 21, and Neto, 27, joined us. Neto brought along his beautiful family: his wife, Naomi, and their chunky baby girl, Nana, my four-month-old granddaughter. We arrived at the former working-class, historically Latiné neighborhood of the Mission where I grew up.

I took them to the top of Bernal Heights, one of the lesser-known hills of San Francisco that offers breathtaking, 360-degree views of the city. You could see both the Golden Gate and Bay Bridges, Alcatraz Island, and all the way across the water to Oakland and the East Bay. I showed them my former home, a small run-down apartment complex behind James Rolph Jr. playground, named after the longest serving mayor of San Francisco, a Republican banker. "Rolph Park" lies next to a dangerous thoroughfare, where the valley of the Mission District meets the foot of Bernal Heights. From the peak, we could see how the Mission is separated from the towering skyscrapers of downtown by the large, imposing freeway.

The trip reminded me of my childhood. At nineteen, my mother, Dolores, a dancer and activist born and raised in the Mission who had been training to support the Sandinista Revolution in Nicaragua, used to walk to the top of the *hill when she was pregnant with me.[1] Sucking on sweet stalks of wild licorice that grew amid the tall grasses, my mother allowed herself respite only once she reached the summit.*

The hill looked similar today as it did when I was a child. Covered mostly in dry grasses, a few trees still surrounding the microwave transmission tower at the top. I took Amina to the peak, just as my mom had taken me. I remembered my mother telling me stories of how she did this walk the day of my birth.

In 1980, when I was three months old, my father, Peter De Jesus Jr., "Piri," was initiated as a priest of Ochún in Santeria. The ceremony took place just two blocks from where he had been born. Before gentrification squeezed the Latiné community from the city, my grandfather had owned a two-story single-family Victorian on 1545 Treat Street, just off Precita Park at the crossroads of the Mission and Bernal Heights Districts.

Amid these narrow, winding streets, my parents came of age. Musicians, dancers, activists, and spiritualists, my family were among the founding members of the first Carnival parade in San Francisco: my aunt, Margaret De Jesus, was one of the main organizers and lead dancers along with the famous African American drummer Marcus Gordan and celebrated Afro-Panamanian dancer Adela Chu. Their contingent consisted of my mom, dad, Auntie Margaret, and Uncle Tobaji making several circles around Precita Park with a few other Afro-Brazilian and Afro-Caribbean troupes and Mexican mariachis.

A mural still graces the side of Leonard R. Flynn Elementary School, across the street from Precita Park, commemorating this time. I took Laurence and the kids to look at the mural, pointing out our family's journey documented in chipping paint on the side of the tall building. The large and beautiful painting features my dad in his late teens. At the bottom center of the mural, he sits next to his good friend, the famous musician Carlos Santana. Just as you would have normally found him at that time, Piri is painted jamming with other musicians, lighting up the park with Afro-Caribbean music. Wearing a black-and-yellow shirt, my dad drums two congas. His dark mustache and Afro show that this painting was made right before he shaved his head to undergo his priesthood ceremony. One of the drums has his signature Puerto Rican flag on the side.[2] Auntie Margaret is also featured in the mural. Wearing a flaring red dress, directly in front of Piri and Carlos, drumming their congas, Auntie Margaret is dancing salsa.

Both of my father's parents were Puerto Rican and very proud of ensuring that we did not lose that culture in our upbringing, regardless of how many generations of diaspora our family went through. Piri's mother, Maria Magdalena, was from Arecibo, Puerto Rico. My grandmother told me the family of her father, Armando Reyes y Ortiz, had gone from Cuba in the late 1800s to work in the rum industry in Puerto Rico.[3] Her mother, Doña Niti, was a spiritual healer from Ponce, Puerto Rico.

My family were members of the first Puerto Rican social club in the United States.[4] In a small narrow apartment at the intersection of Mission and Silver Streets, this club nurtured a tight-knit community of Afro-Caribbean and other Latiné people forging diaspora in the Bay Area. Growing up as a child in this vibrant community of food, music, dancing, festivals, and religion, I had no idea that my family's traditions and practices were seen as a threat.

Bodies

THROUGH MY PATERNAL GRANDFATHER, Peter De Jesús Sr., I came to understand how non-White immigrants and US citizens are criminalized because of the color of our skin. He was born on a sugarcane plantation in Honolulu on December 4, 1922, to Afro-Taíno Puerto Rican cane cutters. After Hurricane San Ciriaco of 1899 devastated Puerto Rico, his family had been recruited by one of the "Big Five" sugarcane companies, along with many other workers, to harvest the fields in Hawai'i.[1] My great-grandparents were promised employment and opportunity in the wake of the natural disaster; however, when they arrived in Hawai'i, they were forced to labor on a plantation under horrible conditions and kept segregated from the local Hawaiian population.[2] This abusive history contributed to the Puerto Rican plantation community clinging to its Puerto Rican identity. To this day, we, the descendants of this migration, continue to identify as Puerto Rican, honoring the struggles of our ancestors.[3]

When he turned eighteen, Peter Sr. attempted to enlist in the US Navy, but although he was born in Honolulu, authorities denied him based on his accent and dark-brown skin color. He became a merchant sailor instead. Aware that race and immigration status could lead to the incarceration of non-White people, regardless of their innocence or citizenship, my grandfather often told how he had worked the docks during the Pearl Harbor attack.

Early in the morning on December 7, 1941, he recalled, the Japanese carrier bomber planes flew over his head as he unloaded ships. He reminded us of the subsequent round ups and incarceration of Japanese immigrants and their American-born children during World War II—whole families and communities were shipped to detention camps.[4] On one of his sailing voyages to Los Angeles, California, Peter Sr. himself was nearly incarcerated in a War Relocation Authority camp because law enforcement suspected he might be Japanese.[5] While my grandfather was proud of the day he finally enlisted in the US Army—on December 3, 1945, in Goleta, California (he would later obtain the rank of sergeant)—he knew that because of his dark skin and Spanish accent, he would always be excluded and criminalized by the nation of his birth.[6]

My grandfather's experience, witnessing the incarceration of Japanese immigrants and Japanese Americans in the 1940s, reminds me of the indefinite detention of Marielitos in the 1980s. Both moments conjure for me the history of the importation of Afro–Puerto Rican cane cutters to Hawai'i in the 1890s and recall the enslavement and forced mass migration of Africans to the Americas since the 1600s.[7]

I see these layers of history echoed in my own lifetime—in the Trump administration's separation of Central American refugee families, for example, who entered the United States at the US-Mexico border since 2017: babies torn away from parents who were indefinitely detained.[8] Still, as I write, over one thousand migrant children remain lost to their families as a result of our country's cruel immigration policies.[9]

I think about how agents of the state, individuals like Rafael Martinez and Charles Wetli, working to classify and categorize those like the Marielitos, factor intimately into this process of criminalizing immigration. I wonder about what goes on inside their minds. What do they think they are doing?

* * *

"It was difficult to gain access to prisons," Rafael Martinez told me in 2021. When he was asked by INS to assist in identifying incarcerated Marielitos in the 1980s, he took advantage of this moment to collect some information about the detainees' tattoos. He brought in a research assistant, Julio Mechoso, who was also a White Cuban émigré: "So, Julio and I did all of the interviews." Martinez had hoped to capture the culture of tattoos. Whereas Charles Wetli was caught up in the initial push to categorize the supposed dangers of Mariel Cubans, Martinez thought that this research was a continuation of his social services efforts. It was only years later that Martinez realized that his efforts had not helped the Marielitos but had instead participated in their criminalization.

When I began to read "Tattoos of the Marielitos," written by Rafael Martinez and Charles Wetli, I was struck deeply by the deliberate and methodical way that racialized criminality is crafted through academic research and scholarship.[10] Martinez and Wetli's symbolic analysis draws on rehashed stereotypes and just plain guessing about the cultural meaning of Marielito tattoos. The text itself is short—just ten pages. The article is made up mostly of photos taken by Wetli of tattoos on dead bodies. These images of gunshot wounds and tattoos are featured with an analysis that is supposed to provide law enforcement with understanding of Afro-Caribbean "cult" symbolism.

In most of the images, the wounded and tattooed body part is featured without showing that it once belonged to an entire person. Most of the photos do not include visible heads, limbs, or other orientations to the human body. We understand that the tattoos come from dead bodies, though, because the captions point out how the people were killed—whether from gun violence or stabbings. And so, the reader is expected to deduce that the individuals' deaths were likely the result of some criminal enterprise in which they were engaged.

Wetli and Martinez render the Marielito tattoo a criminological specimen that they claim to be mining for its value to law enforcement profiling. The images remind me of Martinez's chilling words: "The dead bodies couldn't speak." Throughout the article, they dehumanize dark-skinned Marielitos. The descriptions, the photos, and the handling of the Marielito bodies produce an objectified criminality made visible through the touching, grasping, holding, and dissection of the medical examiners' photographic gaze.[11] I see it as a glimpse into Wetli's criminological sculpting, a way for us to understand how he handled dead bodies.

In this article, Martinez and Wetli posit a seamless link between Marielitos and incarceration. After a brief introduction, the second page shows a large table titled "Results of the survey questionnaire," which displays information that Martinez had collected from detainees held at the Atlanta federal penitentiary. Postcolonial scholars contend that during the seventeenth and eighteenth centuries, the scientific use of tables and diagrams played a role in the establishment of racial and civilizational hierarchies. [12] These visual representations involved the categorization of human beings, which concurrently contributed to the legitimization of scientific knowledge. Through this table, Martinez and Wetli use the Marielitos' tattoos to depict them as destined for incarceration. In answer to the question "Where were the tattoos done?" they tell us that thirty-one people (67 percent) respond "C. Cuban Jail."

Martinez and Wetli conflate and collapse incarcerated Marielitos with dead Marielitos. This slippage leads the reader to see the survey data of living but detained Marielitos as representative of the pictures of the dead Marielito bodies. But no one can speak for the dead Marielitos. No researcher can survey the dead—at least, not like this.

It is troubling to think of this kind of criminological ventriloquism, especially for me, as I was raised within a spiritual tradition that seeks to investigate what the dead have to say. However, in the case of "Tattoos of the Marielitos," the dead Cubans who ended up on Wetli's medical examiner's table were not the same individuals who took Martinez's survey. A bit of "subject juggling" therefore occurs: we are expected to take the survey and interview responses from the small sample of Marielito detainees as speaking for *all* Marielitos—those who ended up dead on Wetli's table and those living people whom law enforcement might encounter on the streets. This flattening produces a kind of blurring, a collapsing of criminality, where the experiences of about 40 Marielito detainees, out of a population of about 3,800 detainees, are rendered as representative of the more than 125,000 Cubans who arrived from the Port of Mariel and who are called Marielitos.

In this article, Martinez and Wetli sculpt criminality as a thing that law enforcement can decipher by reading the hieroglyphs of Marielitos' flesh.[13] Officers are led to believe they can use the tattooed skin as a decoder to determine "criminal specialization"—for example, whether someone was an "executioner," a "kidnapper," a "pickpocket," or an "enforcer," or whether a person was a "prostitute, or active or passive homosexual."[14] Martinez and Wetli thus perform a magic trick of sorts, in which racial science justifies itself through its manipulation of dead Black and Brown immigrants' bodies.

I have experienced this kind of makeshift symbolic speculation by law enforcement during ride-alongs I have conducted with police officers. Officers have shown me the "gang symbols" on people that they have stopped and frisked as evidence that they were correct in conducting their legally questionable searches and seizures. "Tattoos of the Marielitos" is in line with this sort of racial profiling in everyday police patrol, with law enforcement purporting to classify and categorize criminality with no real historical or cultural understanding of the racialized subjects they apprehend.[15]

One disturbing example of the kinds of violations that occur through Wetli's medical examination is revealed in one image, where a White person's hand, presumably belonging to Wetli, is holding down the lower lip of a deceased Marielito, exposing a tattoo on the inner lip.[16] The down-stretched lip of the dead dark Brown man is strikingly juxtaposed with the White ungloved fingers of the living examiner. Wetli's White hand grasping and stretching the lip shows the Marielito's inability to pull his own lip down, his inability to consent to this exposure. It is the touch of White death for this Brown body, made a specimen in Wetli's photographic dissection.

Viewing this photograph, I felt complicit with the medical examiner's touch. The research subject was unable to grant access to this intimate display. Surely, a tattoo on the inside of a man's lip is meant only for him or for his closest relations; otherwise, the man would have tattooed a more visible part of his body. I was embarrassed to be included in the exposure of this man's tattoo on his inner lip, which, I thought, was clearly meant to be private. Wetli's White hand sculpted this man's body in the name of science and rendered him a mere fleshy materiality. I could see the down-stretched inner lip, no longer wet from saliva as you would see in a living body, and I felt culpable.

If it is possible, this moment is made even more unfortunate when what is tattooed on the inside of his lip is revealed: a message of love—"R.P.R. Besame" (Kiss me). This supplication for embrace, addressed to R.P.R. (most likely a cherished relation), should have remained private. Yet I am forced to participate in the violation, complicit with Wetli's racial sculpting through the photographic image. It was even more unsettling for me that Martinez and Wetli's caption under this image tells me that "R.P.R.," the letters identifying the person this man wants to kiss, "are probably the initials of a girlfriend."

What does it do to make this deceased Marielito's loved one a girlfriend? In addition to assuming that this man is heterosexual, it also infantilizes him; it turns him into a perpetual youth. If the initials "R.P.R." had been those of a spouse instead of a "girlfriend," Martinez and Wetli could have provided him with a kind of White American respectability. Perhaps he was a homeowner? Maybe he held a job? Had R.P.R. been a spouse, we might think he had been a father and husband—a person connected to a larger community; *someone who matters*. By not allowing him a spouse, this man is also refused a family or children who might mourn him. Instead, he is no more than a *Latin lover* asking for a kiss.

Martinez and Wetli's caption reduces the dead man to a perpetual "boyfriend." Now that he has been deemed immature, we are led to believe that the grasping White hand is just one of this mouth's many violators. For who would tattoo the initials of a girlfriend on the inside of his lip? Truly only someone who is irresponsible.

The authors' judgment of this man is clear. Anyone who would permanently tattoo a request for a girlfriend's kiss on the inside of his lip must be an ignorant youth, lascivious and foolish. They imply that such a person does not deserve privacy nor consent. His body can be grotesquely displayed, groped, handled, and exposed for analysis and consumption.

Transforming Black and Brown men into perpetual "youths" is linked historically to the Jim Crow South, where White men would use the terms *boy* or *son* to undermine Black masculinity and assert White patriarchal dominance.[17] It is apparent that the powerful symbolic work of casting an adult man into a boyfriend renders him beyond sympathy; the Marielito is written off as temporally immature. Produced as irrational, hypersexual, and thus lacking in education, cultivation, and civilization, the Marielito is likened to other young men who are presumed to be impetuous, irresponsible, headstrong, ignorant, and impulsive. They are also often to blame for the trouble in which they find themselves, *including their own deaths.*

Blame for one's own death is a core element of the syndrome Wetli later invents, which he calls "excited delirium." There is a kind of demonic conjuring happening through Wetli's scientific touch. This infantilizing criminological approach is key to broader techniques of racial classification whereby Wetli crafts his own expertise. By contrast to the lustful Marielito, Wetli makes himself, the White doctor, into a man of reason and respect. The medical examiners' touch, Wetli's kiss of death, is the White embrace of science, converting once-sacred flesh into excavated remains.

Another core element in Wetli's role in criminology can be seen in his embrace of racial and sexual conflations. In the Marielito article, we see such sculptings in how he determines the artistic merit of tattooed flesh. In one passage, Martinez and Wetli discuss the lack of artistic value of the tattoos alongside presumptions of Marielitos as inherently criminal, sexually perverse, and religiously deviant. Melted together, these conflations indicate to officers that they must control these dangerous immigrants:

> As this group of Marielitos came to the attention of law-enforcement authorities and medical examiners, it was noticed that many had peculiar tattoos that were frequently quite elaborate, nearly always had a dull (nearly turquoise) hue, and usually were lacking in artistic merit. Many of the tattoos seemed to have religious significance, but others suggested

criminal alliances of some sort, or were simply pornographic or reflected a streetwise philosophy.[18]

The "pornographic," the "criminal," and the "religious" blend together in the article's racial sculpting of tattooed bodies. Martinez and Wetli claim that Marielitos reflect a "streetwise philosophy," indicating that they operate outside of White liberal American norms. However, Martinez and Wetli's analysis is simply a repackaging of the stereotypes that circulated about Marielitos at the time. It is not coincidental that Marielitos were also labeled homosexual criminal deviants by both Cuban and US officials and the news media. The Cuban government called them "scum" (*escoria*) and suggested that those who left the island did not have enough "manliness" (*hombría*) to support the homeland (*patria*).[19] Meanwhile, people who identified as homosexual, who had been imprisoned in Cuba, were threatened with additional jail time if they did not leave the island during Mariel.[20] In 1980 in the United States, homosexuality was still listed as a reason to exclude migrants from entering the country.[21] And so, Marielitos entered a complicated immigration system that officially excluded people based on sexuality while also claiming to welcome Cold War refugees from communist Cuba.

After the Marielitos arrived, the US news media doubled down on their negative response with stories that Castro had emptied Cuba's prisons, sending "undesirables" such as mental patients, prostitutes, and homosexuals to the US shores.[22] The *Los Angeles Times* was one newspaper that consistently featured stories of Marielito homosexuality as a contagious disease tied to a deviant lifestyle.[23] Falling in step with the news media's hyperfocus on Marielitos as criminals and homosexuals, Martinez and Wetli's work echoed similar themes in their analysis of the tattoos.

Martinez and Wetli saw the deviant lifestyle of Marielitos as etched onto their bodies by their tattoos. They interpreted the lack of "artistic merit" in Marielito tattoos as reinforcing the sexually deviant "streetwise" and "pornographic" lifestyle that made them seemingly destined for jail. For example, Martinez and Wetli's survey of incarcerated Marielito detainees indicates that thirty-five of the respondents, or 75 percent, used a "melted toothbrush" method for creating their tattoos. The authors then analyzed this survey data as reflective of the dead bodies pictured in their article to show a seamless relationship between the dead and the detained Marielitos. The quality of the tattoos, which they described as "peculiar" and "dull," indicates to them that the Marielitos must be hardened criminals. After making this assessment, they jumped to assumptions about Afro-Latiné religions and their connections to Marielito criminality.

Martinez and Wetli infer that the primitiveness of the tattoos mirrors the primitiveness of Afro-Cuban religions. Many Marielitos openly practiced Afro-Cuban religions such as Santeria and Palo Monte, and some of the men were also members of the Abakuá brotherhood, an all-male Afro-Cuban society.[24] On the island, all these religions had been heavily policed and criminalized since slavery. Through a kind of makeshift syncretism, Martinez and Wetli presume that almost every tattoo had a hidden reference to an Afro-Cuban religion that they could decipher for police.

The notion of syncretism has long been used in early anthropology to describe cultural mixing, in which the blending of two different cultures together is seen as forming one (new) culture. Cuban criminologist Fernando Ortiz describes syncretism by using the term *transculturation*, which emphasizes the mutual blending of two or more cultures into something new.[25] These observations refer to how enslaved African peoples were able to maintain their own religious practices by hiding them behind the guise of Catholic saints. Over time, the use of Christian saint "avatars" together with the rituals and practices of Yorùbá orisha created a new religious practice that has become known as *la Regla de la Ocha* (Rule of Ocha) or, more popularly, Santeria.

The article "Tattoos of the Marielitos" takes up this idea by nefariously interjecting White Cuban anti-Blackness into its rendering of Afro-Cuban religious criminality. For example, the authors turn any Christian symbols into opportunities to describe Afro-Cuban syncretism, casting the religions as inherently dangerous through their connections to dead Marielitos. However, Martinez and Wetli's descriptions of Afro-Cuban orisha are both sinister and inaccurate. They draw on White supremacist Christian renderings of African religions as inherently evil and satanic. The description of an arm tattooed with a depiction of Catholic saint Barbara states, for example, "In Santeria, a depiction of St. Barbara represents the god Changó, a virulent and violent deity. The depiction always portrays a chalice and a sword."

To clarify here, Changó in Cuba (also Ṣàngó in Nigeria, or Xangô in Brazil), was once a great living king (Alaàfin) of the Oyo Kingdom in West Africa. In the Yorùbá diaspora, he was deified posthumously and emerged in Afro-Cuban Santeria as an orisha who brings honor and diplomacy to practitioners' lives. Martinez and Wetli, however, portray him as "virulent and violent"—an ignorant description that reflects Catholic misrepresentations and a deep-seated anti-Africanness. Historically, such racist misinformation is an element of the broader stereotypes used by European Christians to justify slavery and colonialism. More recently, as Haitian anthropologist Jemima Pierre shows, the racist tropes drawn from the disparagement of African religions are used by global investors to justify the continued underdevelopment of the African continent.[26] As with adherents of other African-inspired religions across the Caribbean and Latin America, such as Haitian Vodou, Brazilian Candomblé, and Revival Zion in Jamaica, police and local governments continue to persecute practitioners of Afro-Cuban religions through such baseless fears of the religions' inherent primitivism and violence.[27] Anti-African stereotypes are foundational to arguments of White Western superiority.

As we saw with Saint Barbara, Martinez and Wetli interpreted the tattoos of Catholic saints syncretically as reflections of Afro-Cuban religions. These speculations served to fuse Marielito criminality with corruption, suturing Afro-Latiné religions with lawlessness. Martinez and Wetli thus ensured that White American law enforcement personnel would read any symbols on Afro-Latiné bodies as hiding ulterior motives. In one photograph of a deceased man's body showing a visible gunshot wound alongside a dragon tattoo and a Catholic saint, the caption conjures the practice of Santeria religions as innately hostile:

> This tattoo of a dragon symbolizes aggression. The tattoo extended across the subject's shoulder and down the entire length of his back. The tattoo of the right side of the chest is Our Lady of Charity, the patron saint of Cuba, a syncretism with the deity of Ochún in Santeria. (The circular defect in the center of the subject's chest is a gunshot wound.) The tattoo message on the left side of the chest translates as "'I come from a country without law, and I bring a bullet without a name."[28]

Since there are no dragons used in Afro-Cuban religions, this could have been a key moment for Martinez and Wetli to discuss Afro-Asian influences in Cuba—for instance, the role of male Chinese laborers who were brought to the Caribbean in the mid-1800s and who have also formed syncretic practices. Instead, throughout the article, the authors construct practitioners of Afro-Cuban Santeria, Palo Monte, and members of the Abakuá society as the criminals of the island who have now made their way to the United States.

"Tattoos of Marielitos" shows how Wetli handled the bodies that ended up on his examination table as a medical examiner. Beyond just the dissection of the dead, Wetli engaged in a scientific touching, in which he grasped, pulled, stretched, and molded Brown and Black bodies and their cold flesh into specimens of racial science. Tethered to the diagrams and tables of incarcerated Marielito detainees, the figure of Marielito criminality appears to us as if a specter. Haunting us through the captions and descriptions that feature Western misunderstandings of Afro-Latiné religions, we see a scientific narrative emerge that solidifies stereotypes into seemingly neutral facts. The practice of science thus conjures the seething presence of Anglo-European superiority and anti-Africanness. Scientific portrayals, often presented as impartial, are actually haunting manifestations that permeate law enforcement classifications dictating the fates of Black and Brown immigrants.

* * *

Much of the misinformation that Martinez and Wetli conjure in "Tattoos of the Marielitos" mirrors early social evolutionist scholarship from White Cuban and Anglo-European criminologists who have a long history of persecuting Afro-Cuban religions. Classifications through dermatography, or the study of tattoos, was key to early criminology. Research on tattooed bodies fueled White apprehensions and provided grounds for police aggression toward Afro-Cubans by identifying Black (*Negro*) and Brown (*Mulato*) individuals as the antagonists of nineteenth-century Cuba.[29] White Cuban criminologists used tattoo analysis to target Afro-Cuban religious practitioners, and law enforcement raided their homes and temples. Police confiscated sacred religious artifacts, which they then displayed in law enforcement museums.

In 1908, Cuban police inspector Rafael Roche y Monteagudo singled out the Afro-Cuban Abakuá society using tattoo analysis from prisoners he had interviewed under false pretenses.[30] Roche y Monteagudo had a reputation for harboring racist attitudes and targeting Afro-Cuban communities. He called the Abakuá brotherhood "black beasts" (*bêtes noires*), portraying them as a "dark, mafia-like criminal organization" that threatened peace on the island.[31] Drawing on misinterpreted analysis of the tattoos and slang from Black prisoners, Roche y Monteagudo produced an "arsenal of photographs and coarse vocabulary" that cataloged and stigmatized Afro-Cubans.[32] Roche y Monteagudo was not alone in this criminal profiling. The 1916 book *Sorcery and Nañiguismo in Cuba*,[33] written by the "racial criminologist" Israel Castellanos,[34] draws on prisoner interviews and prison archives to posit "a relationship among assassins, men who wear tattoos, and Abakuás."[35] The Abakuá were denounced as a Black Mafia that would overthrow White rule on the island.

Although attempts to eradicate Afro-Cuban religions ultimately failed, the residual influence of these prejudiced scientific studies still shapes perceptions and the criminalization of Afro-Cuban communities and their religious practices today. The efforts of social evolutionists to persecute and prohibit these religions during the early twentieth century were not confined to Cuba; these distorted criminal narratives continued to circulate globally. In the 1980s, the profiling of Marielitos marked a revival of these tactics, all under the banner of Anglo-American racial science.

Prior to this article, Martinez and Wetli submitted a police report of their survey results titled "Tattoos among Cuban (Mariel) Criminals: A Cultural Analysis." It was submitted via the Entrant Misdemeanant Placement and Program Assessment Component (EMPAC) to the office of the Dade-Miami Criminal Justice Council in 1986.[36] This earlier work was crucial to the formulation of Marielitos and Afro-Latiné criminality across the country. Following this report, many police and government documents referred to Charles Wetli as an "expert" in Afro-Caribbean "cults." These records echo the misguided views on Santeria and Palo Monte, treating them as established fact.

The law enforcement crime documents lump Afro-Cuban Santeria, Palo Monte, and Abakuá religious practices into the category of "ritualistic crimes," which include satanic murders and the activities of drug cartels. A 1986 report provided to President Reagan, *The Impact: Organized Crime Today; Report to the President and the Attorney General*, includes Wetli's work. The report describes Marielitos as "hard-core criminals" who had sparked an "unprecedented wave of violent crime."[37] In addition to "robbery, burglary, rape, counterfeiting, bookmaking, auto theft, shoplifting, extortion, and prostitution," the report informs the president and attorney general that "Marielito gangs" were "involved in cocaine trafficking, along with the murders and assaults, which usually are a part of the illicit narcotics trade."[38] The section on Marielitos precedes a section titled "Colombian Cocaine Rings," interweaving the dangers of these Afro-Latinidades together with the Italian Mafia, La Cosa Nostra. The report states, "Gangs of Marielitos have assisted Colombian drug smuggling organizations, and at least once, a *La Cosa Nostra* family has used a Marielito as a hired killer."[39]

These narratives of illicit activities portrayed Afro-Latiné groups—Black Cubans and Black Colombians—together with Italian American mob syndicates, relying on unverified claims that were accepted as truth by law enforcement. The report illustrates how the presentation of rumors as data can confer undeserved authority in Western science. The Reagan administration's war on drugs fostered these ambiguous portrayals of Afro-Latiné criminality, attributing the US government's own questionable activities to Black, Brown, and dark Brown Cubans and Colombians.[40] For example, the 1986 Iran-Contra affair saw the Reagan administration covertly selling arms to Iran, using the profits to support the Contras, a right-wing guerrilla army in Nicaragua known to smuggle drugs to the United States.[41] Fueled by Cold War dynamics, the administration justified these actions as a defense against the perceived threat of Cuban communism. This led to the US government's discreet backing of right-wing factions in Colombia, Peru, and Nicaragua, supplying them with arms and training.[42]

Since *Latinidad* is used to describe a diverse group of individuals irrespective of their specific national or ethnic origins in the United States, the political category hails a broad spectrum of skin colors, from pale sand, peach, or olive tones to deep ebony, rich mahogany, or the many shades of brown in between. Within this classification system, divergent Latiné peoples are blended together through shared experiences facing US racial color lines. In the example of the Reagan administration's war on drugs, US policies reinforce the hardening of color lines, operating in the spaces between Whiteness, Brownness, and Blackness. Marielito Cubans, "lightened" because of their connection to White Cuban exceptionalism, and the government's need to maintain specific ties with Cuban émigrés, were thus portrayed by the US government as Brown. In contrast, Colombians were cast in a darker shade of Brown, reflecting a range of anti-Blackness in policy and practice. Crime manuals demonstrate how racial color lines differentiate between Latiné groups through White supremacist policies, even as they are collapsed together as Brown criminals.

Undoubtedly, the early portrayal of Cuban Americans as White because of their racial makeup and anti-communist sentiments influence the racial landscape of US Latinidad. While Black Cubans have a long history in the United States—both in New York City, as seen in the *afrocubanismo* movement of the Harlem Renaissance,[43] and even earlier in Tampa, where they worked as cigar rollers in the 1860s[44]—the history of Afro-Cuban exclusion by the US government is made visible in these crime reports from the 1980s. The racial categorization of Marielitos as Brown and Black is juxtaposed against a backdrop of White supremacist values. This closeness or distance to Whiteness delineates specific racial boundaries (differentiating Black, Brown, Red, and Yellow subjects) that are then leveraged to validate discriminatory policies, as well as police and military actions.

The deployment of political storytelling is another tactic to obscure police and military aggression. Ethnic studies scholar Dylan Rodriguez points to the work of political pronouncements, such as those announcing a "war on . . ." (crimes, drugs, gangs, terror), as a kind of storytelling that masks domestic warfare.[45] Such political tales serve to endorse the heightened use of force and weapons by the police and military, all in pursuit of safeguarding America's White spaces.[46] Predominantly White suburbs or metropolitan areas are perceived as sanctuaries that must be shielded from the imagined dangers posed by non-White individuals.[47] Criminal profiles like "Tattoos of the Marielitos" transform immigrants into "foreign" menaces to local White enclaves. Law enforcement, in turn, sees non-White people as looming threats, demanding their containment, regulation, and penalization.[48] The preference among White citizens to dwell in places marked by White social cohesion epitomizes this spatial entitlement embedded in the emotional lineage of racial boundaries set by White supremacy.

In delving into the stratification of these various forms of White supremacies, I observed that some Brown and light Brown Cubans, as well as some Black Cubans, aspire to approximate Whiteness. This is manifested by their strong attachment to the White Cuban community in the United States and their reluctance to build solidarity with Black Americans or other Black Latiné groups. Their self-perception is deeply rooted in White Cuban exceptionalism and White supremacy.[49]

Reflecting on my interviews with Rafael Martinez, I recognize he may have unintentionally played a role in this Whitening initiative through his engagement with INS and with Wetli, particularly in characterizing Marielitos as criminal. Martinez, however, was not aware of the far-reaching consequences of his research within the realm of law enforcement. It was I who informed him of the widespread replication of his joint work with Wetli in various law enforcement guides, primers, pamphlets, reports, and training across the country. I shared with him my findings in which substantial portions of their tattoos-focused article and their other collaborative piece, on Palo Monte, were directly replicated in law enforcement resources. Predominantly, these excerpts were used as materials to enlighten law enforcement officials and political figures about the supposed criminal nature of Marielitos and the perceived threats of alleged ritualistic cults.[50] Even the terms *cult* or *occult*, used to describe Afro-Latiné religions, reflect anti-African Christian beliefs that imply these religious traditions are inherently evil and must be exposed.

During our conversation, Martinez pondered the repercussions of his early contributions to the perceptions of Afro-Cubans in the United States. He shared that he had minimal influence over the final drafts of the two articles, because "Wetli was a powerful medical examiner and senior author." Being an immigrant academic with just a master's degree at the time, Martinez felt his hands were tied. He admitted, "It was really bad." As a testament to this power dynamic, even his name, Rafael, was anglicized to "Raphael" without his input.

Martinez expressed regret over Wetli's choice of descriptors, noting, "He used terms like *voodoo*," referencing Wetli's terminology.

"I'm so happy to hear what you're doing with Wetli," Martinez said, "because for years it has sort of like bothered me." Martinez told me he felt responsible for how these misunderstandings about Afro-Latiné religions further criminalized them.

"Really?" I responded, a bit stunned by this revelation. I had been worried that he might be upset that I was criticizing his work.

"Yeah," Martinez told me, "I would try to educate him, you know. And, because those generalizations, I mean it's sort of like, especially when you're teaching cops—you need to present a balanced view. So anyway. Whatever, I'm glad that you're doing it."

"Can you tell me more?" I nudged. I wanted to know what he thought about the role of his own work in reinforcing this racist criminal profiling of Marielitos.

"It's been such a long time," Martinez reflected. "I just thought that he had such little knowledge. So few cases. When you get a case at the medical examiner's office, it's different from, you know, interviewing people and talking to people, and I see the whole holistic approach. I mean seeing that these are all practices embedded in the culture—embedded in cultural change . . ." Martinez trailed off thoughtfully.

Despite noble intent on Martinez's part, his research with Wetli did not help Cuban Marielitos. It is difficult to say whether such research ever could have helped, really. Could studying the "culture" of Marielito tattoos for the medical examiner to create a criminal profile of this community ever truly serve the interest of this group of Black and Brown unjustly incarcerated Cubans?

When I look back, it seems apparent that academic research can easily be brought into collusion with racialized state violence, particularly when dealing with law enforcement. The tattoo study that Martinez conducted served to further criminalize a vulnerable racial-ethnic population that by today's standards would not likely be seen as truly able to grant consent to be "research subjects" in the first place.[51] Frighteningly, I was also uncovering a discernable pattern: Wetli blamed the Black and Brown victims of violence, who ended up on his medical examiner's table, for their own deaths.

Saturday, October 2, 2021
Antioch, California

Unable to stop thinking about police violence today I received a spiritual mass (misa espiritual) to cleanse the energies that were haunting me.

"We ask the Lord Almighty to send us good spirits to assist us, to keep away those spirits who could mislead us, and to give us the necessary light to distinguish the truth from the impostor." I asked Chango Lade, my dear friend, a deep brown–skinned African American elder in her sixties from the San Francisco Bay Area to be the lead medium. She read the prayer to start our communion with the dead.

I was at my family's home in Antioch, California, where I felt safe. Through divination I confirmed that I had "picked up" some spirits while writing the book. I urgently needed to do this misa to investigate whom the spirits were. And what they wanted. I have participated in spiritual masses all my life, but this was the first time I was doing a misa as part of my research method.

I sat in the middle of the group of nine trusted mediums. White plumes rose out of our homemade clay pot where we placed copal tree resin on hot charcoal. The smoke curled around us, cleansing our bodies and the space. We passed around a small gourd (jicara) of sweet rum. With arms crossed, we grasped and then passed the shared drink. Crossed arms protect from the transmission of unwanted entities.

Spirits can be "picked up" like gum on the bottom of your shoe. I found out that by researching this book I had inadvertently attracted unwanted spiritual presences. In our Afro-Latiné practices, we understand that dead spirits can attach to you. If you walk into a space where someone has passed, and the presence has unresolved issues, you can call spiritual attention. Whether you acknowledge their presence or not, you can pick up a ghost. Sometimes this is called a haunting. In Afro-Latiné religions, we call it a muerto pegado, which translates to a "dead" spirit is "stuck" on you.

The group of nine Black and Brown mediums trained in channeling the dead sat around me in a protective circle. Seven glasses of water formed the other half of our circle, completing our union. The glasses provide the deceased with a liquid conduit to facilitate their messages. Xhiyo, a medium-in-training who identifies as Latinx, had prayed over each glass to channel my ancestral and protective spirits. Bubbles began to fill the glasses of water, indicating that the spirits had accepted our invitation. One by one, each medium stood and calmly approached the table.

Dipping her hands in the aromatic flower bath sitting in a plastic tub (palangana) on the floor, Xhiyo, who is learning to channel her ancestral guides, swept the magical waters over her head and down her body. She knocked the table three times in greeting. Gently hovering her hands over the center glass, she asked her spirit guides to lend us their "light."

"Blessings to all the santeros, old and young," Xhiyo finished her prayer.

"Bless you," we all replied.

Mediums sense spirits through the electrical charge in the air. When these energies are harmful or negative, they are called "bad vibrations" (malas vibrations). Spirits communicate in different ways—from dreams to chills, voices to mental images. Even your mood can signal spiritual contact. States of emotional distress are a key sign that an unwanted spirit has fastened itself to you. Depressive or anxious feelings or unusual irritability can be related to the influences (influencías) of the unenlightened or needy spirit. Well-developed mediums learn to decipher the vibrations.

Thick, spicy cigar smoke fused with piney tree resin incense sharpens our senses like a tuning fork. There are different misas that accomplish distinct goals. Masses can investigate spiritual issues (misa de investigación), develop a person's spiritual guides (misa de desarollo), capture negative spirits (capturación), break free from spiritual enslavement (rompimiento), or unite people with their main protector guides (coronación). By strengthening the spiritual cord and elevating any obscure or "unevolved" spirits, people can achieve generational healing, uplift spirits in turmoil, and connect with their own guides. Rather than Western civilizational enlightenment projects based in colonialism, Afro-Latiné elevations are reciprocal forms of energetic intra-activity. The spirits guide us; we rely on their perspective to navigate the world. This misa was an investigation and, if necessary, a capturing.

"Siete con Siete, Siete na mas . . ." My twenty-one-year-old son, Pilli, who led the songs, switched from the slow, Catholic-inspired melody that began the misa to a fast-paced African Congo verse. He has been singing these traditional songs all his life, trained by my father, Piri Ochun, and my padrino (godfather), Alfredo Calvo Cano (ibaé).[1] My eldest son, Neto, also a high priest (Oriate) in Santeria, had just received the sacred batá drums (añá) from my father. He brought out the box drums (cajón) to amplify the energy. The spirits were activated. Mediums all around the circle began to pop off, getting "mounted" (possessed) with their Congo copresences. The Congos always come to defend their own against unwanted intrusions.

"Nsala Malekun." The Congo spirit Siete Rayos came to greet me, grasping my arm. Siete Rayos is a spirit who has long walked with me; he is sworn to stand up in my defense. Siete Rayos said he is not pleased with the spiritual intrusions happening around me. My "book stuff" (academia), he tells me, is a form of calling the dead. "Don't be foolish," says Siete Rayos. "Stop thinking like a White (mundele) person." Siete Rayos advises me to wake up. I need to stop pretending I do not see the connections between academic scholarship and spirit work. Being so long in the academy, I have inadvertently bought into a kind of Western empiricism, a "Whiteness" that he warns me against. I must acknowledge the spirits. "You have to make a decision," Siete Rayos warns. "Allow yourself to be guided or stay stuck," keep being haunted. "You choose."

Murdered

I WAS FEELING THE IMPACT of the hauntings. I kept waking up at 3 a.m., my stomach in knots. Unable to sleep, I used those early morning hours to look through newspaper clippings. My husband and children slept soundly upstairs. Wrapped in a blanket in the kitchen of my rented home near Stanford, I discovered how Wetli had treated murdered Black women.

"The typical scene is in a cheap room, a clump of bushes or an abandoned building," Charles Wetli told reporters. "The woman is naked from the waist down, her clothes are scattered around. . . . At first glance, she looks like she's been raped and murdered."[1] But Wetli insisted that wasn't the case.

When twelve Black women were found brutally raped and strangled to death in Miami between 1986 and 1988, police initially suspected murder, but Wetli convinced them otherwise. As the chief assistant medical examiner of Dade County, Wetli claimed that "the autopsies have conclusively showed that these women were not murdered." Wetli classified the Black women's deaths as "cocaine intoxication accidents," and he would later cite them as early cases of excited delirium syndrome. With this diagnosis, police officers closed the cases.

Wetli initially told reporters that in the summer of 1987, he "noticed the pattern" when three Black women had died "in a cluster." The murdered Black women, many of whom were immigrants from Jamaica, Haiti, and Puerto Rico, in addition to Black Americans, were depicted as sex workers who had overdosed. Instead of finding that the obvious pattern to these Black women's deaths raised suspicions of homicide, Wetli dredged up racist tropes about Black women as hypersexual.

"In each case, death occurred during or immediately after sex," Wetli told reporters, implying that Black women were engaging in consensual intercourse. During slavery, Black women were presumed to always be ready and available for sex with White masters, and that presumption has persisted in stereotypes about Black women's sex lives. For Wetli, these Black women could not possibly have been raped.

"The best theory now, according to Wetli and two other medical examiners," reporters stated, "is that the women died from something like 'cocaine psychosis'—sudden death from low doses of cocaine that cause the victims to go berserk and die within minutes."[2]

"When you put the three cases side by side," Wetli stated, "the low level of cocaine was the common denominator."[3] In October 1987, a fourth case occurred, and Wetli stated that the medical examiners "suspected some cocaine impurity or some other drug mixed with the cocaine as factors that might tie the cases together, but preliminary tests failed to find such a link."[4] Even as tests failed to show that cocaine or some other mix of drugs contributed to the deaths, Wetli and the other two medical examiners ignored the obvious signs of foul play. They did not want to *see* evidence of struggle on the Black women's bodies. Wetli went on a media campaign to convince people that there was no serial killer on the loose; instead, he presented the women as drug users who were just getting what they deserved for their illicit lifestyle.

Wetli had to go to great lengths to convince people to disregard these obvious homicides. The media coverage surrounding the "cocaine-sex deaths," as he called them, was a deliberate public relations strategy; these deaths formed part of an even bigger theory he was building.

Wetli told reporters that the Black women had "only about 1 milligram [of cocaine] per liter of blood."[5] Then he clarified, "or about one-tenth the amount that killed basketball star Len Bias."[6] Referencing the 1986 death of Leonard Kevin Bias, an African American student and basketball star at the University of Maryland who, at twenty-two years of age, had died of cardiac arrest, was strategic. No conclusive answer was ever reached as to whether Bias's death was related to the small amount of cocaine found in his blood. But the idea that his death was directly related to cocaine use fit well into Wetli's argument, and so he mentioned Bias's death.[7] By linking these Black women's deaths to the recent death of a young, healthy Black athlete who had a little cocaine in his system, Wetli was setting the stage for his own racist theories, which would lead him to "discover" excited delirium syndrome.

"For some reason, the male of the species becomes psychotic, and the female of the species dies in relation to sex while using cocaine," Wetli stated.[8]

To make this argument, however, Wetli had to ignore significant evidence that pointed to the fact that the Black women's deaths were homicides. For example, most of the women were found in a similar pattern: nude from the waist down, with their legs spread wide open and their belongings scattered around.[9] Nidia Torres, a thirty-year-old Black Puerto Rican woman, was found in the parking lot of an abandoned building with a bedspread wrapped around her body.[10] How could someone who died in a sex-crazed frenzy wrap herself in a blanket and dump her own body in a parking lot? Another woman, Barbara Ann Black, who was twenty-three years old, was found on someone's lawn. She was naked from the waist down, and the toxicology report noted that there was no cocaine in her system.[11] Police found several women with condoms next to their bodies. Sixteen-year-old Sharminita Gray was found in a stairwell, "leaning against the steps, naked, and her head was thrown back 'as though she had suffered an immediate seizure.'"[12]

With these examples of foul play and strange positioning, bodies contorted and left in abandoned areas, Wetli and his team of medical examiners repeatedly denied finding any trauma on the Black women's bodies that indicated murder. Specifically, they denied that there were any signs of strangulation.[13] Yet, we know now they were not looking closely enough; medical examiners did find hemorrhages in the women's eyes, noses, and lips that indicated asphyxiation. Instead of investigating these horrific tragedies, Wetli used these women's discarded bodies to serve his grander, erroneous theory. And, for a time, this strategy worked.

* * *

"I have trouble accepting that you can kill someone without a struggle when they're on cocaine," Wetli told news reporters.[14] Wetli was convinced that Black people using cocaine, particularly Black women, were endowed with superhuman strength and therefore could not have been murdered. The idea that Black women could not possibly be victims because cocaine made them too strong to be killed regurgitates the long-held myth that Black women are "medical superbodies."[15] Black historian Jennifer Morgan has discussed how this idea can be traced to colonial depictions of Africans and Indigenous peoples as "monstrous races," depictions that then served to justify European conquest and exploration in both Africa and the Americas.[16] In early slaving voyages to West Africa, European traders described African women's strength and suitability for enslavement and reproduction by describing how difficult it was to capture them.[17] Fascinated with African women's abilities in childbirth, Europeans used the myth of Black female "superhuman" strength to justify breeding them like cattle.[18] The rendering of Black women as superhuman extended to their offspring. African women's presumed superhuman abilities justified all African people's enslavement.[19] They were denigrated as beastlike by Europeans, and this type of racial-sexual logic was implicit in African enslavement, Indigenous genocide, and European colonization.

Wetli resurrected the anti-African trope of Black women having super strength together with a "culture of poverty" mentality, stating: "Cocaine is a stimulant. And these girls were streetwise."[20] The "culture of poverty" hypothesis, first coined in 1958 by anthropologist Oscar Lewis, presumed that poverty was a lifestyle attributable to traits that were passed down through generations and that created a vicious cycle.[21] The hypothesis blamed Black American and Puerto Rican women for the reproduction of a pathological family structure headed by single mothers, who, Lewis thought, produced criminal children.[22]

Wetli's use of the term *streetwise* indicates an analysis that draws on ideas like Lewis's about a culture of poverty. Black sociologist Elijah Anderson describes *streetwise* as knowing "'how to behave' in uncertain public spaces."[23] A streetwise person is someone who has developed a sophisticated survival strategy to navigate the dangers of the urban streets.[24] However, for Wetli, *streetwise* seemed to mean that Black women had superpowers, and that with cocaine they became extra-strong. By this time I knew that Wetli also used the term *streetwise* to talk about Black and Brown Cubans who ended up on his medical examiner's table. He stated that the tattoos on dead Marielito bodies "reflected a streetwise philosophy" that "indicated a preference for certain types of criminal activity."[25] For Wetli, being streetwise meant that these Black and Brown people were illicit, criminal, sexually deviant, and therefore responsible for their own untimely deaths.

Charles Wetli told reporters that he could not figure out "why all of the deaths were in the northwest section of Dade, why they were clustered in groups at about the same times, or why almost all of the victims were black."[26] It is crucial to understand that these were Black women and girls who were killed in Black neighborhoods in the Miami area that had long been segregated. For example, most of the women were killed in Overtown, a Black diaspora neighborhood located just northwest of downtown Miami, which during Jim Crow was called "Colored Town."[27] Others were killed in a so-called prostitution zone in the North Miami area, long known for its Black Caribbean and especially Haitian community,[28] and which, in law enforcement circles, is called "North Dade." Another area where police found dead Black women was in the historic Brownsville District, one of the few designated locations in the Miami area where Black people were allowed to own homes during segregation.[29]

Wetli built on the racist history of segregation to criminalize the places Black women were killed in order to undermine the women's credibility. Unable to see the Black women as victims, Wetli went through mental gymnastics to find other causes for their deaths. "'We might find out that cocaine in combination with a certain (blood) type (more common in blacks) is lethal,' he said. 'We just don't know.'"[30] Wetli underscored that there was no telling why minor doses of this particular drug had a lethal effect. At one point he speculated that the rainfall in Peru might have produced a bad shipment of cocaine.[31]

Wetli undertook a strategic media campaign aimed at convincing Miami that these women were streetwise, drug-addicted prostitutes whose deaths were meaningless and whose cases needed no further investigation. In a November 1988 *Miami News* article, reporters Adrian Walker and Heather Dewar highlighted Wetli's findings of "cocaine-sex deaths" in a two-page story that featured a large, bolded "List of Victims" box. Titled "Cocaine-Sex Deaths in Dade Probed," this list included descriptions of the twelve Black women.

Walker and Dewar's descriptions, or "bios," of the victims were designed to blame these women for their own deaths. The bio of Erica Edwards, one of the women police found dead in a field on October 22, 1986, is a prime example of how reporters like Walker and Dewar team up with medical examiners like Wetli to disparage the Black women victims. Using Wetli's "data," Walker and Dewar categorize Edwards as "cocaine-sex death" number 5. They then portray her as a degenerate prostitute immigrant who got what she was looking for:

(5) Erica Marie Edwards—found dead at 8 a.m., Oct. 22
Court records show Edwards, 24, a native of Jamaica, was arrested five times since 1986. Charges included drug possession and prostitution. Between May 1986 and December 1987 she lost 45 pounds. On May 13, she was arrested for flagging down cars at Northwest 79th Street and 12th Ave-

nue. Edwards "was told the hazard of her continued actions," the arresting officer wrote. Four months later, her body was found in a field at 811 N.W., 79th St., two blocks away from the scene of her last arrest. Police said she was last seen standing on the corner at 1 a.m.

Walker and Dewar's characterizations of the other twelve victims were just as damning. In Edwards's case, the reporters tell us that she was a Black immigrant who had been arrested multiple times for drugs and prostitution, and so was *streetwise*. They imply that her recent weight loss indicates poor health from cocaine addiction, and thus her death was likely due to underlying conditions and drug use.

According to the story, Edwards's risky behaviors caused her death; she should have heeded the officers' warnings four months prior. Her death didn't matter much, however, since she was last seen "standing on the corner at 1 a.m.," two blocks from where she was arrested. Details such as these served as proof that the Black women had found exactly what they were looking for. Walker and Dewar intended to ease public fears of an unseen killer, and they also condemned these women. As the *Miami News*'s presumably White readers would see and conclude for themselves, these Black women's deaths were due to so-called Black problems: prostitution, drugs, and crime.

The media campaign itself interfered with the investigation. Wetli convinced the Centers for Disease Control and Prevention (CDC) experts who had been brought in to advise the investigation—people who had been concerned there could be a serial killer lurking in Miami—of his version of the events: "CDC experts have agreed with the theory that the deaths are caused by some female version of cocaine psychosis."[32]

Even before police investigators were told of the medical examiner's findings, Wetli was speaking to the press. Reporters who had interviewed Wetli at the medical examiner's office were the first to notify Lieutenant Clint Wunderly—the Miami-Dade County police officer in charge of investigating the Black women's deaths—about Wetli's conclusions that the women had not been murdered. When asked to comment, Lieutenant Wunderly told reporters that once he received the official findings from the medical examiner's office, he would "close the books" on the cases and "look no further" into the Black women's deaths.[33]

Lieutenant Wunderly ended up doing just that in November 1988, proving Wetli's campaign a success. The police closed the cases, the CDC experts agreed with him, and I imagine that Lieutenant Wunderly believed he had successfully protected the public. However, Wetli's faulty racist logic would soon be exposed.

* * *

In October 1988, just one month before police officers closed the cases, at least five more women were found dead in the Overtown area of Miami, two on the same morning.[34] But even when the rapes and murders occurred right in front of the police, they chose instead to believe Wetli's fabrication. In one disturbing account, an undercover police officer, Robert Beaty, describes walking up to a man having sex with a seemingly unresponsive woman in a trash-littered lot in the Overtown area.

"What's going on?" Officer Beaty asked.

"'Good sex,' the man replied. The woman, lying under the man, said nothing."[35] Ten minutes later, Officer Beaty found Anita Spires dead and the man gone.[36]

But for years, Black women had been trying to tell police that they were in danger, and no one had listened. They identified Charles Henry Williams, a Black man convicted of serial rape, early on as a potential serial killer.[37] Four women had been killed near Williams's family home in Overtown, and he was suspected in at least eleven deaths.[38] The six-foot-one Williams had worked first as a bus mechanic for the county and then as a kitchen worker at Coral Gables Hospital. He had played football at Miami Jackson High, and in 1976 he was arrested for raping a fifteen-year-old girl on her way to school.[39] He got a year for assault. Then in 1977, another fifteen-year-old claimed that Williams had choked and raped her. He was sent to a program for sex offenders.[40]

In court testimony, one of the Black women who accused Williams of raping her, a graduate of Miami-Dade Community College, described how "Williams grabbed her from behind, forced her into a field, raped her, stole her crack, and walked away."[41] She chased him, screaming, just as a police squad drove by. With her pants still pulled down from the assault, she flagged down the police. But the police did not seem to care. They neither took pictures of the scene nor offered to take her to a rape treatment center, even when she insisted. The police told her she "had no business being out there." She stated that the police "were actually believing" the story that Williams was telling them instead of her own.[42]

Even though he was Black, police did not take Williams into custody for the alleged rape of a Black woman. Instead, they arrested him for possession of crack cocaine. Five weeks later, they finally filed rape charges against him, but only after it became apparent that he might be a person of interest in other cases. At his rape trial, prosecutor Susan Dechovitz said in the opening statement that "Williams selected the victim because he thought she wouldn't be believed."[43]

It was the case of fourteen-year-old Antoinette Burns, a Black girl found raped and murdered under a tree in December 1988, that would finally challenge Wetli's claims. When police found Burns's body, Wetli claimed that her death was another "sex-cocaine death of a hooker."[44] Even though the police and public had bought into this racist argument for years, Burns's death was different. First, Metro Sergeant Wesolowski noticed that Antoinette had a hairbrush in her back pocket. "No one—unless forced—would have sex in such an uncomfortable position, he reasoned."[45] Then the toxicology report came back negative for cocaine. Wesolowski and Sergeant Cliff Nelson took their doubts to the chief medical examiner, Joseph Davis—Charles Wetli's boss.

In a careful reexamination of photo slides from the autopsies, Davis found overlooked trauma on the Black women's and girl's bodies. There were visible "lip and neck injuries, as well as minute hemorrhaging in the eyes," which were "all symptoms of asphyxiation."[46] Davis ended up reclassifying fourteen of the deaths that Wetli had claimed were "sex-cocaine deaths" as homicides. When Davis made the announcement that the women's cases were homicides, he said that some of "the signs of asphyxiation were so pronounced that one could see them from 'ten feet away, it's that clear.'"[47]

The Miami Police Department finally realized that the city was dealing with a serial killer. More murdered women continued to be found. The fact that these Black women's murders had so easily been dismissed via the deployment of racist and misogynist stereotypes points to the broader issue of racial science. Wetli's manufactured "sex-cocaine deaths" allowed a serial killer to continue hunting Black women and girls with impunity. Ignoring evidence of struggle, assault, rape, and murder, Wetli excluded these key findings to support his preconceived theories.

* * *

As I continued with my research, it was as though I was being led to all these connections. For example, I read that in October 1988, a woman named Beverly Gunder-James had testified that Williams had "choked her to unconsciousness" and "dragged her off to an alley," where she was rescued by a passerby.[48] However, she was not allowed to tell the jury that earlier that evening she had introduced Williams to her friend Erica Edwards, the Black woman from Jamaica whom I described earlier, who was later found dead in an open field in what Wetli claimed was one of his "cocaine-sex deaths." In the rape trial against Williams, Edwards's death could not be entered as evidence.

Charles Henry Williams would never be held accountable for any of the Black women's deaths. Instead, he died in jail of acquired immunodeficiency syndrome (AIDS) while serving a forty-year sentence for rape, just ten days before the scheduled start of the trial for the only murder he was ever charged with: the death of nineteen-year-old Patricia Johnson, a Black woman asphyxiated in 1984.

Between 1980 and 1989, police suspected Williams of raping and choking at least thirty-two Black women and girls, ranging in age from fourteen to thirty-six.[49] In a 1993 article, Charles Henry Williams described himself as a "sex-crazed crackhead" but claimed that he did not murder or rape anyone.[50] When asked who did, he smiled and said he would not be a "snitch." He then insinuated that he had witnessed the murders and knew who had committed them.

Semen taken from Patricia Johnson's body was found to match Williams's genetic profile. In addition, using Williams's dental records, a forensic dentist "linked a bite mark on Johnson's right breast to Williams's teeth."[51] Even though evidence placed Williams with at least six of the victims, prosecutors never tried him for these killings.[52] As a result of Wetli's racist and sexist campaign to disparage these victims of rape and murder, their deaths remained unsolved.

Taking up these claims, news media invoked the age-old Jezebel trope by exhibiting demonized characterizations of the Black women's lives. The original Jezebel figure from the Bible is portrayed as an enemy of God, a murderer and a prostitute embodying wickedness, promiscuity, and deceit.[53] She is depicted as a dark-skinned woman "with a greedy appetite for sex"; her heinous behavior is used as justification for her gruesome execution, with witnesses delighting in her body being dismembered and devoured by dogs.[54] The public punishment of Jezebel effectively amounts to a public lynching.[55] Similarly, news media condemned the Black women and girls in Miami as "cocaine whores," reassured by the assertion that their deaths must have been the result of immoral behaviors.

What was at stake for Wetli that would motivate him to hold press conferences and do a publicity storm to prove that these Black women were not murdered but instead "crazed" by sex and cocaine? I am convinced that Wetli employed this campaign to make himself into an expert. Through the deployment of a racist narrative of "sex-crazed" Black women, Wetli crafted himself as exactly the opposite. He was able to claim the position of rational White doctor, a man to be taken seriously. White medical doctors have long used Black women's bodies to make themselves into experts. Claims that Black people have a higher pain tolerance have justified horrific experimentation on them in the name of medicine. In early gynecology, for instance, White doctors used the myth of Black women's strength and pain tolerance to experiment on enslaved Black women, forcing them to undergo gruesome procedures that maimed them and their children.[56]

Revered as the "father" of American gynecology, Dr. James Marion Sims started his career by conducting "years of nightmarishly painful and degrading experiments, without anesthesia or consent, on a group of slave women," thus medically training himself on an easily available population.[57] Armed with his scalpel and his faith in racist stereotypes, Sims would cut into the scalps of Black infants on the belief that Black people were prone to low intelligence and perpetual childishness because their skulls closed prematurely.[58] He would then use a cobbler's tool to force the skull bones of Black infants into new positions, causing the deaths of many children.[59] He blamed the children's deaths on the "sloth and ignorance of their mothers and the black midwives who attended them."[60]

I place Wetli's racist science in this lineage of experimentation on Black women's bodies. Just like Sims, Wetli asserted himself as the highly skilled, discerning, and omniscient expert and made himself highly valuable to law enforcement. The way the Black women, after they had been brutally murdered, were blamed, denigrated, dismissed, and condemned by the very people charged with investigating their deaths was similar to how the Black mothers and midwives were blamed for the deaths from Sims's deadly "operations." Never allowed to be victims, even when murdered, Black women were used to reinforce White expertise.

* * *

Black feminist mobilizations have taken the lead on exposing the serial murder of Black women. Black feminist activists have repeatedly sprung into action when no state authority or community cared about Black women's deaths. In 1979, in Boston, Massachusetts, the Combahee River Collective (CRC), a radical, queer group of Black feminists, joined together to decry the deaths of a dozen Black women who had been murdered and whose deaths were not investigated.[61] Most well-known for their *Black Feminist Statement* (1977), the CRC pioneered an intersectional model of activism that they called "identity politics." White liberals would later co-opt their term to dismiss coalition-based activism in favor of less radical politics.

The CRC mobilized for the safety of themselves and their sisters.[62] These Black feminists were frustrated by the initial response to the serial killing of Black women in their community. Police officers told them to find a Black man to protect them, or to stay inside because the police would not protect them. Black lesbian feminist Barbara Smith knew that these suggestions did not address her own vulnerability as a queer woman, or the vulnerability of single mothers.[63] Even heterosexual married Black women could not be expected to always be accompanied by a man or to remain hostage in their homes. Smith and her comrades in the collective began crafting the first of two pamphlets, "Six Black Women: Why Did They Die?"[64] The pamphlet allowed them to address how the serial killing of Black women is part of the "thread of the fabric of the violence against women" more broadly.[65]

At its conclusion, the pamphlet offers fourteen recommendations for "Self-Protection." Several are practical tips like: "If you feel like you are being followed . . . change directions . . . stay calm . . . DO NOT GO HOME . . . run to the nearest lighted place." And the writers also offer an important insight into how Black women will likely not receive assistance from strangers if they call for it. "Yell FIRE!" the collective advises, "if someone is attacking you, people are more likely to come to your aid, than if you call 'Help.'"[66]

Grounding their critique in the political and economic systems of capitalism, imperialism, and patriarchy, the Combahee River Collective argued that all Black women share racial and sexual oppression and must fight back with all women to access safety.[67] They wrote for the "1000s and 1000s of Black women whose names we don't even know. As Black women who are feminists we are struggling against all racist, sexist, heterosexist and class oppression. We know that we have no hopes of ending this particular crisis of violence against women in our community until we identify all of its causes, including sexual oppression."[68]

The CRC offers an approach rooted in the lived realities of Black women. This viewpoint calls for a fundamental change in how to conceive of Black fatalities. I see these deaths not as isolated incidents but as part of broader structural oppression. Terrion L. Williamson, a Black feminist scholar, sheds light on the CRC's perspective by emphasizing that to exclusively view the repeated murders of Black women as "serial killings" maintains the focus on the killers.[69] Law enforcement often emphasizes the way criminals target their victims, perceiving serial killing as merely a sequence of deliberate murders involving three or more victims.

When viewed through the Black feminist perspective of the Combahee River Collective, however, it becomes evident that in order to comprehend patterns of mass racial violence fully, one must see acts of murder as tied to a more extensive pattern that Williamson describes as the "serialization of Black death." [70] Within this framework, we can see that "the serial murders of Black women" represent just one among "many forms of premature death" that have shaped the lives of Black people since the era of colonialism and transatlantic slavery.[71] I perceive this serialization at work—the interplay of multiple and layered oppressions is visible in the campaign against the murdered Black women and girls in Miami whose deaths Wetli unjustly labeled "sex and cocaine deaths."[72]

In writing this book, I could sense the spirits of Black women urging me to link the blatant disregard for their lives, wherein they were unfairly blamed for their own murders, to larger patterns of structural violence. These Black women and girls want me to know that they are more than the sum of their deaths.

Tuesday, November 2, 2021
Stanford, California

I know that the spirits of the Black women and girls who were murdered are helping me through my research. It's All Souls Day, Día de los Muertos, *and I've inherited the gift of spirit from my great-grandmother.*

Juana "Niti" Reyes Borás, my grandmother's mother, was a spiritual healer who left Arecibo, Puerto Rico, in the 1940s, bringing her spiritual techniques with her to San Francisco's Mission District. Doña Niti served clients in the local Latiné community, curing spiritual ailments, removing errant spirits, and helping with illnesses such as susto *(fright) that no one else could resolve. We lived with her when I was a newborn so that my mother could take care of Doña Niti as she aged. She had a room full of potato sacks filled with herbs, which she had brought back from Mexico and the Caribbean, that no one could name. Jars with herbal powders, green potions, and spiritual baths (*baños*) lined her shelves.*

*Doña Niti was a bit of a legend. My father, Piri, said she was known as "hands of steel" (*manos de hierro*) because she could tell whether a person would live or die by touching them. Auntie Margaret remembers Puerto Rican women coming to the house, lining up in the living room, awaiting Doña Niti's healing.*

She wasn't the last one in our family with the gift.

Spirits first possessed my father, Piri, when he was a child. After being haunted for years, when he was fourteen, he found his way to Elpidio Alfonso "Obafun," a White Cuban émigré living in the Mission who was a priest of Santeria from Matanzas, Cuba. Obafun taught Piri how to wield the second sight and provided him with a system to hone his abilities. Rather than dismiss him as mentally ill, Obafun honored this gift, showing Piri how to use his power to heal. My father learned the way of the Ocha (la Regla de Ocha) and became a high priest in Santeria, initiating many people in our community.

When, as young children, Neto and Pilli told me they saw spirits, I knew how to guide them in the ways of our elders. And so, when the Black women spirits reached out to me, I tried to find a healthy way for me to respond to them that honored my family's traditions and my own academic practice. I used my journals to let them write what they wanted me to know. Just sitting here, emptying my mind, they take over. My hands seem to have a mind of their own.

I told Pilli about this practice today, after our Day of the Dead ceremony. I told him that my way of dealing with the ghosts I had picked up through my research was to let them write. He thought that was a way to deal with all the trauma I'm uncovering in this research. Worried that I wasn't sleeping well and had lost my appetite, he knew that the research was getting to me.

When I told him about what I had uncovered, about how this man named Charles Wetli had created this syndrome that was used to justify police violence, he said, "Oh, you mean that fake George Floyd thing."

"What?!" I asked him.

"Yeah," he said, "at first they tried to say George Floyd died from an overdose or something," Pilli remembered the name was something like "excited." After a quick Google search, I realized that, yes, at first, police and media tried to use the excuse of excited delirium syndrome for Floyd, but then it seemed to disappear after the video came out.

How did I not know this?!

I thought back to George Floyd's death in the summer of 2020. I don't recall hearing the term.

At that time, Neto had called me. "Ma, I need to quit my job," he said. Neto had been working as a counselor for "at risk" youth in Oakland, CA. He told me that he had been called to heal after the death of George Floyd. He was going to follow in the footsteps of my father and great-grandmother.

Manic

GEORGE FLOYD WAS ARRESTED for allegedly using a counterfeit twenty-dollar bill to buy cigarettes on May 25, 2020, in Minneapolis, Minnesota. The senior officer in command, Derek Chauvin, knelt on his neck for over nine minutes, ultimately killing him. Floyd was calling for help as he took his last breaths. Many tried to portray him as having overdosed, even though the amounts of fentanyl and methamphetamine in his system were not enough to cause death.[1] Conservative media described Floyd as "hysterical," "on drugs," and "a lunatic."[2]

While police knelt on Floyd, the rookie officer, Thomas Lane, is heard on body camera footage asking whether this might be a case of "excited delirium."[3] During the trial, Chauvin's defense attorneys argued that excited delirium syndrome was real and that Chauvin's lethal force was justified because of Floyd's superhuman strength.[4] Initially, when George Floyd's death was addressed on the Minneapolis Police Department website, the narrative was in line with a medical defense. It stated, "Man Dies after Medical Incident during Police Interaction."[5] The post described Floyd's death as follows:

> Officers were able to get the suspect into handcuffs and noted he appeared to be suffering medical distress. Officers called for an ambulance. He was transported to Hennepin County Medical Center by ambulance where he died a short time later.
>
> At no time were weapons of any type used by anyone involved in this incident.[6]

Initially, the official police statement reassured the public that officers were assisting Floyd. There was a false impression that Floyd just spontaneously died within a short time of interacting with police. If seventeen-year-old Darnella Frazier had not posted her bystander video to Facebook showing Officer Chauvin kneeling on Floyd's neck, the world might never have known that this was far from a person suffering medical distress—rather, it was a public lynching.

As a result of Floyd's death, people started looking into excited delirium syndrome. The National Association for the Advancement of Colored People (NAACP) and the American Civil Liberties Union (ACLU) argued that excited delirium serves as a medical scapegoat for police abuse and is not an actual medical diagnosis. The syndrome is not listed in the *Diagnostic and Statistical Manual of Mental Disorders* (DSM-5) and has no International Classification of Diseases (ICD-9 or ICD-10) code, which means that it cannot be studied statistically as a diagnosis. It is also not recognized by the American Medical Association (AMA), the American Psychiatric Association (APA), or the World Health Organization.[7] However, it is recognized by the National Association of Medical Examiners, which allows for it to be used as a legitimate cause of death in the United States.[8] *CBS News* reported in 2018 that a review of studies found that more than 10 percent of deaths in police custody that year were attributed to excited delirium.[9] The way the US medical system presumes a diagnosis to be stable when it is not is part of how this so-called syndrome has hidden in plain sight for so long.

* * *

In November 2021, the police contacted Jade Ellis and requested that she retrieve the ashes of her father, Jeremy, which had been discovered by a police officer in a random hotel in San Diego. Bewildered by how her father's ashes ended up in the hotel, Jade, who was listed as his next of kin, received the call to collect them. Jade felt a sense of irritation, expressing her reluctance to embark on the two-hour drive, still harboring resentment toward her dad. She recalled saying, "I was like, 'Oh, hell no. I don't want them.'"

The police told Jade Ellis's family that Jeremy was "on drugs" and that he had died because of heart failure attributable to excited delirium syndrome. Jade remembers them saying he just "up and died." For years, Jade had been upset with her dad for the way he had died. She blamed him for leaving her. Even so, despite her initial reluctance, she eventually made the journey to retrieve the ashes.

During that period, Jade was deeply immersed in preparing for her initiation to Santeria. Her guiding orisha is Obatala, known for embodying tranquility and revered as the elder among the orishas. While Obatala typically presents as male, they are among the few orisha who transcend traditional gender roles, manifesting as male, female, and nonbinary genders depending on the moral narrative revealed through divination. Jade's Obatala was determined to be feminine through the cowry-shell oracle (*dillogún*). Being initiated to the orisha of eldership was ironic for Jade, given that many people in her hometown of East Los Angeles, rarely have the privilege of growing old. For instance, Jeremy, who was killed at the age of forty, was considered "old" by neighborhood standards.

Jade told me that her father's spirit was "buggin' lately."

Jeremy had been trying to get her attention, but she had been deliberately avoiding his attempts at communication. Since his death, Jade had learned how to keep Jeremy's pesky spirit at arm's length when she decided to stop "doing him" and be herself. Her journey from wounded child to liberation artist had not been easy. Now an activist, a tattoo artist, a poet, and a soon-to-be priestess, she had endured so much pain and hardship to get to where she was. I was glad Obatala would bring Jade some much-deserved peace.

I suspected that Jeremy's spirit may have become more active because of Jade's upcoming initiation ceremonies. Practitioners of my traditions understand the spirit plane (*ará onú*) as a site where spiritual entities can become more powerful, "developed" (*desarollado*) in death. Through Jade's ceremonies, Jeremy's spirit would be "activated," allowing for more direct interaction with Jade and her spiritual family—even with me. These concepts align with theories of quantum physics that question the fixed nature of matter and have long recognized the interconnectedness of the world through waves, energies, particles, transmissions, and imperceptible forces.[10]

I asked Jade what she knew about how Jeremy had died. She really did not know much. She had been informed that there was a police pursuit, and that Jeremy's heart "stopped" during the incident. To gather further details, Jade connected me with her mother, Carmen.

I felt an immediate bond with Carmen during our phone conversation. Her affection for Jade and Jeremy resonated in her voice. According to Carmen, Jeremy came across as a good listener, but he did not really engage in extensive conversation. He had gained a reputation for illegally acquiring old cars, and his friends would call on him for special orders. Jade had shared with me that there were typically "five cars in rotation" when Jeremy was around. He would refurbish and customize lowriders, selling some and giving others away to spread happiness through the neighborhood. It was his way of beautifying the community, a form of extralegal community art.

Carmen reminisced about meeting him at a lowrider show. Describing "Big Jer" as "the love of my life," with his tall stature, dark complexion, and charming smile, she was immediately taken by his good looks and gentle demeanor.

Jeremy grew up in the heart of "gang land," as Carmen described it; "there was lots of crime and shoot-outs." His mother, Diane, a biracial woman with a Black father and a White mother, gave birth to Jeremy during her eleventh-grade year, at the age of seventeen. Jeremy's father, Marcel, a Black German man, was not around in his life. Diane's struggle with heroin addiction began when Jeremy was young, leading him to be raised primarily by his White grandmother, Bev. Jeremy's aunties, Brenda and Glenda, also resided in the house and were involved in the family business of "boosting," or theft.

According to Carmen, "they were all boosters." Jeremy had told Carmen that while growing up, he recalled having cold packs of frozen meat in his stroller as his mother shoplifted from grocery stores. Bev, his White grandmother, was known for her constant companions: her shotgun, a cup of coffee, and her Pall Mall cigarettes. In one memorable family tale, Grandma Bev was sitting in her favorite spot, a La-Z-Boy recliner on the porch, when a drive-by shooting took place. A bullet pierced her coffee cup, prompting her to calmly say "Get 'em," and everyone in her house rushed out with their guns.

Carmen also fondly recalled Jeremy's aspirations to be a good father to Jade and her sister, Eva. She proudly noted that they had carefully planned both children, ensuring that they were "exactly seven years apart." Carmen wanted a family, and especially children, with Jeremy. "It was fucked up," she remembered of the hurt she saw in Jeremy's eyes when he couldn't be there for their kids. He had not wanted to repeat his parents' mistakes. They often discussed the need to "get our shit together" now that they were parents. Jade's birth—Carmen was convinced the baby would be a girl—marked a significant moment in their lives. Carmen even chuckled about how she had accurately predicted her trans daughter's gender.

Jade holds cherished memories of the times Jeremy was around. Despite being an awkward queer kid, she never faced harassment in her neighborhood because her father was highly respected. "A lot of my safety I owe to that, I think," she says. "I was never bullied nor mistreated by my community. At least not for being gay." Jade's newfound Santeria community is also rallying behind her, recognizing the love and positivity she brings to the world. When we met, the *ile* (house-temple) was generously covering the costs for her initiation ceremonies, which amounted to several thousand dollars and encompassed all the necessary items for the rituals.

When Jeremy passed away on June 11, 2011, he had spent a significant portion of Jade's life in and out of prison. At the time of his death, Jeremy was on parole and had accumulated two prior strikes under California's "Three Strikes and You're Out" law, which meant he would face a life sentence if he were arrested once more. Before he died, his plan was to return to Carmen and the kids, and he had scheduled a date with them on Father's Day. Carmen recounted the circumstances surrounding his death as she had been told: "The police are behind him on the freeway. He knows he's going to go to jail for life. Somehow, they crashed into him. The police didn't do it correctly. They made him crash, and he hit a big semi. Him being on crystal, they said his heart goes out. He crashes into the semi-truck." While she couldn't recall the specific freeway, she remembered that it had made the news. "It was a big car chase," Carmen shared.

"Did they conduct an autopsy?" I inquired.

"No," she replied. "We were just told his heart went out, and he died. That it was unexplainable."

During my conversation with Carmen, I sensed Jeremy's spirit. The atmosphere shifted, and I felt an urgency, as if he wanted me to pay attention to something.

"They made him crash," Carmen asserted. "They made him hit that semi. And they told us his heart failed." It was clear to me that Jeremy deemed this information significant. I could discern his desire for me to include it in the book.

The coroner officially recorded Jeremy's death as "unclassified." Families often receive vague explanations regarding the cause of death. It is occasionally attributed to heart failure and commonly labeled as "unclassified" or "undetermined." Medical examiners across the country use excited delirium syndrome as either the cause of death or as contributing to death, and they attribute the syndrome to some kind of drug-related heart failure. In addition to cocaine, it is now associated with the use of methamphetamine. Medical examiners will usually opt for an "unclassified" designation if they believe further investigation is necessary. Jeremy's death, however, remained uninvestigated. It was only eight years after his passing, following the death of George Floyd, that people started to seriously question the syndrome that police claimed led to his demise.

* * *

In the weeks that followed, I reached out to Jade and told her about the information I had learned from her mother regarding her father's death. Jade was taken aback. "I remember them trying to say my dad was manic and just crazy," she said, referring to the police's characterization of him. "They made him seem like he was drugged out—out of control—and he just died."

Jade's observation is quite accurate, as there exists a historical connection between excited delirium syndrome and the medicalization of mania. In my research on Charles Wetli, I uncovered that he, along with a coauthor, coined the term *excited delirium syndrome* in 1985. Although Wetli and his coauthors would later expand their hypothesis to encompass other drugs, including methamphetamine, their initial focus was primarily on cocaine. In his capacity as the deputy chief medical examiner for Dade County, Wetli collaborated on two articles with his colleague David A. Fishbain, a psychiatrist who supervised the psychiatric emergency services at Jackson Memorial Hospital in Miami, and held an associate professorship at the University of Miami School of Medicine during that period.[11] These two articles laid the foundation for what is now recognized as "excited delirium syndrome."[12]

The articles identified a range of symptoms they claimed were induced by cocaine, including disorientation, hallucinations, disturbed perceptions, impaired thinking, and other manifestations of "delirium." The authors argued that these symptoms resulted from low-level drug toxicity and purportedly led to the death of people in police custody. In 1985, Fishbain and Wetli coined the term *excited delirium syndrome* based on a study of seven cases of people who died between April 1983 and May 1984.[13] To establish a precedent for excited delirium syndrome, Fishbain and Wetli referred to the experiments conducted by Dr. Luther Bell in 1847 at the McLean Asylum for the Insane in Somerville, Massachusetts.

During the Mexican-American War, a number of unexpected deaths occurred among Dr. Bell's hospitalized patients when he conducted experiments on them. The first individual, a thirty-five-year-old woman identified as "E.A.P.," whose husband was serving in the war, was described as "wildly attacking" anyone who approached her.[14] The asylum documented E.A.P.'s display of "mania" and "delirium."[15] She was restrained in a bed, administered small doses of opium, and subjected to leeching for sixteen days. According to medical records, she remained in a state of high excitement, recognizing no one, rarely sleeping, and experiencing diarrhea.[16] The following day, she was described as having "suddenly" passed away. Several similar deaths occurred at the asylum, where Dr. Bell treated patients in like manner—restraining them in beds, applying leeches, and administering opium. Bell documented forty such unexplained deaths between 1836 and 1849, describing the deceased individuals as exhibiting symptoms of "acute exhaustive mania" and "agitated delirium," characterized by "sleeplessness, disconnected delusions, and hallucinations," ultimately culminating in unexplained death.[17] Bell published his findings in the *American Journal of Insanity* in October 1849, and this phenomenon became known as "Bell's mania" or "excited catatonia."

This diagnosis fascinated me. As I kept looking, I discovered that the history of mania is intertwined with the criminalization of spiritualists in the nineteenth century. At the time when Dr. Bell conducted his experiments leading to the coining of the term *Bell's mania*, medical doctors were not universally regarded as all-knowing experts. Healing practices of the era were influenced by a multitude of cultural traditions, with Western doctors vying for prominence. Even scientists in the United States in the 1860s did not dismiss the notion of spirits.[18] Alfred Russel Wallace, who alongside Charles Darwin proposed the theory of evolution, was among those who believed "that spirit communications" validated the existence "of an extracorporeal dimension" to human beings.[19]

However, as doctors sought to establish themselves as the sole authorities on health and medicine, they viewed spiritualists as a threat. A network of physicians, particularly neuroscientists claiming expertise in the understanding of the mind, launched a campaign against spiritual mediums.[20] They labeled spiritualists lunatics and swindlers, contending that spiritualism constituted mental illness, manifesting as neuroses, mania, delirium, and even insanity.[21] They introduced a new disorder known as "medio mania," which posited that mediumship trances resulted from an abnormality in the "upper part of the cerebrum."[22] They even suggested that this condition could be contagious among "séance goers" with "a similar occult deficiency of the nervous system."[23] Medio mania was predominantly seen as a neurotic disorder affecting women, associated with vegetarian diets and uterine issues, although doctors believed that men could also exhibit these symptoms by purportedly mimicking women's behavior.[24] Treatment for this "disorder" typically involved a combination of sedatives, tonics, high-protein diets, and the application of electricity to bodies.[25]

The criminalization of female spiritualists was a direct result of their refusal to conform to the prevailing societal norms for White women's domestication and their challenge to positivist scientific thinking.[26] Police, doctors, lawyers, and politicians targeted spiritualists and fortune tellers with sting operations, lawsuits, and accusations of lunacy. Spiritualists were declared legally insane, leading to the confiscation of their properties and disputes over their wills.[27] By 1893, the National Spiritualists Association (today the National Spiritualist Association of Churches) was formed to defend healers and mediums across the country who were charged with crimes.[28]

Anyone who acknowledged visions—even subconscious ones—was a threat. During the same period, even psychologists faced a reputation as "mad doctors," with skepticism surrounding their therapeutic methods, a stigma that persists to this day. In an effort to counter the perception of irrationality, psychologists embarked on a reform movement targeting individuals who did not conform to neurological models of the mind.[29] Between 1860 and 1875, a coalition of neuroscientists, criminologists, physicians, and psychologists in the United States and Britain joined forces to criminalize spiritual healers and elevate Western medicine as the sole authority in the field. This concerted effort led to a broader cultural shift, in which those claiming contact with spirits were branded as insane.

This systematic criminalization of spiritualism extended to Afro-Latiné religions, and criminologists emphasized the importance of reinforcing Western medicine to uphold White values and prevent what they deemed "racial degeneration."[30] Prominent criminological eugenicists such as Cesar Lombroso, often referred to as the "father of positivist criminology," were instrumental in targeting spiritualists through his research in prisons and asylums.[31] Lombroso, who subscribed to the belief that criminality was hereditary, influenced his student Fernando Ortiz, who later became renowned as the father of the study of Afro-Cuban religions. In his first book, *Afro-Cuban Underworld: The Black Witches* (*El hampa Afro-Cubana: Los Negros brujos*), Ortiz argued that an African "germ of homicide remains latent" in Black people, waiting to be awakened through savage rituals.[32] Although Ortiz later apologized for this racist criminology, it nevertheless contributed to the criminalization of Afro-Latiné religions for generations.

It is not the first time that medical doctors would weaponize mental illnesses like mania as a way to criminalize non-White and nonconforming people. But I was surprised to discover that Wetli and his coauthors had joined Bell's mania with their own blend of American eugenics.

* * *

Even when it became evident in 1989 that the Black women whose deaths Charles Wetli had erroneously labeled "cocaine-sex deaths" had, in reality, been victims of murder, he staunchly clung to the belief that Black people possessed a genetic predisposition to become "cocaine-crazed" and to spontaneously die around police. Building on his earlier claims about the cardiac arrest of the Black basketball star Len Bias, Wetli maintained his argument that young Black males, particularly those with a low body mass index, were at a heightened risk of death from cocaine.[33] Thus, according to Wetli and other medical practitioners who worked closely with police, cocaine would be the ready explanation for the deaths of Black males in the midst of violent encounters with law enforcement.

However, I was taken aback to uncover that in a 1996 article published in the *American Journal of Emergency Medicine*, Wetli and coauthors had referenced a racist news report from 1914, which had been used to justify lynchings during that era.[34] In note 2 of "Cocaine-Associated Agitated Delirium and the Neuroleptic Malignant Syndrome," Wetli and his colleagues cited a *New York Times* article, written by Dr. Edward Huntington Williams, that warned of "negro cocaine 'fiends'" causing havoc in the South.[35] Wetli and his colleagues used this citation as historical support for their claim that Black people exhibit extreme reactions to small amounts of cocaine.

Historians have demonstrated that accounts like Dr. Williams's were prevalent during the Reconstruction period, when Ku Klux Klan (KKK) patrols and police collaborated to maintain White social dominance.[36] Cocaine use became directly associated with Black men during this period. Southern segregationists and northern physicians, including individuals like Dr. Williams, collaborated to promote anticocaine measures, ultimately leading to a national ban on the substance in 1914.[37] The stringent crackdown on the drug served to criminalize Black men and justify White mob violence and the arming of law enforcement with guns.[38] Concerns surrounding cocaine reinforced the stereotype that African Americans were violent, uncivilized, and uncontrollable.[39] Such racially biased narratives fueled terror campaigns against Black people in the South, prompting the "Great Migration" (1910–70) of African Americans to northern cities.

The article cited by Wetli and his colleagues bore the sensational title "NEGRO COCAINE 'FIENDS' ARE A NEW SOUTHERN MENACE; Murder and Insanity Increasing among Lower Class Blacks Because They Have Taken to 'Sniffing' Since Deprived of Whisky by Prohibition."[40] This article depicted southern Black people in fantastical scenarios, portraying them as lascivious individuals engaged in "cocaine orgies," "sniffing parties," and "wholesale murder."[41]

The article's author recounted an incident in which the Asheville chief of police killed a Black man in his own home. The man was reportedly under the influence of cocaine, and instead of subduing him, the police chief beat him to death. Dr. Williams tells us that the chief first tried to shoot the man to "kill him right quick." When the man did not immediately succumb, the chief resorted to beating him to death, all while his family and community members looked on in horror. Dr. Williams noted that, in case the family considered aiding the Black man, the police chief had conserved his ammunition for the impending "mob."

The article concluded with Williams's plea for increased armament of the police. He argued that law enforcement needed more potent weapons to counter Black men under the influence of cocaine, as firearms capable of killing "any game in America" were insufficient to halt "the increased vitality of the cocaine-crazed negroes."[42] Dr. Williams cautioned White readers about the sinister impact of cocaine on Black people:

The list of dangerous effects produced by cocaine just described— hallucinations and delusions, increased courage, homicidal tendencies, resistance to shock—is certainly long enough. But there is still another, and a most important one. This is a temporary steadying of the nervous and muscular system, so as to increase, rather than interfere with good marksmanship.[43]

Echoing the historical rationales for slavery and colonization, the age-old myth of Black superhuman strength was resurrected not only to justify police killings but also to promote a heightened vigilance around Black people. For Dr. Williams would also have us believe that Black people on cocaine somehow gain a new superpower: they become expert marksmen, too.

Penned by a White physician, this *New York Times* article serves as a stark illustration of the close relationship between police violence, medical justification, and lynching. It was the Black investigative journalist Ida B. Wells who initially exposed how southern lynch mobs incited widespread fear through displays of violence against Black men. In her 1892 pamphlet *Southern Horrors*, Wells adeptly demonstrates the connections between the lynching of Black men by White mobs and sexual violence against Black women by White men. She used the term *Southern horrors* to mock the commonly cited pretext for lynching Black men, alleging that they had assaulted White women.[44] Wells illustrated how the portrayal of Black men as rapists effectively placed them "beyond the pale of human sympathy."[45] She further revealed how lynching was employed as a smoke screen to disguise Whites' violent efforts to strip African Americans of their hard-fought rights.[46]

Wells's subsequent book, *A Red Record: Tabulated Statistics and Alleged Causes of Lynchings in the United States, 1892–1893–1894*, published in 1894, meticulously utilized White newspapers to document more than ten thousand lynchings of African Americans, shedding light on the role of media dissemination in instilling fear among readers. Just as in Dr. Williams's article, news media portrayed Black men as "beasts" and served as an endorsement for lynching.[47] Lynching is as much about White spectatorship as it is about racial violence. Historian Amy Louise Woods elucidates how the White audience played an integral role in the mechanics of lynching.[48] As a ritual, lynching consolidated White supremacy by leveraging the wide circulation of lynching stories and imagery. Lynching was not only about the violent act itself; it was also a media campaign that united White viewers through a shared perception of Black threat. The widespread dissemination of lynching images, depicting White power and Black denigration, served to "instill and perpetuate a sense of racial supremacy in their White spectators."[49]

* * *

This legacy of lynching in medical racism persists, often obscuring systemic violence and perpetuating harmful stereotypes. In their 1996 article, Wetli and his colleagues cite Dr. Edward Huntington Williams's argument that Black people had a predisposition to becoming "frenzied" and wild with "mania" when using cocaine, thereby reinforcing their racially biased genetic argument. [50] This citation serves as a disconcerting example of how racist ideas are entrenched in medical science—effectively resurrecting the narrative of lynching media.

One thing I found curious after discovering Dr. Williams's 1914 article was that it does not actually describe a precedent for excited delirium syndrome, as Wetli and colleagues suggest in their citation. At no point does Dr. Williams make the claim that Black people unexpectedly die in police custody. His account instead describes a police officer openly assassinating a Black man who was believed to exhibit superhuman strength.

The narratives like those of the "Negro Cocaine 'Fiends'" provide a platform for White doctors like Edward Williams to assert control over the moral safety of White America. Wetli employed a similar strategy when he classi-fied the murdered Black women as suffering "cocaine-sex deaths." In his own words, Wetli was steadfast in his belief that the Black "species" possessed a racial-genetic predisposition to cocaine that led to their deaths in police cus-tody. Much like Fernando Ortiz's notion of an African "germ" of criminality, Wetli's eugenicist perspective was veiled behind his scientific discourse. Like Dr. Williams, Wetli and his colleagues propagated the notion that cocaine bestowed Blacks with seemingly superhuman strength, especially when con-fronted by law enforcement.[51] This perceived superhuman strength, in their view, served as a justification for excessive police force.

Rejecting the argument that police restraint or "positional asphyxia" could result in fatalities, Wetli and his colleagues contended that it might be "tempting" to attribute the cause of death to "minor injuries" sustained dur-ing police encounters, "such as minor head injury," but they argued that this would lead to unnecessary lawsuits.[52] Defending police violence as "normal procedure" against agitated, coked-out Black people, Wetli and colleagues claimed that the deaths of those with excited delirium syndrome should *al-ways* be attributed to cocaine toxicity, even though some individuals classified as having had the syndrome had "low to modest cocaine blood levels and [did] not behave like patients with massive overdose."[53]

I think about fourteen-year-old Antoinette Burns and twenty-three-year-old Barbara Ann Black, who were raped and murdered with no cocaine in their systems. Yet Wetli labeled their deaths as instances of spontaneous heart failure attributed to "cocaine-sex." His argument concerning the relationship between cocaine-induced delirium and police restraint bears a disconcerting resemblance. He did discern a pattern in police-involved deaths. For example, Wetli and colleagues asserted, "Shortly after being restrained, agitation ceases and the victim is frequently found dead, or near death, just moments later."[54] Indeed, the authors were aware of the role that police violence played in deaths attributed to excited delirium syndrome. In anticipation of this criti-cism, they stood firm, asserting: "Since the victims frequently die in police custody, there are often allegations that death resulted from asphyxia related to hogtying, or other police procedures such as restraining neck hold, pepper sprays, or electrical stun devices. However, it is important to note that many victims of this disorder die suddenly and without the application of any law enforcement restraining techniques."[55]

Consequently, the authors swiftly rejected the evidence that police violence could be responsible for deaths they attribute to excited delirium syndrome.

"When cocaine users with agitated delirium die, cocaine should be considered the cause of death,"[56] the authors state unequivocally. "It is well to remember that in most cases of agitated delirium, death occurs without significant police restraint, and frivolous speculation about the cause or mechanisms of death will only invite needless litigation."[57]

If Wetli had been the medical examiner in George Floyd's case, he would likely have attributed Floyd's death to excited delirium syndrome. I must admit that I continually find myself surprised by these revelations. While I am not oblivious to the role of systemic racism, I am deeply concerned about the extensive influence of medical categorization and diagnosis in concealing this violence. Diagnoses such as medio mania, which criminalized spiritualists, and excited delirium, which targets Black and Latiné people, are not rooted in objective facts. As I observed from Wetli's cited precedents (Bell's mania and "negro cocaine 'fiends'"), these are fictitious medical conditions that only masquerade as truth. It is the underpinning of racial science that enables them to function as seemingly impartial classifications.

Psychiatrist Jonathan Metzl exposes this process in action, illustrating how racism has been ingrained in diagnostic language throughout history.[58] For instance, eugenicist social scientists in the late nineteenth and early twentieth centuries crafted flawed social studies to substantiate the biological supremacy of White races and the inferiority of Black and Brown races.[59] In the "Black extinction hypothesis," statistician Fredrick Hoffman utilized 1890 census data in his book *The Race Traits and Tendencies of the American Negro* (1896) to depict African Americans as highly susceptible to disease, and argued that "their extinction was inevitable."[60] Rather than attributing the shorter life expectancy among Black people to systemic inequality and racist violence,[61] Hoffman, as Erickson relates, reduced his findings to "a simple tautology": Black people "died because they were inferior," and they were considered "inferior because they died."[62]

What I've learned from this history is that while medical categories may appear stable, I do not take for granted that diagnoses are constantly being contested.[63] In the case of diagnosing syndromes, Western medical practitioners rely on individuals' descriptions of their bodily experiences, diagnosing based on reported "symptoms."[64]

I think about the story I traced of how mania leads to excited delirium. However, with excited delirium syndrome, medical examiners "work backward" in identifying the cause of death, as no specific disease can be diagnosed through autopsy. Instead, medical examiners rely on the accounts of police officers and paramedics regarding the behaviors exhibited by the deceased to attribute the cause of death. Since the dead person cannot speak, at least not in a way recognizable to Western medicine, the distinction between classifying someone's death as excited delirium syndrome or as a homicide is often simply what police officers and paramedics report happened at the scene. Yet, by telling this story through the lens of the victims' experiences, as the Combahee River Collective advises, we unveil how these medical diagnoses are little more than racially biased conjectures bolstered by the authority of medical examiners and the law enforcement apparatus that depends on them.

Wednesday, October 13, 2021
Emerald Hills, California

When the dead visit my dreams, I can't hear their voices, but I can sense their intentions. It's not like that for everyone. But that's how it is for me. That's how it was when my stepson, Sito, visited me. He didn't speak with his voice, but he showed me what he wanted me to know.

I still can't believe Sito passed. He was taken from us on September 8, 2019, at the age of nineteen. It is an unimaginable loss. When he was fourteen, he had witnessed the tragic stabbing of a fellow student, a Black Latino boy from the Mission whom Sito had known for many years. Then, Sito was arrested and falsely accused of the boy's stabbing. Even though the police knew Sito was not the killer, he spent four months incarcerated in maximum security at San Francisco's Juvenile Hall, a place notorious for its violence. This experience forever impacted our family and ultimately led to Sito's revenge murder only a few short years later. Sito's story is a different side of the tragic cycle of youth violence and inner-city police corruption. My husband, Laurence, is writing a book about Sito's story. I feared that I couldn't.

Sito is one of the spirits guiding me through my process of uncovering the evidence in this book. At the funeral, his friends said he'd become their guardian angel. Right before his death, Sito had begun the process to be initiated as a priest of Santeria. And even though his ceremony was not completed, Sito is still a powerful copresence. He guides and protects us.

Neto told me that Sito is the reason he decided to start helping people after George Floyd's death. Sito wanted Neto to heal the generational trauma that Brown and Black incarcerated youth lived with. I think this is also why Sito came to me last night. I was feeling overwhelmed and lost, and he was trying to help me.

In my dream, Sito looked just as he did right before he died: tall, strong, with light-brown skin, wearing a red 49ers jersey. His straight, dark hair fell into his eyes. Sito reached for my hand. When he touched me, we were transported to an abandoned lot. It was dark outside, and the place felt eerie. We walked across the street to a field. I could see bodies of Black women. I knew they were the women in Miami whose ends Wetli had labeled "sex-cocaine deaths" but who had actually been raped and murdered by a serial killer. Some of the women were wrapped in blankets; others were nude from the waist down.

Sito leaned down and touched one of the women. Her eyes opened. He held out his hand to her. When their hands met, a bright light shone where they touched. The woman's spirit floated out of her body. It disappeared into the night sky. I sensed that he had somehow helped her spirit. Sito looked at me. This book would assist in such elevations, he wanted me to know.

Sito started jogging down the street, going somewhere urgently. I followed, jogging alongside him. We came to an intersection. It was daytime, there was a bus stop and a corner store. The red-lettered "Cup Foods" sign was unmistakable. Although I had never been to the Twin Cities, I recognized this place. We were at the intersection of Chicago Avenue and Thirty-Eighth Street in Minneapolis, Minnesota, where George Floyd was killed. I stopped and stared in shock. Sito and I stood about thirty feet away from Officer Derek Chauvin kneeling on George Floyd's neck. This image was so deeply etched in my mind, I could not believe that I was there. Then, Sito lifted his palm. A light from his hand illuminated the scene. Now, I could see that a number of floating entities were surrounding Floyd. The whole space was full of spirits. Could I do something? Could I help Floyd? I felt panicked.

I wanted to stay, but Sito pulled me away. I looked back regretfully at the scene, but knew I had to follow. We were in a park. I knew this place. I had come here as a kid. It was San Francisco's Golden Gate Park. We walked past a pond. Ferns, reeds, and palms lined the edge. It was night, but I knew that in the daytime, this little lake had a fountain in the middle. Families liked to picnic here. Sito stopped and pointed toward the bushes. I could make out a homeless man in a sleeping bag. Something was wrong with him. Oh no. He was dead. Sito looked at me. This man's case was important. I had missed something. Sito wanted me to see a connection between the Black women murdered by a serial killer, George Floyd, and the dead homeless man. I needed to understand how the criminalizing of Afro-Caribbean religions was tied to excited delirium.

The next morning, I woke up nervous. I lit a candle for Sito and thanked him for his guidance.

Panicked

AS I CONTINUED DIGGING into Wetli's background, strange connections kept appearing. My research seemed to speed up as if it had a momentum of its own. I would come into my office at the Center for Advanced Study in the Behavioral Sciences (CASBS) at Stanford University and discover some new, odd connection between Wetli and other cases I had been studying for years.

Two days after my dream with Sito, on Saturday, October 15, 2021, I was working late at the Center. Perched atop an eastern hill and located next to Stanford's illustrious golf course, the almost twenty thousand square feet of Center grounds lie just off the famous Junipero Serra Boulevard. The thoroughfare was named after the Franciscan friar and Spanish missionary who participated in the brutal colonization of the local Indigenous people of California. Pope Francis canonized Junipero Serra in 2015, making him the first Hispanic American saint. Local Native American tribes decried the canonization as disrespectful, arguing that it maligned the Indigenous ancestors of the land who had endured colonization under Serra's influence.[1] Indeed, this offense remains, with Saint Serra's name gracing some of the most picturesque sights of Northern California.

Junipero Serra Boulevard spans the length of the volcanic rock and greenstone basalt foothills near the university. This area is known for its robust wildlife, with hungry deer, wild turkeys, dusky-footed wood rats, and even an occasional mountain lion roaming freely. Swallows and woodpeckers flutter amid the shady woodlands of California live oaks and laurel trees that give the setting a light and airy serenity. Locals and tourists flock to the three-and-a-half-mile Stanford Dish Hiking Trail that loops around CASBS's grounds. With its stunning views and natural wildlife, the Center is celebrated as an ideal location for scholars to write books.

Nestled on the hillside are the CASBS Fellows' studies. These small cabins are highly coveted real estate, and Fellows compete for their preference among the fifty-four available offices. Outside each cabin door is a list of former occupants, mostly famous scholars, who "lived" in the room, making up the "Ghosts in the Study," part of the charm and lore of being at CASBS. However, it truly does not matter which study you get. Every cabin, fitted with floor-to-ceiling windows that bring the surrounding area indoors, boasts an equally gorgeous view. My corner office, Study 16, looked out on the campus. The scene was an artistic panorama of woody shrubs and wildflowers. In the distance, the grassy valley of Lake Lagunita, dried up at that time, formed a carpet behind which the Hoover Clock Tower stood tall.

It was a balmy fall day. Northern California is known for its warm autumns. So, I had left my study door ajar. I was quietly reading the materials that the helpful library manager had located for me. As the afternoon sun fell behind the hill, I was engrossed in a police document. Charles Wetli's name appeared in the file as an expert on "Afro-Caribbean cults." The case involved the suspected ritualistic murder of Leroy Carter Jr., a Black homeless man in San Francisco in 1981. When I first started conducting research on the policing of Afro-Caribbean religions in 2013, I was told about this unsolved case by two retired, high-ranking police officers whom I had interviewed in San Francisco.

The coincidences kept coming. There were very few details available about the unsolved case. I decided to do a quick search to see whether anything new had turned up since I had last looked. Much of the information on the web was on crime blogs and mystery fan pages. This case had now become horror-story lore. I managed to find some early newspaper clippings in the archive, but then I came across an article for the travel platform Inside Hook that referenced two of Wetli's cases as part of an inquiry into the 1974 murder of a woman by the name of Arlis Perry, who had been raped and killed in Stanford University's Memorial Church.[2]

From my study at CASBS, I glanced up to look in the direction of Memorial Church, and I could just make out the steeple with its cross on top. Jane Stanford had the church constructed in 1893 as a tribute to her late husband, Senator Leland Stanford. It was modeled after European churches they had seen on their travels. Memorial Church was also a tribute to Leland Stanford Jr., the couple's only son, who died of typhoid fever in 1884, just shy of his sixteenth birthday.[3] The church was meant to be the center of campus. The brilliant gold of the cut-glass tesserae makes up the largest mosaic mural in America. Measuring thirty feet in height by eighty feet in width, the scene impressively reproduces artist Antonio Paoletti's painting of Christ's ascension in the New Testament. The Romanesque feel of the massive columns, rounded archways, and carved natural stone make for a striking experience.

Inside the church, the light filters through stained glass onto polished wood pews. Exquisite frescoes and ornamental woodwork make the structure feel very different from other buildings on campus. When I was an anthropology graduate student in the early 2000s, the department was located right next to "Mem Church," as it is called by students, and I have a cherished photograph from my doctoral graduation in which I and my two young sons, Neto and Pilli, stand in front of the church.

On October 12, 1974, Arlis Perry had wandered into the church to find solace. It was around ten o'clock at night, and she had been in a disagreement with her husband, Bruce Perry, who was a graduate student at the time. The next morning Perry's body was found in a frightening scene. She was lying near the altar and was nude below the waist; someone had driven an ice pick into her skull. A long altar candle jutted out of her vagina, and another was left lying between her breasts. Police were so captivated by the scene and the fears of a cult murder that they ignored the man who found her body, a campus security guard and former police officer named Stephen Crawford, who had called in Perry's death by stating, "Hey, we got a stiff here."[4]

I had already been aware that the so-called Satanic Panic of the 1980s and 1990s had effectively vilified Afro-Caribbean religions in its wake. During this period, a mass public hysteria emerged from evangelical fears and unproven conspiracies. Law enforcement agencies, evangelicals, and child psychologists were convinced that an underground network of Satanists was abusing children and murdering people. From the documents I found, it appeared that Charles Wetli had begun to make a name for himself in this circuit.

The article from Inside Hook details how DNA evidence had finally solved the so-called satanic murder of Arlis Perry. Instead of the ritualistic crime it appeared to be, it turned out that Crawford, the campus security guard who had discovered her body, was the actual murderer. Semen found on a kneeling pillow and the jeans draped over Perry's body that had been collected at the crime scene finally linked Crawford to the murder in 2018.[5] Forty-four years after her death, this DNA evidence proved that Crawford was the killer.

There were claims that Crawford had become upset with Stanford when the police department was reorganized and he was demoted from his position as an officer. His weapon had also been taken from him after he failed psychological tests.[6] Reporter Scott Herhold, who had researched the case since the 1970s, stated that he did not believe Perry "was the intended victim."[7] Herhold argued instead that the "gruesome crime was against Stanford."[8] He suggested that Perry had simply paid the "terrible price" for Crawford's anger.[9]

Reporters speculated Stephen Crawford might have been a serial killer. He was described as "normal" and a "good guy" by neighbors,[10] and his brother was a police officer from Mountain View, California, which seemingly lent Crawford credibility.[11] In another odd coincidence, Crawford was fired from Stanford after he was found to have stolen from the university.[12] Over a number of years, Crawford took hundreds of thousands of dollars in rare books from Stanford's main library, as well as Native American artifacts and art, including a human skull, from the university's anthropology department.[13] A forged Stanford diploma was found in Crawford's home, even though he had never graduated from the university.[14]

As a military veteran, a former police officer, and a security guard on campus, Crawford knew exactly what law enforcement would focus on. The Inside Hook article suggests that Crawford had staged Perry's murder to throw the police off his scent, because he knew that police were caught up in the Satanic Panic. Some believed that Crawford had not only gotten away with Perry's murder but had also killed others.[15] Reporters detailed a few other cases that remained unsolved, including a case that Charles Wetli was involved in as a "cult expert." Between 1973 and 1974, when Crawford was on campus, at least three other unsolved murders had been committed around Stanford that had suspicious similarities to Perry's killing.[16] One of those murders had occurred on Junipero Serra Boulevard, right around the corner from where I was sitting that day.

It was not cold, but I shivered. It was mid-October, just about the anniversary of Perry's murder. I stopped reading the articles and looked out the large window. The striking view felt different now. Time had passed too quickly for comfort. I could have sworn that I had just looked up and it was bright outside. But now the sun was setting, and what had felt so tranquil suddenly seemed unnerving. I heard a noise outside my office and jerked my head toward the open door. Walking slowly to the opening, I peeked around the corner. Two deer nearby were chewing on twigs. They looked at me, ears twitching. I felt silly for being spooked. I was sure no one else was on-site that weekend. My husband, who was also a Fellow, had been working in his study earlier in the day, but he had left for a late afternoon meeting. I was going to rideshare my way home.

Maybe a security guard is on the Center grounds, I thought.

I remembered Stephen Crawford, the campus security guard who had murdered Arlis Perry, and a chill ran up the length of my body. The story had gotten to me. I knew this place too well. For me, Stanford was like a former home that I had lived in as an adolescent and then returned to as an adult. My son Pilli, now a senior there, was majoring in computer science; he had wanted to attend college here because he felt connected to it from having grown up on campus with me when I was a doctoral student. Things looked the same, yet different. I felt as though I was stirring up ghosts. My heart was racing.

As if on cue with my spine-chilling thoughts, a news story started blaring from my laptop speakers. I turned back from the doorway where I was standing; my laptop was across the room on the desk next to the large windows overlooking Mem Church. Leaving my back unguarded, I stared at my screen in disbelief. A reporter was detailing the story of how officers of the Santa Clara County Sheriff's Office had gone to serve Stephen Crawford with the warrant for his arrest.

I rushed over and started clicking through windows on my computer, trying to discover where the offending sound was coming from. I had so many open tabs on my cluttered laptop that I could not find which one was playing. The newscaster continued to recount the gruesome details of Perry's death and then Crawford's final move. In 2018, when authorities finally went to arrest him, Crawford shot and killed himself as deputies stood outside his open front door. The former campus security guard had committed suicide to evade arrest. It was all caught on the sheriff's body camera footage, which they were about to play. When I heard the pop of the gunshot on my computer, I roughly shut my laptop to stop the sound. My computer was possessed.

Panic-stricken, I grabbed my bag, threw my laptop inside, and slammed my office door. Feeling as though I was being watched and followed, I ran down the winding road from the isolated hilltop. I was terrified. I did not even take the time to open my rideshare app. My senses on alert, I looked around frantically as I ran, expecting to see someone chasing me. Afraid I was going to trip and fall on the bumpy road, I finally arrived at the closed gate, gasping for air. The gate was supposed to be a comfort, it was supposed to reassure me that no one without clearance was allowed on these grounds after business hours.

But I now knew that security clearance had not protected Arlis Perry or the others who had been raped and murdered on this campus. I never worked alone at CASBS again.

* * *

On February 8, 1981, Leroy Carter Jr., a Black American homeless man, was found decapitated in Golden Gate Park, San Francisco. Carter was a twenty-nine-year-old Vietnam veteran who was known to spend time in the park but who did not get into much trouble.[17] Carter's body had been found wrapped in a sleeping bag in a woodsy area near Alvord Lake, a man-made pond built in 1833, about two hundred feet west of the Stanyan and Height Street entrance.[18] A mutilated chicken was found nearby.[19] One of the odd elements of the crime was that the wing of the chicken, along with some corn kernels, had been stuffed into the bloody stump of Carter's neck, where the head had been removed.[20] I was first told of Carter's gruesome story by two retired police detectives I had interviewed early in my research on the criminalization of Afro-Cuban religions. They told me this story to explain why, for them, "Santeria" was a "type of crime." Nine years later, I came across this story again as part of the Satanic Panic scare. Arlis Perry's and Leroy Carter Jr.'s murders were seen as examples of the Bay Area's ritualistic crime phenomenon.

In 1981, Officer Sandi Gallant was called to investigate the Leroy Carter Jr. homicide. Gallant recalls not knowing where to start with the bizarre case. She had heard that Charles Wetli was an expert on Afro-Caribbean "cults," and so she reached out to him.[21] Even though at the time, Wetli had very little knowledge of Afro-Cuban religions, he concocted what now seems a fantastical tale.[22] Wetli told Officer Gallant that Leroy Carter Jr.'s killer or killers were most likely practitioners of Afro-Cuban Santeria or Palo Monte.[23]

Despite the absence of any support for the assertion that Santeria or Palo Monte was responsible for this murder, Wetli informed Gallant that the perpetrators would first boil the victim's head to create a potion. He then claimed they would consume this concoction in order to gain magical powers.[24] According to Wetli, "the ritual called for a 21-day period of brewing in a cauldron. After that, the priest would sleep in the same room as the head and the cauldron for 21 more days, ostensibly to connect with them. After this 42-day period, the final step of the ritual would be to return the head to the body's final resting place."[25]

The theory was met mostly with skepticism by the San Francisco Police Department. They did not stake out the park on the forty-second day. However, Officer Gallant and her partner did decide to walk through the park on the morning of the forty-third day. To their astonishment, Leroy Carter Jr.'s missing head turned up near Alvord Lake. Although they never captured the person (or people) who killed him, the infamy of the story would live on to haunt Santeria and Palo Monte practices for decades.[26]

* * *

Leroy Carter Jr.'s unsolved murder remains a mystery to law enforcement and internet sleuths. One crime blog theorized that Charles Wetli himself might be the killer but that he lived too far away for it to be likely.[27] The blogger claimed that the level of detail Wetli knew about the crime was uncanny, especially the specifics about the head reappearing on the forty-second day. At the time, the only people who knew of Wetli's forty-two-day theory were the police. While it may seem far-fetched that someone from law enforcement would be involved in this murder, we need only look to the Arlis Perry murder for an example of a crime in which a former police officer had staged the scene to appear ritualistic.[28] So it is not completely implausible that Carter's murderer might have been someone connected to law enforcement.

We will likely never know whether Leroy Carter Jr.'s murder was inspired by some kind of ritual practice, or whether the homicide was simply designed to look ritualistic in order to throw police off the scent. But we do know that none of what Wetli described is accurate—at least not according to any known Afro-Caribbean religion. In a follow-up interview with Rafael Martinez, I asked about Wetli's theory about the Leroy Carter Jr. case. Martinez had never heard the story before.

"Where did Wetli get this crazy theory?" I asked him.

"Who knows!" Martinez told me.

"But how did Wetli supposedly become an expert of Afro-Cuban religions?" I probed, hoping Martinez might know something.

"Remember, he got information from all these detectives, and some of them actually were practitioners. You know, some of the cops from the city of Miami and Miami-Dade were practitioners, but most had a lot of fear. But yeah, I have no idea where he got that from."

I remembered the police report that Rafael Martinez and Charles Wetli submitted to the Dade-Miami Criminal Justice Council in 1986, "Tattoos among Cuban (Mariel) Criminals: A Cultural Analysis." The report had been circulated among law enforcement early on during the Satanic Panic and had identified Wetli as an expert on Afro-Caribbean "cults."[29] Could that be the reason people in law enforcement thought Wetli was a cult expert? But the report was produced five years *after* Carter's death.

Martinez recounted an unexpected visit by Wetli to his home in 1980. On that day, Wetli arrived to take Martinez to meet a Palo Monte priest. Together they, along with a police officer, went to interview the priest. The *palero*, a practitioner of Palo Monte, had undertaken a sacred promise to his beloved *nganga* spirit, committing to sleep alongside it for the entire forty nights of Lent. In Palo Monte religious traditions, the *nganga* is a spirit dwelling—often taking the form of a cauldron—that holds the sacred source of ancestral power. Unfortunately, the *nganga* has been unjustly stigmatized as malevolent. Recall that traditionally, from its Congolese heritage, the *nganga*, or *prenda*, serves as the repository for the remains of deceased family members. Through the *nganga*, a spirit is enlivened, given a tangible form, and imbued with potent abilities to offer guidance to the living.

Martinez fondly remembers a pleasant conversation with the *palero* in his home. The *palero* was hospitable and willingly shared insights, aiming to provide law enforcement officers with a deeper understanding of the religion. He expressed the hope that by engaging with them, law enforcement might cease its unwarranted criminalization of Palo Monte. It's worth noting that this interview took place in the year preceding Leroy Carter Jr.'s tragic murder in 1981.

Martinez was surprised that Wetli did not reach out to him when Sandi Gallant inquired about the case. If he had, Martinez would have told Wetli that whoever killed Carter did not exhibit behaviors consistent with Palo Monte or Santeria practitioners.

"I don't know where he got that from," Martinez remarked of Wetli's unfounded theory. Wetli's notion that the murderer would sleep with Leroy Carter Jr.'s head might have been loosely inspired by the visit to the *palero*, who had undertaken a forty-night ritual sleeping next to his *nganga*. However, from Martinez's perspective, it was evident that *paleros* were not murderers. In Palo Monte, for instance, ancestral bones are part of the sacred vessels used to reactivate spirits, but these bones are most often obtained with consent from family members before they pass away or legally through medical supply companies—not through homicidal means.

Wetli seems to have drawn upon racist stereotypes surrounding Afro-Cuban religions that depict practitioners as "Black witches" (*negros brujos*).[30] In the early years of the Cuban republic, fictional narratives circulated that propagated the false idea that Black witches were boogeymen who would murder White Cuban children, serving the dual purpose of criminalizing

Black Cubans and scaring children into obedience.[31] Historian Ivor Miller has revealed the deep-seated racial prejudices against Black religious practitioners in Cuba throughout the "colonial, republican, and revolutionary" eras, with authorities consistently displaying hostility toward them.[32] Similar to the Jim Crow South, where unfounded fears about protecting White women served as pretext for violence against Black people, in Cuba many African and Afro-Cuban men faced executions and lynching based on these myths. Afro-Cubans were unjustly characterized as "hypersexual, criminal, and degenerate," a portrayal that aimed to reinforce White male dominance and exert control over the nation's identity.[33]

An egregious example of these baseless claims occurred in March 1875, when the Abakuá society was banned in Cuba on the grounds of claims that they were murdering White children for their blood.[34] The fires were fueled after the November 1904 kidnapping and murder of Zoila, a four-year-old White girl from the outskirts of Havana, which became a national spectacle.[35] For a year, the reporter Eduardo Varela Zequiera convinced the public that Black witchcraft (*brujería*) was to blame. Through his alarmist reporting and demands that police search the household of every Black "witch" in town, he made a successful career for himself.[36]

Without any substantiating evidence, two Black men—Lucumi Domingo Boucourt, originally from Africa, and Victor Molina, a Cuban native—were charged with Zoila's murder. Testimonies from White men claimed that there were rumors suggesting Boucourt was a renowned *brujo*, but the only evidence they had was his African origins.[37] It is important to note that Boucourt resided more than forty-five miles away from the location of Zoila's murder.[38] Following a biased trial in January 1906, both men were subjected to garroting, a form of execution by strangulation with an iron collar or wire. Their brains were preserved for what was presented as a scientific examination of Black witches, purportedly carried out to protect the White population.[39]

Martinez informed me that such stories from Cuba followed Afro-Cuban religions to the United States. After his collaboration with Charles Wetli, he grew frustrated with the discriminatory portrayal of Afro-Caribbean religions to which his and Wetli's work had contributed. "You remember, as a medical examiner, he [Wetli] had a lot of cops that came to him during the investigation of homicides," Martinez told me.

Martinez cited anecdotes shared by Miami police officers as contributing to Wetli's misunderstandings. He emphasized that these anecdotes were rooted in fear and tried to rectify these misconceptions. However, it was challenging; Wetli held a senior position as a medical examiner and doctor, and he wielded significant influence in the law enforcement community.

"What are some of the fears they had around Afro-Cuban religions?" I asked Martinez.

"Don't go out on December 4th," he said, referring to the day that the patron saint Santa Barbara is honored, "because they're gonna kidnap you and drink your blood because, Santa Barbara." He described these as "boogeyman-type" stories propagated by certain zealot cops. He thought Wetli was unduly influenced by this, believing these biased stories to be fact. Martinez recalled that in the first article they coauthored, Wetli had confused Santeria with Palo Monte, and "even called it voodoo." Martinez recalled thinking, "What are you doing?" But he told me that he "never had a chance to correct him."

Martinez cautioned against officers who saw supernatural threats everywhere: "You know, those cult cops. They see the devil all over the place."

I recalled encountering a news story I had found featuring Wetli and his disturbing collection in the *Burlington (VT) Daily Times*, published June 25, 1980, a year before Leroy Carter Jr.'s death. The images portrayed Wetli sitting at an evidence table in the Dade County medical examiner's office alongside a large, ghastly looking human skull in the center. In another photo, Wetli points to different items on the table as he sits next to a White woman, likely another medical examiner. A stark white tablecloth lies coldly underneath the various Afro-Cuban religious items that Wetli had supposedly "discovered," as if from an archaeological dig. The caption, headlined "SANTERIA FINDINGS," reads as follows:

> Drs. Donna Brown and Charles Wetli display the crumbling bones of a woman long dead and the remains of several types of birds (R) in the Dade County medical examiner's office Tuesday after the bones were found in Miami, Fla., cemetery this weekend. The findings are signs that Santeria—a voodoo-like cult mixing primitive African beliefs and Catholicism—is flourishing in Dade County. *Wetli is a self-taught santeria expert.*[40]

These early images circulated widely across the country; I found reprints in newspapers as far away as Texas, California, New England, and New York. There was even a *Roving Report* television episode titled "Santeria or Cuban Occult in Miami, Florida" that aired on Britain's Independent Television Network (ITN) in 1981, which featured Wetli and his gruesome collection.[41] This was during the early years of the Satanic Panic. This press identified Wetli as a "self-taught" expert of Santeria! Officer Gallant must have seen these stories, and she must have contacted Wetli. I was sure this media was key to how he had become known as a cult expert, even when he had no real knowledge about the religions themselves. He used the publicity surrounding his Santeria collection as a means to criminalize Afro-Cuban religions and to make himself into a so-called expert.

The *Daily Times* article quotes Wetli making sensational and erroneous statements about Afro-Caribbean religions, including claims about the use of "animal remains" for "white magic" and human bones for "black magic." Wetli states, inaccurately, that the human remains "could have been a grave robbing, it could have been a murder, or it could have been a completely legal sale of the bones."[42] To anyone with an understanding of these religions, Wetli's statements are undeniably misinformed because these religions honor human life and revere ancestral remains. Yet, alarmingly, they found acceptance among both law enforcement personnel and the general public.

I realized that a central aspect of Wetli's strategy to bolster his own authority was his reliance on deeply entrenched racial biases that many people mistakenly accepted as undeniable truths. He exploited deeply ingrained racist stereotypes associated with Afro-Cuban religions, mirroring the tactics he would later employ to perpetuate racist stereotypes against Black people, thereby fabricating the concept of excited delirium syndrome.

The extensive dissemination of these images through national media outlets transformed a young Wetli into a highly sought-after authority in his field. Six years later, he replicated this approach with his "cocaine-sex" cases, endeavoring to convince the public that the deaths of Black women were not the results of a serial killer. He employed a similar method in the 2000s, crafting the narrative of excited delirium syndrome. Through this repetitive pattern, Wetli strategically utilized media sensationalism to establish himself as an "expert."

Rafael Martinez shared his perspective, suggesting that this phenomenon was part of the broader context of the Satanic Panic. "You know, Santeria and Palo got sucked into it," he told me. "Same as all the other pagan religions. They were sucked into it as if they were evil, malevolent. 'Watch out,' you know, like they're gonna kidnap your kids."

"Let me tell you," Martinez continued, "I was invited to a couple of conferences where those people actually were speakers, and I think they were disappointed after they heard me. Because they thought I was gonna go there and say, 'Let's go hunt these people,' and then when they heard my anthropological take on these practices, they were like, 'Who is this guy?'"

* * *

In a full-page article titled "Satan Sleuths" that appeared in the *Los Angeles Times* on May 25, 1989, Officer Sandi Gallant is photographed leaning slightly forward, with her arm draped over a park bench, and staring confidently at the camera.[43] Her demeanor evokes the aura of actress Joan Collins, famous for her role as Alexis Carrington in the hit 1980s television soap opera *Dynasty*. Alexis was a sultry antagonist, constantly scheming and causing turmoil for other characters. Gallant channels a similar vibe with her subtle smirk and fashionable blond pixie cut, accentuated by an oversized collared shirt featuring exaggerated shoulder pads.

Beneath the photograph, the caption identifies Gallant as "Satanic crime specialist Sandi Gallant of the San Francisco Police Dept." The article describes the evolving landscape of crime investigation, highlighting the shift from drug-related crimes in the 1960s to computer crime in the 1970s to terrorism in the 1980s.[44] It predicts that occult-related crime will be the dominant criminal focus of the 1990s.[45] The article also spotlights the discovery of Leroy Clarke Jr.'s head, which turned up forty-two days after his body was found, and features police officers who were once dismissed by their colleagues but are now in high demand as occult crime "experts." The journalists acknowledge Gallant as a leading authority "among the small but growing number of police officers who have carved out a specialty in crimes connected with the occult."

Officer Gallant was brought to San Francisco to investigate local leads on the Jonestown case, three years before Leroy Carter Jr.'s homicide. In November 1978, more than nine hundred people connected to a San Francisco Bay Area Christian church, the People's Temple, were killed in a mass murder-suicide in Jonestown, Guyana. The group, which included mostly poor Black people and more than two hundred children, was led by a psychopath, a charismatic White Christian named Jim Jones.

To those who followed him, Jones promised liberation from racial oppression, enticing them to abandon San Francisco and establish a new settlement in Guyana. Abused and defrauded, the mostly poor Black people were attempting to leave the colony when they were forced at gunpoint to drink Kool-Aid laced with cyanide. These murdered Black people were part of the serialization of Black death, however the prevailing narrative framed this tragedy as the result of a so-called cult of people taking their own lives. Once again, the blame for the deaths of these Black victims was shifted onto them.

Beyond the Jonestown case, Gallant's role quickly expanded during the Satanic Panic, when she found herself investigating a number of other such cases. In the aftermath of her involvement in both the Jonestown and Leroy Carter Jr. cases, Gallant earned the reputation of being San Francisco's foremost authority on "ritual crimes."

In the 1980s, a coalition of child psychologists, law enforcement officials, and Christian evangelicals collaborated to fuel the Satanic Panic. This hysteria was closely associated with concerns that elements in heavy metal music and video game culture would ensnare the minds of White teenagers, drawing them into the "occult." Manifesting primarily in the United States, the United Kingdom, Canada, and Australia, the Satanic Panic concocted a convoluted narrative involving a network of Satanists who were allegedly engaging in child abuse and murder.[46]

It is important to distinguish the Satanic Panic from the "cult craze" of the 1960s and 1970s. During that earlier period, there was apprehension about White youths being indoctrinated by Asian-influenced practices such as the Korean-Christian movement the Divine Light Mission, the Unification Church, and the International Society of Krishna Consciousness.[47] In the eyes of law enforcement, the satanic scare was considered a new form of "terrorism." The Satanic Panic of the 1980s emerged from a wider evangelical fearmongering against non-Christian religions and youth culture to consolidate law enforcement and psychological expertise.[48]

The beginning of the Satanic Panic is usually traced back to *Michelle Remembers*, a book published in 1980 that became a national sensation. *Michelle Remembers* spawned a genre of copycat books that detailed satanic cults raping, breeding, and killing babies and children. The young woman who is the subject of the book, Michelle Proby, was from Seattle, Washington.[49] She had begun to meet with a Canadian psychiatrist named Lawrence Pazder, who, through hypnosis, helped Michelle "remember" that she had been abused by a satanic cult. Using memories recovered through this therapy, Michelle related that when she was five years old, her late mother abused her and forced her to participate in horrific rituals.[50] During the course of her treatment, Michelle and Dr. Pazder each divorced their respective spouses, got married, and co-wrote this bestselling memoir.

Meanwhile, the election of Ronald Reagan provided White Christian evangelicals with a significant platform to frame the country's moral concerns. Although many of Michelle's claims were eventually discredited, they sparked a nationwide frenzy. Numerous Americans began to similarly "remember" instances of abuse, and Michelle's story became a cornerstone for this widespread alarm.[51] Therapists began to specialize in "satanic abuse," purporting to assist individuals in retrieving suppressed memories. Consequently, a consistent theme of drug use, device-assisted sexual abuse, torture, animal mutilations, human sacrifices, and cannibalism began to characterize such recollections.[52] Similar to the criminalization of spiritualists in the 1860s with the fabricated diagnosis "medio mania," therapists actively worked to convince people they were being "abused" by a "cult."

During this period, there was a notable surge in the field of clinical psychology, as the number of practitioners tripled. A significant portion of these professionals chose to focus on "repressed memory," "recovered memory," and "trauma search" therapies.[53] This emergent specialty was fixated on recovering patients' memories of ritual abuse.[54] The psychiatric diagnosis, initially termed *multiple personality disorder* (MPD) and later rebranded as *dissociative identity disorder*, stemmed from the Satanic Panic phenomenon. A 1992 study identified a link between therapists trained in MPD or "satanic ritual abuse" and those inclined to diagnose MPD.[55] Researchers cautioned that there was a trend of overdiagnosing these conditions.[56] Notably, Child Protective Service (CPS) caseworkers frequently underwent such trainings.[57]

Caseworkers for CPS played a pivotal role in the legal proceedings stemming from this hysteria. The Satanic Panic's first wave emerged in Bakersfield, California, in 1983. A zealous prosecutor formed a "ritual abuse task force."[58] This group collaborated with county social workers and law enforcement to identify and remove children purportedly abused by satanic cults from their homes.[59] The police often depended on CPS caseworkers to interview these children and deferred judgement about the occurrence of abuse to them.[60]

Unfortunately, these investigations, often led by inadequately trained enthusiasts, wreaked havoc on families. Social workers influenced by "satanic abuse" workshops would prematurely surmise the presence of child abuse without tangible evidence.[61] For example, the lead social worker in Bakersfield participated in law enforcement seminars about satanic crimes featuring the book *Michelle Remembers*.[62] The social worker extracted children from their homes and funneled them to these specialized therapies led by CPS caseworkers who were similarly trained. These children began narrating tales reminiscent of earlier claims describing blood-drinking rituals, "cannibalism, rape by chanting people in robes, [and] babies bred for sacrifice."[63]

However, these shocking tales lacked substantial proof.[64] Allegations, such as the ritualistic killing of thirty babies, emerged without any supporting evidence—no bodies were discovered, and no missing infants were reported.[65] The majority of these witnesses were displaced children themselves. One boy initially refuted claims of abuse until subjected to repeated interrogations, and another became an accuser post-hypnosis, while detained by police for two months.[66] In Bakersfield alone, numerous individuals faced charges: twenty-eight were incarcerated, with some serving over two decades in prison. Several more relinquished their children in plea deals.[67] Yet actual convictions were sparse.[68] The media eventually posited that the overemphasis on "blaming the devil" hampered genuine child abuse prosecutions, given the unreliability of children's accounts.[69]

As I delved deeper into my research, I found that Charles Wetli was among the prominent cult experts in Miami initiating training sessions for law enforcement on "ritualistic crimes." This loose network of investigators included former police officers turned cult consultants. In addition to the police, therapists and clergy members contributed to the hysteria by conducting trainings, hosting seminars, writing newsletters, and delivering public presentations. Intriguingly, they propagated satanic conspiracy theories as a legitimate law enforcement model without substantial evidence to back their claims.[70] Wetli, alongside Officer Sandi Gallant, belonged to this tight-knit network of practitioners who garnered financial benefits from both ends of the research-expertise spectrum. It was a lucrative circuit, with cult experts receiving between $5,000 and $10,000 for workshops and training sessions on "ritualistic crimes." These sessions ranged from a day to a full week in duration.[71]

Robert Hicks, once a police officer and now a critic of the Satanic Panic, expressed his shock at the profitability of this cult-expert circuit. He participated in multiple workshops and began tracking the rising popularity of these so-called experts. He observed their frequent appearances on television talk shows, as they addressed parents about potential threats to their children and often shared exaggerated statistics with journalists about human sacrifices in the United States.[72]

Hicks described courses that covered topics like "sects, cults, and deviant movements" and were facilitated by institutions like the Institute of Police Technology and Management at the University of North Florida. These were designated for "intermediate" investigators and purportedly delved into a range of religious practices and psychological disorders linking such disparate subjects as "countercultural Satanism"; "dynamics of paganism"; the "in-depth study of Afro-Cuban-American Santeria, Palo Mayombe, and brujeria";

"multigenerational ritualistic abuse"; and "multiple personality disorder and dissociative states."[73]

Afro-Latiné religions like Santeria and Palo Monte, along with European pagan practices such as Wicca, were grouped together in the Christian hysteria over Satanism, resulting in unwarranted attention from law enforcement. Hicks criticized these workshops for their lack of rigor, inaccuracies, unsupported claims, and "ignorance of anthropological, psychological, and historical contexts."[74]

It is important to understand that the Satanic Panic was not a peripheral issue but was deeply entrenched in all levels of law enforcement and political spheres of the time. In 1988, in the state of Virginia alone, cult experts offered "at least fifty seminars to the public—usually in churches and schools," in addition to the exclusive courses for law enforcement officers who earned in-service certifications.[75] Moreover, institutes like the National Crime Prevention Institute of the University of Louisville, which is considered a serious law enforcement training institute, offered programs linking Satanism to role-playing games and heavy metal music, and Palo Monte and Santeria to drug trafficking.[76] The market was also flooded with books, newsletters, audio recordings, and even software designed to aid in occult investigations, made by the International Protection of Assets Consultants Inc. of Salt Lake City, Utah, which retailed for $995 and included "profiling sexually motivated homicides" as part of the package.[77]

In a pattern that foreshadowed excited delirium syndrome, in which medical examiners depend on police descriptions to diagnose a nonexistent medical condition, the cult child abuse investigations relied on testimonies and inadequately trained experts. Even with minimal evidence pointing to actual victims of satanic ritual abuse, across the country almost two hundred people were indicted and prosecuted. During the Satanic Panic, there were eighty convictions, with a number of people serving lengthy sentences.[78]

This systematic crusade extended to video game culture, with critics alleging that games like Dungeons and Dragons could lure unsuspecting White suburban teenagers into Satanism, drugs, murder, or suicide.[79] Even Tipper Gore, the wife of then Democratic politician Al Gore and the future second lady, supported such claims. She joined BADD (Bothered About Dungeons and Dragons), an anti-satanic conspiracy group, and convinced the Consumer Product and Safety Commission to place warning labels on video games, even though later investigations debunked theories that video games presented a hazard to teenagers.[80]

In 1993, the US Department of Justice published a report, *Satanic Cult Awareness*, highlighting the purported atrocities committed by satanic cults, including everything from sexual torture to forced participation in abuse and murder. Officer Sandi Gallant was personally thanked by the authors of the report.[81] This fabricated threat targeted non-Christian, non-White religious practices and LGBTQ+ communities as un-American. Even some feminist narratives around sexual abuse inadvertently fueled the Satanic Panic by emphasizing the uncovering of repressed memories.[82]

The pervasive and destructive reach of the Satanic Panic, fueled by systemic biases and unchecked power, left an indelible mark on countless communities and individuals. Its consequences extended far beyond mere rumors, affecting real lives.

In 1994, four queer Latina women were wrongly convicted of "satanic related" sexual abuse of two girls in San Antonio.[83] They were imprisoned for fifteen years, until a 2016 documentary, *Southwest of Salem: The Story of the San Antonio Four*, which premiered at the Tribeca Film Festival, unveiled the truth and led to their exoneration. Throughout their trial, the prosecution painted these four Latina women as nefarious lesbians, conflating queer identities with pedophilia.

The key witness for the prosecution, Dr. Nancy Kellogg, head of pediatrics at the University of Texas Health Science Center in San Antonio, made unfounded claims about evidence of sexual abuse linked to "satanic rituals" and "lesbianism." Journalists later exposed significant flaws in Dr. Kellogg's abuse claims. Her identification of purported physical evidence did not follow prevailing medical knowledge. She later retracted her findings.[84] One of the two girls, now an adult, also recanted her story.[85] Indeed, Latiné studies scholars have since emphasized how the intensified border security and the war on drugs during the 1990s likely influenced the San Antonio Four's case.[86]

* * *

Growing up in the 1980s as a child whose family practiced Afro-Latiné religions, I had firsthand experience with the criminalization of the Satanic Panic. Living below the poverty line, my family survived on food stamps and state-subsidized health insurance (Medi-Cal), and so we would periodically need to take trips to the welfare office. I was distinctly afraid that CPS social workers would remove me from my home if they found out my family practiced Santeria. I grew up distrustful of teachers, doctors, and other service providers. Writing this book has caused me to relive some of these difficult moments from my childhood. I now realize why I felt so threatened in my adolescence. These were not misplaced fears. The structural power of the Satanic Panic did indeed mistakenly separate families, launch false child abuse claims, and criminalize non-White, non-Christian worshippers.

As a result of the Satanic Panic, Afro-Latiné religious practitioners found themselves unjustly in the crosshairs of law enforcement.[87] Facing relentless scrutiny from politicians, animal rights groups, and the police, our communities continually grapple with prejudice and endure targeted attacks, racism, and xenophobia. This discrimination provoked two Santeria churches in the 1980s to seek justice through legal avenues.

In 1980 in New York City, Black Cuban, Afro–Puerto Rican, and African American Santeria practitioners started a grassroots campaign after their ceremony was raided by police. They mobilized support, circulating petitions and securing legal representation, aspiring to negotiate with the city for a special permit that would authorize their religious rituals.[88] Although their efforts did not yield immediate success, they laid the groundwork for a landmark case in 1989. The Church of Lukumi Babalu Aye, led by an affluent White Cuban priest named Ernesto Pichardo, took on the City of Hialeah, Florida, over accusations of discrimination. Pichardo's unwavering commitment led the case to the US Supreme Court, where the church would become a beacon of religious freedom.

Friday, December 17, 2021
Stanford, California

Today is San Lazaro's day. It is a holiday in our tradition. In Santeria, the Catholic saint Lazarus is associated with Babalu Aye, the Yorùbá orisha of smallpox and contagious infections. The famous Santeria Church of Lukumi Babalu Aye in Hialeah, Florida, which is named in honor of Saint Lazarus, went to the Supreme Court to fight for religious freedom. The global COVID-19 pandemic we are living in is certainly Saint Lazarus's moment.

In the traditions my family practices from Matanzas, Cuba, he is known as Azojuano, which is the name from the Arará Dahomey peoples, where he was once a living king in Africa. When I was a kid, my dad would set up a special ceremony for Azojuano on December 17, to clean our family and community. With so much sickness and death we've experienced these past two years of quarantine and now, finally, being able to come together in ceremony, our family decided to do an awán *(cleaning ritual) for Azojuano. We pray he will help the world heal from so much illness.*

Priests carefully arrange plates piled high with special African foods around a large basket lined with burlap. Each plate contains different ingredients in a special sequence that activates the healing qualities of the food, which we understand to be medicine. Chopped root vegetables, fruits, meats, grains, lard, oil, coffee, tobacco, corn on the cob, whole red snapper, and meat bones are expertly arranged. The medicinal plant cundeamor (bitter melon stalk) is draped around our necks to cool the hot energy.

As the drumming begins, the officiator (Oriate) sings the collective Arará prayer, "Awan awan awa nu mi we awan se se . . . ," letting Azojuano know that with our hands we place these offerings, to clean ourselves, in the basket. We ask him to respond to our plea.

Each person goes around the circle of plates. With two hands, we bend to pick up the food from each plate, gently touching our forehead, then the back of our necks, then our stomachs. Last, before tossing the small handful into the basket, we breathe onto the offering, infusing it with our life force (aché).

Lined up from eldest to youngest in birth age, we all sing together. Wise, gray-haired grandmothers with dark skin and knowing eyes clean themselves first, while the youths wait in line, to honor the place of the elders. The basket is the earth that contains us all. We know that the earth is hungry, and through divination we learned that the earth is also angry because of human greed, arrogance, violence, and destruction. To calm this anger, we feed it the food-medicines. Once we finish going around the circle, priests clean us with incense, Azojuano's sacred wicker brooms (ajá) and then wash our hands with a mixture of coconut water, wine, and scented oils. I can feel the cooling energy down my body as we settle into the collective prayer through the rhythm of the ceremony.

COVID-19 has brought a kind of destruction that has transformed our planet. I ask Azojuano to provide the world with the healing we need. Azojuano is also the orisha of resurrections. Since he was once living, Azojuano is an ancestor, and like other dead spirits who return to the present, Azojuano communicates through dreams.

It reminds me of when I spoke to Rafael Martinez about how spirits communicated through dreams, and he told me that Wetli haunted him. In the summer of 2020, Martinez had not thought of Wetli for years when out of nowhere, Wetli appeared to him.

"I woke up dreaming with him," Martinez told me. He had lost touch with Wetli in the late 1990s. The last he recalled, Wetli had remarried sometime around 1994. Martinez had attended the wedding, but then he did not see or hear from Wetli after that. Wetli had relocated to New York, and Martinez chalked it up to them drifting apart.

After Wetli appeared in his dream, Martinez searched for him online. "And what do I find over the internet, he had died like three or four days before." Stunned, Martinez told me, "It gave me chills."

This story made me think of Azojuano. I was nervous, but I decided to ask Martinez if he was a practitioner of Santeria. "I am," he told me.

On September 24, 2005, Martinez entered the first level of initiation in Santeria, receiving the elekes, *the beaded necklaces that offer protection. "I remember the day. It was the day of La Mercedes," the Catholic Virgin of Mercy, which corresponds to the orisha Obatala, Martinez told me.*

"What led you to do it?" I asked him.

"I felt like I needed to. I felt it was the right time for me. I've never believed in people telling me, 'You have to do this,' or 'You have to do that.' It had to feel good inside. You know I like to think of myself as not one religion, but anything. So, it felt good. I received the necklaces, and then within two years, at different points, [I received] the warriors, and then eventually Olokun."[1]

I was so surprised to find out that Martinez was a practitioner. Martinez told me about how, like many Cubans, he had an affinity to San Lazaro. The information about Martinez's Santeria initiations may be a sign from Azojuano to show me how we can heal collectively from trauma, particularly racial trauma. Our lineage in Cuba, the Eguardo (*also* Egbado *or* Ewardo), *is known for its special relationships to the orisha Azojuano and Olokun, which Martinez had both mentioned by name.*

My great-grandmother in ocha, Fermina Gomez "Ocha Bi" (ibaé), began the practice of giving the orisha Olokun to noninitiated practitioners (aleyos) in Matanzas, Cuba. Olokun is the guardian of the depths of the ocean and contains all the mysteries of the world. Olokun is a gender nonbinary orisha who activates the souls of those who died at sea, particularly those Africans who succumbed during the Middle Passage. Olokun is a great avenger of injustice. I thought, maybe Olokun and Azojuano had guided Martinez. They certainly must have activated his spirits, his muertos, *as they are called.*

Afro-Latiné traditions call "unenlightened" spirits who have unresolved issues "muertos oscuros" (*dark spirits*). *It is common for* muertos oscuros *to visit people in order to assist the spirit in attaining elevation, and it is also common for them to haunt the living. Was Wetli a* muerto oscuro *who needed light?*

Or perhaps Wetli was haunted in the afterlife by the stigmatizations he created? Martinez himself has always been troubled by the negative depictions that came about from their shared writings. Had Wetli's own experience with Santeria and Palo led him to have a better understanding of the afterlife so that his spirit could contact Martinez, someone Wetli knew would acknowledge him, seek him out, confirm the interaction? Wetli, it seemed, had now become one of Martinez's muertos oscuros.

Tormented

WHAT I HAD NOT REALIZED when Rafael Martinez told me about his new *muerto oscuro* was that while Charles Wetli had taken part in fomenting these racist stereotypes against Afro-Latiné religions, he would also later take part in trying to undo them. That was quite an unexpected find.

I was reading a document produced in the winter of 1989–90 by the California Office of Criminal Justice Planning when I learned that Wetli had testified *on behalf* of the Church of Lukumi Babalu Aye, a Santeria church, as an expert witness. The document was a "special edition" of a research update, which is a kind of police manual that is circulated to advise law enforcement on how to handle particular cases and crime scenes. Titled "Occult Crime: A Law Enforcement Primer," the document features a legal case study on whether animal sacrifice is considered a "Constitutionally-Protected Religious Ritual."[1] It homes in on *Church of Lukumi Babalu Aye v. City of Hialeah*, the Santeria case that would eventually go all the way to the US Supreme Court.[2]

In 1989, after years of harassment by animal rights groups, politicians, and law enforcement, the Church of Lukumi Babalu Aye sued the City of Hialeah, Florida, for religious discrimination when, shortly after the church was established, the city passed ordinances banning animal sacrifice. The case, which the church eventually won in the US Supreme Court in 1993, made national headlines and has become an important precedent on issues of religious freedom. Animal slaughter is one of the sensationalized aspects of religious practice in Afro-Caribbean religions that has received the most attention from media, politicians, animal rights activists, and law enforcement. They have used racist and xenophobic misinformation to demonize ritual killing as "animal cruelty." However, just as in Jewish and Muslim religious slaughter, Santeria practitioners pray over livestock and fowl before conducting humane ritual killing and butchery and then consuming the meat. Since most Afro-Caribbean ceremonies are conducted in people's home temples, police are often called by neighbors who are offended that sheep, goats, or chickens are being slaughtered nearby.

I was astonished to find that at the bottom of the case study, on page 34, it lists Charles Wetli as having testified on behalf of the Santeria practitioners. The document, which portrays Santeria in a negative light, includes a note (in parentheses) to reassure law enforcement that Wetli was still a good person to contact despite his service as an expert witness for the Santeria church: "(Although Dr. Wetli testified for the plaintiff, he initially requested to be a neutral court witness.)" I had to ask Rafael Martinez about this!

"How did Wetli end up testifying for the Santeria church?"

"I'm not sure," Martinez told me. "But you know he later became friends with Migene González-Wippler," he said, mentioning a Puerto Rican Santeria practitioner and anthropologist who has written several books on the religion and other spiritual practices. "He [Wetli] even wrote the foreword to her book."

I went back and looked. He had indeed written the foreword to González-Wippler's 1989 book *Santería, the Religion: Faith, Rites, Magic.* I immediately requested the book from the library at Stanford.

The foreword was four short pages, signed "Charles Wetli, M.D., Deputy Chief Medical Examiner, Dade County, Florida." Wetli describes the need for this book in light of the "distrust and misunderstandings of Santeria by the general public."[3] Even those "who make a genuine effort to learn about Santeria are quickly frustrated," he states.[4] Wetli mentions the lack of factual information about the religion and that stereotypes have impacted how people see Santeria. I thought about Wetli's early years, when he considered himself a "self-made expert."

"Most who have only casually heard of Santeria picture 'voodoo dolls' pierced with needles, the ritualistic sacrifice of defenseless animals, and totally incomprehensible states of possession," Wetli writes.[5] He states that these misunderstandings have "thereby deprived" people of the knowledge of this "fascinating religion with a most interesting history, colorful ceremonies, a rich mythology and a profound philosophy."[6]

It seemed Wetli had shifted his perspective on Santeria. Remembering images from his "Voodoo" collection that were widely circulated in the early 1980s media, I couldn't believe that he was now denouncing the myths his research had perpetuated. In the foreword, Wetli emphasizes the need for a more informed approach: "Clearly, both factual information and meaningful dialogue are needed if Santeria is to gain acceptance in modern-day America."[7]

Delving into Wetli's testimony on behalf of the Santeria church, I found that he told the court, "To my knowledge, there have not been any health-related problems due to the disposal of a sacrificed animal."[8] The City of Hialeah had singled out the Santeria church, basing its opposition on three concerns that drew on the moral panic of the time. First, with the backing of animal rights groups, the city contended that Santeria should be banned for its practice of "animal sacrifice."[9] Although Santeria's method of slaughter is comparable to other forms of religious killing, wherein the carotid arteries of fowl and livestock are swiftly severed in a humane manner, the city argued that it was worse than commercial forms of slaughter. The city also took issue with Santeria religious stores (*botanicas*) that sell live animals to practitioners and, like pet shops, house animals in cages, feeding them and giving them water.

Second, in the midst of the Satanic Panic and the heightened anxieties about child safety, the city proposed that children witnessing "animal sacrifice" would undergo psychological distress and sustain long-term trauma. Lastly, the city suggested that Santeria posed a public health risk, citing instances of animal remains discovered in public places like railways, rivers, and wooded regions. Recall that Wetli's first encounter with Santeria and Palo Monte stemmed from discarded chicken remains and Palo cauldrons. To the extent that the discarding of animal remains is an issue for Afro-Latiné religious practitioners, it can be remedied with the provision of disposal bins at these sites. Yet, without evidence, the city made bold claims about "tens of thousands" of animal remains polluting the streets if *santeros* were permitted to conduct religious slaughter.[10] At the time, animal remains had been found only once in the City of Hialeah, a fact Wetli testified to.

In the city, White Cuban politicians, animal rights groups, and Christian evangelicals were ardently opposed to the foundation of a Santeria church within their working-class community. The police department's chaplain in Hialeah labeled Santeria followers as "demon" worshippers, denouncing the faith as sinful and "an abomination to the Lord."[11] The Ecclesiastical Board of Hialeah went on to describe the Santeria method of animal slaughter as "'barbaric,' 'medieval,' and 'satanic.'"[12]

During the city council meeting, when city attorneys Bill Wetzel and Richard Gross told council members that prohibiting the church's establishment was unlawful—as the religion was entitled to the same freedom as other groups—they were met with intense fury and angry shouts. City council member Silvio Cardoso retorted, "Hogwash, Mr. Gross," to cheers. Cardoso further declared, "They are in violation of everything this country stands for. I believe this council has the authority to stop these people."[13] The council's initial intention was to pass resolutions that would completely prohibit Santeria within the city. On their lawyer's counsel, however, they opted for a series of ordinances against "animal sacrifice."

* * *

The Hialeah City Council made "animal sacrifice" into a legal category and adopted new city ordinances to prohibit Santeria slaughter, referencing Florida's animal cruelty statute. However, Florida's statewide law superseded the city's ordinances and already allows for "the practice of killing animals humanely."[14] In fact, the Florida state animal cruelty law specifically exempts "slaughterhouses and the religious slaughtering of animals."[15] As such, the ordinances did not truly prohibit Santeria ritual slaughter. However, the primary intent of the city was evident: it was about discriminating against the religion and sending a clear message that Santeria was not welcome.[16]

The trial unfolded in the summer of 1989, with Judge Eugene Spellman, a Miami-bred Catholic Democrat, at the helm. Early on, there seemed to be an evident bias from Judge Spellman against the Cuban American attorney and plaintiffs, and even against the expert witness, Charles Wetli.

"Slaughtering animals for religious sacrifices in Dade County causes no public health problems," Wetli declared under oath in the courtroom.[17] His statement was echoed by three other county officials.

The Santeria church enlisted Wetli as an expert witness to provide a counter testimony to that of the prosecution's witness, Dr. Michael Fox, a veterinarian. At the time, Fox held the position of vice president at the Humane Society of the United States (HSUS) in Washington, DC.[18] Notably, he played an instrumental role in steering the HSUS toward more aggressive legal approaches in its animal rights activism. This new approach specifically targeted minority cultural practices, ranging from Indigenous sealing and whaling to Jewish and halal ritual slaughtering, sales of freshly slaughtered poultry in Asian American markets, and Afro-Cuban Santeria rituals. Despite having never witnessed Santeria slaughter, Fox contended that the descriptions provided by plaintiffs did not sound humane or pain-free. His testimony centered primarily on chicken slaughtering, emphasizing that, because of their anatomy, an instant or painless death was "highly unlikely."[19]

Wetli, on the other hand, spoke from his experience as a forensic pathologist who had directly observed Santeria slaughter. He asserted that, in his professional opinion, Santeria's method "resulted in rapid death."[20] Yet he also acknowledged that he wasn't in a position to comment on whether the pain experienced by animals was in a manner comparable to human sensation.[21] Judge Spellman focused on this point, arguing that he found Fox's testimony as a veterinarian "more convincing" than Wetli's, stating that Fox's "specialized knowledge, is more credible in this area" because he knew more about animal pain.[22]

The court discussion devolved into Christian notions of "suffering," likening animal meat harvesting to human religious experience. The debate shifted to whether animals feel pain similar to humans and if Santeria slaughter inflicted more pain than mainstream commercial slaughter methods. Instead of concentrating on the primary concern—the infringement of religious freedom and targeted discrimination—Judge Spellman seemed to support the city's stance. His final judgment was influenced by his personal conviction that Santeria slaughter caused chickens more distress than commercial slaughtering.

From the onset, Spellman seemed biased against the Cuban plaintiffs and attorney. He expressed skepticism about Ernesto Pichardo, the head priest, doubting his credibility and seeing him as insincere.[23] The judge also had a contentious interaction with the church's Cuban American attorney Jorge Duarte, a Buddhist, even going as far as threatening him with contempt of court.[24]

On October 5, 1989, Judge Spellman upheld all of the city's ordinances. He described Santeria as an "underground religion" that was not "socially accepted by the majority of the Cuban population."[25] Echoing the city's sentiments, Spellman voiced concerns about children, stating, "The City has shown that the risk to children justifies the absolute ban on animal sacrifice."[26] Skeptical of Wetli's assertions regarding the humane nature of Santeria slaughter, the judge concluded that "the animals perceive both pain and fear during the actual sacrificial ceremony."[27]

It did not matter that hundreds of thousands of animals are slaughtered for food every day in ways that are far less humane than the form of killing performed by Santeria rituals. Instead, Spellman was influenced by the prevailing prejudices of the time. His ruling effectively reinforced the idea that

Santeria and its followers were outsiders and should not be given the same constitutional rights as other American citizens.[28] On the steps of the courthouse, the ACLU, along with attorney Duarte, addressed reporters. "It is a dark day for religious freedom," Duarte remarked. "We've made criminals out of 70,000 people in South Florida."[29]

* * *

Learning this history made me wonder, *Could Wetli have had a change of heart after experiencing the secondhand racism aimed at Santeria?* Associated with a Black Caribbean religion, Wetli was already discredited in the eyes of Judge Spellman. Wetli had written the foreword to González-Wippler's book that same year. Things had also changed quite a bit since 1980. Wetli's "cocaine-sex" cases had recently been ruled homicides, and police were now looking for a serial killer whom Wetli's theories had inadvertently helped to keep free. Maybe he regretted how his early misunderstandings had demonized the religion?

However, in 1996, Wetli was still claiming that Black people had a genetic defect that led to excited delirium syndrome.[30] And he had made sure that the 1989–90 "Occult Crime: A Law Enforcement Primer," discussed earlier, noted that he was a reluctant witness for Santeria—that he had asked to remain "neutral."

Nevertheless, given his testimony and what he wrote in his foreword to González-Wippler's book, Wetli appears to have undergone a slight shift in his thoughts on Santeria. He had started conducting law enforcement trainings as well, meeting new practitioners, many of whom were police officers themselves. Martinez told me that Wetli was friends with a number of police practitioners. In his foreword, Wetli acknowledges that there had been much confusion by "non-Hispanics, like myself" in attempts to understand the religion. "Obviously, there is a need for intelligent, nonemotional, and nonconfrontational dialogue to avert religious and legal conflict," he writes.[31]

Wetli was born in Green Bay, Wisconsin, and was raised for a bit in Manhasset, Long Island. On both sides of his family, he had German ancestry.[32] His paternal grandmother, Marie Wetli (née Berendson), was born July 15, 1875, in Green Bay, Wisconsin. Her father, Bernardus "Bernard" Martinus Berendson, had been born in the Netherlands, immigrated to the United States, and had fifteen children in Green Bay with his wife, Barbara. Berendson was a register of deeds in Brown County, and by the time of his death in 1901, he owned more than one thousand acres of land.[33] Marie married Wetli's grandfather Charles Joseph Wetli, after whom Charles Wetli was named. Charles Joseph Wetli was a German American farmer who died at the age of fifty from blood poisoning that resulted from a leg infection.[34] Marie Wetli had to raise her five children alone as a widow. From her obituary, I saw that she devoted herself to Christianity.[35] She was a member of the Third Order of St. Norbert and of the Christian Mothers Society of St. Mathew's Church.[36] As part of this society, Christian mothers pledge to raise their families closely in line with Christ's teachings.

To what extent did Charles Wetli's German Catholic upbringing influence his perspective as a medical examiner, as well as his engagements with Afro-Latiné religions? All four of Wetli's grandparents and his father were buried at the Allouez Catholic Cemetery and Chapel Mausoleum in Green Bay, where there was a family plot.[37] Raised as a devout German Catholic, Wetli attended the University of Notre Dame, a Catholic university, and as a student he worked as a pumpkin picker.[38] As I looked a bit further, I found a fascinating connection: Wetli's paternal uncle was a renowned missionary in Latin America.

Born on February 2, 1910, in Earl Park, Indiana, Cletus Wetli, Charles's father, was the eldest of the Wetli siblings. A close second, his younger brother Elred Joseph Wetli arrived on September 27, 1911. I imagine the two were particularly close owing to their proximity in age. Tragedy struck when they were sixteen and fifteen: they lost their father. It's plausible to think that, being the oldest of the five Wetli children, Cletus and Elred shouldered considerable responsibilities, supporting their mother in upholding the family's deep Catholic values as guided by the Christian Mothers Society. This devout upbringing likely influenced Elred's spiritual path, leading him to embrace life as a Benedictine monk.

After his World War II military service, Elred Wetli took on the monastic title "Brother Elred" in 1950 and joined the Benedictine Holy Cross Abbey in Cañon City, Colorado.[39] By 1951, he and five fellow monks journeyed to Volcan, Panama, to establish the San Benito Agricultural School. Despite the church's call to return to the United States, Brother Elred chose to remain in Volcan, dedicating himself to teaching English at the school. His profound impact in South America led Pope John Paul II to honor him with the Order of Saint Gregory the Great, a prestigious papal knighthood, in 1990.[40] Many regarded Brother Elred as a "living saint" for his missionary contributions.[41] There were even intentions to commemorate his legacy with a towering nine-foot statue in Volcan.[42]

When Charles Wetli wrote the foreword to González-Wippler's book and testified in court in 1989, his uncle Elred was about to receive the medal from the pope.[43] Did Charles ever share his insights on Santeria with Brother Elred? Was Charles trying to carve out his own legacy by becoming a living saint?

I imagine that Charles Wetli's deep Catholic roots shaped his initial perceptions of Santeria. However, his stance evolved significantly upon delving deeper into the religion, especially after forging bonds with Santeria priests like the Puerto Rican anthropologist-practitioner Migene González-Wippler. It would seem that even his camaraderie with Rafael Martinez was important in developing his newfound respect for other cultures. I broached this topic with Martinez, curious about his own history and perspective.

* * *

"I ended up in Colombia doing a novitiate," Rafael Martinez told me of his youth, after coming to the United States from Cuba as a Peter Pan kid.

"What's a novitiate?" I asked.

"The novitiate is the first year when you join a Catholic order, like nuns, or priests or brothers, these were brothers, you go through a training period." Laughing, Martinez told me, "It's sort of like a version of an *iyawo*." A person is an *iyawo* during the yearlong initiation period when becoming a Santeria priest. Rafael Martinez told me that he had been raised a practicing Catholic. He became disillusioned after his time training with the Christian Brothers, however.

The Christian Brothers is a global order that goes as far back as 1684.[44] A Roman Catholic lay organization, the Christian Brothers educate poor Catholic boys, with a special emphasis on the marginalized.[45] According to historian Barry Coldrey, Christian Brothers associations toe "a thin line between extreme severity and sexual abuse," where they exhibit a "strange mixture of caring and corruption."[46] It was the emphasis on educating Christian boys that led the Christian Brothers to care for orphaned, delinquent, and neglected children.[47] In the past few decades, many Christian Brothers schools across the world have been shut down.[48]

Hailing from Cuba, Martinez grew up in Catholic traditions. He had vague recollections of his grandmother engaging in spiritual practices, but the specifics eluded him. In Cuba, it is not uncommon for people who practice Santeria to also identify as Catholics. While the Catholic Church claims that 60 percent of the island identifies as Catholic,[49] this number encompasses a significant portion who are believed to follow Afro-Cuban religions.[50]

The Catholic Church sometimes appears to recognize syncretic practices across Latin America and the Caribbean, such as Santeria, but only when it suits their agenda. An instance of this was during Pope John Paul II's visit to Cuba in 1998. He held an "ecclesiastical reunion" with religious leaders from Jewish and Protestant faiths but notably excluded representatives from Afro-Cuban religions. Cardinal Jaime Ortega, then the archbishop of Havana and the head of the Catholic Bishops' Conference of Cuba, responded by describing Santeria practitioners as "members of the Catholic family."[51]

"They are baptized Christians," Cardinal Ortega stated, "and we cannot engage in ecumenism with a part of the Catholic Church itself." Ortega then suggested, confusingly, that by refusing to meet with Afro-Cuban religious leaders, the pope was being inclusive. Ortega asserted that the pope was simply considering Afro-Cuban religious practitioners as members of the Catholic Church, and thus they did not require separate representation.[52]

Rafael Martinez had initially joined the Christian Brothers with aspirations of teaching, but after six months in Colombia he returned to Miami in 1969 feeling "disconnected." This led him away from the church, but it was his anthropology class that reshaped his worldview. "I have to say this, it was Mercedes Sandoval's courses that really opened up my mind to diversity and cultural relativism. At that age, young, it was an awakening. You know, 'all religions are good.'"

Mercedes Cros Sandoval, an anthropologist originally from Santiago de Cuba, taught at Miami-Dade College during the 1970s. At the time, she was among a few scholars studying Santeria from a cultural health lens.[53] Sandoval penned her observations on how the Catholic Church's declining reputation, marred by corruption and sexual abuse scandals, had led individuals to Santeria.[54] She argued that Santeria played a therapeutic role for many in the exiled community, aiding in their adaptation.[55] Advocating for a collaborative approach, Sandoval emphasized that mental health professionals should work in tandem with *santeros* for a culturally informed perspective, recognizing the significance of "obtaining the backing of 'supernatural power in caring for the soul.'"[56]

Following Sandoval's teaching, Martinez proudly declared to me, "I'm a cultural relativist!"

Cultural relativism was a concept introduced by Franz Boas in 1887; it urges researchers to set aside their own moral judgments when examining unfamiliar cultural traditions.[57] While some feminist anthropologists propose moving beyond cultural relativism to a more "relational" approach—

emphasizing interconnectedness and fluidity among cultures—Boas's teachings encouraged a generation of American anthropologists to interpret people based on their unique cultural perspectives. For Martinez, *cultural relativism* is more than just a "buzzword."

When he was a young anthropologist in the late 1970s, Martinez embarked on his fieldwork on Santeria by visiting a *botanica*. "I remember his name was Osvaldo," he said. Martinez shared with me that Osvaldo was a priest of Ochún, the goddess of the river, love, and riches. He told me, "The *botanica* doesn't exist anymore"; it used to be Botanica Iyalorde. Martinez recalled how Osvaldo opened up to him and shared with him the intricacies of the religion.

Martinez's father's friend introduced him to a man named Julio Garcia Cortéz, who wrote the 1971 book *El Santo (la Ocha): Secretos de la religion Lukumi* (The Santo: Secrets of the Lukumi religion). Cortez hosted spiritism sessions every Friday at the *botanica*. Martinez attended and documented meticulously. He watched as patrons participated in the rituals, providing him with foundational insights even before he collaborated with Charles Wetli.

Martinez is considered an *aleyo* in Santeria—a practitioner who has not undergone the priesthood ceremony. Martinez mentioned that he has a *padrino* (godfather) in the faith, a scholar-practitioner and trusted collaborator. Emphasizing the significance of having a therapeutic system within his line of work, he informed me of an upcoming drumming ceremony, or *tambor*, for San Lazaro (Azojuano). Their focus was understanding the role of trance in the religion. Martinez understood that his own work was to utilize the tools of cultural anthropology to undo ignorant stigmas.

When Martinez began conducting research on Santeria, he was taken by the religions' inclusivity. He saw how "gay practitioners" were widely accepted. "You know, I'm gay!" he told me with a big smile.

"I'm aware," I responded with a chuckle. "I've met your husband." We reminisced about our first meeting almost a decade earlier. Martinez confided that after his anthropology course, part of his distancing from the church was an affirmation of his identity as a gay man. "I don't need to be part of an organized religion that doesn't accept who I am," he said.

Eventually, Martinez enrolled in a master's program in anthropology at the University of Florida. "I'm a frustrated anthropologist," he confessed. His ambitions had once extended to obtaining a doctorate in anthropology, but work commitments took precedence. "So, eventually after working in Miami I decided to go to school at night, but there was no anthropology degree offered in the area. So, I went for the education degree."

* * *

When Martinez first met Wetli, he was transitioning from Christian-Brother-in-training to a cultural relativist. Around the same time, Wetli was navigating pivotal moments in his life. He had married his first wife, Buddie, in 1977, a year after his return from service in the US Army. Subsequently, he joined the Dade County medical examiner's office, where he worked for almost two decades. In the early 1990s, after testifying on behalf of the Santeria church, Wetli began leading law enforcement trainings in Florida on ritualistic crimes. Despite the Satanic Panic, the "Santeria 101" training sessions were successful in expanding officers' perspectives on Afro-Cuban religions, according to Martinez.

In 1993, the US Supreme Court ruled in favor of Santeria religious practitioners, strengthening religious freedom in the country. This decision led to more culturally inclusive police trainings, albeit under the title "Ritualistic Crimes." When Martinez took over the "Santeria 101" program from Wetli in the early 2000s, he inherited the course's name. Police department officials advised Martinez to keep that title in order "to get approval by the accrediting agencies," so they would be seen as aligning with "crime investigation." For Martinez, however, the goal was "always cultural competency" and promoting "respect and understanding."

Each session saw around thirty law enforcement officers from various agencies across Miami-Dade County. Because of its popularity, Martinez introduced an advanced, week-long course titled "Ritualistic Crimes: Investigation." The curriculum explored Afro-Latiné religions' "*potential* for criminal involvement." Martinez said it was important that "potential" was emphasized.

A significant portion of the trainings addressed the contentious topic of the ritual slaughter of animals, a frequently misunderstood aspect of the religion. Misinformed police actions around these rituals have led to public embarrassments, lawsuits, and trauma for the religious practitioners. Thus, Martinez ensured that both the basic and advanced courses provided comprehensive insights into the subject.

Each course concluded with a "cultural immersion" exercise. An *Oriate* (high-ranking Santeria priest) would perform a ritual that included animal slaughter. Martinez recounted an instance in which an *Oriate* slaughtered a goat at the Miami River, illustrating that it was a humane practice. While there were "a few objections from participants," most officers found value in the demonstrations. One officer, a member of PETA (People for the Ethical Treatment of Animals) recognized the importance of religious freedom and referenced the Ernesto Pichardo case in which the Supreme Court concluded that religious slaughter was constitutional.

Taken on a voluntary basis, the course was consistently full. The best training participants, Martinez shared with me, were those officers who were also religious practitioners of Afro-Cuban religions such as those initiated to Santeria, Palo Monte, or *Ifá* (a Yorùbá diaspora divination system). Not only were these police officer–religious practitioners trainers in the course, but they also enrolled as students. In fact, it was police practitioners who had originally introduced me to Rafael Martinez. They initially approached me, informing me about the trainings. Their concern was that since these courses were discontinued, there had been a resurgence of discrimination against Afro-Cuban religions in the agencies where they worked.

In 2005, police departments discontinued the courses because of budgetary constraints, as explained to Martinez. So, while I was not involved in any ritualistic crime trainings, which at that point were defunct anyway, I did begin investigating officers' training programs across the country. My research revealed that misconceptions about Afro-Latiné religions from the Satanic Panic era persisted in law enforcement. Additionally, I discovered that specific cases continued to haunt the religions long after their misconceptions were believed to have been clarified.

* * *

In the spring of 1989, the border regions between the United States and Mexico were heavily militarized as a result of President Ronald Reagan's antidrug initiatives.[58] The Reagan administration escalated the criminalization of Latin American immigrants after the indefinite incarceration of Marielitos.[59] Citing Cold War motives, Reagan accused Cuban and Nicaraguan communists of smuggling drugs into the United States. A special South Florida task force was set up, led by Vice President George H. W. Bush, that brought together the US Army and Navy to police the sea.[60] Consequently, drug activity intensified along the US-Mexico border, elevating the significance of the borderland cartels. By the mid-1980s, Mexican cartels provided "90 percent of the cocaine" entering the United States.[61]

The region around Matamoros, Mexico, and Brownsville, Texas, became a stronghold for two dominant and brutal drug cartels: "the Gulf Cartel and Los Zetas, now known as the Northeast Cartel."[62] The Matamoros case gained notoriety when, in addition to drug smuggling, Adolfo de Jesus Constanzo, a White Cuban American, integrated aspects of the Palo Monte religion into his criminal enterprise. Martinez shared that Constanzo's followers were instructed to kidnap a White American student because he wanted to extract "the brains of a smart person to give those powers to the *nganga* to imbue it with intelligence." Inspired by the early twentieth-century myths of *negros brujos* (Black witches) murdering people, Constanzo decided to incorporate human sacrifice into his practice. Palo Monte does not involve any human sacrifice; however, Constanzo believed it would give him an edge against law enforcement in his drug operations.

The police in Brownsville, Texas, called Charles Wetli in April 1989 and requested that he accompany them to the borderlands of Matamoros to help with this sensational case of ritualistic drug murders. According to Martinez, Wetli replied, "I cannot go, the one who has to go is Dr. Martinez." And so, Rafael Martinez went to Santa Elena Ranch in Matamoros.

"This whole thing was brought to the attention of the authorities because this guy Mark Kilroy had disappeared," Martinez explained. In March 1989, Kilroy, a White American college student from Texas, disappeared during spring break.[63] "They thought he had got drunk or was in some Mexican jail," said Martinez. Flyers were posted, and Mark Kilroy's family collaborated with the police search of the Brownsville, Texas, area. "And by chance, they ran into the Santa Elena Ranch, where the bodies were found."

Until Kilroy's disappearance, Constanzo had been murdering Mexicans without garnering any attention. "Of all the bodies that were found there [on the Santa Elena Ranch], many of them were simply drug rip-offs. People would go there to buy drugs and he would just kill them to keep their money," Martinez related. "But there was a fourteen-year-old kid that was beheaded. There was another guy that was tortured."

Constanzo used murder to instill fear in his drug smuggling operation. Inspired by the Hollywood horror genre, Constanzo required members of his ring to watch the 1987 horror film *The Believers* fourteen times.[64] The movie, which features actor Martin Sheen as a police officer who uncovers a network of Santeria followers in New York City practicing human sacrifice, mobilizes the Satanic Panic fears to further entrench the White fantasy that practitioners of Afro-Latiné religions are nefarious. It also inspired the psychopath Constanzo: police uncovered fifteen bodies buried at his ranch.

I consider it ironic that the White fantasy about Black witches that had circulated for decades to criminalize these religions would actually be taken up by a White Cuban American—an example of life imitating racial science. The fictitious tropes whipped up in the early evolutionist logics of White

Cuban racial fantasies were reenacted by a White Cuban who thought these myths might actually make him invincible. They did not.

Adolfo Constanzo fashioned himself into the feared *negro brujo*, a trope that draws from a combination of racially charged narratives. It first stems from the long-standing biases within Cuban society that amplified inaccurate fears of Black criminality. Recall how such tales were told to White Cuban children to scare them into obedience, stories of the evil Black boogeyman who murdered children for their blood. Fake stories that would shape the minds of people like a young Constanzo, who would later craft his own version of the *negro brujo*. I liken Constanzo's tragic performance to a kind of Afro-Latiné minstrelsy, in which he embodied his own racist fantasies using Palo Monte as blackface.[65] Martinez speculated that Constanzo might have also been influenced by tales of Aztec human sacrifice.

Martinez recounted the palpable fear among the Mexican police officers when he arrived at Rancho Santa Elena. They deemed him mad for venturing into the compound where Constanzo stored his narcotics and religious cauldron.

The US government aided in amplifying the violence and unrest in Mexico and Central America through the war on drugs and the Cold War because the government supplied weapons to the drug smugglers and counterinsurgency groups.[66] "Constanzo felt pressure because the police were cracking down on drug trafficking in the area," Martinez said.

Martinez was convinced that Constanzo and his followers committed additional murders in Mexico City, but that they "were never investigated." Rumors abound that, in addition to drug syndicates, Constanzo was the spiritual advisor to high-profile politicians and law enforcement officers in Mexico.

Constanzo was very organized in his criminal witchcraft. Authorities found ledgers and notebooks at his house that detailed his clients' names and the dates of spiritual services rendered. He documented which ceremony each had received and for what purpose. Martinez speculated that Constanzo used this information for potential blackmail, noting that pages had been torn from certain ledgers.

"When I got there, Constanzo was on the loose," Martinez recounted. Authorities were anxious that Constanzo would return to the ranch to collect his religious items. Little did they know he was en route to Mexico City. This tale would culminate with a shoot-out with police.[67] Stories circulated that Constanzo had commanded one of his followers to kill him before he could be arrested.[68] Others claim that the police executed him to safeguard the identities of his high-profile clients.

* * *

While in Matamoros, Martinez held a training for the local police to set them straight, "They were blaming *paleros* for everything. And I said, 'Listen guys, there are many Palo Mayombe practitioners that are law-abiding citizens, and they don't kill people. No, this is an aberration. It's like how Jim Jones gave Kool-Aid to all those Christians. This is self-made Palo, he created it.'"

The panic spiked. "This became very sensational," Martinez said. "And all kinds of people became experts overnight on Palo." It garnered so much attention that Martinez found himself on *El Show de Cristina*, a popular Spanish-language talk show on Univision in the 1990s. The host of the show, Cuban American journalist Cristina Saralegui, has been called the Oprah Winfrey of Latinos.[69] A special segment of *El Show de Cristina* featured the Matamoros case, and Rafael Martinez appeared along with one of Mark Kilroy's parents.

Later that year, Wetli and Martinez were approached by the Florida Department of Law Enforcement to create an "intelligence update." Their September 1989 report, titled *Palo Mayombe*, was provided to the Investigative Analysis Bureau. The ten-page report details the Matamoros case and clarifies that Constanzo practiced a "deviant" form of Palo Monte. Their report informs law enforcement that Palo Monte had "not posed a significant problem" to Florida; however, some inaccuracies remained. It suggested that Palo Monte "is practiced among Hispanic drug organizations, and its associations with these groups can pose a threat to law enforcement officers."[70]

Despite Constanzo's being a Cuban American born in Miami, the report also referenced the notorious case of the Mariel Cubans. "Within the last 25 years, with the influx of Cuban immigrants, and especially the Mariel Cubans, the malevolent practice of Palo Mayombe has become predominant."[71] Labeling Palo Monte as "malevolent" has roots in the historic anti-Black Cuban sentiments that have cast the religion in a negative light. However, the report clarifies that the human bones found in Palo Monte *nganga* are not the product of homicide. It also references Wetli's medical examiner expertise in determining the origins of religious items:

> In Dr. Wetli's examinations of Palo Mayombe artifacts, most of the human bones have been found to be of origins other than American. In addition, none of the specimens examined were the result of murder or human sac-

rifice. The human bones and skulls used in the Nganga can come from a variety of places, such as a biological supply company or on the black market. There have even been instances where individuals have advertised these items for sale in newspapers.[72]

The emphasis on the non-American origin of Palo Monte bones might comfort some White people, but this perspective leads to its own set of assumptions. It shapes the parameters around how societies should perceive and interact with the deceased—determining what is considered appropriate, modern, and thus an acceptable way to engage with human remains.

Still, there is a need to reflect on the historical context of retaining human bones in the name of science. For example, in Cuba police officers and researchers kept the brains of wrongly accused Afro-Cuban men for scientific purposes.

The confluence of science and the exhibition of human bodies dates back to nineteenth-century eugenics practices. One significant instance of racial objectification happened to Sara, or Saartjie Baartman, who was denigrated by White audiences, and dubbed the "Hottentot Venus." Exhibited in European sideshows and museums because her curvaceous body deviated from European beauty norms, Baartman was a spectacle for the bourgeoisie.[73] Following her early death, Baartman's remains underwent extensive scientific examination and dissection, and they were on display for over a century.[74]

The trend of dissecting Black bodies in the name of science, from Saartjie Baartman to the surgeries conducted by Dr. James Marion Sims on enslaved women, is its own form of Western cannibalism. Feeding off the frenzied racist spectacle of White supremacy, the scientific consumption of Black and Brown flesh produces malevolent energy. The emotional, psychological, and spiritual waves of scientific racism are a tangible force that manifests and affects people and communities. The ripple effects of this prejudice can be seen in how racist actions and sentiments spread, reinforcing racist stereotypes. We can see the sociocultural ripples of these negative waves in Adolfo Constanzo's distorted perceptions of Palo Monte rituals.

Combatting this negative racist power requires delving into the historical and cultural truths of Palo Monte rituals in order to dispel the myths and counteract the stereotypes often linked to these practices. Central to Palo Monte practices is the veneration of ancestors, activated through bones, which are loved and cared for, as precious treasures of cultural knowledge. Tracing back to Central Africa, Palo Monte traditions have endured despite transatlantic slavery, and the practices are a testament to the resilience and strength of the African diaspora. Aiming to balance humans' relationships to the spirit world, Palo Monte enhances people's deep connections to the natural environment. Misunderstandings of Palo Monte as "sorcery" or "dark magic" have contributed to its history of criminalization.

I know of Palo Monte practitioners whose homes have been searched by police, and even though they were not charged with crimes, their *ngangas* were confiscated, never to be seen again. The loss of an *nganga* can impact the long-term health and well-being of the practitioner who is united with its energy. Since the time of his work with Wetli, Martinez has gone on to work with other scholars and to advocate for law enforcement to take a more ethical approach to the dissection of Palo Monte *ngangas*: "We recommend that medicolegal professionals excavate *nganga* assemblages responsibly."[75]

Martinez and his colleagues suggest that the medicolegal community begin to consult with Palo Monte practitioners before they examine an *nganga*.[76] They should not automatically assume that a Palo Monte *nganga* is illegal; rather, they should first ascertain whether the *nfumbe* was "legally sourced." Martinez is using his more recent work to "correct" some of the mistakes he made earlier in his career, when he cowrote articles with Wetli.

"It always bothered me," Martinez told me as he described how some of the things that they wrote had continued to criminalize Palo Monte.

In a more recent 2017 article, "Afro-Cuban Ritual Use," Martinez and his colleagues advised law enforcement and medical examiners to be aware that Palo Monte should not be seen as *always criminal*:

> The criminal component of certain Palo nganga assemblages can guide medicolegal investigations, and investigators must always consider the possibility that Palo remains are illegally sourced from cemeteries. However, we urge that the medicolegal community refrain from a default association of Palo practices with other criminal activities. Conducting taphonomic studies of Palo remains and engaging in interviews with informants can assist in determining when remains have been legally or illegally sourced. In those *rare* cases where ritual remains are ascertained to be the legal property of a Palo practitioner, we recommend returning these ritual objects to their owners.[77]

Unfortunately, from this passage we can see a lingering presumption of Palo Monte criminality. This article still subtly hints that Palo Monte is questionable. It states that medical examiners should consider the "possibility" that Palo Monte remains have not been secured legally; "in those rare cases" in which Palo Monte remains are "legal property," the authors recommend returning the objects to the owners. However, these statements perpetuate the troubling association of Palo Monte practices with wrongdoing.

The widespread presumption of inherent guilt stems from the deeply in-grained anti-Blackness that influences perceptions of Afro-Latiné religions, particularly the specific demonization of Palo Monte since slavery. I do not point this out to condemn Martinez's genuine efforts to assist in cultivating better understandings between law enforcement and Palo Monte; however, I cannot help but recall how this invokes Fernando Ortiz's early assertions that there is a latent "germ" of African criminality that exists in all Black religions.

At this point in my research, I realized that all these medical, legal, and criminological research practices make up a *racial laboratory*. Together, they establish the foundation for making race appear invisible through scientific procedures. The perceived absence of racism is central to how our societal structures function, appearing impartial. Tied to the procedures legitimizing Western scientific understanding, the racial laboratory is shaped by means of research, analysis, categorization, testing, and experimentation. Over four centuries, with the shadows of chattel slavery, apartheid, and Jim Crow segregation lingering, the roots of White supremacy are deeply entrenched and institutionalized.[78] I now recognize how, through this process, academics, criminologists, police, and medical-legal practitioners solidify time-worn tropes of Black and Brown criminality into empirical truths through the racial laboratory.

* * *

In 1989, in a seeming end to the Matamoros case, the Mexican police mobilized Indigeneity against Blackness in the fate of Rancho Santa Elena. "Do you know what the Mexican police did?" Martinez asked me. "They brought a shaman, a healer." As the ranch was considered damned, the police did not know what to do with it. According to Martinez, the Indigenous shaman first tried to "exorcise the space" by sprinkling it with cologne, sage, and holy water to be rid of the black magic. Ultimately, the Mexican authorities ended up burning the ranch down: "The whole thing went up in fire."

It is curious that Mexican police used an Indigenous healer (*curandero*) to eliminate the so-called black magic of the White Cuban. In a recuperation of the "noble savage" trope, the Mexican state, which has waged war on its own Indigenous population, is also more comfortable with *curandero* healing practices than with those of Afro-Latiné religions.

There are not many differences between the *curandero*'s techniques—using sage, candles, cologne, and holy water—and those of *santeros* and even *paleros*, who also draw on these tools to calm turbulent spaces and call on the spirits. However, the Mexican police did not understand that what they were attempting to "exorcise" (a Christian term that Martinez used to describe their intent) was the ether of White supremacy, which had led a White Cuban American, Constanzo, to invent his own ritualistic murder based on Hollywood inspiration and racial fantasies. I wonder how many spirits they stirred up in the process.

* * *

While I was finishing the first draft of this book and trying to submit it to the press, a series of negative occurrences took place that made me feel I was not going to be able to finish. First, while we were packing to move out of our rented home near Stanford, a nearby fire forced us to evacuate for five days. Then, my son Neto and his wife, Naomi, started experiencing harassment from White neighbors and local city code enforcers who wanted them to stop practicing healing rituals in their home. They had to mobilize quickly as church members were threatened with slurs, and people were surveilling their property. During all this I got sick with COVID-19 for the second time, and then my husband and our two young children also became sick with COVID-19. The children stopped sleeping because of the lingering effects of the coronavirus, also called "long COVID." It was a very difficult time. The elder priests with whom I grew up would probably say that Charles Wetli's spirit did not want me to finish this book.

Wednesday, March 16, 2022
Stanford, California

The high-tech conference room at the CASBS, *with its wood paneling and wall of windows, captured the natural beauty of the grounds. Today, however, the room felt especially intimidating. All Fellows give a thirty-minute "seminar" on their work, followed by thirty minutes of questions and answers. What had begun as friendly weekly presentations had become increasingly tense. When scholars who worked on race, gender, inequality, or power (mostly Fellows of color) asked questions, we were met with incredulity. Answers ranged from reinforcing racist stereotypes about people in Africa or Asia to not engaging with the questions at all.*

Dealing with this tension during the ongoing COVID-19 *global pandemic, as we underwent weekly testing to be on campus and were caught in cycles of sickness, everyone was at their worst. After almost two years of exclusively online exchanges, many of us were not accustomed to being around other people, especially not large groups.*

I was mic'd up and had my presentation cued. I had decided to present on excited delirium syndrome and deliberately chose to include how dead spirits had led me to this discovery. I titled the talk "The Dead Lead the Way: Excited Delirium and the Policing of Afro-Latiné Religions."

I talked about how Afro-Latiné practitioners were drawing on alternative frames to fight against police violence. I discussed how my interactions with Jade

Ellis and her father's spirit, Jeremy, have been key moments that unexpectedly shifted my research.

I asked: "What would it do to the research process if we took seriously Afro-Latiné religious practitioners' active engagements with the dead?" Might it call for a shift in our social scientific methods and also ourselves? I challenged that it would disrupt the racial laboratory to acknowledge the presence of dead spirits and other immaterial copresences as research interlocutors.

When I finished my talk, the room was eerily quiet. The first two questions came from Black scholars who wanted to hear more about how I was thinking through the idea of the "racial laboratory." I discussed how I was inspired by the work of Christina Sharpe, who talks about the slave ship as a "floating laboratory," where doctors and medical researchers took "advantage of high mortality rates to identify a bewildering number of symptoms, classify them into diseases and hypothesize about their causes."[1] Building on this racial science, medical examiners have experimented on Black and Brown bodies, offering findings that reinforce White supremacy and launch their own careers as experts.

A famed Latino economist applauded the "bravery" it took to admit that I encountered spirits. He challenged me to go deeper, to look at other spirits, besides Jeremy's, with whom I have been working all along. He suggested I add my own story into the book. He was addressing the bravery it takes to confront Western positivism. Positivism is a self-reinforcing worldview that holds that "truth" can be determined only by verifiable science, empirically based evidence, or mathematical calculations.[2] Positivism has such a powerful hold on truth claims that non-Western cultural perspectives are always diminished as fanciful "beliefs." Even anthropologists who claim to deeply submerge themselves in other cultural formations are unable to acknowledge or admit to engagements with spiritual entities without being dismissed as having "gone native." I argued that it is time that we decolonize our methods to take spirits as seriously as the people we work with do. If we do not, how can social scientists truly claim to have a deep understanding of non-White, non-Western perspectives?

Then, a White woman, a philosopher, commented, "I'm sympathetic to alternative epistemologies, and I'm sympathetic with decolonizing knowledge, but what I struggle with in so many ways is spirituality." This incredulousness has come from her mother's Christianity, she said: "So this is a question if you can help me get along with my mom?" When her mother says, "You were safe because I prayed for you," the philosopher responds, "How many other mothers are praying for their daughters who aren't safe?" She asked me how I can reconcile this problem with my decolonial theory of spirits.

I explained that in Afro-Latiné understandings, spiritual impact on the world is not as physically dense as touching and moving an object. Instead, we must think through spiritual effects as vibrational influences. Many people and places are haunted. And not all spirits have the same level of impact on the material world. There are precise techniques that enable the dead to access more agency. Jeremy, for example, became activated through Jade's healing techniques. Some entities do have direct impact without intervention, as, for example, in the countless hauntings known throughout time, or in near-death experiences in which people encounter deceased family members as they pass.

This series of fruitful questions gave me hope. People were taking the idea of spirits seriously and not just dismissing my assertions out of hand. Then, a scientist raised his hand. "I'm on Einstein's side of this," he said, referencing the popular opinion that famed physicist Albert Einstein had once attempted a séance with his friend, the well-known author Upton Sinclair, and that Einstein dismissed spiritualism as "nonsense."

"Most of your talk was describing things that require no spirits," he told me. "You are entirely persuasive. I can see how the experiences, practices, and techniques are wholly real, effective, and evidence of the phenomenon you are talking about—spirits coming from the other side and influencing action, you know, changing people's physical . . . [having] a material impact on the world. But most of your talk was describing things that require no spirits. You could describe excited delirium as a cover for police violence without ever invoking anyone's parents. So, I'm curious, you know, how you deal with the obvious criticism from an old, cis, White empiricist, who says the story you tell is incredibly powerful and important, but the explanatory apparatus is unswallowable for me."

I wish I would have responded to him that excited delirium gets its origins from the assault on Afro-Latiné religions. Instead, what I told him seemed to come out of nowhere. I leaned into the microphone and said, "Well, when you go to sleep at night, maybe the spirits will talk to you themselves."

I chuckled almost involuntarily before composing myself. Then I continued with my original response: "I can offer a method that stems from a decolonial approach that is grounded in an alternative epistemology, and I'll find people who disagree with this method. But I'm not going to convince you against your Western skepticism. That is something that is inherently tied to the anti-Black racism that I have been describing throughout the talk."

After the talk, I was frustrated. The question referencing Einstein still bothers me now as I write down my thoughts. I did not see the scientist for the rest of the day, so we could not continue the conversation. But I wanted to say more.

Later that day, one of the Fellows, an African philosopher, thanked me for taking African understandings of spirits seriously. She said that she had never heard anyone talk about African notions of spirit presence as truth in an academic setting until my talk, and it made her feel validated. That alone made my talk worthwhile.

Leaving CASBS, *I thought to myself, How does anyone deal with the horrors of police violence without being able to pray?*

Brutalized

MY RESEARCH TOOK ME DEEPER into the brutality of policing, and I realized I could not separate the criminalization of Afro-Latiné religions from the violence against Black and Brown immigrants. Remembering what the Fellow had said to me about how you can explain police violence without mentioning spirits, I wish I had thought to bring up the case of Abner Louima.

In 1997, New York Police Department (NYPD) officers sexually assaulted and tortured Haitian immigrant Abner Louima. And yet, Louima's brutal treatment did not end with his assault. It continued through character defamations and accusations. News media, police, politicians, pundits, and the courts targeted Louima with racist tropes against Black religions simply because he was Haitian. Labeled a "voodoo" priest despite having no associations with Vodou practices, Louima was portrayed as the aggressor, a Haitian immigrant who had somehow corrupted the once-good, all-American White cops through his black magic.

Louima's story reflects how police brutality and immigrant stereotypes weave through American racial color lines. It shows how racial and religious criminality is imprinted on Black and Brown people, justifying torture and brutality.[1] For police officers, use of force is a spectrum of violence where "handcuffs, choke holds, [and] other excessive methods of police restraint, such as hog-tying," emerge from the long histories of White domination.[2] Hortense Spillers warns that there is a kind of pornographic spectatorship that occurs in the exercise of brutality against Black people, wherein White viewers find it irresistible to watch the destruction of the captive Black body.[3] I recall how lynching media circulated photographs of smiling White faces next to what Billie Holliday woefully described as "strange fruit" hanging from trees to engender a unified White public.[4] There is a similar titillation induced today through the constant circulation of police killing videos, which are increasingly recorded in high definition on smartphones and posted to social media platforms.[5]

Although I am weary of reproducing the depraved excitement that can accompany accounts of Black suffering, I must engage the Louima case to show how brutality is at the core of how Black people experience America's police. In the historical echoes of racial violence, I see what legal scholar Katherine Franke suggests is a thin line between police brutality and sexual arousal.[6] Franke argues that police brutality is inherently sadistic, meaning that officers derive pleasure and sexual gratification from inflicting pain, suffering, and humiliation on non-White people.[7] The Louima assault reveals how the lines between sexual, racial, and religious deviance are merged, influencing the wider public's view on victim versus perpetrator.

* * *

Thirty-two-year-old Abner Louima was at Club Rendez-Vous listening to his favorite music group, the Phantoms, on August 9, 1997, when a minor fight broke out.[8] It was a "Haitian night" in the Brooklyn nightclub, so he and a large number of the local Haitian community were at the club when police barged onto the scene and began to violently break up the crowd. One of the officers, Justin Volpe, claimed that Louima hit him.[9] Despite Louima's not being the assailant, he was roughly detained and taken to the Seventieth Precinct by Officers Volpe, Charles Schwartz, and Thomas Wiese.[10] They halted twice en route to assault Louima. Officer Wiese eventually intervened, suggesting they "deal with him down at the precinct."[11] Patrick Antoine, another Haitian man leaving his friend's house near the nightclub, was also apprehended and beaten, along with Louima, as the officers mistakenly assumed he was involved in the initial altercation.

After assaulting Louima and Antoine at the station, an officer, believed to be Officer Schwartz, escorted Louima to the restroom and handcuffed him in view of the other officers. As Officer Schwartz restrained Louima, Officer Volpe rammed a broken broomstick up Louima's rectum, rupturing his colon and bladder.[12] Officer Volpe then smeared the mixture of blood and feces across Louima's face, forced the stick into his mouth, damaging his teeth, and threatened his life if he spoke out. They left Louima injured and bleeding in a cell for hours. Fellow detainees raised alarms because of the overpowering odor, and Louima was taken to a hospital. He suffered severe injuries, including a perforated rectum and a torn bladder.[13] He underwent three emergency surgeries, was in the hospital for two months, and had to have a colostomy.[14] While Louima was at the hospital, a nurse referred to him as "the man who had beaten up a police officer."[15] Hearing this, Louima responded, "Lady, do you think I'm stupid? I'm a Black man. Do you think I would beat a police officer in New York City?"[16]

A nurse from the hospital reached out to the NYPD's Internal Affairs Bureau, reporting the serious injuries. However, no one logged the complaint for thirty-six hours, nor was it reported to the district attorney's office, as required by law.[17] If not for an anonymous tip to Mike McAlary, a savvy *Daily News* reporter, this incident might have gone unnoticed. McAlary managed to bypass the police stationed at the hospital and secured Louima's testimony. Within a week of the story breaking, fourteen officers from the Seventieth Precinct were reassigned, put on desk duty, suspended, or arrested.[18]

When eventually questioned, the officers implicated in the appalling incident provided misleading accounts, suggesting Louima had sustained his injuries from a consensual homosexual encounter. They tried to depict Louima as a queer, aggressive Black man. In a statement to the Federal Bureau of Investigation (FBI), Officer Thomas Bruder, who was in the car with Officer Volpe that evening, described over one hundred "unruly" people at the club.[19] Officer Bruder further labeled the initial disturbance as a "lesbian fight" and asserted that he discovered an advertisement for an "All-Male Review" and a flyer of a shirtless man among Louima's belongings. But Officer Bruder claimed to have discarded them.[20] By introducing these elements, the officers tried to weave a misleading narrative steeped in racial and sexual stereotypes to hide the truth of their cruelty. The media would follow their lead.

* * *

At the time the assault occurred, Louima, who had been an electrical engineer in Haiti, worked as a security guard in New York City. He lived with his family and was in a committed heterosexual marriage. Despite his harrowing ordeal, the media depicted Louima in a negative light. Journalists used racially charged, homophobic, and xenophobic language to tarnish his reputation. The press labeled Louima as a dubious individual who assaulted an officer.

During the trial, media outlets continuously referred to Club Rendez-Vous as a "gay" venue, insinuating that Louima was homosexual.

Religion also played into the vilification of Louima. Newspapers portrayed him as a Black witch doctor who had put a spell over the NYPD's *normally* good cops.[21] At one point, Justin Volpe's father, Robert Volpe, a retired detective with the NYPD, claimed that he feared Louima's "voodoo" magic and stated that he had started carrying around spiritual protection.[22] Rumors suggested that Justin Volpe might have staged the assault to look like a "voodoo" ritual. This theory was drawn from the unsolved 1996 murder of Claude Michel, a Haitian doctor discovered near the Seventieth Precinct in Brooklyn, where Officer Volpe served. Michel was found in his Nissan Pathfinder with a slashed throat, holding his own severed penis. A person claiming expertise in ritualistic crimes baselessly suggested that this heinous act bore the hallmarks of Haitian "voodoo."[23] In response to these erroneous speculations, Louima would always have his uncle, a Protestant minister, by his side during interviews with press. In Haiti, Protestants are known to reject Vodou practices completely.[24]

Still, the prejudices persisted. James Ridgway de Szigethy, a "cult cop" affiliated with the National Police Defense Foundation and known for his right-leaning views, was friends with the Volpe family. A conspiracy theorist most known for suggesting that the actor Johnny Depp was part of a satanic network,[25] de Szigethy also alleged that Louima practiced "devil worship."[26] Observing Louima's testimony about the brutal assault, de Szigethy tried to discredit him, leveraging Louima's Haitian heritage.

He told reporters: "It was something that I'd suspected from the beginning about Louima . . . that he might be involved in the practice of voodoo."[27] De Szigethy took it upon himself to probe into Louima's background, asking people in "Little Haiti to confirm his eerie hunches."[28] In court, as Louima recounted the harrowing night of torture by Justin Volpe, de Szigethy expressed disbelief, claiming that Louima gave him "the willies."[29]

In a December 2003 crime blog, de Szigethy drew parallels between his investigations into criminality through examinations of the punk rock movement's body art and tattoos and the work of law enforcement strategies documenting tattoos of Cuban Marielitos in the 1980s. Without directly referencing Charles Wetli and Rafael Martinez's work, de Szigethy cites inspiration from those law enforcement experts who studied tattoos to gain insight into the perceived criminal aspects of Marielitos and Haitians, and their religious practices like Santeria and "Voodoo." His description of Marielitos might sound familiar. He characterizes the Marielitos as "the thousands of criminals and mental patients that the government of Fidel Castro had dumped into the United States."[30] He labels them "violent and dangerous," attributing this to their Santeria beliefs and "an eagerness to commit murder and traffic drugs."[31] De Szigethy further insinuated that Louima had unleashed "voodoo" and "phantoms" on the Volpes as retaliation for the acts perpetrated against him.

Haitians and Marielitos have long been tethered together by authorities and policymakers, and unjustly branded as dangerous criminals. It is important to note that in 1980, the same year as the Mariel boatlift, ten thousand Haitian immigrants fleeing the Duvalier dictatorship sought refuge in the United States.[32] I remember that Haitians and Marielitos were called "boat people," and both were incarcerated for long periods, with many Haitians being forcefully deported.[33]

The treatment of Black, Brown, and dark Brown immigrants is rooted in racism. Echoing sentiments from White politicians of the time, news media in Florida declared, "We Don't Want No Goddamn Black Refugees!"[34] Reviving a policy from 1954 that had been abandoned since Ellis Island's closure, the Reagan administration interdicted boats, holding Haitian asylum seekers "in detention camps in Florida and Arkansas."[35] When Haitians sought legal recourse against their detention, the US Immigration and Naturalization Service (INS)—which was restructured after 9/11 into Customs and Border Protection (CBP), Immigration and Customs Enforcement (ICE), and the US Citizenship and Immigration Services (USCIS)[36]—argued that Haitians, unlike Cubans, were not fleeing political repression but were merely trying to escape poverty in their homeland.[37]

Haitians fought their detention through litigation and won. In 1982, Judge Eugene Spellman, the same federal judge who seven years later would oversee the Santeria church case against the City of Hialeah, ordered the release of 1,900 Haitians detained in camps to local community organizations. Judge Spellman found that the Haitians had also been denied due process and had been treated in a discriminatory manner by the INS, similar to the Marielitos.[38] Led by then associate attorney general Rudolph Giuliani, the US attorney general's office appealed the decision, but it was upheld in appellate court.[39]

The Abner Louima case highlights the prejudice against Haitians, which is intricately tied to the broader discrimination against Black religious practices. This discrimination encompasses African traditional religions from the continent, African diaspora practices, and Afro-Latiné systems like Haitian

Vodou, Jamaican Revival Zion, Congos del Espiritu Santo from the Dominican Republic, Şàngó practitioners from Trinidad, Brazilian Candomblé, Puerto Rican Espiritismo, and the Afro-Cuban religions of Abakuá, Palo Monte, Santeria, and Espiritismo Africano. These religions, which have fostered Black empowerment, face opposition both in their native countries and in the United States. Regrettably, outdated and baseless tales about African cannibalism, barbarity, and intellectual inferiority—once propagated to rationalize African enslavement—still persist and are used against African descendants today.

Following the 1804 Haitian slave revolution that is said to have begun from a Vodun ceremony, fears surrounding Black religions spread throughout the United States and the Caribbean. The global backlash against Haiti and Black religions resulted in the persecution and deaths of numerous Black people, even those only suspected of being connected to Afro-Latiné religious practices.[40] It is disheartening yet unsurprising to witness these age-old fears resurface in modern narratives that unjustly portray Haitians and Marielitos as disorderly people in need of control.

In the United States, these racist fears have been mobilized in medical discourses of Haitians as contaminating vectors. In 1915, the US military occupied Haiti using allegations of "voodoo" barbarism to justify targeted repression of Vodou religions on the island.[41] These stigmas carried over into Americans' treatments of Haitian refugees, who were met with violence and hatred. For example, early in the AIDS pandemic, there were false stories circulating that associated Vodou practices with the creation of AIDS.[42] Haitian anthropologist Jemima Pierre reflects on her childhood in Miami in the 1980s, where cruel American children would taunt Haitians and falsely associate them with AIDS or unpleasant odors.[43]

Taken up by television, newspapers, and even scholarly publications, the erroneous narrative of Haitians as carriers of AIDS "posited a scenario in which Haitian professionals who had fled the Duvalier regime ended up in western Africa and later brought the new virus back to Haiti, which introduced it to the Americas. AIDS was said to proliferate in Haiti because of strange practices involving voodoo blood rituals and animal sacrifice."[44] We see a similar type of racist origin story with the 2019 coronavirus as coming from Chinese meat consumption, a belief that has also spawned violent attacks against Asian and Asian American people in the United States.

In the early 1980s, the US government used unfounded rumors linking Vodou rituals to the onset of the AIDS pandemic as a pretext to mandate HIV tests for Haitian asylum seekers.[45] These misconceptions, which combined notions of blood contamination with misguided fears about Vodou religions, played a role in the establishment of the "world's first and only detention camp for refugees with HIV."[46] A *New York Times* editorial commented on the importance of keeping blood donations "untainted" when describing a 1983 policy of the Centers for Disease Control and Prevention that prohibited blood donations from the "'Four H Club' (homosexuals, hemophiliacs, heroin users, and Haitians)."[47]

In the 1990s, stigmas of Black and Brown "boat people" with tainted blood and "voodoo" religions would contribute to attempts at forced repatriation of Haitians and Marielitos. As Tavia Nyong'o argues, there was a blurring of racial and sexual contagion, in which these Black queer bodies were seen as irrational drug users who were bringing deviant sex, rituals, and disease to White America.[48]

In 1994 Rudy Giuliani was elected as the mayor of New York City with a pledge to restore "law and order" by bolstering police authority. He urged the NYPD to take stringent measures on areas he labeled as "dirty" with the intent of making them "clean," which largely resulted in the targeting and arrests of Black and Brown people.[49] Three years after Giuliani's election, the controversial "stop and frisk" strategy paralyzed Black and Brown men in the city and contributed to the rise of mass incarceration. This area of aggressive policing also fostered an atmosphere of racial and sexual dominance, with officers like Justin Volpe feeling emboldened to commit heinous acts.

Abner Louima was not the only Black man sexually assaulted by White police officers at the time. Six other Black immigrants reported being abducted by the NYPD and taken to isolated locations in Queens where they were anally raped.[50] What is unique in the Louima case is that the officers were arrested and charged with a crime.[51]

Historically, sexual assault as a form of race-based terror has been weaponized in the United States to subdue Black men and reinforce White male superiority.[52] In conversations with the FBI, officers involved in the Louima assault not only denied any wrongdoing but also described Louima as "sweaty" and "cracked up." These descriptors are used to identify people exhibiting so-called excited delirium syndrome, and were a way for the police to signal to other law enforcement officers that Louima was not a credible witness. Attempting to tarnish Louima's reputation, the officers insinuated that the injuries he sustained were likely from drug abuse. For instance, Officer Bruder pointed out Louima's missing teeth, implying that narcotics abuse could be the cause. However, Louima's teeth were knocked out by Officer Volpe when he thrust the bloody, feces-covered broomstick into his mouth.

As we reflect on Katherine Franke's assertion that police power embodies elements of sexual sadism, it's clear how sexual violence is infused with racialized state power in this case. After the horrendous act against Louima in the NYPD's Seventieth Precinct bathroom, Officer Volpe paraded the tainted, bloodied broomstick with pride, announcing to his fellow officers, "I broke a man down."[53] Officer Volpe's appalling behavior showcased a perverse arousal, serving as a form of camaraderie among the White officers. It was as if he were partaking in a twisted rite of passage, in which Officer Volpe also reportedly proclaimed, "I took a man down tonight."[54]

Building on this perspective, policing scholar Paula Ioanide suggests that Officer Volpe's boastful behavior post-assault, brandishing the broken broomstick, reflected a wider display of White male supremacy.[55] The officers' celebration of their brutal actions toward Louima evoked the painful history of chattel slavery and colonial dominance.[56] I also understand this overt display of camaraderie as tied to smaller, everyday displays of racial and sexual aggression that bond police together. A mere eighteen months after Louima's torture, Amadou Diallo, an unarmed Black man from West Africa, was fatally shot by four NYPD plainclothes officers. The forty-one-plus bullets that tore into Diallo came from an anticrime unit with the chilling motto "We own the night."[57]

Police are able to wield sexual violence with impunity, anchored in the misconception that Black people are predators. This research has revealed how the myth of the Black predator is a deeply entrenched narrative; it is a White fantasy of Black criminality.[58] The myth is weaponized in courtrooms, justifying extreme uses of force against Black people. Even when video evidence counters the claims of Black people as threats, White fear is mobilized as a successful defense.[59]

* * *

One of the most striking examples of the Black predator myth in action is evident in the case of Rodney King, a Black motorist who was brutally beaten by police. On March 3, 1991, this chilling beating was captured on film from a nearby balcony. George Holliday, awakened by the commotion, recorded four Los Angeles Police Department (LAPD) officers as they assaulted Rodney King, who lay curled on the ground while they punched him, kicked him, and even deployed a stun gun on him.[60] The first video to go viral showing police enacting brutal violence against Black people, the grainy, out-of-focus film, captured on Holliday's recently purchased video camera, circulated around the world as a prime example of excessive use of force against Black people.

The LAPD officers' subsequent acquittal a year later proved even more jarring. Despite the video being presented as evidence to showcase the officers' abuse of power, the jurors in Simi Valley, California, were swayed by the officers' assertions. They were convinced that, even as King lay on the ground shielding his face and body from the relentless blows of the White officers, he was the real threat. Merely being a Black man in America, it seemed, marked him as dangerous. Astonishingly, after the verdict, a White juror voiced her belief that "Rodney King was in 'total control' of the situation."[61]

The jurors' acquittal of the White police officers in the Rodney King case underscores the long cultivation of White paranoia in the United States.[62] As scholars have elucidated, it is entrenched in White American consciousness to consider Black, Brown, and other non-White people an existential threat.[63] In this context, the police are seen as the guardians of White safety, especially against the perceived danger of the mythic Black predator. This perpetuates a cycle of distrust, in which aggressive police actions are justified by projecting fear onto Black people. Consequently, all officers need to say is that they *feared for their lives* to exonerate themselves from being seen as instigators.[64]

Laurence Ralph describes how this distorted reality emerged from the menacing figure of the "Knife-Wielding Black Man with the Bugged Out Eyes" that was used in the South to justify violence during Jim Crow segregation.[65] This trope traces back to the 1915 film *The Birth of a Nation*, directed by D. W. Griffith, which depicts the Black male as a criminal who, in the aftermath of the Civil War, raped White women, murdered, and wreaked havoc on the genteel White South. Based on the 1905 novel *The Clansman*, the film is credited with bringing about the rebirth of the Ku Klux Klan.[66] *The Birth of a Nation* captivated White audiences across the country and is known to have inspired thousands of lynchings. Ralph ties the myth of the "Knife-Wielding Black Man with the Bugged Out Eyes" to the historical underpinnings of the slave patrol in New Orleans, Louisiana. He shows how police were not armed in the South until they felt that the Black population, regarded as dangerous, needed to be suppressed.[67]

The trope of the Black male threat that White mobs used to keep Black people *in their place* is continually resurrected. An example can be seen in the killing of Emmett Till, a Black teenager from Chicago who, while visiting family in Mississippi, was falsely accused of whistling at a White woman. The White woman, Carolyn Bryant Donham, who later admitted to lying, told the jury in her husband's defense that Till had grabbed her. It took an all-White, all-male jury one hour to acquit her husband, Roy Bryant, and his half brother, J. W. Milam, of all charges.[68] In his closing statement, Sidney Carlton, the defense attorney, told the jurors that if they didn't free Milam and Bryant, "your ancestors will turn over in their grave." He went on, "I'm sure every last Anglo-Saxon one of you has the courage to free these men."[69]

In its current iteration, the fear of Black people is often evoked in the justification of lethal police shootings. More recently, the trope of the "Knife-Wielding Black Man" was infamously resurrected in the police shooting of seventeen-year-old Laquan McDonald, another Black teenager from Chicago who in 2014 was shot sixteen times.[70] His death was also caught on video. Police officer Jason Van Dyke said he feared for his life because McDonald was holding a knife. However, the video showed that McDonald was walking away from the officer when he was shot.[71] Ralph notes how the "fantasy of Black predatory violence is so ingrained in US culture" that a police officer can evade a murder conviction by persuading jurors that a seventeen-year-old whom he shot sixteen times possessed extraordinary strength, enough to bring a knife to a gunfight and emerge as the victor.[72]

The logic of the slave patrol, which Ralph describes as embedded in police violence, ties back to controlling the threat of Black rebellion. These sentiments reflect an earlier era of chattel slavery, when a prevailing narrative depicted Black people's attempts to escape enslavement as nefarious and mentally unstable. Even before the tremors of the Haitian Revolution struck fear into the hearts of White slave owners globally, the 1739 Stono Rebellion in South Carolina had already sown seeds of unease about Black uprisings and their associated religions. The rebellion was led by a group of enslaved Kongo people originally from Angola. Utilizing African drums and traditional instruments of war, they rallied others to join their liberation movement.[73] Later, the antebellum planter class twisted the African religious facets of the uprising into propaganda that portrayed the enslaved as savage, predatory, and lacking in intellect.[74]

Dr. Samuel A. Cartwright, a physician from pre–Civil War New Orleans, formulated several theories to pathologize and rationalize the actions of enslaved people seeking freedom.[75] These included *drapetomania*, a claimed ailment that drove slaves to flee captivity; *rascality*, an alleged condition that led slaves to engage in criminal activity such as theft; and *dysaesthesia ethiopica*, which purportedly rendered slaves unresponsive and indifferent to punishment.[76] These fabricated mental disorders were employed to reinforce the notion that enslaved people should accept their bondage without pursuing liberty. Those who dared to seek freedom were labeled as criminal and insane, posing a perceived threat and instilling fear in White slaveholders.

Such medical narratives like drapetomania, which aimed to pathologize resistance to slavery, are earlier roots of the current fictitious syndrome called *excited delirium*. This idea that Black people possess an inherent inclination to act wildly and irrationally in the presence of White authorities is part of the long history of controlling Black communities and maintaining White supremacy through the use of fear.

By the time of the Haitian Revolution (1789–1804), White fears became so stirred up that they reverberated throughout the Americas, resulting in the ramping up of slave patrols in the United States and the Caribbean, as well as the transformation of enslavement practices and sugar production.[77] Unlike the unsuccessful Stono Rebellion, the Haitian Revolution, for slaveholders, was the "realization of their worst nightmare."[78] The backlash was so profound, Haitian anthropologist Michel-Rolph Trouillot notes, that Whites were unable to fathom the idea of a free, armed Black nation, and so attempted to erase the fact of the successful slave revolution through a collective historical silence.[79] Indeed, the US government declined to acknowledge the Haitian government until 1862, even when France finally did so in 1825, nearly two decades after Haiti's independence.[80]

This silence persists and is evident in the treatment of both Black individuals and Black religions. As Haiti was shunned and marginalized, misinformation about Vodou religions as malevolent and barbaric continued to circulate in order to demonize Black governance globally. In New Orleans, accusations of "voodoo" practices were used to target African Americans and Haitians during Reconstruction.[81] Newspapers run by ex-Confederates in New Orleans regularly included "salacious accounts of Voodoo rituals and ceremonies" to claim that Black people were unfit to vote.[82] Meanwhile, White politicians invoked ominous tales of "voodoo" to support racial segregation and the intensified policing of Black communities.[83] As I delved more into this history, I recognized that the logic of the slave patrol is closely connected to White misguided anxieties concerning Black religions. This unsettling pattern resurfaced in the cruel treatment of Abner Louima.

* * *

Abner Louima may not have been a practitioner of Vodou, but that did not stop practitioners from coming to his spiritual defense. Anthropologist Karen McCarthy Brown cautiously discusses how her longtime interlocutor Mama Lola, the famed Vodou priestess in Brooklyn, had admitted to doing spiritual work to aid in the defense of the battered Louima.[84] Indeed, the Haitian and African American community that rallied around Louima was powerful. Crowds of demonstrators marched holding plungers (initially it was thought that Officer Volpe had assaulted Louima with a plunger). Taking hold of Manhattan and the Brooklyn Bridge, they demanded accountability for the atrocities suffered at the hands of sadistic police officers.

McCarthy Brown brings us to the scene of the protests during that period. The NYPD, she informs us, had arrived at the protest prepared for battle, while members of the Haitian American community came with a vibrant display of dancers, singers, drummers, and colorfully dressed people carrying signs of protest.[85] They boldly asserted, "Justin A. Volpe is a sexual sadist!" During the protest, at least two people were "possessed by Vodou spirits." One embodied *Papa Gede*, the spirit associated with "sex, death, and humor," with a face covered in white powder, while another embodied *Azaka*, wearing the characteristic embroidered blue denim of Vodou temples in the Haitian countryside.[86] The protesters squarely placed the blame on Mayor Rudy Giuliani's "tough on crime" approach, exemplified by one sign depicting Giuliani himself, not Louima, with his pants pulled down and head submerged in a toilet bowl. McCarthy Brown vividly describes the scene outside city hall, where a multitude of toilet plungers bobbed as Reverend Al Sharpton addressed the crowd.

For three years, Mama Lola kept her lamps burning. On December 13, 1999, Justin Volpe, who had pleaded guilty, was sentenced to thirty years in prison. Still, it took a second trial for the three other officers to be found guilty. The suspicions fabricated around Louima led the jury in the initial trial to question the credibility of his testimony. All charges related to the beatings on the way to the police station were dismissed. Officers Bruder, Schwartz, and Wiese were finally found guilty in March 2000. Schwartz was sentenced to fifteen years and eight months, and the other two officers each received five years in prison.[87] Louima has since become an activist against police violence.

The influence of empowered Vodou spirits and the extreme brutality of the sadistic torture made this case a rare instance in which White police officers were held accountable for their violent actions against a Black person. However, the media continued to portray the officers as isolated "bad apples" who had supposedly fallen under a "voodoo" spell. Nevertheless, this triumph did not undermine the persistent workings of the racial laboratory. As my interlocutors understand it, dismantling this system remains an ongoing effort across all realms.

Tuesday, December 2, 2021
Stanford, California

It's the anniversary of Mario Woods's death. San Francisco police killed twenty-six-year-old Woods, another Black youth who was walking down Third Street in the Bayview district on December 2, 2015.[1] I remember how deeply it shook our San Francisco community. The Bayview is one of the last Black neighborhoods of the city. Five police officers shot Woods twenty-one times. They stood in a half-circle, execution style. They said it was because he had a small pocketknife. Local schoolchildren riding the bus home captured the killing on their cell phones. The video made national news and sparked outrage across the country.

My uncle Baba Tobaji and his wife, Iya Wanda, two Black American priests born and raised in San Francisco, formed a group of practitioners to conduct ceremonies on behalf of the spirits and families of Black men killed by police violence. At the one-year anniversary of Woods's death, they held a ritual to cleanse Woods's family and the location of his killing. Mario Woods's family and protesters from the Justice for Mario Woods Coalition carried signs: "Mario is our son" and "Jail Killer Cops."

Uncle Tobaji and Iya Wanda dressed all in white. Standing on the sidewalk where police killed him, they sang A umba wà orí, the Lukumi song of the dead, to sacred batá drums (añá) at an altar they created.[2] With small marks of white eggshell chalk (efun) *on their foreheads, acknowledging this moment as a rite of the dead, the group poured water on the ground. Ritual libations and prayers cool the space to shift the hot vibrations.*

In our traditions, proper deaths and burials are important so that ancestors won't haunt the living. Without such ceremony, the spirit lingers restlessly and can cause harm. A violent death leaves an impression, making the location haunted. In Africana beliefs, the family of the deceased must make proper amends for the spirit to find peace. Woods was killed in that very spot.

Uncle Tobaji, now in his seventies, shared with me that African drums and rituals have the power to awaken something in people. He mentioned that regardless of one's faith, these practices have the ability to "shift vibrations." He told me that "a lot of people are being touched by these traditions."

"The thing that we have in common is the trauma," he explained. Uncle Tobaji taps into our traditions to ignite something profound in people. "You make people realize there's something else."

"It's not just the words or the harmony but it's the vibration of the drums," he shared. The sacred melodies and the rhythm of the batá *have the power to transform spirits. The sound creates a shift in vibrations; they are like "ancient text messages."[3] In West Africa,* batá *drums were used to alert neighboring communities of war or danger over great distances.[4]*

The ceremony's vibrations resonated with Mario Woods's family. Uncle Tobaji told me that the family felt a small sense of relief. He recognized that while the ritual cannot change the injustice of Woods's death, it had the power to bring about an energetic transformation.

My deceased godfather, Alfredo Cano Calvo (ibaé), *a high priest of la Regla de Ocha, master drummer of the sacred* añá *drums from Matanzas, once told me that the drums are like a telephone that calls the orisha.[5] Padrino Alfredo explained the vibrational, radiating power, or* aché, *of the drums as tapping into a great "mystery in the world."*

"There are divine forces that radiate around and through us. And the radiance from our own religious strength is what leads us to give love, worship, and continue," Padrino Alfredo guides us.[6] Afro-Latiné vibrational activisms connect wavelengths of social justice. Now, Woods's death anniversary always makes me think about the Lukumi song of the dead:

A umba wà orí. A umba wà orí. A wà òsùn. àwọ o ma. Lerí omá.
Lẹ̀awo. Ará orún kawúre.

We have heads. We have heads. We have the sacred paint.
We have children.
On the head of this child, we are gathering back the secret.
All the ancestors in heaven, we wrap you with prayers.[7]

As this year comes to a close, I hope to wrap all our children in the protection of our ancestors.

8

Excited

IYA WANDA AND UNCLE TOBAJI started organizing Lukumi death ceremonies (*itutu*) for local Black men killed by the police in 2016, on the day
Oscar Grant would have turned twenty-nine. Grant was shot by BART (Bay
Area Rapid Transit) police officers seven years earlier, in the morning hours of
New Year's Day at the Fruitvale Station in Oakland, California. The officers
claimed that an overexcited crowd, consisting mostly of Black youth, had
made them fearful, leading to their aggressive and confused behavior.[1] One
of these officers, Johannes Mehserle, shot Grant in the back while forcibly
restraining him, even though Grant was face down. Mehserle later claimed
he had mistaken his firearm for a Taser and attributed the tragic error to
the presence of an agitated crowd.[2] Grant's killing marked one of the initial
instances of an unarmed Black man being shot by police that was captured
on cell phones and circulated widely. The story was immortalized in the ac-
claimed film *Fruitvale Station* (2013), starring Michael B. Jordan, who portrayed Oscar Grant.

It was the fallout from police shootings like Grant's and others that led
journalists and politicians to advocate the use of electroshock weapons over
firearms as a "safer" alternative. Law enforcement considers the Taser, the most
commonly used electroshock weapon, as "less than lethal."[3] Researchers and
advocates, however, challenge the putative safety of Tasers. Taser International
Inc. (now Axon) has disputed any claims that Tasers cause injury and death.
Among Taser International's main defenses is excited delirium syndrome.

* * *

One of the first people whose death led observers to question whether excited delirium syndrome was an actual medical condition was Natasha McKenna, a thirty-seven-year-old Black mother. Police arrested McKenna on January 26, 2015, after she called them to report an assault.[4] According to the officers, McKenna already had an existing warrant "for assaulting an officer in Alexandria, Virginia," which they cited as the basis for her arrest.[5] She was subsequently detained in a jail in Fairfax County, Virginia. After a weeklong delay in McKenna's transport, her mental health began to deteriorate.[6]

On February 8, 2015, while still held in jail on charges of attacking a police officer, McKenna refused to leave her cell. A forty-five-minute struggle ensued. The Sheriff's Emergency Response Team reported that it took six deputies to "extract" the five-foot-three, 130-pound McKenna from her jail cell. According to a *Washington Post* article, McKenna was so thin that a standard-size restraint belt could not be used to immobilize her because her torso was too small.[7] Nonetheless, her slight stature was used to justify the excessive force.[8]

The Taser's electroshock incapacitates people unlike any other weapon. Taser International came up with the term *electro-muscular disruption* (EMD) system to describe how the weapon operates on the body. Consisting of a canister of compressed gas, the Taser discharges two barbed projectile probes, which are connected to the weapon by copper wires. The wires deliver the voltage that disrupts the electrical muscular control of the person.

"Each sound of the click that you hear. Each click, it's like getting punched by a heavyweight boxer," said Officer Johnson, whom I interviewed about what being tased feels like during Taser trainings. He told me, "It locks you up. You can't move." Police officers must yell "Taser, Taser, Taser" when they fire, to let people know that the Taser has been activated. Upon the deployment of a Taser, small pieces of confetti called "aphids" are released; they contain tiny serial numbers that identify the Taser that was fired and who fired it. Because one can never pick up all the aphids, there is always a trace left.

Taser International claims that no one has died from a Taser-induced heart attack. In its "Medical Safety Information," the company describes its rigorous testing for safety; it claims to have purposefully attempted to disrupt the heartbeat of animals while tasing them, and to have seen no indications that Tasers are dangerous.[9]

McKenna was tased at least four times during the struggle with six deputies, amounting to the delivery of more than 100,000 volts of electricity.

After losing consciousness, McKenna stopped breathing and suffered a heart attack.[10] No charges were filed, and the medical examiner ruled her death an accident.[11] McKenna's death was captured on video and classified as a cardiac arrest due to excited delirium syndrome. It would not be until five years later, following the death of George Floyd, that reporters began focusing on this questionable diagnosis.[12]

Excited delirium syndrome seems designed to distract from this type of excessive use of force. When I first found McKenna's story, I did not know that excited delirium syndrome was used as a successful defense in twenty-nine of the thirty wrongful death lawsuits against Taser International.[13]

Perhaps I was too willing to see Charles Wetli as a changed man, given his Supreme Court testimony in favor of a Santeria church. I thought he might have regretted his choice to use his research to criminalize Black and Brown people. Considering his ambitions, I probably shouldn't have been surprised to find out that Wetli had not only served as an adviser for Taser International—conducting research into the safety of the Taser electroshock weapon—but was also one of the company's expert witnesses in court.[14]

* * *

"I've never seen a case where I could say that a Taser actually contributed to the death," Wetli stated.[15] "As far as interfering with the heart rhythm," he added, "there's never been any convincing evidence that that can actually take place."[16]

Wetli had relocated from Miami to New York in 1995, when he became the chief medical examiner for Suffolk County, Long Island.[17] In the early 2000s, Wetli was approached by Taser International and "retained as the company's expert witness in more than a dozen lawsuits."[18] Wetli testified that when cocaine and other drugs are involved in a death, excited delirium syndrome must always be the cause.[19]

Wetli was one of five coauthors of a document claiming that although the Taser causes "great pain," the weapon itself does not cause death. This document, "Medical Examiner Collection of Comprehensive, Objective Medical Evidence for Conducted Electrical Weapons and Their Temporal Relationship to Sudden Arrest," is available on the US Department of Commerce's National Institute of Standards and Technology website.[20] On the document's disclosures page, Wetli and Dr. Steven Karch, a coauthor, are both listed as having been "retained as consultants / expert witnesses for Taser."[21] The document's other coauthors were all affiliated with Taser International in some manner, whether as consultants, expert witnesses, or active board members. The disclosures page ends with a bullet point: "All authors are frequent expert witnesses for law enforcement."[22]

A Reuters investigation found that since 2000, there have been more than a thousand incidents in the United States in which people have died after being stunned with a Taser. Nearly all these incidents also involved other uses of force, such as beatings or choke holds. This same investigative report found that excited delirium syndrome was listed in the autopsy reports of at least 275 Taser-involved deaths.[23] Amnesty International found that between 2001 and 2008, excited delirium syndrome was cited in 75 of the 330 deaths following the deployment of a Taser. Indeed, excited delirium syndrome has been key to Taser International's legal defense strategy.[24]

Perhaps unsurprisingly, race is a factor in the deployment of Tasers. A 2010 study found that in the United States, when the Taser was the first type of force used by police officers, Latiné suspects were twice as likely to be tased as White suspects. Researchers argue that "the enhanced use of Tasers against Hispanic suspects can be interpreted as akin to racial profiling in the sense that it involves disparate treatment of suspects on the basis of race, and to that extent it raises the same questions concerning the accuracy of officers' judgments about the dangerousness of individual suspects."[25]

Disproportionate use of Tasers based on race is not a concern in the United States alone. A 2020 study by the Independent Office for Police Conduct (IOPC) in the UK found that Black suspects were tased by police for five seconds longer than White suspects.[26] In almost one-third of the cases studied by the IOPC, the researchers found that police deployed Tasers rather than other de-escalation techniques and were not always following official guidance on Taser usage. After the study's completion, several of the cases reviewed were sent for criminal prosecution or disciplinary action.

Attorneys representing families of individuals who have died after being tased have alleged that Taser International has unduly influenced medical examiners.[27] The company has spent millions of dollars enlisting researchers who back the company's argument that the Taser is harmless. According to Reuters, Taser International actively sought out medical examiners to establish "a cause of death in Taser-involved deaths, sometimes mere hours after a death, lobbying the medical examiner in favor of a finding of excited delirium."[28] Reuters specifically identified Charles Wetli as one of these medical examiners who received substantial payments for testifying in support of this conclusion.[29]

Sponsored by Taser International, the realm of training and research on excited delirium syndrome has evolved into a significant business venture.[30] When experts testify in court, they command fees ranging from "$500 to $1,000 an hour for testimony and depositions."[31] According to the *New York Times*, a private entity known as Lexipol: Public Safety Policy and Trainings Solutions charges "thousands of dollars to review and write policies for police departments."[32] The article further reveals that the Institute for the Prevention of In-Custody Deaths (IPICD), a company that positions itself as "a global leader in training Excited Delirium to law enforcement all over the world," also charges for its training programs.[33] On its official website, IPICD, established in 2005, states that the organization primarily focuses "on providing Train-the-Trainer and forensic instruction through its seminal scientifically- and legally-based excited delirium, arrest-related death, sudden in-custody death, forensics, suicide, amendment-based use-of-force, and other risk management programs."[34]

In 2017, former Taser CEO Rick Smith testified in court, expressing the company's belief that excited delirium syndrome training "saves lives."[35] Smith acknowledged that the company's connection with the Taser weapon was "polarizing" owing to criticism from organizations like the ACLU and other critics who argue that the weapons are lethal.

"We're never going to run from Taser," Smith said. "It's something we're proud of, and we think the facts are on our side. But we don't want to be having the Taser debate every time we talk about something else."[36] Coincidentally, in 2016, after the police shooting of Mario Woods, my aunt Petra De Jesus, a San Francisco police commissioner at the time, debated Steven Tuttle, a senior official at Taser International.[37] Concerned about the lack of appropriate warning advisories on the Taser product, she stressed the need for accountability for lethal police incidents.[38]

Commissioner De Jesus drew attention to how the business of law enforcement weapons is very lucrative.[39] In 2017, Taser International rebranded itself into Axon and moved into the weapons software industry by expanding its consumer products to include body cameras, patrol car cameras, and software subscription packages to "manage digital footage generated by these cameras."[40] In addition to the Taser electroshock weapon, which at the time provided the bulk of the company's revenue, Axon offered body cameras to police agencies for free, along with the first year's subscription to Evidence .com, the company's online software for managing recorded content and other evidence.[41] "The Axon brand will let the company market its cameras and records management software to police departments without the controversy the Taser brand can generate," Smith said.[42]

It is not lost on me that the same company that manufactures the weapons used to electrocute Black, Brown, and dark Brown people also gets paid to film these same people on dashcams and bodycams they provide to police departments for free, all so that they can turn a profit from police violence.

* * *

When Iya Wanda and Uncle Tobaji started working with family members of Black people killed by police violence, they saw how the government and law enforcement community treated the families like criminals. Iya Wanda told me that authorities and medical examiners would give families misleading information. "It felt like the whole system was rigged," she told me.

"Everybody's lying to them." Iya Wanda explained how police tried to force families to stay quiet or take settlements. "Police know they're wrong. There's a systematic way that they handle killings, which involves lying," she told me, exasperated. "Sometimes they will not let you know that the person is already dead when they know they are, or they lie to you about which hospital they are in." She described how families are sent on a chase for the truth. This troubling reality is amplified when medical examiners work directly with companies like Taser International and the police, raising concerns about how they interpret their findings.

A December 26, 2021, *New York Times* exposé, titled "How Paid Experts Help Exonerate Police after Deaths in Custody," shed light on an "industry" of experts, particularly medical examiners who have built careers around defending cases of police violence. According to the article, this industry employs the concept of excited delirium syndrome to obscure instances of police abuse, including deaths related to Tasers and excessive use of force. Since George Floyd's death in May 2020, when Officer Derek Chauvin knelt on Floyd's neck for more than nine minutes, there has been a growing realization that something is fundamentally flawed with the medical terminology of "excited delirium syndrome." The *Times* article makes it evident that Charles Wetli did not just invent this syndrome, but was also a significant figure in the process of sanitizing police-involved killings within the law enforcement sector.

Another one of these experts, Dr. Deborah Mash, a student of Wetli's who coauthored multiple articles on excited delirium syndrome with him, has also come under scrutiny. In 2017, allegations surfaced that Mash worked too closely with Taser International and law enforcement agencies to conceal Taser-related fatalities. Mash's association with the company came into question after the death of Israel Hernandez-Llach, an eighteen-year-old Latiné man who died of cardiac arrest in Miami Beach, Florida, while being tased by a police officer. According to Reuters, a mere four hours after Hernandez-Llach was pronounced dead, Taser International reached out to the Miami Beach Police Department via email, specifically requesting the collection of brain tissue samples from the deceased teenager. Taser International's representative told the police to send these samples to Mash for testing.[43]

According to court records, Mash played a significant role in providing testimony and written research that Taser International utilized as part of its defense strategy.[44] Between 2005 and 2009, Mash served as an expert witness in a minimum of eight wrongful death lawsuits involving Taser International.[45] Her academic tenure lasted thirty-one years, during which time she held the position of professor of neurology and molecular and cellular pharmacology at the University of Miami Miller School of Medicine. Her retirement, in 2018, came just one year after the Hernandez-Llach case.

While actively engaged with the Miller School of Medicine, Mash directed the University of Miami's Brain Endowment Bank. This institution boasts a nationwide network of pathologists whose primary mission is to coordinate the posthumous donation of brain and spinal cord tissues.[46] This practice of preserving brain and spinal cord tissues for scientific study mirrors a disturbing historical continuum of retaining Black people's brains, as seen in the cases of Afro-Cuban men accused of witchcraft in early republican Cuba. In this current context of excited delirium syndrome, Mash's utilization of these brain tissue samples was aimed at substantiating the existence of the fabricated disease and defending cases in which a Taser was alleged to have contributed to the cause of death.

Todd Falzone, the legal representative for the Hernandez-Llach family in their liability lawsuit, raised concerns about the close alignment between Taser International's research and its defense tactics. "From the minute they find out someone dies, they're doing everything they can behind the scenes to set up . . . so the case goes away," he stated.[47]

Medical examiners, forensic pathologists, and organizations such as IPICD and Lexipol have built careers around the concept of excited delirium syndrome and other medical excuses for police misconduct. In a disconcerting example of this, Mark Kroll, a biomedical engineer without a medical degree who holds a position on the corporate board of Axon (formerly Taser

International), was cited at trial in former officer Derek Chauvin's defense. Kroll contended that an officer applying "body weight on someone facedown does not cause asphyxia."[48] Furthermore, in a 2019 webinar training, Kroll expressed a desire for the creation of a medical term that would exonerate police violence. He stated, "Hopefully in the future we'll have something like sudden infant death syndrome, just 'arrest-related death syndrome' so we don't have to automatically blame the police officer."[49] Paradoxically, such a syndrome has already been in use—excited delirium, originally conceived of by Wetli and associates—allowing for the medicalization of police violence.

The *New York Times* article sheds light on how this network of medical examiners works. The article described a "self-reinforcing ecosystem," an intricate web of companies and organizations, where paid experts conduct trainings, produce policies, and carry out research studies to reinforce the concept of excited delirium syndrome. What is particularly striking is that nearly three-quarters of the research studies aimed at justifying police violence by framing it as an appropriate use of force involve at least one author from this network."[50] The article identified Wetli as occupying a prominent role in this group. These experts are then compensated once more to provide testimony in court, asserting the safety of restraint techniques that can be fatal, thus reaping financial gains at both ends of the research spectrum. From choke holds to electric shocks, and from exerting body weight to hog-tying, excited delirium syndrome operates as an invaluable exoneration tool for law enforcement officers while simultaneously serving as a lucrative enterprise for the expert defense industry.[51]

* * *

Just eighteen months into his tenure as the head of the Long Island medical examiner's office, Wetli encountered what was described as "one of the most difficult cases" of his career. On July 17, 1996, Trans World Airlines (TWA) flight 800, a Boeing 747 departing from John F. Kennedy International Airport en route to Paris, plunged into the Atlantic Ocean. A mere twelve minutes after takeoff, a catastrophic fuel tank explosion, likely caused by faulty ignition wiring, resulted in the loss of all 230 lives. Initially, authorities recovered only 99 bodies, and it took the navy three months to retrieve most of the other remains. It was not until ten months later that the final remains were recovered. It was a protracted four-year-long investigation. Speculation about terrorism loomed, and frustrated family members believed crucial evidence was lost in the delay. Many were upset with the lengthy identification process, but Wetli adamantly declined external assistance, stating, "I don't need thirty dentists at eight o'clock in the morning."[52]

Through my research I've come to recognize Wetli's response to the TWA crash as emblematic of his approach. He chose to rely on his close-knit team and rejected outside aid. Given that the explosion "had sheared the skin, clothes and limbs from many passengers," the bodies were difficult to identify.[53] Wetli claimed that he wanted to shield families from the gruesome remains, and he was lauded for successfully identifying all the victims using dental records, fingerprints, and other means. This case prompted me to contemplate how Wetli's conclusions often appear to align with broader political interests. I recalled his role as a medical examiner for the US Army in 1975, when he garnered acclaim for averting an international crisis by attributing the deaths of seven South Korean soldiers in a tunnel to toxic concrete rather than North Korean aggression. Similarly, in 1988, he managed to convince the CDC and Miami police that the murders of Black women and girls were linked to cocaine, possibly even tied to a contaminated batch resulting from toxic rainfall in Peru.

The TWA flight incident highlights a similar, subtle hubris to his practice, characterized by his consistent refusal of external assistance and unwavering commitment to claims, whether or not they were accurate. I reflected on how, even when faced with evidence contradicting his stance, such as in his "genetic defect" theory regarding Black people and cocaine, Wetli remained resolute. It led me to question whether, in the TWA victims' identifications, his close-knit team might have reached conclusions that aligned with Wetli's preconceived notions.

Considering these patterns in Wetli's practices, I could not help being alarmed at his assertion that the Taser electroshock weapon was safe. The more I delved into Wetli's involvement with Taser International, the more it echoed his previous endeavors as a cult expert on Afro-Latiné religions. In the past, Wetli had conducted research on Marielitos and leveraged his findings to generate additional income as an expert. Much like his career in providing police trainings on cults during the Satanic Panic of the 1980s and 1990s, he appeared to employ a similar strategy when conducting profitable training sessions on excited delirium syndrome in the 2000s.

Looking back on Wetli's role in the medicalization of police violence, I began to recognize how his racist criminalizations sparked an entire industry designed to conceal the deaths of Black and Brown people who have, in reality, fallen victim to police violence. It is evident to me that Wetli helped to establish a system of White expertise that revolved around the criminalization of deceased Black people, from Marielitos to Black women and girls, and those killed by police violence. His medical categorizations proved so effective that, until the day he died, Wetli continued to obscure cases of police violence. In his final role as an expert, he did not even need to invoke excited delirium syndrome—a fact that may be the most dangerous part of the Ricky Ball case.

In 2020, Wetli was called upon to serve as an expert witness in the prosecution of Officer Canyon Boykin, who stood accused of the murder of Ricky Ball, a twenty-six-year-old Black father from Columbus, Mississippi. The Ball case was fraught with disturbing accounts of police violence and racially motivated aggression. On October 16, 2015, Ball was shot, tased, and ultimately killed during a questionable police interaction with Officer Boykin, a member of the Columbus Police Department's Special Operations Group (SOG). Officer Boykin, known for his aggressive approach, had been accused of racially profiling people in the area.[54] He also was purported to have personal issues with Ricky Ball, stemming from Ball's romantic involvement with Officer Boykin's stepcousin Laura Hines, a White woman.[55]

During a previous interaction captured on body camera audio, Officer Boykin expressed his intention to forcibly remove Ball from his car, using profanity and allegedly racial slurs.[56] Ball, however, managed to escape on that occasion. Several months later, Officer Boykin confronted Ball and fatally shot him. The case raised several red flags. Initially, two conflicting police reports emerged from the Columbus Police Department (CPD),[57] and it was later revealed that the gun supposedly found in Ball's possession actually belonged to Officer Boykin's friend Officer Garrett Mittan, another SOG member. Officer Mittan, who was the first officer on the scene with Ball and Officer Boykin, had not reported the gun as stolen until twelve days after Ball's death.[58]

Ball's family asserted that Officer Boykin had pursued Ball, opening fire and injuring him.[59] Witnesses from the community claimed that Ball fled through the neighborhood desperately seeking help, screaming "They gonna kill me." The family alleges that Officer Boykin dragged Ball for fifty feet, tased him, and left him to bleed to death.[60] Bystanders emerging from their homes attested that CPD officers prevented paramedics from promptly attending to Ball. No oxygen mask was placed on him, nor were lifesaving efforts made at the scene. Following the incident, community members reported being intimidated by the officers, who aimed their weapons at them and attempted to force them out of the area.[61]

In a civil deposition against Officer Boykin, a Mississippi Bureau of Investigation officer testified that Ball's fingerprints were absent from the gun and cited "discrepancies in the Taser log."[62] A grand jury indicted Boykin in September 2016, leading to his termination.[63] Additionally, the assistant police chief, Tony McCoy, and the narcotics officer, Joseph Strevel, resigned.[64] Ball's family filed a wrongful death lawsuit against the city, alleging that Mittan, who had resigned by then, had planted the gun.[65]

However, with the 2016 election of Donald Trump, who had advised officers to "rough people up more," the climate around policing shifted.[66] Police departments across the country stopped allowing scholars to conduct ongoing research, halting interviews, ride-alongs, and ethnographic study of policing. This political transformation played a pivotal role in altering the course of the Canyon Boykin case.

In 2017, Boykin filed a wrongful termination lawsuit, claiming that his dismissal was racially motivated, as he was "White and the deceased was Black."[67] The department argued that Boykin was fired for failing to activate his body camera during the incident, having his fiancée in the police car without permission, and making derogatory remarks on social media targeting African Americans, women, and disabled people.[68] Nonetheless, the city settled with Boykin for an undisclosed amount.[69]

State attorney general Lynn Fitch, a conservative Republican, assumed office on January 9, 2020, and regarded Boykin's case as a top priority. She replaced the former Democratic attorney general's prosecutors involved in the case and initiated an investigation to determine whether prosecution should proceed. Fitch personally selected Charles Wetli as her expert, providing him with the various case materials, including scene photographs, Ricky Ball's autopsy images, the autopsy report, and a 2017 affidavit. Wetli also reviewed Boykin's grand jury indictment.

Despite the autopsy performed by deputy medical examiner Lisa Funte, which indicated that Ball had been shot "from back to front," Wetli challenged her findings, concluding that "Mr. Ball was not shot from behind."[70] Consequently, in May 2020, at Fitch's behest, the manslaughter charge against Boykin was dropped, and Fitch also requested that the judge dismiss the case "with prejudice," meaning that the same charges can never be revived or brought back to court.[71] Former prosecutors on the case expressed shock and dismay, contending that the decision to drop charges hinged on a narrow interpretation of evidence, as well as the omission of crucial evidence against Boykin.[72]

Despite retiring as medical examiner in 2006, Wetli remained active as an expert on cases until shortly before his death on July 28, 2020. Two months after submitting his report on the Ricky Ball case, Wetli succumbed to lung cancer in a Manhattan hospital at the age of seventy-six, leaving behind a legacy marked by his controversial involvement in cases related to police violence.

* * *

The Ricky Ball case unveils the collaboration among medical examiners, police officers, and politicians in concealing instances of police abuse against Black and Brown victims, offering a stark reminder of how legacies are often reshaped and obscured in the aftermath of police violence. History would seem intent on casting Charles Wetli's impact in a different light. His obituary dedicated a mere one-line mention of his expertise in "drug-related deaths, deaths in police custody and the relationship between the rituals of certain Afro-Caribbean religions and forensic investigations."[73] In stark contrast, two pages were reserved for the TWA flight, emphasizing his triumphant identification of all the Boeing passengers. I could not help being upset at this revisionist narrative. I kept thinking that Wetli should be known instead for his role in fostering an industry that conceals police violence.

The Ricky Ball case serves as a stark reminder of how medical examiners are strategically deployed by politicians, corporations, and lawyers to manipulate the justice system in favor of law enforcement. I should not have been surprised, but I admit that I had naively thought that perhaps Wetli's change of heart in relation to Santeria practices might have impacted his other views. Through the Ricky Ball case, it became clear to me that the racial laboratory is not solely about a specific term or syndrome used to cover up police violence. It would be too easy to believe that simply eradicating the use of the fake syndrome might solve the problem. I now understand that the role of the expert itself is deeply troubling within the framework of White supremacy.

Anthropologist Kamari Clarke's insights shed light on how the role of "expert witnessing" traces back to medieval juridical processes, notably emerging during the Salem witch trials of 1692, when a medical doctor acted as an "aid to the court" to provide his "medical opinion that a female defendant had bewitched victims."[74] Experts, far from providing impartial counsel, play a central role in shaping the frameworks that legitimize dominant institutions.[75]

This research underscores what many have observed: the medicalization of police violence is ingrained in the fabric of America. Excited delirium syndrome is just one instance following a historical precedent of categorizations used to conceal police killings. In the 1990s, for example, officials in California deployed the "No Humans Involved" (NHI) acronym to dehumanize Black males in South Central Los Angeles. NHI facilitated the medicalization of police violence wherein Darryl Gates, the Los Angeles chief of police at the time, argued that "Black males had something abnormal with their windpipes," making them more susceptible to being fatally crushed by police.[76]

Akin to Black feminist Sylvia Wynter's critique of NHI as a tool for justifying police violence, I recognize this medicalization as rooted in eugenics.[77] The medicalization of police violence reinforces evolutionary ideals, with White medical expertise institutionalizing hierarchies among racial groups (Black, Red, Brown, Yellow, and White), categorizing them in a scale from least to most human. This system of classification originated from European global domination and was perpetuated in the racial laboratories of slave ships and plantations, and it remains entrenched in today's institutions, from universities to hospitals to police departments.[78]

Within these racial laboratories lies the role of the White expert, the seemingly impartial outsider believed to provide a neutral perspective, yet who instead actually reinforces the entire structure of violence. In Afro-Latiné perspectives, the White expert would be considered a type of negative spirit, one that attaches to you and can potentially infiltrate your very being.

Saturday, January 8, 2022
Oakland, California

I saw Iya Wanda at a drum ceremony. We sang and danced with the orisha, and it lifted my spirits. After, we sat and ate stewed goat and black beans and talked about how Black and Latiné children are in constant danger from the police. Iya Wanda mentioned that our children are in desperate need of safe places to be themselves and learn the traditions.

When I was a kid, Iya Wanda held a Lukumi "Sunday School" for us at her house. She'd have activities that taught us about the orisha, and we'd learn songs and Lukumi prayers. Iya Wanda wanted to bring something like that back.

During our conversation we discussed what had initially led me to this research. As a single mother, I took my two boys from the San Francisco Bay Area to Cambridge, Massachusetts, in their formative years, when I was pursuing a tenure track job at Harvard University. My fear as a mother to Brown teenage boys led me to study police violence.

It was February 2012, and the snow had been piling up in Harvard Yard. Being from California, I was still unaccustomed to the winter weather even after two years of living on the East Coast. The red brick pavement was slippery. Workers shoveled and salted the paths. I carefully made my way across the icy streets, late to meet my two children for dinner. Sixteen-year-old Neto and ten-year-old

Pilli went to school just down the block, and we'd meet up at different restaurants in Harvard Square.

Even though snowy Cambridge made a picture-perfect scene, I was chilled by news of the death of another Black boy. I remember it being early evening when I found out about Trayvon Martin's killing. During a lecture at the university, an alert appeared on my phone. I thought it was my kids, so I checked and saw the headline. As I walked to meet Neto and Pilli, two students talked about what had happened, how Trayvon "was stalked," that "they did not arrest the killer." I eavesdropped.

Two years earlier, we had moved into a faculty apartment in one of the Harvard University "houses," just off Harvard Yard. It had seemed like a fairy tale. The steepled brick building covered in snow, with a courtyard that gave the impression of an old English village. The ringing bell tower reinforced the gravitas. The dining hall could have been taken directly from Hogwarts. Bright canary-yellow walls with white roman columns and intricate white crown moldings framed the tall ceilings and large antique crystal chandeliers. Bustling students with trays piled with food found their way to seats at long wooden tables.

Harvard calls the large compound a "house"; it is where mostly undergraduate students live. During the winter, beautiful lights twinkle against the white snow. The offer of after-school hot chocolate had sold us on living in here our first year on campus. I thought I was giving my kids a once-in-a-lifetime opportunity. The first day we moved into our new apartment was our reality check. My large, Brown, fifteen-year-old boy had gone to the convenience store around the corner, just as Trayvon did. Like Trayvon, my son wore his usual hoodie. When he tried to get back into our apartment, he was stopped.

"What are you doing here?" he was asked. "This is private property," he was told.

At first, he was afraid, then insulted. In the end, I knew we were lucky that it was just humiliation that he suffered.

9

Forced

FEBRUARY 26, 2012, marked a fateful day, when Trayvon Martin, a seventeen-year-old Black teenager in Sanford, Florida, went to the store to buy some iced tea and Skittles. Little did he know that he would never make it back home. What should have been an ordinary errand turned into a tragic encounter with a vigilante neighborhood watchman named George Zimmerman. This man deemed Trayvon's appearance "suspicious," leading to a horrifying sequence of events where Zimmerman followed, attacked, and fatally shot the Black teenager who was wearing a hoodie, solely because he was walking in the suburban neighborhood. I remember being terrified for my children.

The Trayvon Martin story compelled me to study policing. About a week after Trayvon's tragic death, I received a call from police officers who were practitioners of Santeria in Florida and asked whether I could look into the reemergence of the criminalization of Afro-Cuban religions. They had noticed a troubling rise in racism among the Florida police force. I recall watching the trial of George Zimmerman unfold on television, alongside students and colleagues at Harvard University. Media coverage attempted to downplay the possibility that Zimmerman had racially profiled Trayvon, citing his mother's Peruvian heritage as evidence to the contrary.

Amid online conversations and news punditry at the time were discussions about Florida's Stand Your Ground law, which grants individuals the right to "meet force with force" if they perceive themselves to be threatened.[1]

There was uncertainty about whether Zimmerman would employ this law to justify his actions. Some argued that Trayvon, in fact, had the right to stand his ground, given that he was being pursued by Zimmerman. Ultimately, Zimmerman's defense team opted not to not invoke the Stand Your Ground law but instead chose to argue plain self-defense. They appeared to bank on the notion that it would be relatively simple to portray an unarmed seventeen-year-old Black youth as the aggressor when faced with a grown man with a gun.

* * *

On that fateful day, Trayvon had made a quick run to the corner store to get some snacks so he and his cousin could eat while watching a football game. On his way back it started raining, so Trayvon took shelter under a store awning until the shower passed. When George Zimmerman spotted Trayvon waiting for the rain to subside, he called the police with baseless suspicions. "This guy looks like he's up to no good, or he's on drugs or something."[2] Zimmerman then proceeded to stalk Trayvon, who, in a frightened call to a friend, voiced his apprehension about the stranger following him.

As tensions escalated, Trayvon attempted to evade Zimmerman, who had declared to the police, "These guys always get away," stating his intention to continue pursuing Trayvon.[3] Despite the 911 operator's instructions for Zimmerman to stand down, he disregarded the advice. When he caught up with Trayvon, a confrontation ensued.

Witnesses in the neighborhood provided conflicting accounts: Selma Mora testified that she observed George Zimmerman straddling Trayvon immediately after the gunshot, after which, she claimed, he "stood up and began pacing."[4] Two other neighbors claimed that Trayvon was the one on top.[5] Nevertheless, when the police arrived at the scene, Trayvon lay face down with his arms beneath him, contradicting Zimmerman's assertion that he had turned the victim over, spread his arms, and checked for weapons after the shooting.

The pivotal question in the case revolved around determining who was on top and thus considered the aggressor. It did not matter that Zimmerman was explicitly told by the police not to pursue Trayvon. The final judgment would hinge on the analysis of gunshot evidence.

Don West, George Zimmerman's attorney, reached out to Vincent Di Maio, a medical examiner known for his expertise in gunshot analysis. The case was all over the news, and Di Maio was already familiar with some of the basic facts. Later, Di Maio would admit that even before examining the evidence, he had already formed his conclusions.[6] Based solely on what he saw in the news coverage, Di Maio was convinced that Trayvon Martin was the aggressor and George Zimmerman the victim. When he told Don West his theory, West knew that the whole case could rest on Di Maio's testimony, and this turned out to be true.[7] The defense's strategy was set. It centered on portraying Zimmerman, armed with a 9-millimeter pistol, as a victim of Trayvon Martin, who they alleged used the concrete sidewalk as his weapon.[8]

In a subsequent book, *Morgue*, Di Maio provided further insights into why he believed George Zimmerman had valid suspicions to pursue Trayvon Martin. Di Maio claimed that because the neighborhood demographics were changing, from a White suburb to a more racially diverse neighborhood, Zimmerman was justified in stalking Trayvon.[9] Di Maio attributed a sinisterness to the Black people entering the neighborhood: "Strangers came and went. Low-end people from the wrong side of the gates drifted through. Gangsta boys in low-slung, baggy pants and cockeyed ball caps started hanging around."[10]

Di Maio's biased portrayals were disturbingly obvious. He described Trayvon Martin, a seventeen-year-old high school student who liked video games and had a few tardies on his academic record, as a large, intimidating "badass" who was "flirting with thug life."[11] By contrast, he depicted George Zimmerman, an unemployed adult approaching his thirties with known anger issues and a penchant for spying on his neighbors, as a clumsy "former altar boy," a "part-time college student," and the "son of a Virginia magistrate" who aspired to become a judge.[12] The world would continue to see Zimmerman's penchant for violence in 2015, when he was arrested for domestic violence and suspicion of aggravated assault with a weapon.[13]

After a three-week trial, it took the jury two days to acquit George Zimmerman. The all-female, predominantly White jury, with only one Latina member, agreed with the defense's narrative. Even though Trayvon Martin was minding his own business and walking home when he was stalked, assaulted, and fatally shot by Zimmerman, the jurors blamed Trayvon for his own demise. They believed the argument that he used the sidewalk as his weapon against a gun. The entire case relied on the medical examiner's testimony that Trayvon had been on top of Zimmerman in the final moments. Shockingly, the prosecution did not present a rebuttal witness to contradict Vincent Di Maio's testimony.

Some have argued that the prosecution deliberately undermined the case by not bringing in a rebuttal witness.[14] Di Maio, who was paid $400 an hour, was known to tailor his testimony to align with the defense's theories in high-profile cases.[15] Before testifying for Zimmerman's defense, he had appeared on talk shows and expressed views of the evidence that contradicted his court testimony.[16]

Yet prosecutors did not contest these assertions. They could have argued against the "unscientific manner" in which Di Maio had decided that Trayvon's sweatshirt was separated from his body.[17] Di Maio admitted that he was unfamiliar with baggy hoodies, and so had used his own fitted men's dress shirt to come to his conclusions. He argued that Trayvon must have been leaning forward because the imprint showed that the clothing was not up against his skin. The prosecutors failed, however, to question why Di Maio did not test his theories on the actual clothing Martin was wearing. Hoodies are designed to be loose fitting, which allows for many possible explanations for Trayvon's sweatshirt not being against his skin. The prosecutor did not challenge this argument and instead used the cross-examination time to joke with Di Maio that they were both old White men who did not wear hoodies.[18]

Dr. Shiping Bao, the original medical examiner who was never called back for rebuttal, contested the idea that gunshot residue held the key to this case, calling this assertion "absurd and refutable."[19] Bao felt strongly that "no one could tell who was on top and who was on the bottom at the time of the shooting" based on the gunshot residue alone. "We just don't know," he stated.[20]

In reality, Trayvon Martin's case was never adequately presented. The mostly White women jurors seemed to parallel the outcome of the trial of Emmett Till's murderers, driven by a defense attorney's manipulative rhetoric that drew on the fear of Black youth as inherent predators.[21] Zimmerman's trial was widely decried as a sham. Even President Obama acknowledged the racial injustice, stating, "You know, if I had a son, he'd look like Trayvon."[22]

The verdict deeply disturbed me, fueling my outrage and determination. With a Black president in the White House, the tragic outcome showed me that our society could not change without real, systemic reform. I decided to focus my research on policing as a means to contribute to this change, and the following summer I began conducting ride-alongs with police officers.

Little did I know that six years before Trayvon's killing, the same medical examiner responsible for concocting George Zimmerman's acquittal scheme, Vincent Di Maio, had coauthored a book titled *Excited Delirium Syndrome: Cause of Death and Prevention* with his wife, Theresa, a nurse. Their book, rooted in Charles Wetli's theory, argued that excited delirium syndrome existed, and that innocent police and paramedics were unjustly accused of killing people simply because American society had a desire to assign blame.[23] The Di Maios' book also defended the safety of Taser weapons. Tellingly, Taser International had purchased more than a thousand copies of the book to distribute to forensic pathologists nationwide.[24]

I could not believe the coincidence that the medical examiner I had watched during George Zimmerman's trial also had a connection to my research on excited delirium syndrome. I decided to delve deeper into Vincent Di Maio's background, wanting to understand his motivations, how he came to his conclusions as a medical examiner. I found another book, written by Vincent Di Maio and Ron Franscell, titled *Morgue: A Life in Death*. In that book Di Maio distances himself from deep contemplation, stating, "I don't seek profound meaning in the behavior of humans, or the stars, or the alchemy of little coincidences."[25] When bodies come to his medical examiner's table, Di Maio says he sees them only as "evidence." The person is "long gone," the spirit "seeped out."[26]

Di Maio's assertions jumped off the page at me. In contemplating how the spirits led me through the discoveries in this book, I thought about this limited view of Western positivism that he expressed, how it only allows a very narrow grasp of reality. I reflected on how Di Maio's approach is unable to comprehend the layers of racism that lead to those bodies lying on medical examiners' tables in the first place.

It also made me consider the role of medical examiners and their relation to police violence. When people think about police reform, they often limit their analysis to those specific agencies and institutions. This research has allowed me to see that we must trace the networks of institutional collusion more broadly. Indeed, the community of medical examiners is actually quite small, comprising approximately "five hundred board-certified forensic pathologists" in the United States.[27] I now understand that they wield significant power. I needed to take a closer look at how medical examiners seem to use a sleight of hand, turning prejudice into immutable facts. Their conclusions are far from neutral observations; rather, they have the power to obscure the suffocating grip of racism that people of color in the United States continue to endure.

* * *

Antonio Valenzuela, a forty-year-old Brown Latiné man, was tragically killed on February 29, 2020, in Las Cruces, New Mexico, when officers tased him twice and then placed him in a "vascular neck restraint" commonly known as a choke hold. He was a passenger in a pickup truck that the police pulled over; officers said they thought Valenzuela was reaching for a gun and feared for their lives. No gun was found. Officer Christopher Smelser asserted that, as Valenzuela tried to escape, he tased him twice, wrestled him to the ground, delivered blows, and employed a choke hold until he stopped struggling. During the incident, Officer Smelser threatened Valenzuela, declaring, "'[I'm going to] choke you out, bro.'"[28] Meanwhile, Officer Andrew Tuton, Smelser's partner, added to the body compression by pressing his knee onto Valenzuela's back as he lay unconscious, face down in the dirt.

A medical examiner's analysis attributed Valenzuela's death to "asphyxia injuries due to physical restraint," revealing swelling in his brain and hemorrhaging in his eyes, indicative of neck and chest compression.[29] The examination further revealed severe injuries, including a crushed Adam's apple and a deep muscle hemorrhage in his neck.[30] Unfortunately, it would take several months for Officer Smelser to face termination and manslaughter charges.[31] Notably, there was a stark absence of protests in response to Valenzuela's death, as Amy Andrea Martinez and Humberto Flores point out.[32] Indeed, it was not until six months later, after the murder of George Floyd, that Smelser was charged with involuntary manslaughter, a charge later elevated to second-degree murder. Throughout Smelser's trial, his defense attorney argued that physical restraint alone did not kill Valenzuela and that he must have "also experienced the toxic effects of methamphetamine use," which, as we have seen, is a veiled allusion to claims of excited delirium syndrome.[33]

In their book *Excited Delirium Syndrome*, the Di Maios employ similar forensic manipulation tactics as seen in the Trayvon Martin case, downplaying the severity of injuries sustained during encounters with police and paramedics. They argue that injuries like neck tissue hemorrhages, sustained from having an arm placed around the neck, or fractures of the thyroid cartilage or the hyoid bone should not be equated with death by strangulation.[34] The Di Maios, a medical examiner and a nurse, respectively, tell us to ignore injuries like the ones suffered by Antonio Valenzuela. Instead, they claim that these injuries are mere "markers" indicating pressure was applied to the body. They effectively shift the blame away from excessive police force to the public's "interpretation" of events.[35]

Much of the Di Maios' writing in *Excited Delirium Syndrome* revolves around convincing readers that restraint techniques and force tactics employed by police officers, including Tasers, are benign. The book attempts to medicalize deaths occurring during violent restraint in police custody and in mental institutions, attributing them to a "cascade of physiological responses" triggered by an unidentifiable "syndrome"[36] called excited delirium. To the question "What is the cause of death?" they reply: "It is the authors' contention that death is due to a combination of the normal physiologic changes seen in a struggle, combined with, depending on the case, the use of illicit drugs, medications, and natural disease."[37]

According to the Di Maios, excited delirium syndrome deaths are, by definition, those in which "an autopsy fails to reveal evidence of sufficient trauma or natural disease to explain the death."[38] Consequently, they imply that autopsies in cases of excited delirium syndrome should be disregarded since they yield little helpful information.[39]

The medicalization of police violence involves ignoring obvious indicators of assault and the damage done to the body by law enforcement. However, a memorandum by US deputy attorney general Lisa Monaco, dated September 13, 2021, contradicts the Di Maios, clearly designating techniques like choke holds and carotid restraints as "inherently dangerous."[40] Vascular neck holds "apply pressure to the throat or windpipe and restrict an individual's ability to breathe," while carotid restraint techniques limit "blood flow to the brain causing temporary unconsciousness."[41]

Despite these glaring risks, the Di Maios assert that such neck holds do not result in death.[42] In their book, they even dispute other medical examiners who do find that choke holds and restraints cause fatalities. In their assessment of Tasers, the Di Maios assert that the electroshock weapon is safe and nonlethal.[43] They argue that deaths attributed to Tasers are merely "blamed" on them, and they refer to a report in the *Arizona Republic* that details ninety deaths, between 1999 and 2005, following the deployment of a Taser.[44] The Di Maios say that after reviewing "the details of these deaths," they believe all were actually cases of excited delirium.[45] They claim that the people did not die immediately after being "Tasered" and were also under the influence of illegal stimulants.[46]

Furthermore, the Di Maios advocate for hog-tying, a practice that restrains people's hands and feet together behind their back, forcing them into a painful arch.[47] They argue that hog-tying people should not cause "positional asphyxia," where individuals die from restricted chest expansion and impaired breathing. The Di Maios suggest that many police departments unjustly banned hog-tying, fearing it was the cause of in-custody deaths, rather than excited delirium syndrome.[48] While they emphasize one study involving healthy individuals to support their claim in favor of hog-tying, they dismiss numerous other studies indicating that restraints can be lethal.

A study conducted by Ron O'Halloran and Janice Frank in 2000, mentioned but dismissed by the Di Maios, argues that rather than the term *positional asphyxia*, which suggests that death results from being in forced positions, the correct term in these cases should be *restraint asphyxia*.[49] O'Halloran and Frank contend that physically restraining people can lead to deadly consequences: "It is not a new concept that a person can die from the application of body weight."[50] Crowd stampedes, human pileups, and being pinned down are all common scenarios leading to fatalities, including instances in which people are sat upon, or "smothered." It is widely recognized that homicides occur "by kneeling or sitting on the back of a prone victim or suspect, or by hog-tying."[51]

O'Halloran and Frank caution against alternative explanations for sudden deaths in custody, such as "excited delirium / acute exhaustive mania," which cannot be reliably verified as a cause of death.[52] They argue that theories attributing such deaths to "cocaine-induced brain disorder" or to "cardiac arrhythmias" often lack "significant autopsy findings."[53] Autopsy results, they note, tend to be "minimal" to support the idea of "excited (agitated) delirium," a concept they call "loosely defined as a condition." Aditionally, O'Halloran and Frank argue that in cases of "so-called 'cocaine delirium,'" the cause of death is likely restraint related or some other form of forceful violence.[54]

Scant attention has been paid to the numerous Latiné men like Antonio Valenzuela who have tragically lost their lives to police restraint-related force because their deaths are often attributed to excited delirium syndrome.[55] In 2013, the death of Jesse Aguirre in San Antonio, Texas, was classified as excited delirium syndrome, but his autopsy showed he died by positional asphyxiation when, after a violent struggle with police, he was held face down.[56] On April 21, 2020, in Tucson, Arizona, just one month before George Floyd's murder, twenty-seven-year-old chef Carlos Ingram Lopez, a Latiné father of a two-year-old daughter, was restrained with a spit hood by multiple officers who pinned him face down for twelve agonizing minutes.[57] Despite his pleas of being unable to breathe, he died at the scene; the autopsy listed "sudden cardiac arrest, with physical restraint by officers and cocaine intoxication as contributing factors."[58] The manner of his death remained "undetermined." The heartbreaking moment was captured on video footage: Lopez calls out for his "nana," his grandmother, while complaining of being unable to breathe before he loses consciousness and succumbs.[59]

The Di Maios do not dispute that most of those deaths attributed to excited delirium syndrome occur during arrests involving a violent struggle, culminating in the often fatal restraint of the person, who "typically" dies within "minutes" of police engagement.[60] *Excited Delirium Syndrome* concludes with the suggestion that these deaths could be prevented by the "rapid administration of sedative medications at the scene."[61] As a lifesaving measure, they recommend coordination among emergency medical services (EMS) personnel, police, and emergency room staff to identify symptoms and administer sedatives to individuals suspected of exhibiting excited delirium syndrome.[62] Indeed, this approach, endorsed by medical examiners like Charles Wetli, has been widely implemented across the country with alarming consequences.

Neither the medical data nor the logic aligns with the concept of excited delirium syndrome. For instance, the Di Maios propose that uncontrollable individuals exhibiting excited delirium syndrome can be calmed down if offered a cigarette.[63] If such de-escalation tactics do not work, they then suggest that police officers and paramedics should "use overwhelming force" and apply chemical restraints like ketamine.[64] Finally, they simply give up: they state that excited delirium syndrome likely means the person will die in custody and emphasize the need for responders to "be prepared for the potential for death to occur."[65]

The Di Maios dedicate their book to "all law enforcement and medical personnel who have been wrongfully accused of misconduct in deaths due to excited delirium syndrome."[66] They express shock at accusations against police officers in cases where deaths are attributed to restraints or positional asphyxia.[67] The Di Maios' defensiveness reminds me of Wetli's reaction when, instead of considering the possibility of the Black women's murder, he could not fathom why people questioned his diagnosis that they had died from "cocaine-sex." Just as Wetli initially dismissed suspicions of foul play, the Di Maios' perspective overlooks critical evidence and alternative explanations for these tragic deaths.

* * *

I went deeper into Vincent Di Maio's background, searching for any connections he might have had with Charles Wetli since they were both prominent medical examiners during the same period.[68] Although no direct links emerged, Di Maio, like Wetli, served in the United States military. He was chief of legal medicine at the Armed Forces Institute of Pathology in Washington, DC, in 1970 before relocating to Dallas, Texas, where he assumed the role of chief medical examiner. In 1981, he took over as chief medical examiner in San Antonio, ultimately retiring from this post.

Over his career, Vincent Di Maio faced criticism for actively pursuing high-profile cases that thrust him into the media spotlight, and for providing expert witness testimony that conveniently aligned with those who hired him.[69] Interestingly, it seemed that these tendencies also ran in the family: Vincent Di Maio's father, Dr. Dominick Di Maio, also had a penchant for high-profile cases.

In 1974, Dominick Di Maio achieved his longtime aspiration of becoming chief medical examiner in New York City, after a twenty-six-year wait.[70] His tenure was short-lived, however. Suspicions arose that he would provide expert testimony "for a price."[71] Allegations of improprieties also surfaced during his time as acting chief medical examiner, culminating in his resignation after just four years on the job.[72]

Dominick Di Maio began his journey as a medical examiner in 1950, when he joined the New York medical examiner's office, working for sixteen years at the King's County Hospital branch in Brooklyn. Neither his predecessor, Dr. Milton Helpern, nor Mayor Abraham Beame wanted him as the chief medical examiner.[73] Reports emerged of illicit activities occurring at the New York City morgue during his tenure, including claims of "nighttime prostitution, gambling and drinking."[74] During the city's investigation, the commissioner, Nicholas Scoppetta, uncovered that Dominick Di Maio had accepted "$4,000 from a California research group for compiling city statistics on narcotic deaths," and that he freely used the city morgue for his private autopsies.[75] Dominick Di Maio defended his actions, stating, "I would do it again."[76]

Yet the accusations of corruption in the Office of Chief Medical Examiner in New York City would neither begin nor end with Dominick Di Maio. His successors, who had worked as medical examiners alongside him, faced allegations of mishandling autopsy cases to cover up police abuse and receiving kickbacks from morticians.[77] They were investigated for issuing misleading autopsy reports and altering "other doctors' findings in 'police custody cases.'" Dr. Elliott Gross, who assumed the role of chief medical examiner in 1979, instituted a policy of performing "all autopsies" of people who died "in police custody" in his Manhattan office, leading to accusations that he attempted to "cover up the cause of death" in cases involving police brutality.[78]

Following his forced retirement, Dominick Di Maio, like his son would do later, turned to a new career as an expert witness for defense lawyers in high-profile cases. In one such case, he provided testimony that supported

Bernhard Goetz's self-defense argument. Goetz, a thirty-seven-year-old White man in New York City, shot four Black male teenagers on a subway train on December 22, 1984. Goetz became famously known as the "Subway Vigilante"; he claimed that he shot the teenagers in self-defense because they were robbing him. But Goetz shot eighteen-year-old Darrell Cabey as he was cowering and terrified. He reportedly told Cabey, "You don't look too bad, here's another" and shot him in his back, severing his spinal cord and causing permanent brain damage and paralysis.[79]

Nevertheless, people supported Goetz as if he were the real victim. He was acquitted of murder and assault charges, serving only 250 days in prison for illegal gun possession.[80] Dominick Di Maio's testimony played a pivotal role in Goetz's acquittal, as he asserted that none of the Black teenagers "could have been seated or running away when Goetz fired," corroborating the self-defense argument.[81]

The Goetz case rapidly gained national attention and played into the broader narrative of fear and hostility toward Black youth. This case was part of a larger trend in the 1980s as stories of urban crime, often involving young Black teenagers, were widely covered by the media, contributing to the stigmatization and racial profiling of Black youth. The National Rifle Association (NRA) capitalized on this climate of fear and racial tension, launching a successful campaign to ease concealed-carry laws on firearms, and using the Goetz case as a prominent example of self-defense against perceived racial threats.[82]

Certainly, the testimonies of both Dominick and Vincent Di Maio, father and son, can be viewed as emblematic of the larger societal struggles surrounding racial tensions during their respective eras, as evident in the Bernhard Goetz case and the George Zimmerman trial. These two cases share some striking similarities in how they played out, the roles of White experts in perpetuating fear of Black youth, and ultimately the reinforcing of White supremacy. In their testimonies, the Di Maios contributed to these narratives by providing expert opinions that aligned with the defenses' arguments, effectively lending their authority to the idea that violence against Black youth is warranted.

Tellingly, before the emergence of the concept *excited delirium syndrome*, Dominick and Vincent Di Maio seemed to have held different perspectives on homicides and violent struggles. In 2001, they cowrote the book *Forensic Pathology*, which discussed how to classify certain deaths. "There are cases in which the cause of death would ordinarily be considered natural, but it is a homicide," they wrote.[83] This was illustrated with an example of a violent struggle, such as a burglary in which a homeowner, taken by surprise, dies of a heart attack. In such cases, they argue that although the "mechanism of death is a cardiac arrhythmia" owing to "severe coronary atherosclerosis, . . . the manner of death is homicide, in that the arrhythmia was brought on or precipitated by the struggle."[84]

It is worth noting the curious shift in Vincent Di Maio's approach just five years later, when he seemed to suspend this logic in his assessment of excited delirium deaths. The only significant difference was that these cases involved violent struggles and the excessive use of force by police officers, rather than an imagined burglar.

Both Dominick and Vincent Di Maio's track records of validating vigilante violence when it is lucrative and convenient must be considered within a broader historical framework to illuminate the deeply rooted racial dynamics that are intertwined with the use of restraint in the United States.

* * *

The inherent violence of restraints has historical precedents that date back to the era of chattel slavery. Contemporary forms of restraint conjure the legacy of enslaved Africans shackled together during the Middle Passage in horrific conditions. Hundreds of human cargo, tightly packed like sardines at the bottom of ships, manacles rubbing skin bare, and the use of iron muzzles to silence the wails of women ripped from families and home.[85] Recall the disgusting practice in which fifty-pound iron neck-chain collars marked enslaved Africans on plantations to punish runaways, causing deep cuts, sores, and scars.[86] Neck chains, in particular, "were unique in their form of restraint because they were worn for extended periods of times."[87] To remind ourselves of the brutal use of violent restraints and manacles during that period underscores the enduring legacy of such practices in the current context of police violence.

Black medical anthropologist Leith Mullings argued that we must account for the long-term health consequences of structural racism.[88] A similar type of accounting is needed in the relationship between slavery, policing, and prisons, wherein restraint and captivity continue to commingle in the daily life of Black and Brown people. One cannot think about police violence without understanding how it crosses into the "suffocating oppression" of prisons, as noted by Orisanmi Burton.[89] In these sites, captivity enhances a multitude of forms of domination: prison guards and inmates reproduce intimate forms of aggression—from hog-tying to gagging—mirroring what occurs on the streets during police interactions. In the violence of American democracy, the police, prisoners, and prison guards are interrelated elements of a larger structural dynamic tied to racialized violence and restraint.[90]

Scholars have pointed out that the use of restraints to physically detain or incapacitate individuals in custody is itself a form of intimate violence.[91] Forced restraint has been known to cause adverse effects on the body, including pressure ulcers, agitation, infections, necrosis, bodily impairments, asphyxiation, and strangulation.[92] Such violent restraints are particularly exacerbated in mental health settings, where they contribute to racialized incidents that can blur the lines between care and violence.[93] Increasingly, psychologists and lawyers have argued that restraints are inherently violent and should not be used as a treatment technique for the elderly or mentally ill.[94]

It is draining to witness the recurring pattern of how aggressive restraint leads to death without a seeming end. On April 19, 2021, in Alameda, California, Mario Gonzalez, a twenty-six-year-old Latiné man calmly sitting in a park, died after police unnecessarily put him in a restraint, pinning him to the ground and putting a knee on his neck for over two minutes. He also complained about not being able to breathe before he lost consciousness. The medical examiner claimed that Gonzalez died from the "toxic effects of methamphetamine with the physiologic stress of altercation and restraint, morbid obesity and alcoholism contributing to the process of dying."[95] Even though, after George Floyd's death, medical examiners seem to no longer use the term *excited delirium syndrome*, they continue to use the same medicalized justifications to cover up police killings.

Consequently, medical practices like those suggested in the Di Maios' book *Excited Delirium Syndrome* continue to be employed, increasing the precarity for Black and Latiné communities, particularly among those who are undocumented. Since September 11, 2001, the US government has deputized police officers to apprehend undocumented people. The war on terror, immigration enforcement, the prison system, and everyday policing became intertwined. The *Washington Post* has documented in its Fatal Force database that Black people were killed by police "at the highest rate in the United States (31 per million residents) between 2015 and April 2020," and that Latiné "people followed with the second-highest rate of 23 per million residents."[96] Important work has been done showing the relationship between racist policing and immigration enforcement; for example, the everyday act of driving is becoming a high-risk activity in Latiné communities because of violent police encounters. As of January 28, 2022, the *Los Angeles Times* showed, "49 percent of all police killings since 2000 in Los Angeles County were Latinx."[97]

I find myself disheartened by how White supremacy has perpetually morphed throughout history, evident in acts of genocide, warfare, and violence directed at Indigenous, Black American, Latiné, Afro-Latiné, Asian, Arab, and Muslim people, and also by fostering divisions among these groups. These histories are resurrected in law enforcement actions. In the shift from slave shackle to police handcuff, anthropologists have noted that the violent policing and incarceration of Black and Brown people en masse is "intergenerational"—that is, a deadly cycle of captivity and aggression that spans across Black life, passed down across generations of families.[98] Jaime Amparo Alves emphasizes the interconnectedness of Black captivity and democracy, stressing that these forces are not in conflict.[99] Alves points to examples in Brazil, where the state's anti-Black racism has created a vicious cycle of racial injustice leading to intergenerational captivity and hindering the flourishing of Black social life.[100]

A similar dynamic is at work in the United States, where there exists an intergenerational connection between mass incarceration and police violence. Through my research on the medicalization of police violence, I have come to understand the interdependence between law enforcement, legal apparatuses, and medical examiners, which plays a pivotal role in concealing this successive generational violence. Examining the historical corruption and defense of police, as evident in the actions of New York medical examiners, I discern a precedent for the expert industry that figures like Charles Wetli were part of, profiting from the creation and maintenance of excited delirium syndrome. This pattern of systemic cover-up, I realize, itself crosses generations, and in the case of Dominick and Vincent Di Maio, this practice was directly passed down from father to son.

Tuesday, March 22, 2022
Stanford, California

After my CASBS *talk last week, I went back to my office and investigated the story of Albert Einstein's engagement with spirits. I recalled Einstein having had a more complicated relationship with spiritism than what the Fellow had recounted. Indeed, the story was as I had remembered. Although some newspapers claimed that Einstein dismissed spiritism, the actual story was more nuanced. Einstein had not only participated in the séance with his friend Upton Sinclair, he had also actually been enthusiastic about spiritual metaphysics.[1]*

Early nineteenth-century physicists who challenged the solidity of matter did not actually dismiss spirits.[2] Wireless telegraphy, X-rays, and other frequencies beyond visible light were just being detected.[3] The concept of "ether" was also central to early physics. Ether, the unseen world all around us, was understood as filled with vibrational waves and energy. These electromagnetic waves were thought to enable the transmission of unseen forces.[4]

The idea that Einstein was opposed to spiritualism is a later revision of positivist rhetoric. In addition to séances, Einstein met with several psychics, hand-readers, and other mediums.[5] He is said to have been a great fan of the work of Madame Blavatsky,[6] a clairvoyant and psychic who had paranormal experiences beginning in childhood.[7] Einstein was actually more concerned with people using his name than with dismissing spirits. In 1930, when Upton Sinclair wrote

Mental Radio, *which documented experiments on his own wife's psychic abilities, Einstein offered, of his own accord, to endorse the work if Sinclair did "not use his name."*[8]

The day after my talk, I received an email from the skeptical Fellow: he wanted to have lunch. I was looking forward to enlightening him about his mistaken views on Einstein. I wanted the Fellow to see how people like him made it difficult for scholars to undo Western positivism. Even a celebrated scholar such as Albert Einstein was afraid of publicly acknowledging the possibility of spirits.

Today, we were able to meet for lunch. The director of the Center, Margaret Levi, a well-known feminist political scientist, joined us. She reserved a small round metal table. Margaret acted like a cross between a referee and a devil's advocate. As a committed collector of Aboriginal art, she mentioned how the Afro-Latiné understandings of spirits I discussed had resonated with her understandings of spirits as portrayed by Indigenous artists she knew.

I was still frustrated with the skepticism of the Fellow; however, before I could bring up that Albert Einstein was not allergic to the idea of spirits, the interaction took an unexpected turn.

I noticed a grimace of discomfort cross the Fellow's face. Then he told us that he had lost his father as a child. Soon afterward, his father had started to visit the Fellow's dreams. These visits haunted him. This experience was one of the reasons he was so opposed to believing in spirits. Rather than embrace the evidence of his father's sprit, he became a deep skeptic. Looking torn, he told me, "You could not have known that when you said that to me"—when I had said, "When you go to sleep at night, maybe they'll talk to you themselves."

The pain in his face made me forget about Albert Einstein. In Afro-Latiné practices, this moment is called una prueba *(proof) from the copresences. They are providing you a confirmation* (confirmación), *and you should take notice. I told him so. I said, "For practitioners of Afro-Latiné religions, your story would serve as confirmation of spirit contact." They would see this as evidence that the spirits are sending you messages. He said that he imagined that they would think this. Then he told me that his father had also been a scholar. In fact, he had been a Fellow at* CASBS. *He told me that in many ways his whole career, even being at* CASBS *at that very moment, was him following his dad.*

This moment made me think of how Jade Ellis lost her father at a young age. How Jeremy's spirit had "stuck" to Jade. She recalled how she ended up "doing" Jeremy for a while; she became him.

I saw this scholar differently today. He was not just a Western skeptic dismissing my talk because he found it fanciful. I saw the hurt boy who had lost his father too young. And when that father's spirit tried to make contact, this boy refused to see him. Rather than be able to acknowledge the presence of a father's spirit after death, the Fellow had convinced himself it was not real. He could not allow himself to acknowledge the truth of those visits, and it deeply hurt him. My talk triggered that pain, and so it was "unswallowable" for him. It was so sad.

And yet, his father's essence never left him. Even if he refused to acknowledge this copresence, his father's geist had shaped the Fellow in his likeness. Much like Jade, he was "doing" his father. Even decades later, he would occupy the very same fellowship his father had had when he was alive. The idea of "real science" that the Fellow clung to would not allow him to see his father still trying to contact him.

Did the spirit of his dead father want me to communicate with him precisely so we could have this conversation?

I asked him whether I might include his story in my book. He laughed and said he should have known better than to speak to an anthropologist.

Delirious

UNCOVERING CHARLES WETLI'S CASES was making me feel delirious. The connections were overwhelming. I knew he had used racist tropes to make himself into an expert, first on Afro-Cuban Marielitos and then on the "cocaine-sex deaths" of Black women murdered by a serial killer. Now I was seeing another pattern in his racist science. He used media to criminalize Black and Brown people and to craft his own expertise. He leveraged the legitimacy afforded to him as a White physician and subsequently published this flawed research to profit within the expert circuit. Is it possible that my efforts could help to break this cycle of racist scapegoating and expose the profitable industry peddling prejudiced science?

There were so many connections and too much pain. I was not sure I was up to the task the spirits had given me. The scope of violence was vast, with its far-reaching tentacles revealing a complex system of complicity designed to rationalize and perpetuate racial social control. Initially, I thought I had grasped the mechanics of this violence through my research on police training and the police academy. As I delved deeper, however, I realized that medical examiners and even paramedics played a role in this intricate web of death. The realization was dizzying; excited delirium had become a disturbingly effective tool capable of concealing a multitude of violence, operating almost unnoticed. When I was discussing the medicalization of this racist science with a colleague at CASBS, they asked if it connected to the latest incident of police violence in the mainstream news. Regrettably, it did.

* * *

On the fateful evening of August 24, 2019, at 10:43 p.m., Elijah McClain, a twenty-three-year-old massage therapist in Aurora, Colorado, was strolling home from the convenience store. He was listening to music, his headphones engrossing him in soothing sounds.[1] It was a cool sixty-seven degrees outside; a chill in the air prompted him to don a ski mask, as he suffered from anemia. An unsettling call to the police described this unarmed, gentle Black man as "sketchy."[2] Officer Nathan Woodyard approached Elijah McClain and, shockingly, within a mere ten seconds, initiated his physical detention, despite McClain's having committed no crime. The self-described "introvert" politely asked the officer to "leave him alone" and "respect his boundaries," all while carrying the iced tea that he had just purchased from a nearby convenience store.[3]

"I have a right to stop you because you're being suspicious," Woodyard told McClain, even though he lacked any probable cause. Within the brief span of two minutes, Woodyard subjected McClain to a "carotid control hold" and, together with two other officers—Randy Roedema and Jason Rosenblatt—forcibly brought McClain to the ground. The combined weight of these three officers amounted to roughly seven hundred pounds, crushing McClain.[4]

In those initial two minutes, Officer Rosenblatt menacingly brandished his Taser and threatened to use it on McClain as they struggled to handcuff him. "Taser, Taser, Taser!" he yelled. Officers Woodyard and Roedema warned McClain, "You're going to get tased this time, stop fighting,"[5] Yet the electroshock weapon was never administered. McClain, in desperation, pleaded with the officers, explaining that he could not breathe as their collective body weight bore down on his chest. Struggling to catch his breath, McClain implored them to see him for who he was, exclaiming "I'm here!" and identifying himself, "My name is Elijah McClain!" Amid his groans, he consented to comply with their demands, uttering "Alright! I can't breathe, please stop!" and "It hurts!"

Body camera footage tells a harrowing tale. Officers ordered McClain to "stop tensing up" as he asked them for help, even vomiting in the process. "Throw up right there, OK. Don't throw up on me," Officer Rosenblatt instructed McClain. At 10:46 p.m., just three minutes after the officers first encountered Elijah McClain, he lay handcuffed on the ground, awaiting the arrival of paramedics. Within minutes, eight more officers swarmed the scene. In the footage, McClain lay motionless on his side when K-9 Officer Matthew Green, who had just arrived, threatened him: "Dude, if you keep messing around I'm a bring my dog out, he's going to dog bite you. You understand me? Keep messing around."[6]

For five agonizing minutes, Officer Roedema subjected McClain to various painful techniques while he was on the ground. These included wrist and arm control methods, and he even applied an arm bar maneuver, a wrestling technique known for exerting excruciating pressure on the elbow joint. Such a maneuver is notorious for causing unbearable pain that swiftly immobilizes an individual and can result in broken bones. Officer Roedema himself recalled hearing McClain's shoulder "pop" when he applied the submission hold. Throughout this ordeal, McClain could be heard coughing, wheezing, and gasping for air.

When EMS arrived at the scene, paramedic Jeremy Cooper told investigators that he had reached the conclusion, after just one minute of observation, that McClain was "hyper aggressive" and likely exhibiting "excited delirium."[7] Cooper's assessment, however, stands in stark contrast to what was captured on body camera footage: McClain lying motionless, in a prone position, complaining of trouble breathing, all while enduring the forceful holds by multiple officers. Cooper described his rationale:

> It took all these guys to get him down and even then [unintelligible] . . . no pain compliance . . . [unintelligible] still fighting, still fighting when we got here. He's super diaphoretic [sweating profusely], he's tachycardic [high pulse rate]. He's having excited delirium, and that's why we hit him with five of the ketamine.[8]

Cooper determined that McClain, who was five feet seven and 140 pounds, was suffering from "excited delirium" and administered five hundred milligrams of ketamine.[9] This potent sedative medication is commonly administered to people suspected of exhibiting excited delirium syndrome during police encounters. When Aurora Fire Rescue paramedics arrived, they did not speak to McClain. Without his consent, and while he was already handcuffed and restrained by police, Cooper injected him with a dosage typically intended for someone weighing 220 pounds.[10] According to established medical guidelines, McClain should have received a dose of 320 to 350 milligrams of ketamine, aligning with his body weight. Paramedics later told police investigators that they mistakenly thought McClain weighed 190 pounds. Consequently, he was sedated to a level comparable to that of general anesthesia, with the inherent risk of respiratory arrest. Tragically, while still on the scene,

McClain went into cardiac arrest. Six days later, on August 30, 2019, he was declared brain dead and removed from life support.

* * *

Paramedics frequently administer ketamine, a potent sedative, to individuals they suspect may be experiencing excited delirium—a practice that is in line with the recommendations outlined in Theresa and Vincent Di Maio's book *Excited Delirium Syndrome*. Officers claim that ketamine helps mitigate the fight-or-flight response in people they are attempting to subdue, arguing that involuntary ketamine injection avoids harm. But the administration of potent drugs such as ketamine, without prior knowledge of a person's medical history and without consent, remains a significant concern. Emergency medical services personnel responsible for administering sedatives are expected to provide cardiac monitoring and be prepared to deliver medical resuscitation in case of an adverse reaction.

Ketamine is a distinctive dissociative agent known to induce hallucinations and catatonic states. First synthesized in 1956 and approved for use in the United States in 1970, ketamine has seen various applications: from serving as a tranquilizer on dogs and horses to becoming the primary surgical anesthesia during the Vietnam War. In recreational contexts, it is referred to as "Special K" or "Kit Kat" and is among the most common date-rape drugs.[11] Available in both powder and liquid forms, it can be smoked, snorted, and ingested. Ketamine is notorious for being slipped into drinks, causing individuals to enter hallucinogenic states and become detached from reality or catatonic. Victims of ketamine spiking typically report a bitter taste followed by a dreamlike altered state of awareness, often leading to unconsciousness and amnesia, particularly alarming in cases of sexual assault.

Ketamine shares similarities with other dissociative or hallucinogenic substances like MDMA (ecstasy), PCP (phencyclidine), and LSD (lysergic acid diethylamide), although it is considered to be less addictive with fewer side effects. Consequently, ketamine has become a lucrative product in the pharmaceutical industry.[12] In 1964, after successful animal testing results, Parke-Davis commissioned Dr. Ed Domino to conduct human studies, commencing tests on incarcerated people at Jackson State Prison in Michigan.[13] Domino coined the term *dissociative anesthetic* to describe ketamine, owing to its ability to function as an analgesic and produce hallucinations and catatonic states. Approved by the Food and Drug Administration (FDA) in 1970, ketamine has been hailed as a miracle drug, finding applications in various medical treatments, including treatment-resistant depression and fibromyalgia.[14] Some individuals have reported experiencing an unpleasant reaction known as a "K-hole," characterized by intense auditory or visual hallucinations accompanied by a profound sense of detachment from reality.[15]

Police and paramedics often work together to subdue and detain individuals, and the use of ketamine is pivotal in these types of chemical restraints. Concerns have emerged regarding the close working relationships between law enforcement and paramedics, leading to potential confusion about whom paramedics are working for and a general lack of concern for the patients they are supposed to be treating. Within this dynamic, officers employ "code words" as signals to paramedics, suggesting the possibility of excited delirium syndrome and encouraging the administration of sedatives. These codes, laden with racial implications, have become ingrained in the everyday language shared between police and paramedics. This linguistic practice was evident in the Elijah McClain case: officers described him as possessing "incredible strength," "crazy," "pouring [with] sweat," and "obviously on something." Regrettably, these descriptions led to the administration of a ketamine overdose, despite his restraint, prone position, and handcuffed state.

The alarming trend of law enforcement officers and paramedics collaborating to administer ketamine to individuals considered unruly is part of a larger medical–law enforcement complex. MPD Involvement in Pre-Hospital Sedation, a 2018 study conducted by the Office of Police Conduct Review (OPCR) in Minneapolis, found that between 2010 and 2018, ketamine sedation increased drastically. In 2017, 40 percent of the cases where paramedics administered ketamine were to Black men aged eighteen to thirty-four.[16] But Black men were not the exclusive victims of this "weaponization of medicine."[17]

On January 11, 2018, a year before McClain's tragic death, Jerica LaCour, a twenty-nine-year-old Black mother of five in Colorado Springs, also received a fatal dose of ketamine from paramedics. It is essential to highlight that LaCour, who displayed no signs of combativeness or violence, was walking in a park, crying, when police, firefighters, and other EMT personnel approached her. Despite her compliance with their instructions, she was strapped to a gurney and placed in a spit hood when paramedic Jason Poulson of the American Medical Response Ambulance Service injected her with four hundred milligrams of ketamine.[18] Shortly after being injected, LaCour stopped breathing.

Leah Grissom, an EMT affiliated with the Cimarron Hills Fire Department who was on the scene, objected to the administration of ketamine, pointing out that LaCour was calm and already restrained.[19] Poulson, however, disregarded Grissom's concerns, asserting that LaCour "was fine" even after Grissom noted that she was not breathing.[20] Poulson failed to promptly transport LaCour to a hospital, and a doctor pronounced her dead upon arrival. The LaCour family filed a lawsuit, objecting to the administration of ketamine. Their attorney, Daniel Kay, remarked that "LaCour's behavior did not fit the criteria of excited delirium."[21]

I worry about the argument that the injection of ketamine was not justified because Jerica LaCour did not fit the supposed criteria for excited delirium syndrome. I refuse the idea that administering ketamine as a means of chemical restraint is ever warranted. Indeed, as this research has uncovered, the use of the term *excited* to describe the type of delirium said to kill Black and Latiné people in police custody invokes troubling imagery of hypersexuality, aggression, and danger associated with Black people since slavery. It is disconcerting that this language continues to lend credibility to this fabricated syndrome, leaving excited delirium unchallenged and perpetuating the medicalization of police violence.

* * *

I take a moment to reflect on the interconnectedness of the weaponization of medicine and the racialization of drug use. The roots of ketamine's role in "treating" excited delirium syndrome can be traced back to the racial history of cocaine. Originally derived from coca, an Indigenous medicinal plant from South America, cocaine had been used for centuries as a tea to combat fatigue. European scientists transformed this plant medicine into a drug.[22] In the early 1900s, cocaine was extracted from the coca plant and became a popular medical anesthetic and legal recreational narcotic. Even the original Coca-Cola soft drink contained cocaine until 1903.[23] Cocaine's criminalization and prohibition only occurred in 1914, when it was associated with Black men in the South and used as a scapegoat in justifying lynching. Medical professionals began to emphasize cocaine's high addictiveness and detrimental effects during this period.

From the 1890s to the 1910s, ideas on race and criminality were wielded as tools of political reform, targeting different substances with racial associations. Cocaine was associated with Black men, marijuana with Mexican men, and opium with Asians, particularly the Chinese.[24] When cocaine made a comeback in the 1970s, it was Whitened. Portrayed as a glamorous drug for the young and wealthy, cocaine was nicknamed "Snow White," "white gold," "blow," and "white rock." However, there were two types of cocaine: the

White kind that was mostly left alone by law enforcement, and the Black kind, known as "crack," which faced heavy stigmatization and criminalization.[25] Crack cocaine—produced by baking soda to remove the hydrochloride, resulting in crystal-like rocks that make a crackling sound when heated[26]—was colloquially referred to as "sleet," "hail," and "black rock."[27]

Historians have demonstrated the connection between drug policies and racial politics.[28] In the 1970s, the Nixon administration initiated the war on drugs as a means of suppressing Black radical movements.[29] A startling revelation comes from John Ehrlichman, one of Richard Nixon's Watergate co-conspirators, who had previously served as the president's domestic affairs adviser and later faced conspiracy, perjury, and obstruction of justice convictions.[30] Referring to the war on drugs, Ehrlichman openly confessed to journalists:

> You want to know what this was really all about? . . . The Nixon campaign in 1968, and the Nixon White House after that, had two enemies: the antiwar left and black people. You understand what I'm saying? We knew we couldn't make it illegal to be either against the war or black, but by getting the public to associate the hippies with marijuana and blacks with heroin, and then criminalizing both heavily, we could disrupt those communities. We could arrest their leaders, raid their homes, break up their meetings, and vilify them night after night on the evening news. Did we know we were lying about the drugs? Of course we did.[31]

Following this strategy, in the 1980s and 1990s right-wing conservative media and politicians targeted Black and Brown women, particularly mothers, labeling them as "crackheads" and depicting them as criminals who were mentally unstable and expendable.[32] Their children were branded "superpredators," a term that found its way into the rhetoric of prominent figures, including former first lady Hillary Clinton.[33] The term *superpredators* was originally coined by John J. DiIulio Jr., a Princeton University professor of politics who declared: "Based on all that we have witnessed, researched and heard from people who are close to the action . . . here is what we believe: America is now home to thickening ranks of juvenile 'superpredators'— radically impulsive, brutally remorseless youngsters, including ever more preteenage boys, who murder, assault, rape, rob, burglarize, deal deadly drugs, join gun-toting gangs and create serious communal disorders."[34]

Later, DiIulio deeply regretted the term *superpredators*. In 1996, during a Palm Sunday prayer at his Roman Catholic church, he experienced what he described as an "epiphany," stating that he felt "a conversion of heart, a conversion of mind."[35] He realized that he needed to renounce his racially biased "superpredators" theory, acknowledging that he had been "misdirected."

"I knew that for the rest of my life I would work on prevention, on helping bring caring, responsible adults to wrap their arms around these kids," DiIulio said.[36] By this time, however, the "superpredators" theory had taken root. Based on DiIulio's racial social science, President Bill Clinton signed the consequential 1994 Violent Crime Control and Law Enforcement Act into law. This legislation resulted in the incarceration of an entire generation of Black and Brown youth.[37] This pattern of criminalization laid the foundation for mass incarceration, a phenomenon that Michelle Alexander has referred to as the "New Jim Crow" and that, as historian Elizabeth Hinton has shown, traces its origins through the "war on poverty."[38]

Through this unearthed history, a recurring pattern has come into focus. Time and again, I've witnessed the persistent portrayal of a fabricated archetype: the drug-addled, unhinged, superhuman Black person. This fictitious construct serves as a pretext to justify police violence and racist policies. Recall the 1914 *New York Times* article by Dr. Edward Huntington Williams advocating for a heavily armed police force—needed, he argued, because ordinary firearms were insufficient to subdue "negro cocaine fiends." This article laid the foundation for the narrative that Black individuals are inherently dangerous with drug use. Charles Wetli, in turn, perpetuated this damaging stereotype, citing Dr. Williams's notion of the "negro cocaine fiend" as evidence that Black people possessed a genetic defect that led to irrational behavior and sudden death when encountering law enforcement.

Indeed, these stereotypes continue to resurface with deadly consequences. During the trial of Jason Van Dyke, the officer who fatally shot Chicago teenager Laquan McDonald, the defense attorney, Dan Herbert, described McDonald as "some kid whacked out on PCP, acting really bizarrely."[39] Herbert then implied that McDonald's death was legitimate because he was a young Black menace. Contrasting McDonald with the quintessential image of White boyhood innocence, Herbert stated, "If this was a kid in a Boy Scout uniform just walking down the street with a knife and Jason Van Dyke shot him, yeah, it probably wouldn't be justified."

* * *

I spoke confidentially with a medical professional who worked at the hospital where Elijah McClain was treated before he was taken off life support. I will refer to them as "Jessie." Jessie told me that the hospital issued a "Do Not Resuscitate" (DNR) order within hours after McClain was brought to the hospital, before even speaking to his family. It was later changed to a "Full Code" order, which means doctors and nurses should do whatever they can to fully resuscitate McClain. These orders are crucial so that the patient's health-care team knows how to proceed. The initial DNR order alarmed the hospital professional I spoke with because medical doctors normally make such orders only after discussing treatment options with families. After too many attempts at resuscitation, DNR orders, which are considered a last resort, may be necessary since it is difficult for the body to sustain repeated resuscitation attempts.

Jessie was upset that early on there was a DNR order stating, "Given that he was young and healthy and that his family was not there, the standard practice would be to keep resuscitating or stabilizing him until his family could be consulted." In the end, however, the doctors managed to stabilize McClain's body until his family was notified. Unfortunately, he was pronounced dead because of brain damage.

Making the situation even more heartbreaking, when Sheneen McClain, Elijah's mother, finally arrived at the hospital, the staff treated her with suspicion and hostility. There were hospital staff who interacted with her as though she were a criminal, portraying her as a drug addict or absentee mother. Jessie described Sheneen McClain as a "polarizing figure" among the hospital workers, with some nurses and doctors understanding her heartbreak while others treated her with disdain and even anger. Many hospital workers expressed frustration at Sheneen McClain's search for answers. They seemed to take her pain personally, portraying her as disruptive, unreasonable, and unhinged.

Adding to the emotional weight of the incident, Sheneen McClain had to deal with medical practitioners who communicated directly with law enforcement while providing care for her son. The police had informed Elijah's nurses and doctors that they needed to be notified of any changes to his health, claiming that they were concerned his death would cause a "riot." Although Elijah McClain was not charged with any crime, two to three police officers stayed by his side, twenty-four hours a day, during his time spent in the hospital in a coma.

"They even accompanied him to get a scan to evaluate him for brain death," Jessie related to me, frustrated with how this violation of medical procedures accommodated law enforcement at the expense of the McClain family. "It was very confusing."

To justify their presence at the hospital, the police intimated that McClain was likely a dangerous criminal. He could revive at any time, police asserted, and put nurses and other hospital staff at risk. So convinced that McClain was a violent offender, police expressed frustration to hospital staff that they were unsuccessful in locating a match after they ran McClain's tattoo through their crime database. Law enforcement agencies and prisons photograph tattoos on arrested and incarcerated individuals. Placed in nationwide databases, these images aid law enforcement in investigations. Tattoo recognition also allows authorities to connect suspects to a longer criminal history.

In McClain's case, police told hospital staff that the lack of a database match for his tattoo must have been due to a blurry image. The truth, however, was that McClain's tattoo was not in crime databases because he had never been arrested or charged with any crime. The tattoo in question was not a gang symbol, as police had imagined. McClain's tattoo conjured another group of people—those who play string instruments in a band or orchestra. A treble clef is a curly stylized *G*, a musical symbol positioned at the front of the horizontal lines in sheet music to indicate the high-pitched sounds of instruments such as flutes or violins. McClain was a dedicated violinist. In addition to the treble clef symbol, he had tattoos of musical notes along with an exuberant declaration, "Music is life." On his lunch break from his part-time job at Petco, McClain would play the violin for stray animals at a shelter.[40] Similar to the mistaken tattoo analysis of deceased Afro-Cuban Marielitos in the 1980s, Elijah McClain's tattoos were weaponized against him.

Sheneen McClain was justifiably outraged that the police remained at her son's bedside day and night while he was in the hospital. She confronted hospital staff who were working with the police, and she harbored suspicions that the medical personnel had ulterior motives. Sheneen expressed concerns that doctors were pressuring her to harvest her son's organs. Because the police never informed the hospital that no charges had been filed against Elijah McClain, the officers' presence remained in place. Engaged in a struggle with the hospital for respect and denied access to her son during his care, the grieving family reached its breaking point. After only a few short days, his body was removed from life support and his organs were donated.

"It was heartbreaking!" Jessie told me. "The family had to leave the bedside, but the police remained for another twenty-four hours before his organs were procured. And when he was taken off life support, the police were still there. Who's the threat now? Who are you protecting?"

Many of the hospital staff who took care of Elijah McClain were trauma-tized by this case. "For months I stopped sleeping, I could not eat, I developed migraines," Jessie confided. Jessie felt complicit with the hospital and the police. "He was such a sweet kid. But even if he wasn't, is death what he deserved?"

Jessie and other hospital staff felt compelled to make a change in hospital policies and practices. A few have taken up diversity, equity, and inclusion (DEI) work to transform practices between law enforcement and medical professionals.

"There are so many things about this case," Jessie told me. "I saw the video of him at the convenience store where he went to buy some iced tea, and I just wept. He was so polite and cordial to those around him and bowing to the cashier. It was so tragic how everything was, and how the mom was treated by us—in our hospital. These are my people; these are my friends and col-leagues." Then Jessie's attention turned to Elijah McClain's mom. "She was grieving. She was a mother who just lost her son."

* * *

Sheneen McClain was treated like a drugged-out criminal while her son Eli-jah was treated like a "superpredator." From the police to the hospital, they never had a fair shot. Sheneen's ordeal and Elijah's tragic death are intercon-nected elements of a broader phenomenon: White supremacy.

It was in a fitful dream that I realized this whole racist system was an excited delirium—not a syndrome, but a White fantasy of racial and sexual criminality. I awoke and understood that this delirium is connected to the original European fantasy that African people were savage. The very concept of "delirium" is based on rendering African peoples as living a flawed reality or "fetish."[41] Sigmund Freud, another medical practitioner who became an "expert" and founder of his medical practice of psychoanalysis, drew on rac-ist European colonial stereotypes of African religions in his theories of what constituted "normal" and "healthy" behavior for White people.[42] In Freud's views, which reflected the beliefs of the time, Europeans were considered the epitome of civilization, a perception that was believed to explain their global dominance.[43] The idea of mental illness, dementia, delirium, mania, hysteria, and other so-called sicknesses of the mind all begin with the pathologizing of African religions.

Black Caribbean political philosopher and psychiatrist Frantz Fanon dis-cusses this experience as being *Blackened*. The process of Blackening refers to how colonialism and slavery produced a split racial fantasy wherein the

European "settler paints the native as a sort of quintessence of evil" to make the settler himself the epitome of civilization.[44] Fanon called this racial fantasy a "Manichean delirium," and he saw the entire colonial world as enveloped in this racial fabrication.

Fanon described his own initial experience of being objectified as Black, depicted as "savage" when he saw himself through the eyes of White people, and it physically destabilized him. He felt a sense of vertigo, then nausea, and finally tears involuntarily sprang from his eyes. Fanon stated, "On that day, completely dislocated, unable to be abroad with the other, the white man, who unmercifully imprisoned me, I took myself far off from my own presence, far indeed, and made myself an object."[45]

* * *

In September 2020, the City Council of Aurora, Colorado, paused the use of ketamine by emergency responders until an investigation into Elijah McClain's death could be completed.[46] Things might have been different for McClain had police in Colorado been aware of a 2018 report by an independent group in Minneapolis, the Office of Police Conduct Review, which raised concerns about police requests that paramedics inappropriately administer sedatives to people deemed uncooperative.[47] However, police disregarded these recommendations. During a training on how to handle cases thought to be excited delirium syndrome, the Minneapolis Police Department appears to have instructed officers to ignore the report.[48]

The report documented similar incidents of inappropriate collusion between police and medical personnel as seen in the Elijah McClain case. It detailed, for example, how officers inappropriately ask paramedics to administer ketamine and even go so far as to restrain people while they are forcefully injected.[49] In one incident, police restrained a jaywalker for using profanity against an officer, then proceeded to punch the individual in the face while they were strapped to a gurney. Despite the jaywalker's objections, paramedics continued to administer ketamine. The report noted that an officer at the scene had referred to ketamine as "the good stuff."[50] In another case, a man was sedated with ketamine and became catatonic, and an officer referred to the man as having "just hit the K-hole."[51]

It was George Floyd's death that led to the reexamination of Elijah McClain's death. Consequently, in 2021, the American Medical Association (AMA) took a stance against the use of ketamine in treating excited delirium syndrome. The AMA completely rejected the notion that excited delirium syndrome is a disease, stating that the association's new policy "opposes 'excited delirium' as a medical diagnosis and warns against the use of certain pharmacological interventions solely for a law enforcement purpose without a legitimate medical reason."[52] In addition, the AMA stated that "the term 'excited delirium'" had been used to justify "excessive police force" against Black men, and that the association opposes "pharmacological interventions such as ketamine."[53]

It was Elijah McClain who helped me see the true nature of my scholarly intervention. In my conceptualization of the term, *excited delirium* is not merely a fabricated genetic syndrome in which sweaty Black people with bulging eyes up and die spontaneously around police, as Charles Wetli had claimed. Excited delirium is the White racial fantasy of Black and Brown predatory violence that is sanitized through racial science. Through a complex network of law enforcement practitioners, so-called experts, and medical personnel, this moral panic is medicalized—which is to say, it is institutionalized through the racial laboratory. Structural racism produces an excitement and delirium that obscures this dynamic. What I have come to understand through the process of writing this book, in other words, is that excited delirium is the White gaze of the racial laboratory itself.

Sunday, April 10, 2022
Emerald Hills, California

It is my twenty-second anniversary united with the orisha Aganyu. I was think-ing about my family's journey and how far we've come.

On February 2, 1980, the year of the Mariel boatlift, my father became a priest of Ochún. I was his first and only child alive at the time, and the divination por-tion of Piri's ceremony (itá) addressed my spiritual health and well-being. The oracle divined that my life was to be guided principally by the orisha Aganyu, the volcano, giant, ferryman, who is also the spark of life. From that point, I was considered presa, *or "in debt" to the orisha. In la Regla de Ocha, being in spiri-tual debt is also called* Iroso, *which refers to the* oddu *(moral sign) by the same name and means that the person is expected to give back to others. You must help heal generational trauma. Touching both pointer fingers to the two sides of the face just under the eye socket, the diviner pulls the skin downward, telling you, "Open your eyes." The sign warns, "Look around you and beware." There are great mysteries in the depths of the sea.*

In 1994, Piri took his young children from San Francisco to Matanzas, Cuba, where he met Alfredo Calvo "Oba Tola" (ibaé), who gave Piri the honor of be-coming the owner of sacred batá *drums (añá). Piri had been drumming most of his life, and this was a heavy responsibility. Swapping children, Padrino Alfredo initiated me in 2000, and two years later, Piri became the* padrino *to Alfredo's* twin sons, Cosme and Damian. Over his forty-plus years in Ocha, my father has officiated and crowned hundreds of people's priesthoods in the United States and Cuba.

I can feel my godparents' spirits with me here. Padrino Alfredo, and his daughter, my madrina (godmother), Juana Regla Calvo "Oba Bi" (ibae), urge me on with little signs. I remember sitting in Padrino Alfredo's house in Matanzas, Cuba. He rocked in his chair with a cigar and a cold beer as he told us stories. Madrina Juana Regla would be busy preparing the room for the ceremony.

Today, while setting up my altar (trono) as my godmother had taught me, Javi, a Latiné transman and iyawo (new priest) initiated to Changó, returned from the grocery store with an exclamation. "I don't know why, but I had to buy this! Do you know what it means?" Javi asked me.

As soon as I saw the camouflaged, foam-padded neoprene beer sleeve designed to insulate beverages, I smiled. There was no way for Javi, who had never met my godfather, to know that Padrino Alfredo would never be without his beer sleeve. To keep the heat from ruining his drink, Padrino Alfredo would carefully wrap the sleeve around his Cuban-brand beer. It was rare to see him without a sleeve-wrapped bottle in his left hand and a cigar in his right.

Padrino's spirit reminded me to not forget his needs, today, on our anniversary. Placing the sleeve-clad Heineken on the altar in response to his request brought me so much joy.

As our traditions understand them, the spirits are already engaged and challenging us, even if we do not acknowledge their observations. My father describes how spiritual observations emit their own energetic waves—they transform that which they discern. Physicists describe this phenomenon as "the observer effect": anything we focus our attention on, whether an animal or an atom, is fundamentally changed through the act of observation. The observer effect is one of the puzzles of the natural sciences. It is seen as a pesky issue in ensuring verifiable calculations because, even at the macroscopic level, ignoring "the observer effects can cause errors in experiments."[1] The same can be said for ethnographic observations. We fundamentally transform that which we observe.

Conjured

I EAGERLY WAITED on the front steps of CASBS. The Center allows Fellows to invite guests to dine amid the natural beauty of the grounds. With her striking cobalt-blue and dark-red African-style head wrap, Professor Amara Smith smiled as she walked toward me. A scattering of freckles accentuated the deep taupe of her high cheekbones, which framed her penetrating gaze. I had invited Professor Smith to join me for lunch in mid-spring of 2022 to think through excited delirium with someone I trusted, someone who was both a scholar and practitioner.

I have known "Iya Amara" since I was a child in the San Francisco Bay Area orisha community. She is a celebrated dancer, scholar, and Black queer artist from Oakland. As we embraced, I admired her unabashed African-inspired dress. With full set of *elekes* (sacred beaded necklaces) on display to the world, she does not hide the fact that she is an orisha practitioner. Iya Amara has been initiated for more than thirty years to the orisha Yemaya, the owner of the ocean, mother of the world. Yemaya is also the womb and spinal cord in the human body. The orishas connect human bodies to elements of nature; they balance our divine connections with the world.

As we chatted in the lunch line waiting to get our food, Iya Amara stood out like a bright star against the striped collared shirts, preppy blouses, and beige slacks of the mostly White Fellows. I noticed a few stares. I have become accustomed to academics remarking on my own tempered "ethnic" dress. I bring in aspects of my culture through color, toeing the line of business casual but never fully committed to the more radical style of my youth—a toned-down version of myself, most certainly. Still, my own presence always seems to engender commentary in academia: "Wow! You like color!" or "You always have so many *unique* hairstyles!" But Iya Amara in our lunch line is an unapologetic breath of Africana power. As we sit at the outdoor table, the sun warming us, I ask her, "Can I record our discussion?"

"Of course," she agrees warmly.

In addition to teaching at Stanford, Iya Amara founded a group of other Black queer diasporic women in the East Bay who together reclaim the streets through dance and performance rituals. Uniting through shared notions of oppression, Afro-Latiné and other Black and Latiné peoples have historically come together in healing networks, rituals of solidarity such as Iya Amara's group, House/Full of Black Women. These types of communities have historically organized themselves in transformative collectivities, where Black Latiné consciousness has flourished.[1] African diasporic networks have called themselves *antillanos* to locate their experience within a shared Caribbean archipelago, or they have signaled Black unity across the Americas through use of terms such as *afro-descendientes* (afro-descendants), *afro–latino americano*, *Negro* (Black), and *mulato* (mixed), among many other terms.[2] These racial formations are circuits of Blackness and Latinidad that defy nation-states and have produced their own religious inspirations.[3]

"Through being colonized in a patriarchal belief system," Iya Amara told me, "we have been disempowered to, you know, in a way, forget that we are the embodiment of the answer, and the greatest mystery, and the biggest question in our own bodies." Iya Amara's critique resonates with other queer people of color and feminists who guide communities to activate Indigenous and African teachings to navigate today's challenges, allowing for healing despite the enduring legacies of colonialism and slavery.[4]

Iya Amara offers a decolonial approach cultivated among other Indigenous, Black, Chicanx, and Latiné feminists, such as Gloria Anzaldúa, Cherríe Moraga, Audre Lorde, Octavia Butler, and many others. In this sense, the work of House/Full of Black Women echoes the scholarship of Black Caribbean feminist scholar M. Jacqui Alexander, who suggests that we acknowledge our sacred connections to one another as humans, particularly as cis and trans women of color who are actively challenging colonial oppressions.[5] Speaking to Afro-Latiné crossings, Alexander describes grieving with and being in ceremony with Chicanx women, sisters in solidarity.[6] Similarly, Chicanx feminist Gloria Anzaldúa writes about such spiritual activism as "a weapon in the fight against colonization," where her scholarship and poetry offer a remedy to "cure the stunted spiritual condition of internalized" oppression.[7]

Iya Amara's group of Black diasporic women had inadvertently created a spiritual space when they came together in 2015—in the wake of the killing of Michael Brown and the subsequent uprising in Ferguson, Missouri—that led to the Movement for Black Lives. Iya Amara's group commenced as a space for Black women to grieve together in the Bay Area. On their initial Sunday gathering, they named their meeting "Grievances and Greens." Iya Amara had released an open announcement through social media. Black women from all over Oakland and the East Bay attended. Iya Amara and the other organizers were uncertain what was to come. "We just desperately needed a space to vent and be together," she told me.

"As a spiritualist I should have known," Iya Amara reflected. The moment the Black women crossed the threshold into the home, they began experiencing possession by different spirits. Iya Amara immediately sensed that these spirits were in need of healing. As she recounted the experience, she put her hands to her neck and mimicked a choking gesture, simulating coughing and retching sounds, to illustrate that the women seemed to be struggling to breathe. It became evident that the spirits taking possession of the women were unable to find peace. Iya Amara quickly discerned that the tormented spirits were of Black people who had been lynched, manifesting themselves within the attendees at the "Grievance and Greens" event.

Iya Amara sensed that these spirits were likely the ancestors of the Black women being stirred and activated through this healing space that she had initiated. Without anticipating this response, both she and another organizer, Iya Tobe, sprang into action. This was not a Regla de Ocha religious function, yet their experience as Lukumi priests allowed them to respond effectively. They began aiding both the women and the awakened spirits. Using ground eggshell chalk (*efun*), holy water, and perfume, they were able to coach the women back to their normal state.

Iya Amara came to the realization that all her gatherings held a spiritual dimension. From that moment, she understood, in fact, that all her endeavors were deeply spiritual. Consequently, she began enlisting trained priests to assist at her artistic events. As a priest herself, she understood that her position entailed not only "calling the spirits" but also tending to the well-being of the community of Black women, both living and deceased. Recognizing the need to offer appropriate care, Iya Amara embarked on the journey to heal the traumatized spirits that had been deeply affected by the long histories of violence.

* * *

"Black women are more likely to be sexually assaulted by the police than we are to be killed by them," declares Alicia Garza, one of the Black queer women who cofounded the Black Lives Matter organization. "Yet police kill us too: Natasha McKenna and Sandra Bland were killed while in police custody, and questions still remain after their deaths."[8] Although Black women are killed by law enforcement at lower rates than Black men, this fact does not diminish the precariousness of Black women's circumstances. In the case of Natasha McKenna, the routine invocation of "excited delirium" as a "syndrome" devised by agents of the state such as medical examiners, paramedics, and police drew on racial- and gender-based reasoning in their assessment of her as physically stronger than an average White woman. As a result, the police deemed it necessary to use more force to subdue her.

In light of their vulnerable positions, it is crucial to recognize that the precarity of Black women's lives makes them particularly susceptible to racial, gendered, and sexual violence. For instance, Daniel Holtzclaw, a police officer in Tulsa, Oklahoma, sexually assaulted thirteen Black women while on duty. Like Charles Henry Williams, Holtzclaw claimed that he targeted Black women because of their "lower social status," which meant that no one would believe their stories.[9]

"It is hardly even newsworthy when Black women, including Black trans women, are killed or violated by law enforcement," Keeanga-Yamahtta Taylor asserts, "because they are generally seen as less feminine or vulnerable."[10] Because of the perception of Black women's lives as having less value compared to White women, they face a higher likelihood of experiencing brutality and violent deaths.[11]

Even as my research delved into the influence of how the Black predator stereotype has historically been deployed against Black men, I have been continuously reminded that the aggression against Black women is strikingly less visible. This concealment, due to the intersections of race and gender, makes it difficult to discern the profound pain of Black women. It is sometimes only in the examination of traumas in other realms, such as the women attendees of the "Grievance and Greens" event, where one can fathom the deep roots of this violence. It is therefore essential to examine the nuances within data to truly unearth the branches of this horrible historical tree, made up of racial- and gender-motivated pain and torture.[12]

Attorney-activist Andrea Ritchie highlights the unique police brutality in which law enforcement officers target Black pregnant women, detailing a number of cruel cases of police deploying Tasers on them, claiming they could not tell the women were expecting.[13] At eight months pregnant in June 2012, Tiffany Rent, a Black woman from Chicago, was dragged from her vehicle, forced to the ground, tased, and handcuffed while her two young children watched in horror.[14] She gave birth shortly after the incident and received a settlement from the city.

It has been documented that, as opposed to White women, Black women are frequently tased, multiple times, as part of their arrests. According to the Invisible No More Database, in 2007 thirty-five-year-old Milisha Thompson in Oklahoma City died after being tased twice by police.[15] "The death was ruled accidental, and the electrical stun gun was not listed as contributing to the death."[16] Although Thompson was restrained on the ground with handcuffs when she was tased, her death was attributed to excited delirium syndrome.[17]

The occlusion around violence against Black women often makes it difficult to obtain basic information about what occurs to them when they are killed in police custody. Alicia Garza refers to the infamous case of Sandra Bland. Police ruled Bland's death in police custody on July 13, 2015, a suicide. A civil rights activist from Chicago, Sandra Bland was found hanged in her jail cell. After being pulled over for a minor traffic violation, the arresting officer, Brian Encinia, perceived Bland to be disrespectful because she questioned why she had been pulled over.[18] Bland was in Texas for a job interview.

The partly released footage of Bland's arrest appeared to be edited, and it caught Officer Encinia threatening to tase Bland. "I will light you up," he tells her because she refuses his commands to put out her cigarette and leave her car.[19] Three days later, police found Bland hanging in her cell from a plastic garbage can liner. There is no footage from inside her cell, and her feet were still touching the ground.[20] Her friends and family say that she displayed no signs of contemplating suicide prior to this event. In fact, she had recently received news that she had been offered the job she interviewed for.

Sandra Bland's death sparked public outcry. Across social media, hashtags #WhatHappenedToSandraBland and #SandySpeaks questioned the official police story of her death by suicide. As a result of this online activism, a more extensive recognition of the bias against Black women emerged, giving rise to the #SayHerName campaign.[21] This social media movement facilitated an intersectional coalition, affirming people's commitment to pursuing justice for Black women. It emphasized the importance of prioritizing both antisexist and antiracist efforts to shed light on how societal issues like police violence and the school-to-prison pipeline affect more than just heterosexual cisgender Black men.[22] The #SayHerName social justice movement has helped shift the precarity of Black women's lives and engender public attention.[23]

However, the fight to protect Black women from police violence continues. The same month that police found Bland's body, there were five other cases of Black women dying in police custody, including eighteen-year-old Kindra Chapman, who was also found hanging in her cell. In many cases where Black women die in police custody, "the cause of death varies—apparent suicide, lack of access to necessary medical attention, violence at the hands of police officers—but ultimately, no matter the circumstances, these women's deaths are also a product of the policing practices that landed them in police custody in the first place: racial profiling, policing of poverty, and police responses to mental illness and domestic violence that frame Black women as deserving of punishment rather than protection, of neglect rather than nurturing."[24] In the case of twenty-three-year-old Korryn Gaines, total disregard for her and her child's life was displayed when police fatally shot her as she held her five-year-old son in her arms on April 1, 2016, near Baltimore, Maryland.[25] Miraculously, her son survived the shooting.

Of the fifty cases of Black women killed by police since 2015, not one officer has been convicted of an offense.[26] Kimberlé Crenshaw and colleagues released the report *Say Her Name: Resisting Police Brutality against Black Women* through the African American Policy Forum and the Center for Intersectionality and Social Policy Studies. This report argues that "the failure to highlight and demand accountability for the countless Black women killed by police over the past two decades . . . leaves Black women unnamed and thus underprotected in the face of their continued vulnerability to racialized police violence."[27] The report confirms that this erasure is not just about missing facts. Rather, the framing narratives of police profiling and lethal force used on Black people need to be accounted for by race, gender, class, and sexuality.

Black feminist cultural critic and Rutgers professor Brittany Cooper discusses this precarity in an important *Salon* article, in which she states that she "could have been Sandra Bland." She recalls that she has given "attitude" to police by asking questions about their unfair harassment on at least three occasions. Cooper had also told police she disagreed with their treatment of her. She notes how asking questions of police while being a Black woman in America can be deadly:

> I have had the police threaten to billyclub me, write unfair tickets, and otherwise make public spaces less safe, rather than more safe, for me to inhabit, all out of a clear lust for power. On the wrong day, I could have been Sandra Bland. And if a police officer pulled me over for a bullshit-ass reason, I absolutely would have given him the business on the side of the highway. By this, I don't mean I would have made threats. I mean I would have asked questions.[28]

Seen as threats or as suspects, Black women are easily discarded. This was apparent with the treatment of Elijah McClain's mother, Sheneen, who as a Black mother was not allowed to grieve the loss of her son. As a result of the historical dehumanization of Black women, their deaths continue to go unnoticed. As Black anthropologist Dána-Ain Davis shows, Black women are constantly at risk, perceived as menacing, and their behaviors never cease to be inspected.[29]

Black trans women are especially vulnerable. In June 2020, guards placed Layleen Xtravaganza Cubilette Polanco, an Afro-Latiné trans woman, in solitary confinement after a fight at Rikers Island. Polanco could not afford her $500 bail and had let officials know that she had epilepsy. Guards mandated that Polanco spend twenty days in solitary confinement. Left for long periods without welfare checks, she died on the ninth day.[30] In footage released by Rikers, guards waited ninety minutes before calling for help.[31] No jail guards were charged with any crime in her death.

I see the history of blaming Black and Brown women as especially apparent in the racial laboratory of the social sciences. In 1965, White sociologist turned politician Daniel Patrick Moynihan wrote a presidential report, *The Negro Family: The Case for National Action*, that argued that Black women emasculated Black men and were thus the cause of so-called broken families.[32] The Moynihan report casually suggested that most crimes in the 1960s were committed by Black American and Puerto Rican people, and that female-headed single-parent households were implicated in the reproduction of poverty.[33] Moynihan saw Black and Latiné mothers as greedy, lazy, and ignorant women producing children out of wedlock, which led to a cascade of pathological effects.[34] Many Black scholars and communities condemned Moynihan's "blame the victim" approach for not taking into account structural racism and slavery.[35] Still, the deep impact of the Moynihan report lingers long after its initial publication. Before he became the first Black American president, Barack Obama famously praised the Moynihan report. First, in his bestselling book *The Audacity of Hope* (2006), he emphasized the need for Black people to take personal responsibility to overcome intergenerational poverty; and then later, as president, Obama called out what he saw as a "tangle of pathology" in the Black American community that he thought needed tending to, like gardeners prune their plants.[36]

The pruning of unruly Black and Brown women takes shape in the policies aimed at our reproduction. For instance, in 1927 the US Supreme Court authorized the sterilization of women's bodies to "reduce the number of 'feeble-minded'" people in society.[37] Nonconsenting Indigenous, Black, Mexican, Puerto Rican, and disabled White women were subsequently sterilized as a form of eugenicist population control.[38] Large clinical trials tested the first birth control pill on Puerto Rican women, and between the 1930s and the 1980s, nurses and doctors sterilized one-third of Puerto Rican women on the island.[39] My grandmother Maria Magdalena remembered that as a teenager in Puerto Rico, she hid from American nurses who came to force her and her friends into operations.[40] After Puerto Rican women delivered children, on the advice of their physicians, many would undergo tubal ligation as a form of birth control, unaware that this was permanent sterilization.[41] When my grandmother gave birth to her eldest son in Puerto Rico, she told me that without her consent, the doctors had injected her with a medication to dry up her breast milk, so they could force her to use the unpopular infant formula that was being peddled.

These histories of scientific testing, population control, police violence, and blame are etched onto Black women's bodies. I saw this most poignantly in the tragic death of Breonna Taylor, a twenty-six-year-old Black emergency room technician shot to death by police on March 13, 2020, in Louisville, Kentucky. Taylor and her boyfriend, Kenneth Walker, were asleep in bed when, based on faulty information that Taylor's ex-boyfriend lived at the residence, a group of officers barged into their apartment with a battering ram. The raid was part of an effort to clean up so-called blight in the neighborhood and utilized police violence to prepare the area for a new housing development.[42] Louisville police, which had a pattern of violating constitutional rights, fired thirty-two rounds into the dark home.[43] Six shots hit and killed Taylor. Police claimed that they were "confused by the burst of their own gunfire;" one officer stated that "he did not realize he had fired his weapon until after the fact."[44]

The police did not have an ambulance waiting for Breonna Taylor—the inclusion of an ambulance is a common procedure in these types of heavily armed drug raids. Police also wasted crucial lifesaving minutes before tending to Taylor once they realized that they had shot her. Yet the medical examiner said it did not matter that those police officers waited more than five minutes before assisting Taylor, telling reporters from the *Courier Journal*, "Ms. Taylor most likely died less than a minute after she was shot and could not have been saved."[45] Her boyfriend, Kenneth Walker, disputed the medical examiner's claim. Walker, who was with Taylor when she succumbed to death, witnessed how she "coughed and struggled to breathe for at least five minutes after she was shot."[46]

Tragedies such as Taylor's, and those of the many other women killed by police, are part of the long history of disregard for Black women's lives. From medical testing to prison experiments and sterilization campaigns, Black, Indigenous, and Latiné women have endured the consequences of structural violence, racism, and unjust blame that perpetuate our vulnerability and precariousness. Yet we persist in our struggles despite the lack of accountability and justice. As evidenced by Iya Amara's group, these women conjure healing methods and acts of love that enable survival even amid genocide.

* * *

Iya Amara's group of Black women take over the streets of Oakland, turning them into ritual spaces. Drawing on traditional *Egúngún* (the collective spirits of the dead) practices from the Yorùbá, the women enact renegade spiritual activism in city streets, parks, and neighborhoods. Iya Amara recounted how, in one of their ritual performances, the group cleansed an alley in Oakland known for sex trafficking. Among the group was a survivor, a woman who had been trafficked. The Black woman told Iya Amara how that street had been transformed for her.

Iya Amara ensures that these rituals "serve" the Black women as well as the community. "It's not about us going out and getting exhausted and not getting cleansed ourselves," she explains. To ensure that they facilitate mutual healing and cleanse the spaces involved, they incorporate their own ceremonial practice during every art project. Like the radiating forces activated by the *añá* (*batá*) drums, where the practitioners are simultaneously able to clean people, spaces, and themselves, Iya Amara's ritual processions are what she describes as "shifting vibrations."

In Afro-Latiné traditions, there is no such thing as objectivity. Instead, the spirits and orisha are understood to harness shifting power dynamics to mobilize transformation. This is what Iya Amara refers to as "shifting vibrations." We are taught that the energy of the Great Mother vulture, the spirit-bird (Èyẹ́ Ọ̀rọ̀) in orisha philosophies, harnesses alternative forms of justice.[47] The Èyẹ́ Ọ̀rọ̀ is a "force that is beyond definition."[48] She is considered the womb of the universe that channels the energy of the cosmos, and she is recognized as a protective container that shields you from danger. Orisha practices use an enclosed calabash, or clay pot, as the protective covering to channel this power, mirroring the roundness of the mother's belly and the embrace of the earth.

The *Àjé* are described in Western terms as "witches," however they conjure the feminine energy of life and death. The *Àjé* use the medicines of the living energy of plants and trees, which are themselves understood as portals of power, to make healing potions and powders.[49] They are considered warriors who, with their bird's-eye gaze (Èyẹ́ Ọ̀rọ̀) and medicinal abilities, behold and judge action in order to exact cosmic judgment.[50] They are feared as "the ones with two bodies" (*abaarà méjì*) because they grasp the destinies of humans. These "mysterious flying beings" function as an alternative formation of justice.[51]

Iya Amara tells me about how her group of diasporic women conjure these flying abilities in their cleansing rituals in the streets of Oakland, California. *Brujas* have always been seen as fearsome by patriarchal cultures precisely because of their ability to expose, she reminds me. Feminine power has the ability to soar "above the landscape of daily life, with eyes that can penetrate the darkness," uncovering secrets to reveal what is hidden.[52] The observing and enforcing energy of the sorceress-bird is thus a form of Afro-Latiné sacred justice that, unlike the "eye for an eye" logic of Christianity that renders accountability through punishment, produces energetic change through observation. These spiritual examinations are like infrared light or radio waves that allow us to pierce through dense fog or detect molecules—they are the observer effect.

Priests like Iya Amara draw on this energetic sensibility to shift the world in particular directions. Even as this force has been significantly diminished through Western positivism's hold on modern society, there are many who continue to wield this energy in order to produce alternative models of justice and accountability.

For example, two weeks after the street cleansing procession against sex trafficking, Iya Amara told me that several officers of the Oakland Police Department (OPD) were arrested for trafficking an underage girl.[53] Iya Amara is confident that the ritual cleansing helped that abuse come to light: "I won't say we take full credit for that [OPD sex scandal], but I will say that we were a part of that vibrational shift."

Sitting there with Iya Amara, thinking about the Black diasporic women who came together in ceremony and the lynched spirits who showed up at Iya Amara's "Grievance and Greens" event, asserting their presence to have a kind of contemporary reckoning, I thought of the Black women victims of Charles Wetli's racist diagnosis, and sensed that they had stirred something in me. I realized they did not want me to be sad *for them*, but instead observant *with them*. Wetli's media campaign to assassinate their spirits after they were murdered did not work. In the tradition that Iya Amara and I share—as well as in this book—they are resurrected as revolutionary spirit guides who are working to dismantle the racism that tried to cover up the crimes committed against them from the afterlife. Reinforcing the quest of this collective *egun*, Iya Amara reminded me to validate my own body's sensings.

You know what spirit feels like; you cannot allow coloniality to strangle your powers.[54]

Iya Amara urged me on: "You have an important story to tell. And you're the person they've called to tell it."

Wednesday, May 25, 2022
Antioch, California

It has been two years since George Floyd's death sparked a global public out-cry. I remember like it was yesterday. I had given birth to Langston ten days before that day, and we were in our fourth month of strict quarantine from the COVID-19 global pandemic. Those of us who had not died from coronavirus complications were sick, exhausted, depressed, hurt, lonely. When the bystander video circulated that showed Officer Chauvin kneeling on George Floyd's neck for more than nine minutes, it was just too much. The world watched Floyd take his last breaths, and protests erupted globally at the horrific public lynching. People masked up and took to the streets. There was a sense of historic reckoning. Demands for police reform, reparations, and an acknowledgment of the struc-tural injustices against Black people became part of public discourse, if only for a short time.

My eldest son Neto's father, René, who owns a printing company, Movement Ink, in Oakland, California, had printed five hundred masks that read "Stop Killing Black People" for the Movement for Black Lives (M4BL) in Washing-ton, DC. When he tried to ship the masks to protesters, they were "seized by law enforcement."[1]

Orisha priests I knew across the world started to mobilize collective rituals as part of their activism.[2] Neto, initiated to the orishas as a child, had not been looking for a new path. He was content working for the Oakland Unified School District as the Newcomer Program director for violence and gang prevention, assisting Latiné youth with job training and counseling services. But the death of George Floyd changed that. He and Naomi started making free spiritual baths (baños) for Black and Brown people who were suffering with grief from the trauma of racial violence. They posted the free baths on Instagram. Filling empty juice containers they had collected with the sacred waters, they left the baños outside the door of their rented home in East Oakland. People drove by and picked up the baths, without ever meeting.

Then they started asking Neto and Naomi for more help: "Do you give readings?"

They started doing Zoom consultations, cowry-shell divination readings for Black and Brown people for free. Finding healing through this spiritual work, a number of them asked Neto to initiate them into the religion. It was hard for him to work at the school district and help this growing group of people in need of healing. A good number of them were queer and trans youths who had no one else to turn to; that was how Neto met Jade.

"I asked Ochún if I could keep working and do Ocha [la Regla de Ocha] on the side and she said, 'No,'" Neto told me. Through divination, Ochún, the goddess of the river, wealth, love, and sweetness, had guided him to leave behind the safe salaried job working for the city and dedicate himself full time to helping people. "I'm going to start a church," he told me.

Empower

THE PANDEMIC OF POLICE KILLINGS CONTINUES. Every day, even as I write this, additional Black and Brown people are killed in police interactions. On January 3, 2023, Keenan Darnell Anderson, a Black teacher in Los Angeles, was held down by police after a traffic stop. He shouted for assistance, "They're trying to George Floyd me!" Then he was tased repeatedly and died four hours later. Police claim he died from a "medical incident."[1] Although the term *excited delirium syndrome* has been widely discredited, authorities continue to employ the same signals and coded language to medicalize police violence. Anderson was described as "agitated," "uncooperative," and "resisting officers" despite placing his hands behind his head and lying on the ground as officers applied unnecessary restraint techniques and continued to tase him.

Four days later, on January 7, 2023, after another traffic stop, twenty-nine-year-old Tyre Nichols was tased, pepper sprayed, and beaten to death by police in Memphis, Tennessee. Nichols could also be heard on video calling for his mother. In an unusually quick turnaround, just three weeks after the incident, the video footage was released, and the five officers were all indicted, facing charges of "second-degree murder, aggravated assault, two charges of aggravated kidnapping, two charges of official misconduct and one charge of official oppression."[2] The officers, who are all Black, have been described by different media as a "gang," as "human monsters," their actions "heinous."[3] There is no doubt that what they did was indeed heinous, but this moment should not be made exceptional. These cops are not simply "bad apples"—certainly not because they are Black police.[4] As this book has uncovered, this type of brutal violence and abuse of power directed at Black and Brown people is a product of the violent institution of policing, and the interconnected networks of medical and legal practices that cover up this violence. It does not matter whether officers are non-White; they are still made to embody White supremacy.[5]

The spirits of people classified as experiencing excited delirium demand we discover a means to halt these systems of violence. The teachings of Regla de Ocha show us that "the dead lead the way"; as the Lukumi saying goes, "*Iku lobi ocha*" (*El muerto para el Santo*). Our practices reveal the work of spirit observers, who offer alternative expressions of power and provide invaluable insights often overlooked by Western positivism.

These diasporic teachings are exemplified in Black sociologist W. E. B. Du Bois's concept of double consciousness. DuBois wrote about being "born with a veil," with what he described as a "gift" of "second-sight" that allowed him to better understand the inner workings of White supremacy.[6] Du Bois associated this "clairvoyance" with the unique abilities attributed to special children born with "a caul" (the gauzelike film of the amniotic membrane that sometimes covers an infant's face at birth). Such children are believed to possess psychic abilities.[7] Du Bois's systematic dedication to understanding the workings of White supremacy led him to call for a collective reimagining of society to return to the goals of an "abolition democracy" that could lead to a more just world built on antiracist ideals and radical equality.[8]

In Afro-Latiné traditions, we would attribute Du Bois's clairvoyance to his having good *muertos*, or spirit guides, who provide him with unique input to assess the racism he encountered. Through this research I have come to understand Jade Ellis's father, Jeremy Ellis, a Black cholo chased to death by police, as one of my *muertos*. Jeremy's spirit also deserves credit for taking me on this journey of discovery to uncover what excited delirium really is: it is the distorted gaze of White supremacy. Excited delirium is the stupor that prevents society from looking beyond the White perspective that unfairly associates Black and Brown people with criminality and danger. It is a deceptive fantasy that contributes to racial genocide.

Jeremy and the Black women and girls falsely labeled with excited delirium compelled me to investigate their murders and expose this phantasm. They revealed to me how my Afro-Latiné traditions' attunement to spirits provides a unique perspective to access their stories.

In acknowledging their guidance, I want to demonstrate how spirits impact our lives.[9] By revisiting the moments before George Floyd died, crucial evidence has been overlooked. George Perry Floyd Jr. died on May 25, 2020, almost two years to the day after his mother, Larcenia "Cissy" Floyd, died.[10] He worked as a security guard in a local nightclub and had recently lost his job when the club shut down because of the COVID-19 pandemic.[11] Floyd was in a slump, like many of us who lost so much during the global quarantine. Despite this, he was known for his caring, generous, and open nature. It was common for him to proclaim "I love you!" to members of his large extended family.

In the video that captured his murder, Floyd can be heard expressing his love for Cissy. This call to his deceased mother resonated widely. When former prosecutor Lola Velasquez-Aguilu was invited to take on the case against Derek Chauvin for Floyd's killing, she mentioned that she accepted the role from a mother's perspective, stating, "When George Floyd called out to his mom, he activated all moms."[12]

The interaction between Floyd and his deceased mother serves as significant evidence often disregarded in Western positivist analysis.[13] I see this exchange as providing insight into Du Bois's "second-sight."

In the bystander video, Floyd is heard calling out:

"Mama, mama, mama. All right. Oh my God! I can't breathe! I can't breathe! I can't breathe, man. Mama, I love you."

"Mama, I can't do nothing."

In Western cultures, stories about end-of-life experiences acknowledge the idea that deceased loved one's welcome kin as they transition to the afterlife. By understanding how the departed engage the living, we can discern that Cissy's spirit was by her son's side, which is evident in the video as Floyd speaks to her, asking for her assistance. "Mama," he calls to her, "I love you. I can't breathe."

These words echo Eric Garner's last words, "I can't breathe." It is undeniable that the violence against Black people is endemic in American policing, as evidenced by the number of restraint asphyxiation deaths among Black and Brown people across the country. Garner, who was wrestled to the ground in 2014 for selling "loosies," or individual cigarettes, uttered the immortal phrase, now a rallying cry that reveals the "suffocating nature of racism."[14] Across the world, protesters stage die-ins to acknowledge this call for help.[15] Why is the right to breathe so contentious for Black people?[16]

The intake of air should not be an ethical plea to exist. In Afro-Latiné traditions, Oya, the mistress of the winds and owner of the cemetery, embodies all aspects of the living and dying breath. As the protector of spirits, she is also the lungs in our body and the air we inhale. A tireless warrior, Oya was enslaved by her trusted friends and lovers. She was held captive by her husband, Ogun, the ironsmith, who uses the bellows to harness her raw power to forge weapons. And yet, Oya, the tempest—who also represents hurricanes, lightning, and storms—can never be contained for long.[17] You see her vengeance screeching through the sky in a passionate strike, or you hear her calmly whistling through the leaves.

Breath in Afro-Latiné practices is a point of connection between our bodies and the worlds we inhabit; breath has the power to shift space. This thinking is in line with quantum physicists who acknowledge that space, time, and materiality are entanglements that involve layers of seen and unseen forces, such as air, waves, vibrations, and consciousness, that act in relation to each other.[18] Cissy's spirit is entangled with George Floyd's. When George cried out for her, she responded. As an unbound agent, Cissy created a vibrational shift, insisting that others pay attention. She forced bystanders to stop, take notice, film. Activated by her vibrations, our traditions would allow for Cissy to have influenced those bystanders to make noise, become agitated, yell at the police, fight back, stay as witnesses, and testify at trial.

The great flying mothers of Africana traditions teach us how to hold people accountable. They provide what anthropologist Christen Smith calls "radical Black mothering," wherein the act of Black mothering is itself a revolutionary formation in the face of anti-Black state violence.[19] By invoking the spiritual mothers of my religious tradition, I mean to suggest that Black mothering is not limited to just biological mothers, as Black feminist Patricia Hill Collins explains; rather, Black mothering is about care, reciprocity, humanity, and justice.[20]

Certainly, Black mothers bear a special burden.[21] They are often held responsible for a wide range of social issues, labeled as "vectors of disease," and unfairly depicted as "monstrous," disobedient, and criminal.[22] This bias also extends to how Black children are perceived as equally unruly, as seen in the "culture of poverty" argument.[23] Black mothers, consistently portrayed as antagonistic figures, are often refused any association with maternal purity. As a result, Black maternal grief is often regarded as unworthy of American remorse, and if it is allowed it must be perceived as nonthreatening.[24] When their children are killed by police, Black mothers are expected to be stoic, unflappable, and incapable of displaying human emotions such as anger, sadness, or grief.[25]

Recall the open hostility with which Sheneen McClain was met when she grieved her son, Elijah, and demanded he receive proper care. As shown by the Mothers of the Movement collective—a group of women whose children have been killed at the hands of police—these Black mothers did not choose to become national icons or activists.[26] Sybrina Fulton, the mother of seventeen-year-old Trayvon Martin, for example, addresses how, even ten years later, the pain of losing her son has not subsided and never will: "My chest still hurts," she says. "I still have a hole in my heart."[27]

Afro-Latiné traditions would place Cissy Floyd as a spirit member activist with the Mothers of the Movement; she is a Black mother who, in the afterlife, ensured that her son's death would not be rendered invisible. Like Mamie Till-Mobley, who in 1955 exposed the violence against her son Emmett Till for the world to see the reality of lynching, I credit Cissy Floyd's spirit with ripping open the workings of excited delirium.

* * *

Excited delirium might have erased the death of George Perry Floyd had it not been for the bystander video posted to Facebook. At first, the police tried to get the public to ignore Floyd's death.[28] Excited delirium syndrome was used by Derek Chauvin's defense to argue that Floyd might have killed himself.[29] At one point during the trial, Eric Nelson, the defense attorney, homed in on the video, cruelly describing what he called the "finger and knuckle testimony" and "toe lifting testimony."[30] Showing close-up slides of Floyd pushing his finger against the asphalt to try to lift his shoulder, the expert witness for Chauvin argued that his toe and finger pointed to his ability to breathe. Chauvin's knee in Floyd's neck could not possibly be the cause of death, his defense attorney claimed; look at Floyd's toe lifting. But the ruse did not work this time.

On April 20, 2021, Chauvin was convicted on all counts of murdering Floyd; he was later sentenced to twenty-two years in prison.[31]

After the death of George Floyd, millions of people across the world took to the streets in protest. In the United States alone, an estimated twenty-six million people participated in protests.[32] From New York to Chicago, North Carolina to San Francisco, and across the world in Hong Kong, Australia, the UK, and Germany, chants erupted of "Black Lives Matter!" "Let Us Breathe!" and "Abolish the Police!"

A collective reimagining of the world without the police became seen as a realistic possibility. Calls to defund police and abolish the police led to several cities taking such action. In 2021, major US cities across the country reduced their policing budgets and began to reinvest those resources in their communities.[33] San Francisco, New York, Los Angeles, Austin, Philadelphia, Baltimore, Seattle, Milwaukee, Chicago, and Minneapolis pledged to divest funds from policing and place them instead toward health programs, workforce training, and social services. Moving away from a crime approach toward a health-care approach, Austin, Texas, redirected money to homeless people and substance abuse programs, and provided access to food, housing, and health care. Austin City Council member Gregorio Casar said, "We are showing the country how reinvestments from the police budget can actually make many people's lives so much better and safer."[34] Local governments in the United States spend $100 billion annually on law enforcement; simply by removing the police from schools, some cities across the country saved a collective $840 million.[35]

Abolition has a long history that begins with the movement that ended chattel slavery and extends to the more recent demands to end sex trafficking, prisons, police, the military, and Immigration and Customs Enforcement (ICE). In the United States, the movement for the abolition of chattel slavery, led by people such as Harriet Tubman, William Lloyd Garrison, John Brown, and Frederick Douglass, understood that the institution of slavery defined democracy globally.[36] Du Bois took this up when he argued that legal reform itself was not enough, because the oppressive conditions of slavery were not undone with its legal elimination.[37] The prison abolition movement, developed most famously in the work of Angela Davis, drew upon Du Bois's strategy, arguing for a notion of abolition that is not "a negative process of tearing down," but instead a shared "re-imagining [of] institutions, ideas, and strategies" that create new institutions.[38]

Scholars followed activists to call for abolitionist approaches.[39] Medical doctors and health-care workers have taken up this question by advocating for an "abolition medicine," in which medical professionals understand the "structural factors that produce racial health disparities, while actively recruiting, retaining, and supporting Black and other minoritised faculty, staff, and students."[40] These health-care workers are joining the national call for "police abolition and using their social power" to build capacity for mental-health-care programs, "youth development, education, and employment, as well as harm reduction efforts around drug use, housing insecurity, and incarceration."[41]

The abolitionist medicine movement intervened most poignantly in dispelling the myth of excited delirium syndrome, which has for too long reinforced scientifically inaccurate notions of biological race, and in countering treatment guidelines on the injection of ketamine that reentrenched racial health disparities. This work must continue. The deaths of Keenan Anderson and Drew Washington show how police are continuing to kill people and medicalize away their deaths.

Nevertheless, Floyd's death created an opening that cannot be ignored. Until 2020, mainstream reform movements viewed the police as a necessary institution that seemed insurmountable. A world without law enforcement was once deemed unimaginable to many Americans, as police are traditionally viewed as the guardians of "civilized" society.[42] This perspective is rooted in settler colonialism; the White male police officer is envisioned as safeguarding White humanity from Indigenous and Black "savage beasts."[43] Indeed, this mindset is an excited delirium.

An example of this mentality can be seen in the "Thin Blue Line" argument that arose in reaction to the Movement for Black Lives. This police slogan is symbolized by a black-and-white American flag with a blue line across it. The world, in this mentality, is mythological, full of warfare and predatory Black people.[44] It is the belief in the myth that the police are essential to secure all that is said to be core to "'human' existence: liberty, security, property, sociality, accumulation, law, civility, and even happiness."[45] Yet property, accumulation, security, and law do not constitute "the core" of human existence. Neither do they guarantee liberty, sociality, civility, or happiness. Such unbalanced views of humanity keep us enslaved to excited delirium, the delusion of White fear.

As a result of my research, I now see how law enforcement abuse is perpetrated, how a cover-up system was fabricated to protect those who abuse us, and how this system is vast and irredeemable. Increasingly, there is a recognition that policing is rooted in violence, and reform agendas only further this violence.[46] There can be no real transformation without true acknowledgment of this history. Ruth Wilson Gilmore argues that people hoping for change should aim for a "radical abolition" that utilizes our energies and resources to work toward "the goal of freedom."[47] We must "get out of the trap of reformist reform," Gilmore teaches. If reform within a history of slavery and violence "is the pattern for change, it can only result in a 'changing same.'"[48] We cannot stand for a changing same.

The plantation is not behind us, it lingers and persists.[49] Approaches to abolition, Joy James advises, should not serve merely as intellectual pursuits.[50] She cautions that most academic approaches to abolition desire only to study oppression, refusing to imagine a process that dismantles predatory structures. This type of academic abolition, she argues, is not interested in offering pathways to change. Nor will it support those "who take the risk to try and draw up a blueprint" for radical transformation.[51] The aim, James asserts, must be in creating avenues for change.[52]

Abolition in this context serves as a foundational step, a beginning point in a radical democracy, from which to construct lasting alternatives to punitive structures like incarceration and policing. Abolitionist activist Mariame Kaba reflects on this idea when she affirms, "We have been so indoctrinated with the idea that we solve problems by policing and caging people that many cannot imagine anything other than prisons and the police as solutions to violence and harm."[53] She continues, "People like me who want to abolish prisons and police, however, have a vision of a different society, built on cooperation instead of individualism, on mutual aid instead of self-preservation. What would the country look like if it had billions of extra dollars to spend on housing, food, and education for all? This change in society wouldn't happen immediately, but the [George Floyd] protests show that many people are ready to embrace a different vision of safety and justice."

* * *

Exactly one year to the day after I first interviewed Jade Ellis, I spoke to her again. On September 17, 2022, she told me how her life has transformed since her initiation to Regla de Ocha. "Everything is different in such a beautiful way."

Jade told me she is finally able to find healing. It is something she is compelled to share with the world, just as she did when she first lost her dad and became an activist, poet, and artist. "It makes me excited that I have all these new tools to offer people, and to sew into the other different parts of my life. I know that my dad led me to Ocha and all of these new ways to exist." Now, she said, she finally feels her body.

"This is one of the first times in my life where I feel like my life is really happening and I'm present enough to be really healed. This is the first time where I don't feel like I'm in an episode of *Survivor*. My life has been constant moments of trauma and how I survive them. It has always felt like I'm drowning, and this is the first time I feel like I'm really standing up. I'm fully walking. I'm awake. And I know it's because of my ancestors and Ocha."

The members of Ile EgbadoSito aim to repair and empower their community through prayer and collective mobilizations. The *ile* is reworking capitalistic and patriarchal human relations to engage reciprocally with plants, animals, and each other to make change in the world. Through collectively purchased land, this Santeria church is providing pathways to disrupting intersecting oppressions. Meat slaughtered during religious services goes to a community pantry to target food insecurity where sacred meats are eaten and shared. In the fullest vision of the *ile's* food pantry, it will provide fresh herbs, ritually butchered meats, and collectively sourced vegetables from the garden that members cultivate and harvest together.

As they work collectively toward liberation, the focus is on cultivating healing through understanding the interconnected relationship to ancestors, each other, their many copresences, and the world. A childcare collective assists parents with young children, allowing for a feminist ethics to religious work so that cis and transgender women are able to take lead roles in ceremony. Reconceiving of how to provide members with a sustainable approach to living in one of the most expensive places in the country, the San Francisco Bay Area, there is housing assistance and communal living.

The *ile* even connects to transnational religious family members. In Matanzas, Cuba, where Padrino Alfredo's temple (*cabildo*) has struggled through both the Trump and then Biden administrations' suffocating policies directed at the communist island, Black practitioners of Santeria are dying from lack of food, water, and medical supplies. Ile EgbadoSito has organized to support this vulnerable transnational religious family, providing resources and other infrastructural support to ensure access to clean water and food for children and the elderly, as well delivering medicines, clothing, and other provisions for Cuban *santeros*.

Founded in the wake of George Floyd's death, the *ile* draws on queer of color and feminist teachings in their actualizing of Afro-Latiné religious traditions. This was how Jade was able to find her own healing. Most Santeria *iles* continue to invest in gender binaries, either excluding trans people completely or forcing them to undergo initiation in the gender they were assigned at birth. Furthermore, some practitioners uphold a deep-seated anti-Blackness that allows White Latiné practitioners to withhold knowledge from Black American practitioners to maintain power and control in the religion. Ile EgbadoSito challenges these types of exclusionary practices and racist gatekeeping. Drawing on the vibrational activism, the Santeria church supports its most precarious members—undocumented people, trans and queer people, and Black women. I offer this decolonial abolitionist collective as a radical Afro-Latiné blueprint for imagining new institutions that foster repair.

Jade had been upset with Jeremy for so long, holding him responsible for his death and, ultimately, for leaving her. The police and medical examiners had fed her a false narrative, causing her to feel judged as an extension of her father. She felt both angry and guilty. Now she has gained perspective. Most important, she has *him*. Knowing Jeremy's presence is with her has been profoundly healing.

"After he passed, that was really hard," Jade told me. "Because I thought it was something that I lost and something that I wouldn't be able to get back. And, I have that now. And it is so clear. I know how to identify him in a room now. I know he's here, and I know he's always here. And that feels really good."

Jade had not seen her grandmother Diane, Jeremy's mother, since her father's funeral when she was a child. Jeremy's spirit has brought them back together. They met when Jade unexpectedly took a job near Diane's new home, and Diane reached out to Jade. "I'm extremely aware of my father's influence in my life. My relationship to my family is so different now. I met my grandma recently and I know that's not a coincidence. I know that's him," Jade said.

Until she found Afro-Latiné teachings, Jade had been barely making it. When the police labeled Jeremy's death as caused by excited delirium, it had almost killed his spirit and hers. Jade told me that Jeremy's spirit is now empowered. Together with Jade, he has found peace; they are energetically vibrating.

"Thank you for letting me share your story," I told her.

"This whole process has been such an honor for me," Jade responded. She said that participating in this book has helped her see how Jeremy's story fits into larger hidden injustice. It helped her forgive him.

* * *

After Uncle Tobaji and Iya Wanda's *itutu* ceremony to refresh Mario Woods's spirit, a federal judge narrowly allowed a civil rights lawsuit on behalf of his mother, Gwendolyn Woods. The ruling found just enough evidence to show that officers acted with "reckless disregard for Woods' rights."[54] However, for Black mothers fighting for justice, like Ms. Woods, such success is bittersweet. Charges were never filed against the officers involved in Mario's shooting. And only a year after his death, San Francisco Police officers killed Luis Gongora, a Mexican immigrant, in an eerily similar way to Woods: multiple officers shot him several times because he held a knife.[55]

When Uncle Tobaji sang the death rite, *A umba wà orí*, he created a pathway for Woods's spirit to effect change. Our traditions would understand this prayer as having provided Woods's spirit with the empowerment needed for him to recognize his own spiritual presence. Such ritual incantations weave harmony and rhythm to expand his spirit's energetic force, which can be sensed by mediums through spiritual "signs" that include an uncanny sense of connection or an intuitive confirmation.

One such intuitive confirmation occurred for me at the halftime show of Super Bowl 50. On February 7, 2016, at Levi's Stadium in Santa Clara, California, the R&B singer Beyoncé performed her hit song "Formation" with her backup dancers dressed in outfits inspired by the radical Black Power movement of the 1960s. It was fitting, given the history of the San Francisco Bay Area, particularly Oakland, as the location of the formation of the Black Panther Party for Self-Defense. The Bay Area was still reeling from the death of Mario Woods, who had just passed the year before.

After Beyoncé's performance, a Black Lives Matter protester sneaked onto the field and handed the dancers a sign. When I saw the tweeted image, I had that uncanny feeling of connection that I have learned marks the presence of spiritual engagement. The photo that went viral had Beyoncé's backup dancers, still on the football field, wearing black berets, Afros, and tight black leather shorts and vests. They were holding a "Justice 4 Mario Woods" sign with their arms thrust in the air, making Black Power fists.

For me, knowing the vibrational activism of Uncle Tobaji and Iya Wanda, I could not help but see this image as confirmation of the activation of Mario Woods's spirit. I could see his copresence conspiring to publicize his death and celebrating such a significant moment. It was a further empowerment of the symbols of Black liberation that had already infiltrated the all-American Whiteness of the iconic event that is the Super Bowl. Indeed, this tweet would launch Woods's case to national attention. It also caused some trouble for Beyoncé, who faced a backlash from people upset with her radical turn. Still, I continued to read the tweeted photo as an example of vibrational activism. In 2019, the city would finally settle with Gwendolyn Woods for $400,000, the largest amount San Francisco has ever paid to a family.[56]

Deaths are vibrational in mysterious ways. After the attention brought from the killing of George Floyd and the questioning of excited delirium syndrome, there was a reexamination of the Elijah McClain case.[57] On February 22, 2021, the City Council of Aurora, Colorado, released a 157-page report of an independent investigation that the council had commissioned to investigate the officers' and paramedics' decision to inject McClain with ketamine.[58] The investigation found that the officers did not meet the constitutional requirement to stop or detain McClain.[59] It also found that the vast majority of the pain compliance techniques and restraint maneuvers McClain had endured were excessive, and that the administration of ketamine was not properly executed.[60] McClain was not resisting officers in the presence of EMS, and paramedics injected him after only one minute of observation. Finally, the investigation found that the initial internal affairs unit did not objectively probe the incident, asking instead questions that were meant to exonerate the officers.[61] These findings ultimately led to wholesale challenges of excited delirium as a medical diagnosis.

In the first week of October 2023, California became the first state to ban the use of "excited delirium syndrome" as a cause of death. Mike Gibson, the California assemblyman and former police officer who drafted the law, stated: "If a police officer has someone in custody, and a person dies from positional asphyxia, it should be placed on there that this person died from positional asphyxia, cutting off oxygen flow to someone's brain. It should conclude that. It should not be made up of a term to try to cover up something."[62]

The following week, the Association of American College of Emergency Physicians (ACEP), one of the few professional organizations that had initially endorsed the term, retracted their support.[63] In 2009, after a sponsored meeting by Axon (formerly Taser International), this group had authored a white paper endorsing excited delirium syndrome despite ongoing disputes about its validity as a legitimate medical diagnosis. However, on October 13, 2023, ACEP admitted its error, withdrawing its support and leaving no remaining medical association backing for Charles Wetli's fabricated disease.

In October 2023, Officer Randy Roedema, who had restrained Elijah McClain with painful wrestling moves, was found guilty of "criminally negligent homicide and third-degree assault."[64] That same jury found Officer Jason Rosenblatt not guilty. Rosenblatt was one of the officers who texted "ha ha," making fun of a memorial to McClain. In December 2023, Peter Cichuniec and Jeremy Cooper, the two paramedics who injected McClain with ketamine, were also convicted of criminally negligent homicide.[65] In addition, Cichuniec, who administered the drug, was found guilty of assault in the second degree.

Despite these convictions, just one month earlier, on November 6, 2023, Nathan Woodyard, the former officer who initially approached Elijah McClain and immediately restrained him with a carotid neck hold, was acquitted of manslaughter and criminally negligent homicide.[66] Woodyard admitted in court that he had violated police policy. Nevertheless, the successful defense rested on his tearful account that he feared McClain. "I was expecting to get shot, and I thought I would never see my wife again," Woodyard testified.[67] Although the prosecution presented Roger Mitchell, a forensic pathologist, who testified that there was a clear connection between Officer Woodyard's neck restraints, the administration of ketamine, and McClain's death, the jury ultimately accepted the age-old narrative that a White officer's fear of a Black youth justified the excessive use of force.

My heart aches for Sheneen McClain, who sat in the courtroom, erupting in tears upon hearing the not-guilty verdict. In my own need for solace and comprehension, I seek assistance from my spirit guides. I admit that merely three years after George Floyd's killing, the excited delirium is taking hold yet again. The White public is growing weary of protests over police violence, while politicians and conservative groups launch assaults on scholars and activists by targeting the instruction around the history of racism in our country.

I summon the revolutionary insistence of spirits such as Jeremy's, Cissy's, and Mario's, who have worked to disrupt the excited delirium of the racial laboratory. I draw on the conjuring work of Africana drums and Jade Ellis's poetry to continue to offer vibrational shifts for liberation.[68] I am aware how spirits and energies move people and spaces, how dead observers provide us with blueprints for freedom, if we are able to follow their lead. Afro-Latiné techniques do not aim for salvation in a heavenly afterlife. Instead, they follow an abolitionist logic that seeks a "radical reconfiguration" of the present.[69] I offer this partial blueprint as a *decolonial abolition*, a modality for transformation carved out of Afro-Latiné spiritual pathways (*caminos*) for change.

Energetic activism alone will not undo the ongoing violence that our communities face. However, these strategies afford us modalities for repair in the longer aim of liberation. Undoubtedly, the weight is heavy for the mothers who prematurely lose children to the excited delirium of racist violence. Striving for a "radical abolition" as Ruth Gilmore calls for, or an "abolition democracy" as W. E. B. Du Bois suggested, is more than just undoing powerful institutions. Rather, it is about "figuring out how to work with people" to make that change happen.[70] Abolition is therefore also an energetic charge. Such was the charge from the abolitionist spirits who guided me through this book. I know they will continue to challenge scholars to find better ways to articulate their claims—or they will haunt you until you do.

Thursday, September 8, 2022
Princeton, New Jersey

It was three years ago today. The most unimaginable anguish, losing a child. My chest heaved. My eyes hurt, but I could not stop sobbing. My stepson, Louisito, whom I had just spoken to a few days before, was dead. Murdered. I had my ticket to fly out the following week to mark his priesthood. He was going to be initiated into Santeria like his brothers. Neto and Pilli were with him that morning; later that night he was killed.

On that day, Neto had made a shrimp and crab boil, Sito and Pilli's favorite. They sent me pictures of the three of them, smiling, holding up crab legs. This could not be real. The pain was so deep. I did not know how I could live with such anguish, such loss. The guilt. I had not gotten there quickly enough. I should not have postponed my trip. I ended up taking my flight to San Francisco for Sito's funeral instead of his marking ceremony. I had failed him.

I remember how day had turned into evening as I sat sobbing on the couch. Then I felt Sito's presence behind me. It was soothing. I felt the pressure of a hand on my shoulder. It'll be OK. *He wanted to remove my guilt.* I'll be back.

Two weeks later, I was pregnant with Langston.

Afterword

I HAVE ALWAYS KNOWN IN MY GUT that academic work is a form of conjuring. As a doctoral student, I had come to anthropology struggling with poverty and racism. For so long, I had been a young single mother barely making ends meet. Education was my way out of a cycle of violence. I struggled to feed my two kids as I worked my way through school. With three part-time jobs and a full academic load, I was able to finish my undergraduate degree with honors only with the assistance of my copresences. When I was accepted to the doctoral program in anthropology at Stanford University, I knew that this opportunity would change my life. And it did. Through academia, I built a successful career as a professor and scholar. Rather than being a research subject studied by anthropologists, I am now known as an anthropologist who studies Afro-Latiné religions. I split myself.

But when I was still a graduate student, there was one moment when I came too close to the veil between academia and spiritual conjuring. It was during my second year of the doctoral program, and I was engrossed in critical and feminist theory. I was assigned to cover the French Marxist philosopher Louis Althusser for my seminar Theory and Political Economy. After putting my kids to bed, I stayed up all night reading On the Reproduction of Capitalism: Ideology and Ideological State Apparatuses. *I do not drink coffee, and so I was surprised the next morning that, despite having pulled an all-nighter, I was energized rather than exhausted. I had somehow taken nineteen pages of notes. I felt oddly eager and even giddy to take on the class.*

To say I took over the class is an understatement. I did not let anyone else speak! As if I had written the book myself, I argued the concepts with a manic fervor. At one point, I detailed Louis Althusser's theory of interpellation, in which people become subjects of the state. According to Althusser, the state has the power to create and maintain social order through ideological messages that people internalize as a sense of identity and belonging. Althusser wrote of how the state "hails" individuals by calling out to people through various mechanisms such as laws, educational institutions, media, and cultural practices. By responding to the state's call, people recognize their roles and positions through what he describes as "interpellation," which involves a process of ideological conditioning that shapes people's consciousness and perception of themselves and each other.

With a strange passion, I stood at the long oval seminar table, giving the classic Althusserian example of the policeman who calls on someone to stop: "Hey, you there!" Noting my excitement, the professor, Miyako Inoue, a linguistic anthropologist who studies gender in Japan, joked that it seemed as if I were Althusser himself. Immediately, I exclaimed without thinking, "I am Althusser!"

When class ended, a fellow grad student approached me. He thanked me for my discussion and asked if I had heard the story of Louis Althusser. I had not. He said, "Well, Althusser was known for being a manic depressive. Every morning he would throw his window open and exclaim, 'I am Louis Althusser!' Just as you did during our class." Then he told me that Althusser had murdered his wife, Helene. On November 16, 1980, while massaging her neck, Althusser crushed her larynx, killing her with his bare hands. Shortly after murdering Helene, Althusser threw his window open and yelled to the neighbors, "I am Louis Althusser, and I just killed my wife!" Because he was deemed to suffer from psychosis, he was considered unfit to stand trial.[1]

I was stunned. In that moment I knew I had inadvertently conjured Louis Althusser. I recalled the manic excitement and giddiness I felt in class.

I had always sensed that reading (and citing) academic texts called up the spirits of their authors. At that moment, however, I knew that the divide between the spiritual and the academic was much thinner than I had believed.[2] After this experience, I did not want to inadvertently channel spirits through their scholarship again. I suspected then that much of what we do as academics is itself a form of incantation. I am not the first to make this assertion.[3] However, this is not just a metaphor. As someone raised in Afro-Latiné traditions, I know that spirits respond and react to our attentions. I have since become very aware that scholars must be careful about the theories that we read and the people that we invoke, as our scholarship itself is a kind of séance.[4] Many others believe that academia conjures spirits, whether we acknowledge them or not. Solimar Otero has described these kinds of ephemera as "archives of conjure," how the dead are active agents that work through our research in forms of creative influence.[5]

I decided that I did not want to allow academic spirits to enter me so easily. Without realizing I had done it, I had formed a barrier to academic spirits in an attempt to not allow them to penetrate me. I wrote my dissertation and first book with this barrier erected. I made sure to tiptoe around their presences. I tried hard to not allow them to enter me, to become my copresences—that is, part of my body-world.

As I worked on this book, however, which deals with so many violent deaths and so many people with unfinished business, there was no way for the spirits to not demand a different type of recognition.

Jeremy Ellis's spirit irrevocably shifted my research world. The spirits wanted me to show how people have been murdered, scapegoated, and blamed for their own deaths. They provided me understanding of these interconnected patterns and systemic cover-ups. It became clear to me that my background as a social scientist who was raised in a decolonial spirituality helped me see how excited delirium syndrome ties into the criminalization of Afro-Latiné religions.

More important, the spirits wanted me to confront the very notion of expertise itself. Even my own carefully crafted Western episteme needed to be undone. Early on in researching this book, like Rafael Martinez, I had believed that maybe better police training, by "real" experts, would be able to change the criminalization of Afro-Latiné religions and transform racist policing. But the spirits, particularly those whose deaths have been labeled as caused by excited delirium, were demanding much more. They wanted me to show how expertise itself has allowed for the cover-up of their deaths.

Modupué

There are many whose names I cannot know who made this book possible. So much more than ethnographic interlocutors, I thank the spirits, falsely labeled excited delirium, who were the copresences that with me theorized this book, ensuring its manifestation until the very end. To Sito, Padrino Alfredo ObaTola, Padrino Alfonso Obafun, Madrina Juana Regla Oba Bi, Kiki Oba Bi, Damian Oloyu Oba, Diane McKelhiney Egbin Kolade, Cristobal Puertas Ara Bi, Roberto Clemente Aña Bi Osun, Martin Bonney, Jeremy Ellis, and my many other ancestors who rest at the foot of Olodumare, I praise you.

My grandparents Maria Magdalena "Margie" and Peter De Jesus Sr. sat with me when I was an undergraduate student in Chicano and Latino studies at UC Berkeley writing an honor's thesis on Puerto Ricans in the San Francisco Bay Area. I continue to return to the gifts of those interviews, cherishing the lessons they taught me.

I am grateful to the *poderes* who walk with me, attuning me to alternative notions of justice, and empowering me to find my voice as a decolonial scholar, mother, partner, and practitioner.

* * *

I am so grateful for my close-knit family unit, my husband and children. Laurence Ralph, my love, this book would not be possible without your love, guidance, support, and feedback. You continue to push me beyond my boundaries and believe in me. To my children, Neto, Pilli, Sito, Amina, and Langston, you make me so proud and have given me the greatest gift. Thank you for teaching me the most important lessons in life. Neto, you are an amazing leader, father, husband, brother, son, and priest. I'm so proud of what you've been able to overcome. Pilli, your intelligence and care always leaves me humbled, you nurture the world and are a balm to my soul. Amina, you are so powerful, brilliant, and fierce, I cannot wait to see the great things you will do. Langston, you are our heart, you make the world a better place with your love, talent, luminosity, and grace. To my daughter-in-law, Naomi, you have brought calmness to our world. You and Neto are models of leadership and eldership, and I am so proud of your bravery, honesty, and dedication to liberation. To my granddaughter, Nayari "Nana," you make us complete.

* * *

I grew up with a complicated and beautiful community that, rather than fear spiritual power, taught us to cultivate and hone these knowledges. I am grateful to my father, Peter "Piri Ochun" De Jesus, for giving us these Afro-Latiné traditions and for sitting with me through many conversations to ensure I had gotten our family's story right. To my mother, Dolores Beliso, an activist, spiritualist, dancer, social worker, and priest of Yemaya and Ogun, thank you for your love. Thanks to Steve Weymouth for reading this book with your attorney's eye, and to Veronica De Jesus for supporting our family.

Many thanks to Auntie Margaret for providing me archival documents; for tracing our lineage back through Puerto Rico, Nigeria, Senegal, Taino Indigenous communities, Spain, Portugal, and Cuba; and for telling me stories of racism, passion, and dance. To my Auntie Petra, the former San Francisco Police commissioner who fought against police use of Tasers, debated corporations, and called for a stop to the violence against Black and Brown communities, I am grateful for your voice and courage.

To Uncle Tobaji and Iya Wanda, thank you for the work you do healing those left in the wake of police killings. I am so grateful for your words, knowledge, and commitment to justice for Black people. To my cousin Nailah, thank you for being a sister to me and a godmother to Amina and Langston. Thank you to the Ralph family—Michael Sr., Lynette, Wole, Mike Jr., Fari, Semai, and Sofia—for your inspiring commitment to family, your strength, and your unwavering love. I am grateful to my siblings and close cousins: Barbara, Geno, Anya, Damian, Mateo, Lee Sandra, Amber, Izzie, Ixchel, and their children, Lulu and Luna.

To all the practitioners of the San Francisco Bay Area who make up our community, I give praise. Elders such as Afro-Cuban singer and priest of Obatala Bobi Cespedes; Afro–Puerto Rican priest of Yemaya Edgar Chamorro Aquelle Olorun; Cuban American priest of Yemaya, Jay Perez Somileke; and my godmother of Catholicism, one of the first Asian Americans initiated in Santeria to Ochún, Christina Velasco Olo Oñi Iya, thank you for raising me in a vibrant community. Rene and Maya, I am so grateful to you both and our blended family. Chango Lade, my friend, comrade, and sister, I am so honored to have you in my life, helping me co-mother my children, and being an elder in our circle and *ile*. To my godchildren, Stefan, Alyssa, Scotty, Erica, Michelle, Barbarita, Henny, Eugene, and Erikita, I admire your generosity, commitment, and strength. May Egun and Aganyu bless you, always.

Mama Linda and Andres, and the other elders and *iworo* of Ile Egbado-Sito, thank you for providing care and healing to our youth. Xhiyo, Maria, Twinkie, Chi Chi, Caro, Oba Ibu Ayacua, Sólana, Summer, Eugene, Aleah, Yose, Marita, Deja, Jay, Thalia, Natalie, Brittany, Bri, Bee, Jorji, Vannah, Marilyn, Ursula, Adrian, China, Stef, Jacqui, and so many more, you inspire me every day. You show me how we can challenge racism, homophobia, and transphobia and live the blueprint. I also want to thank my god siblings and close friends, Milagro de la Caridad Velasco Oviedo, Toribio and Aneity Villamil, Mansunsun, Cosme Calvo, Agustín Calvo, Alberto Calvo, Oriana Ides, and Marynez Carrasco.

I am grateful to Jade Ellis, her mother, Carmen, and sister, Eva, for allowing me to share their story. For Iya Amara, Iya Tobe, and the other Black Latiné diaspora women, thank you for your conjure work. It has been an honor to reconnect with Rafael Martinez, who shared his misgivings and allowed me to include his story. Through your honesty, you model how we can always take a second look and transform ourselves and our work.

—*Modupué.*

Acknowledgments

This book would not have been possible without the support from a number of institutions, including Princeton University's Effron Center for the Study of America, the Department of Spanish and Portuguese, and the Center on Transnational Policing in the Department of Anthropology; the Wenner-Gren Foundation; the Association for Black Anthropologists (ABA); *Transforming Anthropology* journal; the Department of Anthropology at Stanford University, and the Center for Advanced Studies in the Behavioral Sciences (CASBS); Harvard University's Divinity School, the Safra Center, the Weatherhead Center, the Hutchins Center for African American Studies, and the Women's Studies in Religion Program at Harvard Divinity School.

At Princeton, I owe special thanks to President Christopher Eisgruber, Dean Gene Jarrett, Deputy Dean Toni Turano, Vice-Dean Fred Wherry, and Blair and Cheryl Effron for cultivating a shared goal of a more equitable future.

There are so many colleagues across a number of universities who shaped me and this book. My thanks to those of you who continue to teach and inspire me every day: Joyce Bell, Jemima Pierre, Peter Hudson, Michael Ralph, Erica Williams, Jonathan Rosa, Elizabeth Hinton, Aimee Cox, Sylvia Yanagisako, Amy Hollywood, Paulla Ebron, Jim Ferguson, Renato Rosaldo, Miyako Inoue, Kamari Clarke, Sean Brotherton, Faye Harrison, Deborah Thomas, John Jackson, Arlene Davila, Jafari Alllen, Skip Gates, Ayesha Chaudry, Rumi Ahmed, Ross Gay, Alyssa Mt. Pleasant, Kris Manjapra, Bertin Louis, Riché Barnes, Lee Baker, Ramón Grosfoguel, Purnima Mankekar, Akhil Gupta, Shannon Speed, Reiko Yamada, and Kristiana Kahakauwila.

To the CASBS community, Margaret Levi, Jennifer Gómez, Hakeem Jefferson, Jennifer Richeson, Lauren Davenport, Mpho Tshivase, Julie Livingston, Megan Finn, Teresa McCarty, Jules Naudet, and Manuel Pastor, I cherished our lunches and conversations. To the TA crew—Michiko Tsuneda, Christen Smith, Whitney, Battle-Baptiste, Ryan Cecil Jobson, Junaid Rana, Vanessa Díaz, Sarah Bruno, Chelsea Carter, Tiffany Peacock, Michelle Rodgriguez, and Khytie Brown—I thank you.

I am especially grateful to those who read previous versions of this book and provided crucial feedback: Laurence Ralph, Judith Weisenfeld, Michael Ralph, Amara Smith, Junaid Rana, Solimar Otero, Patricia Fernández-Kelly, Jade Ellis, Chango Lade, Mitchell Duneier, Shamus Khan, Karyn Greco, and Rafael Martinez.

Thanks to my colleagues at Princeton University: Yarimar Bonilla, Lorgia García Peña, Allison Carruth, Stacy Wolf, Bill Gleason, Judith Hamera, Kinohi Nishikawa, Carolyn Choi, Shamus Khan, Mitchell Duneier, Rachael De Lue, J. Kēhaulani Kauanui, Paul Nadal, Matt Desmond, Anne Cheng, Sarah Rivett, Monica Huerta, Brian Herrera, Alison Isenberg, Yaacob Dweck, Beth Lew-Williams, Rosina Lozano, Laura Leibman, Hanna Garth, Ruha Benjamin, Tera Hunter, Wallace Best, and Eddie Glaude. Thank you for your encouragement and solidarity.

Special thanks to Karyn Greco, for your honesty and trust. I am truly grateful to Patricia Fernández-Kelly for all the laughs and tears we share. Thanks to the love and democracy team at the Effron Center for the Study of America: Patricia Fernández-Kelly, Karyn Greco, Jordan Dixon, Sarah Malone, NicQuwesha Toliver, Yelz Góchez, Genesis Manyari, and Barron Bixler.

I am deeply indebted to Ken Wissoker and Duke University Press and the anonymous reviewers who provided invaluable feedback and patience. Thank you for editorial, indexing, and library support from Jason Gonzalez, Brad Erickson, Paula Durbin-Westby, and Cathy Cambron.

While copyediting this book, Cathy Cambron, an editor I had never met, wrote me the following brave note with which I will end. She told me I could include it if I would like to, and I think it offers insight into the many seen and unseen forces whom I owe thanks:

> I haven't been sure whether to mention this, but it is clear to me that the spirits are very involved with this manuscript! I was having all kinds of very

odd problems with the file until I learned that, each day before starting work, I needed to address the spirits who were concerned about the work and humbly ask for their help in assisting you to find a wide readership for your book. All the issues I was having ceased immediately!

My deepest thanks to those persistent spirits.

Glossary

abaarà méjì Yorùbá term translated directly as "two calabashes," signifying the ones with two bodies, who are feared because of their flying ability. Can also refer to sacred twins.

Abakuá An all-male Afro-Cuban society with origins in West Africa, known for its music, dance, and religious practices.

aché *(also Àṣẹ)* In Yorùbá-influenced religions across the world, it refers to the interconnected energy or life force of all creatures. In Santeria, it also represents the ability to manifest change through rituals and ceremonies.

Aganyu *(also Aganjú)* An orisha in Yorùbá diaspora religions like Santeria, associated with volcanoes, lava, and fiery forces. A powerful ferryman, correlating with the Catholic saint Christopher.

ahijados Godchildren.

ajá A broom used in Azojuano ceremonies to energetically cleanse people.

Àjé Supernatural beings with the ability to cause harm or misfortune; seen as shape-shifters who turn into spirit-birds (Èyẹ́ Òrò) and can be associated with witchcraft. Black feminist practitioners have reclaimed this energy as a potent modality to harness female power of retribution and justice.

Alaàfin *(also Àlàáfìn)* A Yorùbá title denoting a king or ruler, often used in Nigeria to refer to a monarch who holds significant authority.

aleyos Noninitiated practitioners of Santeria.

añá Consecrated sacred *batá* drums in Yorùbá diaspora religions. *See also* batá drums.

ará onú Name for the spirit realm in Cuban Santeria.

awán Cleansing ritual done for the orisha Azojuano.

Azaka Haitian Vodou spirit-energy (*lwa*) associated with agriculture, farming, and the earth.

Azojuano *(also known as Babalú-Ayé)* Refers to the orisha associated with healing, disease, and infectious illnesses, who was the king of the Dahomey peoples. The Catholic association is Saint Lazarus.

baños Spanish word for *baths* that refers to spiritual cleansing potions.

batá drums Yorùbá diaspora two-headed drum played in a set of three.

botanica Religious store catering to Afro-Latiné religions.

brujería Spanish word for *witchcraft*.

cajón Spanish word for *box*, referring to the wooden box drums that are played for the dead in Afro-Cuban music.

caminos Spanish word for *roads* or *paths*.

Changó *(also Ṣàngó or Xangô)* Refers to the orisha associated with thunder, lightning, fire, dance, and passion. A powerful and charismatic figure who symbolizes strength, vitality, politics, and the tongue in the body.

confirmación Spanish word meaning "confirmation." In Afro-Latiné spiritual practices, it describes a spirit's communication of information to a medium.

Congo African-inspired group; also the name for the spirit of enslaved peoples from the Kikongo tradition.

coronación Spritualism term used to describe the crowning ritual that unites mediums with their primary spirit guide.

curandero A traditional Indigenous healer in Latin America who uses a combination of herbal remedies, rituals, prayers, energy work, and other healing techniques to treat a wide range of physical and spiritual ailments.

desarollo Spiritualism term to describe the "development" or enhanced connection among mediums as they tune their perceptions toward spirits.

dilloggún Cowry-shell divination used in Yorùbá diaspora religions like Afro-Cuban Santeria to communicate with the orishas and gain spiritual guidance for practitioners.

efun Eggshell powder chalk used in African diaspora rituals.

Eguardo or **Egbado** *(also Ewardo)* A branch of Santeria practices that hails from the enslaved groups of "Egba" people, a Yorùbá ethnic group who came from the Abeokuta region, in the Ogun State in southwestern Nigeria.

egun Spirits of the dead in Yorùbá diaspora religions like Santeria.

Egúngún *(also Ègúngún)* A traditional Yorùbá masquerade festival honoring ancestral spirits. Participants wear elaborate regalia and masks that represent the spirits of their ancestors to connect with and pay homage to the spirits of deceased.

elekes Sacred necklaces in Santeria.

escoria Spanish word for *scum*.

Espiritismo   A Spanish term used to refer to spiritism practices; a spiritual and religious movement that emerged in the nineteenth century, based on communication with spirits, through mediums who have the ability to communicate with the spirit world. Practitioners engage in séances where they establish contact with spirits and receive messages or guidance from them.

Espiritismo Africano A syncretic form of spiritism that combines elements of African, Indigenous religions, and other spiritual traditions; practiced in various parts of the Americas, particularly in regions with African diaspora populations, such as Cuba, Puerto Rico, and Brazil.

Èyẹ́ Ọ̀rọ̀   The sacred spirit-bird of the Àjé (sorceresses) in Yorùbá religions, often identified as the vulture and considered the messenger of the ancestors. A figure in Ifá divination who allows for spiritual communication.

hombría   Manliness.

ibaé   Yorùbá term that means "homage," used in Afro-Cuban Santeria religious contexts to pay respect to the ancestors who have passed on.

Ifá *(also Ìfá)*   Yorùbá diaspora divination system associated with the orisha Orunmila. There are different styles of practice, most prominently the Ifá from Nigeria as well as the one developed in Cuba. Both are highly respected and used for seeking guidance, solving problems, and understanding the will of the Orishas by consultation with male priests, known as "Babalawos" or, in Nigerian style, also with female priests known as "Iyanifa."

Iku lobi ocha *(El muerto para el Santo)* A saying in Afro-Cuban Santeria that means the orisha are born from the ancestors.

ilé *(also Ilè)*   House or "home" in the Yorùbá language. In Yorùbá diaspora religions, it refers to a sacred or spiritual house-temple dedicated to the worship of orisha and ancestors.

influencías   Spiritualism term used to denote the different negative and positive spiritual influences that surround people's body-worlds.

Iroso *(also, Irosun)* A sign from Ifá and *dilloggún* divination systems.

itá   A Yorùbá diaspora divination ritual in which a diviner interprets messages from orisha that provide guidance for the practitioner's life path.

itutu ceremony Ritual of the dead; also cool water to refresh the spirits.

iyawo   New initiate of Santeria priesthood, also word for *bride* in Yorùbá.

jicara   Gourd bowl used in rituals.

la Regla de Ocha The Rule of the Ocha, another name for Santeria.

Latinidad   A Spanish term encompassing the cultural and social identity and experiences of individuals and communities who identify as Latino/a/

x/é or are of Latin American descent in the United States, regardless of their specific country of origin.

Lukumí *(also Lucumí)* Originally meaning "friend," the term was used to describe groups of enslaved Yorùbá people from West Africa after they arrived in Cuba. It is also the name of the creole ritual language used in Santeria, and it is more generally used to describe the religion itself.

madrina Spanish word for *godmother*.

malas vibraciones Spiritism term to describe when a medium senses negative vibrations in the spiritual field.

misa de capturación A specific spiritism mass to capture a negative spirit.

misa de investigación A specific spiritism mass to investigate a medium's spiritual court, which refers to the spirits who walk with people to assist them in their life pathways.

misa espiritual A spiritual mass or séance.

muerto Dead spirit.

muerto pegado A spirit who has become "stuck" on a living person, causing problems.

muertos oscuros A spirit who remains in the dark and can wreak havoc in the lives of the living. Such spirits require rituals to elevate them and bring them into the light.

mulato/a A Spanish word to describe a person of mixed-race European and African ancestry in Latin America and the Caribbean. In some countries, it may be considered racist and outdated, while in others, like Cuba, it is still used widely.

mundele In the Kikongo language from Central Africa, it refers to a foreigner or a person of European descent. In Afro-Cuban Palo Monte practices it refers to White people.

Negro Spanish word for the color black. Also used to refer to Black people.

negro brujo A pejorative Spanish term that translates to "Black witch."

nfumbe In Palo Monte, it refers to the spiritual essence or the ancestral spirit of a deceased person.

nganga A Palo Monte sacred object, typically in the form of a consecrated cauldron, pot, or container assembled with various ingredients, such as herbs, roots, bones, and other items, that hold spiritual power and connections to ancestral spirits and deities.

Nsala Malekun *(also Nṣálà Màlèkùn)* A respectful greeting that hails from Islam, used in African diaspora religions like Palo Monte.

Obatala *(also Obàtálá)* One of the major Yorùbá diaspora orisha associated with purity, creation, wisdom, and peace. Associated with the mountain, the head, and the elderly. The Catholic avatar is the Virgin Merced.

Ochún *(Also Ọ̀ṣun)* The orisha associated with love, beauty, fertility, wealth, rivers, and sweet waters. The Catholic avatar is Our Lady of Charity of El Cobre.

oddu *(also odu)* A moral-story or sign from Ifá and *dilloggún* divination. It refers to one of the 256 possible sacred patterns that are used for divination readings.

Olokun *(also Ọlọ́kùn)* One of the prominent orisha of the deep sea, wealth, mysteries, and the unknown. This deity is genderless and said to have taken in the souls lost during the Middle Passage.

Oriaté Religious officiator in Santeria.

Orisha *(also Orichá in Cuba, Orịṣa in Nigeria, Orixa in Brazil)* The deities or spirits in the Yorùbá diaspora religions associated with various aspects of life, nature, and human experience and serve as intermediaries between humans and the divine. Each orisha has specific attributes, characteristics, and domains, and they are venerated through rituals, ceremonies, and offerings by practitioners of these spiritual traditions.

padrino Male, godfather.

palangana Spanish word for plastic tub.

palero Priest of Palo.

Palo Monte *(also Palo Mayombe)* Afro-Cuban religion that originated in Central Africa and merged with elements of Catholicism. A complex spiritual system that centers the veneration of ancestral spirits, natural forces, and the use of ritual objects, or *ngangas*.

Papa Guede One of the prominent spirits or *lwa* (loa) in Haitian Vodou, the custodian of the cemetery, who guides the souls of the deceased into the afterlife.

patria Spanish word for nation or homeland.

poder Spanish word indicating spiritual power.

prenda Another name for Palo cauldron that means "precious jewel." *See also* nganga.

preso/a Indebted or enslaved to the orisha.

prueba Spiritism term to describe when someone receives validation of spiritual existence.

rayamiento Initiation ceremony in Palo Monte.

rompimiento A ritual to break a curse, hex, or negative spirit.

Santeria *(also Santería)* Afro-Cuban religion that combines elements of Yorùbá religious practice and some Catholic inspiration, involving the worship of orishas, rituals, divination, and the use of sacred objects to find balance and healing in practitioners' body-worlds.

santero/a Priest of Santeria.

Siete Rayos   One of the prominent spirits in Palo Monte associated with lightning, honor, and the power to overcome enemies.

Yemaya *(also Yemọja, Nigeria, Yemanjá, Brazil)* Yorùbá diaspora orisha associated with the ocean, motherhood, and fertility. She holds a significant place in the pantheon of deities. Her Catholic avatar is Virgin of Regla.

Notes

Introduction

Epigraph: Selection from Khalisa Rae's poem "Epilogue for Banned Books," dedicated to Alice Walker in *Ghost in a Black Girl's Throat*, 81.

1. In keeping with anthropological norms, I employ pseudonyms for research interlocutors. The names of colleagues, family members, and friends remain unchanged, except when requested.

2. See the important work of Christen A. Smith, "Facing the Dragon," in which she talks about the lingering effects of police violence on families and communities through her term "sequelae."

3. Ghosts, specters, and haunting have long been deployed as metaphors in academic scholarship. Even as this work departs from using spirits as analogies, I am still shaped by and indebted to the work of sociologist Avery Gordon, whose important book *Ghostly Matters* showed haunting as a paradigm from which to theorize the complications of life and the sociological enterprise. In addition, the work of Jacques Derrida's "hauntology" launched a whole "spectral turn" in the 1990s, drawing on ghosts and haunting as metaphors for capitalism. See Derrida, *Specters of Marx*. Subsequently, an interest emerged in haunting as an analogy in poststructuralism. Haunting was ripe in literary studies, cultural studies, and social theory, which even produced a literary subfield called "spectral studies." See Blanco and Peeren, *Spectralities Reader*.

In this book, however, I do not talk about my haunting as a useful theoretical model. Indeed, some would say that this metaphor has already worn thin. Instead, this work is more in line with the memoir of Black feminist law professor and critical race theorist Patricia Williams, *The Alchemy of Race and Rights*. Williams honestly divulges her rage, paranoia, and depression that results from being an academic living with racism, which she sees as a lively phantom; this phantom of racism comes after Williams with its powerful presence. Williams also describes the power of her late godmother's bedroom. Williams tried to empty its contents, only to find that the room would assault her: "The room asserted itself, came rushing and raging at me. . . . The force of its spirit still drifts like an odor throughout the house" (49). This work contributes to how Black and Brown experience with spirits demands a different attunement to time, space, place, and presence.

4. "State AG to Investigate Angelo Quinto's Death in Antioch Police Custody," *Bay City News*, September 7, 2022, https://www.nbcbayarea.com/news/local/east-bay /angelo-quinto-antioch-death-investigation/2997166/.

5. For example, even though Avery Gordon speaks of ghosts as a useful language with which to ground the way the past haunts the present, she aptly captures how spirits are a "seething presence" that meddle with "taken-for-granted realities." Gordon, *Ghostly Matters*, 8. Gordon talks about how apparitions reveal something lost. In her case, she also found herself compelled to conduct certain research because of the "persistent and troubling ghosts in the house" (8).

6. See the important work of Chicanx feminist Gloria Anzaldúa, *Borderlands/La Frontera*, in which she writes about her poetry and scholarship as "spiritual activism." Her poetic scholarship has been described as "a weapon in the fight against colonization" (Hartley, "Curandera of Conquest," 155–56). Hartley calls her a "Curandera of Conquest" because of her ability to both "challenge and problematize Western epistemology, but also to heal it and us from its violent processes and colonial legacies" (135). Anzaldúa's poetry and scholarship are a form of spiritual activism, revealing how we have "inherited and embodied" colonial legacies, especially in our reproduction of "dominant forms of inquiry" (155–56).

7. My interlocutors in this book would switch between the terms *Latiné*, *Latinx*, *Latina*, and *Latino*. Some advocate for *Latinx* as a new form born of millennial social media activism concerning gender fluidity, while others have argued that this term is another English-centric product of US imperialism that is difficult for Spanish-speaking peoples and does not reflect Indigenous people from the Americas. I decided to use *Latiné* because it seems to flow a bit more easily off the tongue and also bridges across other transnational solidarity movements in Latin America, Mexico, the Caribbean, and the United States. When quoting other scholarship or when people self-identify as *Latina/o/x*, I use those terms. Ultimately, language is fluid, and our terms are imperfect. *Latiné* itself continues to privilege the coloniality of Spanish and Portuguese relations and ignores other racial formations such as Blackness, Indigeneity, and Asian influences. See also "Latine vs. Latinx: What They Mean, Why They Matter," LATV Media, August 10, 2021, https://latv.com/latine-vs-latinx.

8. Sandín and Perez, *Contemporary U.S. Latino/a Literary Criticism*, 2.

9. Milian, *Latining America*. See also the important works of Jorge Duany ("Nation on the Move") on how Latiné nationalisms travel between colonial relations, and Lorgia García Peña's *Translating Blackness*, which shows how diaspora has been used to destabilize national borders.

10. Queer of color scholars E. Patrick Johnson and Ramón Rivera Servera call these blends "Blacktino." Johnson and Rivera-Servera, *Blacktino*, 3. I use *Afro-Latiné* here to also refer to the intimate and creative blends of Blackness and Latinidad in religious

practices that emerged through specific histories of chattel slavery, colonialism, and Indigenous genocide in the Americas, and that have traveled and transformed with practitioners who remake these inspirations in and through diaspora. *Afro-Latiné* allows for the gender fluidity, radical consciousness, and racial and ethnic play that animate my interlocutors' social spaces with the living and the dead.

11. Racialized state violence in Brazil is also very important for Afro-Latiné formations. Brazil is home to 70 percent of the world's Afro-Latiné people. Practitioners of Candomblé in the United States tend to return to Brazil for their ceremonies, and so experience a different kind of visibility and policing in the United States. See Matory, *Black Atlantic Religion*. See also Colin M. MacLachlan, review of *Afro-Latin America 1800–2000*, by George Reid Andrews.

12. López, *Unbecoming Blackness*. See also Román and Flore, *The Afro-Latin@ Reader*, 4–5.

13. People in the United States are made into "colors" (Black, Brown, Red, Yellow) because of their relation to Whiteness and White supremacy. They also then interact and "cross" with one another through this racialized power structure. See Milian, *Latining America*, 12.

14. I use the terms *Brown*, *dark Brown*, and *light Brown* to reference the complexity of race, emphasizing their relevance both in the context of Black identities as well as in relation to distinct forms of White supremacy. The varying shades of Brown highlight the nuance and ambiguity of racial distinctions and how racial color lines shift across the United States, the Caribbean, and Latin America.

15. As Antonio López shows, Latiné people who are racialized as Black must navigate the violences of "an Anglo white supremacy" that determines our life chances in the United States, while also contending with "a Latino white supremacy" that "reproduces the colonial and postcolonial Latin American privileging of *Blanco* over *Negro* and *Mulato* (mixed-race) identities. López, *Unbecoming Blackness, 5*.

16. I first coined the term *copresence* in my article "Santeria Copresence." Then I developed the term further in my book *Electric Santería*.

Chapter One. Nightmares

1. The energy of the Great Mother (*Èyé Òrò*) in orisha philosophies is one such frame with which we can harness justice. Orisha craftings use an enclosed calabash, or clay pot, as the protective covering to channel this power, mirroring the roundness of the mother's belly and the embrace of the earth. T. Washington, *The Architects of Existence*, 8, 85.

2. Lexie Verdon, "Thousands in Cuba Ask Peruvian Refuge," *Washington Post*, April 7, 1980, https://www.washingtonpost.com/archive/politics/1980/04/07/thousands-in-cuba-ask-peruvian-refuge/987ab70f-3cbe-4ad3-afcd-a6fcb9152d93/.

3. Karen Juanita Carrillo, "The Mariel Boatlift: How Cold War Politics Drove Thousands of Cubans to Florida in 1980," History.com, September 28, 2020, https://www.history.com/news/mariel-boatlift-castro-carter-cold-war.

4. Alfonso Chardy, "Mariel Boatlift Tested Miami's Strength, Then Made It Stronger," *Palm Beach Post*, March 31, 2021, https://www.palmbeachpost.com/story/news/state/2012/03/31/mariel-boatlift-tested-miami-s/7611908007/.

5. Katharine Q. Seelye, "Charles Wetli, Medical Examiner for T.W.A. Flight 800 Crash, Dies at 76," *New York Times*, September 7, 2020.

6. Seelye, "Charles Wetli, Medical Examiner."

7. Beliso-De Jesús, *Electric Santería*.

8. See the excellent work on ritual waste in Santeria by Kristina Wirtz, "Hazardous Waste."

9. Ochoa, *Society of the Dead*.

10. Hamm, *Abandoned Ones*, 62.

11. Hamm, *Abandoned Ones*, 62.

12. Hamm, *Abandoned Ones*, 62.

13. Hamm, *Abandoned Ones*, 62.

14. By 1989, 169 Marielitos were locked down for twenty-three hours a day at the US Penitentiary. See Miles Corwin, "Cuban 'Detainees' from Mariel Boat Lift: 2,500 Prisoners of U.S. Face No Charges," *Los Angeles Times*, August 27, 1989, https://www.latimes.com/archives/la-xpm-1989-08-27-mn-1741-story.html.

15. Corwin, "Cuban 'Detainees.'"

16. Bradford, "Operation Pedro Pan."

17. Rafael Martinez told me the goal of the CHIC Program was to assess Cuban detainees and provide them with support.

18. Hamm, *Abandoned Ones*, 60.

19. Garcia, "Situating Race, Navigating Belongings."

20. Portes and Stepick, *City on the Edge*, 190.

21. Marielitos were met with racism, violence, and xenophobia. Their relationship to Cuban Whiteness, and hence Cuban American "success," is ambivalent at best.

22. Yolanda Martinez-San Miguel argues that "intracolonial migrations" of communities who enter the United States, England, or France with "legal" citizenship as a result of the imperial and colonial power relationships are often missing from studies that address only undocumented migration. Caribbean migrants, in particular, are often excluded from this work, and thus are not accounted for in broader questions of ethnic and race relations. Martínez-San Miguel, *Coloniality of Diasporas*, 2–3.

23. Marielitos and Haitians were seen as deviant, unwanted, and criminal. The Carter administration had criminalized Black Haitians since the 1970s, "subjecting them to a near-blanket detention and deportation." Kristina Shull, "Somos los Abandonados," 3.

24. Immigration and Ethnic History Society, "Cuban Adjustment Act of 1966," *Immigration History*, accessed January 3, 2023, https://immigrationhistory.org/item/cuban-adjustment-act-of-1966/.

25. Beginning with Marielitos and Haitians, detention and denial became the unilateral immigration policy for Caribbean and Latin American asylum seekers. In 1980 and 1981, there were also fifty thousand Haitian immigrants fleeing repressive re-

gimes and attempting to enter the United States. Reviving a 1954 policy that had been abandoned since the closing of New York's Ellis Island, the Reagan administration interdicted boats and placed any undocumented Haitians found "in detention camps in Florida and Arkansas." O'Brien, *Animal Sacrifice and Religious Freedom*.

26. Portes and Puhrmann, "Bifurcated Enclave," 43–44.

27. Frances Robles, "'Marielitos Face Long-Delayed Reckoning: Expulsion to Cuba," *New York Times*, January 14, 2017, https://www.nytimes.com/2017/01/14/us/cuba-us-migrants.html.

28. Laura Parker, "Many Marielitos Languish in Prison as Special Justice Dept. Reviews End," *Washington Post*, June 25, 1991, https://www.washingtonpost.com/archive/politics/1991/06/25/many-marielitos-languish-in-prison-as-special-justice-dept-reviews-end/6e33dbbb-139a-413d-aedb-526508de1172/.

29. Hamm, *Abandoned Ones*, 19–20.

30. Despite gruesome news media depictions of the prison siege as carried out by "wild" criminals wielding homemade "machetes," after the siege was over, there was only one known injury to a hostage between the two complexes. A number of the hostages stated that they had been "warned in advance of the planned insurrection and were told by detainees that they should immediately leave the prison." Hamm, *Abandoned Ones*, 18. The end of the eleven-day rebellion was brokered by the Catholic bishop Agustin Roman, a Mariel detainee advocate who had been outspoken against their indefinite imprisonment. Bishop Roman was brought from Miami to negotiate with the Marielitos (19–20).

31. With freezers full of meat and commissaries still standing, detainees worked in groups to prepare meals while wearing "plastic gloves and caps," offering "enough food to provide three meals a day for detainees and hostages throughout the crisis." Marielito detainees provided hostages with food, medicine, showers, and protection, bringing a "healthful living, safety, stability, and intense playfulness" to what was described as a "riot." Hamm, *Abandoned Ones*, 20.

32. Hamm, *Abandoned Ones*, 20.

33. Robles, "'Marielitos Face Long-Delayed Reckoning."

34. My next book will expand more on a system that arose during the 1980s incentivizing immigrant incarceration, later known as "crimmigration." This approach stitched together criminal and immigration law practices through a series of legislative acts, such as giving Latiné migrants lengthy prison sentences and tethering prisons to immigrant detention. See García Hernández, "Creating Crimmigration"; see also Stumpf, "Crimmigration Crisis," 367.

35. Lee, "'Yellow Peril,'" 537. See also the work of Gina Marchetti, who describes how the "yellow terror" was a colonial metaphor that led to the Chinese Exclusion Act (1882). "Rooted in medieval fears of Genghis Khan and Mongolian invasions of Europe, the trope combines racist terror of alien cultures, sexual anxieties and the belief that the West will be over-powered by the irresistible dark, occult forces of the East." Marchetti, *Romance and the Yellow Peril*, 2.

36. Santa Ana, *Brown Tide Rising*, 73–76.

37. In *Black Skin, White Masks*, Frantz Fanon talks about being "completely dislocated" from himself, and "unmercifully imprisoned" by the White gaze (112).

38. Lennox, "Refugees, Racism, and Reparations."

39. Lennox, "Refugees, Racism, and Reparations," 688.

40. Lennox, "Refugees, Racism, and Reparations," 688.

41. Geggus, *Impact of the Haitian Revolution*.

42. Finch. *Rethinking Slave Rebellion in Cuba*, 22.

43. See Edwards, "Christianity's Role in Colonial and Revolutionary Haiti."

44. See Michel-Rolph Trouillot's, *Haiti: State against Nation*, which documents the disjuncture between how the Caribbean nation and the state formations themselves developed independently as a result of military occupation and colonial interference. The important work of Yarimar Bonilla, "Ordinary Sovereignty," extends this by identifying a false sense of stability given to certain Caribbean sites as they rationalize colonial rule. On the question of colonialism and natural disaster specifically, see the noteworthy contributions of Pinto, "Denaturalizing 'Natural' Disasters," e193; and Bonilla and Marisol LeBrón, *Aftershocks of Disaster*.

45. De Moya, "Protesting the Homeland."

46. Joseph, "Treatment of Haitian Bahamians."

47. Estrella, "Muertos Civiles." See also Hazel, "Sensing Difference"; Aber and Small, "Citizen or Subordinate."

48. Santos-Febres, *Boat People*. See also Grosfoguel, "Race and Ethnicity or Racialized Ethnicities?"

49. My use of the terms *Brown* and *Black* extends beyond their application in identity formations to point to the role of racial color systems in operations of White supremacy. This approach challenges conventional separations of racial categories to emphasize the nuanced interrelations between White, Black, and Brown color lines. It is important to recognize how spectrums of Brownness blur into both Blackness and Whiteness. These color lines are not distinct; rather, they are messy, often shifting among the same bodies and communities. Shades of Black and Brownness, especially "dark Brown," as a way to classify distinct Latiné or Arab groups, reflect the complicated workings of different White supremacies.

Journal Entry. Saturday, September 25, 2021, San Francisco, California

1. We have no relation with my mother's biological family, except for her half brother Tony, who is Black, and with whom she reconnected as an adult. Her mother, a White woman, was abusive to her as a child, and my mother left home at fourteen. Ambiguously racialized (she confirmed later that her father was Filipino), Dolores grew up identifying with the Latiné community in the Mission, where she found a home and family. As a youth, Dolores was an activist involved in anti-imperial politics and revolutionary organizing for liberation struggles in Latin America. She started dancing Afro-Cuban and Afro-Brazilian dance as a teenager, which was how she met my father, who was a drummer in the community. My dad's family welcomed my mom as their own.

2. In 1948, to criminalize the independence movement on the island, US-appointed legislators enacted *La Ley de la Mordaza*, also known as the "Gag Law," banning the display of the Puerto Rican flag. Punishable by up to ten years in jail, it allowed the police to search and seize property in a person's home without a warrant or probable cause.

3. My great-grandfather Armando Reyes y Ortiz was born in Arecibo, Puerto Rico, and my family has been told that his parents or grandparents made their way to Puerto Rico from Havana, Cuba. From conversations with my family and the historical record, I'm unable to verify who Armando's parents were or whether they, or their parents, had come from Cuba. The 1920 US Census shows Armando listed as a "cousin" living with family members at the age of five. His background is a bit of a family mystery, but my grandmother told fond stories about how her father's family had come from Cuba in the late 1800s to work in the rum industry in Puerto Rico. US Census, Year: 1920; Census Place: Islote, Arecibo, Puerto Rico; Roll: T625_2046; Page: 13B; Enumeration District: 188, s.v. "Armando Reyes y Ortiz," Ancestry.com.

4. Many people are not aware that the first Puerto Rican social club in the United States was established in San Francisco on February 25, 1912. El Club Puertorriqueño is also the oldest Latiné cultural club in the United States. Clara Galvano Rivera, "El Club Puertorriqueño de San Francisco," *Centro Voices*, August 8, 2017, https://centropr-archive.hunter.cuny.edu/centrovoices/chronicles/el-club -puertorrique%C3%B1o-de-san-francisco.

Chapter Two. Bodies

1. "Hurricane San Ciriaco," *The World of 1898: The Spanish-American War*, Hispanic Division, Library of Congress, June 22, 2011, https://loc.gov/rr/hispanic/1898 /sanciriaco.html#:~:text=On%20August%208%2C%201899%2C%20Puerto,and%20 property%20damage%20were%20immense.

2. Darde Gamayo, "How the First Puerto Ricans Arrived on Hawai'i Island," *Center for Puerto Rican Studies*, September 14, 2017, https://centropr-archive.hunter.cuny.edu /centrovoices/chronicles/how-first-puerto-ricans-arrived-hawai%E2%80%99i-island.

3. López and Forbes, "Borinki Identity in Hawai'i."

4. Tetsuden, *Judgment without Trial*.

5. My aunt Margaret describes a story Peter Sr. told in which—even though he was not an officer—he described picking up guns and firing at the onslaught during Pearl Harbor.

6. "Electronic Army Serial Number Merged File, 1938–1946," RG 64, Box 00541, Reel 47, National Archives, College Park, MD.

7. Indigenous scholar Jodi Byrd uses the term *arrivants* to signify those Black people violently forced to the Americas through European conquest, slavery, and colonialism, as a way to disrupt the settler-colonial Whitewashing through the false narrative of the immigrant American dream story, which ignores relationships between anti-Blackness and Indigenous genocide. Byrd, *Transit of Empire*, xix.

8. Pistol, "The Historical Presidency."

9. Ted Hesson, "Close to 1,000 Migrant Children Separated by Trump Yet to Be Reunited with Parents," Reuters, February 2, 2023, https://www.reuters.com/world/us

/close-1000-migrant-children-separated-by-trump-yet-be-reunited-with-parents-2023
-02-02/.

10. R. Martinez and Wetli, "Tattoos of the Marielitos."

11. I have chosen not to reproduce the images from "Tattoos of the Marielitos" here so as not to reactivate the dehumanizing depiction of these people's remains. I do not wish to participate in the (re)production of Black and Brown people as specimens.

12. Jones, "Definitions and Categories," 177.

13. In an article I discuss a hieroglyphics of the flesh that emerges from Western scholarship. Beliso-De Jesús, "Hieroglyphics of Zora Neale Hurston."

14. R. Martinez and Wetli, "Tattoos of the Marielitos," 319–20.

15. Martinez and Wetli, "Tattoos of the Marielitos," 319–20.

16. Martinez and Wetli, "Tattoos of the Marielitos," 319–20.

17. See Kelley, "'We Are Not What We Seem.'"

18. R. Martinez and Wetli, "Tattoos of the Marielitos," 315.

19. Peña, "'Obvious Gays,'" 484. See also Hufker and Cavender, "From Freedom Flotilla to America's Burden."

20. Peña, "'Obvious Gays,'" 486. See also Capo, "Queering Mariel," 89.

21. Capo, "Queering Mariel," 89.

22. Peña, "'Obvious Gays,'" 486.

23. Hufker and Cavender, "From Freedom Flotilla to America's Burden," 331.

24. See the great work on the Abakuá society by historian Ivor Miller. I. Miller, "Cuban Abakuá Chants"; I. Miller, *Voice of the Leopard*.

25. Ortiz, "Del fenómeno social de la transculturación."

26. Jemima Pierre shows how White supremacist racist stereotypes of African savagery are used by the International Monetary Fund, the World Bank, and other development entities to justify the underdevelopment of the African continent. Pierre, "The Racial Vernaculars of Development."

27. On the criminalizing of Santeria, Abakuá, and Palo in Cuba, see D. Brown, *Santería Enthroned*. See also R. Román, "Ritual, Discourse, and Community"; and Maguire, *Racial Experiments in Cuban Literature and Ethnography*.

28. R. Martinez and Wetli, "Tattoos of the Marielitos," 318, figure 2.

29. Cuban criminology as a science itself emerged through these evolutionary studies. Afro-Cuban religions were painted as the island's very own dark "underworld," allowing for the disgust and desire to emerge where fantasy and fascination erupted in the theater of White terror. These grotesque displays of White fear circulated in Cuban newspapers and museums as well as through rumor mills and salacious gossip. See Font and Quiroz, *Cuban Counterpoints*. See also Michalowski, *Crime and Justice in Socialist Cuba*; and Fernandez, *Revolutionizing Romance*.

30. See I. Miller, *Voice of the Leopard*, 22.

31. D. Brown, *Santería Enthroned*, 57.

32. Font and Quiroz, *Cuban Counterpoints*, 41.

33. Castellanos, *La brujería y el ñañiguismo en Cuba*.

34. Israel Castellanos, as described in Moore, *Nationalizing Blackness*, 32, accessed at http://www.historyofcuba.com/history/oriente/Castellanos.htm.

35. I. Miller, *Voice of the Leopard*, 24.

36. R. Martinez and Wetli, "Tattoos of the Marielitos," 317. The authors state that they originally discussed the results of table 1's survey in this report to the "Dade/Miami Criminal Justice Council" office in 1986.

37. President's Commission on Organized Crime, *The Impact: Organized Crime Today; Report to the President and the Attorney General* (Washington, DC: Government Printing Office, April 1986), https://babel.hathitrust.org/cgi/pt?id=pur1.32754060288960&view=1up&seq=3/.

38. President's Commission on Organized Crime, *The Impact*, 113–14.

39. President's Commission on Organized Crime, *The Impact*, 113. Emphasis in original.

40. See A. Miller and Damask, "The Dual Myths of 'Narco-Terrorism,'" 128.

41. See "Iran-Contra Affair," History.com, last updated January 17, 2020, https://www.history.com/topics/1980s/iran-contra-affair.

42. See A. Miller and Damask, "Dual Myths of 'Narco-Terrorism,'" 128.

43. Guridy, *Forging Diaspora*, 108.

44. Louis A. Pérez Jr., "Cubans in Tampa." 130.

45. Dylan Rodriguez indicates the use of "different varieties of covert ops, urban guerilla war, and counterintelligence warfare." D. Rodríguez, "Terms of Engagement," 163.

46. D. Rodríguez, "Terms of Engagement," 163.

47. D. Rodríguez, "Terms of Engagement," 158.

48. D. Rodríguez, "Terms of Engagement," 158.

49. See Evelio Grillo, "Black Cuban, Black American," in Román and Flores, *The Afro-Latin@ Reader*, 104.

50. I found another article written by Charles Wetli and Rafael Martinez that was also cited in law-enforcement literature and documents. See Wetli and Martinez, "Brujeria."

51. Abuse of human subjects in scientific research has been widespread, and minority groups have been used as guinea pigs without proper consent. African Americans have been distrustful of research for years, especially since the 1940s Tuskegee syphilis study, which did not offer treatment to its subjects even though penicillin was available. Instead, to "study" the disease, the researchers simply observed as the men in the study deteriorated and died. The legacy of this study and many others has made it difficult for Black people to agree to be subjects of research. Freimuth et al., "African Americans' Views on Research." Throughout the 1940s and 1950s, Puerto Rican women were sterilized without informed consent. Gutiérrez and Fuentes, "Population Control by Sterilization." Research with Indigenous communities has also had a troubling history with informed consent, which has been discussed as a "human rights" issue by scholars. Hanna and Vanclay, "Human Rights, Indigenous Peoples." In Canada, Indigenous groups were studied due to a false hypothesis that saw them as living ancestors for diabetes research. Sarma, Richardson, and Neary, "One Hundred

Years of Solitude." In the United States, the DNA of members of the Havasupai Tribe was used without their consent by Arizona State University researchers. Reardon and TallBear, "'Your DNA Is Our History.'" The improper testing of Aboriginal peoples in schools has also had troubling outcomes. Mosby, "Administering Colonial Science."

Journal Entry. Saturday, October 2, 2021, Antioch, California

1. *Ibaé* is the Lukumi term that honors a priest who has passed into the ancestral realm.

Chapter Three. Murdered

1. Wetli, as quoted in the *Miami News* article in a statement given to reporters. Adrian Walker and Heather Dewar, "Cocaine-Sex Deaths in Dade Probed," *Miami News*, November 24, 1988, https://www.newspapers.com/image/299052298.

2. Walker and Dewar, "Cocaine-Sex Deaths."

3. Walker and Dewar, "Cocaine-Sex Deaths."

4. Walker and Dewar, "Cocaine-Sex Deaths."

5. Walker and Dewar, "Cocaine-Sex Deaths."

6. Walker and Dewar, "Cocaine-Sex Deaths."

7. Keith Harriston and Sally Jenkins, "Maryland Basketball Star Len Bias Is Dead at 22: Traces of Cocaine Found in System," *Washington Post*, June 20, 1986, https://www.washingtonpost.com/wp-srv/sports/longterm/memories/bias/launch/bias1.htm.

8. Walker and Dewar, "Cocaine-Sex Deaths."

9. Walker and Dewar, "Cocaine-Sex Deaths"; Donna Gehrke, "Police Determine a Pattern in Deaths of Dade Women," *Miami Herald*, September 5, 1989.

10. Walker and Dewar, "Cocaine-Sex Deaths."

11. Walker and Dewar, "Cocaine-Sex Deaths."

12. Walker and Dewar, "Cocaine-Sex Deaths."

13. Donna Gehrke, "How Investigation of 32 Deaths Kept Going Astray: As Deaths Rose, Police Denied Serial Killer Lurked," *Miami Herald*, April 27, 1990.

14. Brianna da Silva Bhatia, Michele Heisler, Joanna Naples-Mitchell, Altaf Saadi, and Julia Sherwin. "'Excited Delirium' and Deaths in Police Custody: The Deadly Impact of a Baseless Diagnosis." PHR: Physicians for Human Rights, March 2, 2022. https://phr.org/our-work/resources/excited-delirium/.

15. Owens, *Medical Bondage*, 131; Owens, review of *The Politics of Reproduction*.

16. Morgan, *Laboring Women*, 23.

17. Morgan, *Laboring Women*, 25.

18. Europeans described the "strength" of African women, stating it "was much to be marveled at, for not one of the three men who came upon her but would have had a great labour in attempting to get her to the boat." Morgan notes that the Europeans would use the children to capture mothers: "And so one of our men, seeing the delay they were making, during which it might be that some of the dwellers of the land would

come upon them, conceived it well to take her son from her and to carry him to the boat; and love of the child compelled the mother to follow after it, without great pressure on the part of the two who were bringing her." Morgan, *Laboring Women*, 30–31.

19. Morgan, *Laboring Women*, 25.

20. Kara Grant, "Debunking the 'Excited Delirium' Diagnosis for Deaths in Police Custody: Report Breaks Down How the Term Was Created and Misused for Years," *Med Page Today*, March 3, 2022, https://www.medpagetoday.com/special-reports /exclusives/97491.

21. Lewis, "Culture of Poverty."

22. Harvey and Reed, "Culture of Poverty."

23. E. Anderson, *Streetwise*, 6.

24. E. Anderson, *Streetwise*, 6.

25. Martinez and Wetli, "Tattoos of the Marielitos," 315.

26. Walker and Dewar, "Cocaine-Sex Deaths."

27. See George, "Colored Town."

28. Janey Tate, "A Treasure Map of Gems to Visit in Miami-Dade's Predominately Black Neighborhoods and Cities," *Hylo News Miami*, February 18, 2022, https:// hylonewsmiami.com/2022/02/18/a-treasure-map-of-gems-to-visit-in-miami-dades -predominately-black-neighborhoods-and-cities/.

29. Bea L. Hines, "Martin Luther King Jr. Stayed in This Miami Neighborhood. It Is Now Getting Its Due," *Miami Herald*, May 1, 2020, https://www.miamiherald .com/news/local/community/miami-dade/edison-liberty-city/article242421261 .html#storylink=cpy.

30. Walker and Dewar, "Cocaine-Sex Deaths."

31. Walker and Dewar, "Cocaine-Sex Deaths."

32. Walker and Dewar, "Cocaine-Sex Deaths."

33. Walker and Dewar, "Cocaine-Sex Deaths."

34. "Charles Henry Williams, South Florida Serial Murder during the 1980s, and the Birth of a Modern Police Myth," Reddit, accessed January 7, 2023, https://www .reddit.com/r/LPOTL/comments/n9kwif/extremely_long_writeup_charles_henry _williams/.

35. Gehrke, "How Investigation of 32 Deaths Kept Going Astray."

36. Associated Press, "Rape Suspect Linked to Miami Death," *Gainesville (FL) Sun*, May 17, 1989, https://news.google.com/newspapers?id=VktWAAAAIBAJ&sjid =MeoDAAAAIBAJ&pg=6954%2C6355002.

37. Associated Press, "Rape Suspect."

38. Donna Gehrke, "Dead Women Had Links to a Man Jailed in Two Rapes," *Miami Herald*, September 6, 1989.

39. Donna Gehrke, "Man Suspected in a String of Rapes Indicted for Murder," *Miami Herald*, July 31, 1992.

40. Gehrke, "How Investigation of 32 Deaths Kept Going Astray."

41. Gehrke, "How Investigation of 32 Deaths Kept Going Astray."

42. Gehrke, "How Investigation of 32 Deaths Kept Going Astray."

43. Gehrke, "How Investigation of 32 Deaths Kept Going Astray."

44. Donna Gehrke, "Police Determine a Pattern in Deaths of Dade Women," *Miami Herald*, September 5, 1989.

45. Gehrke, "Police Determine a Pattern in Deaths of Dade Women."

46. Gehrke, "Police Determine a Pattern in Deaths of Dade Women."

47. Da Silva Bhatia et al., "'Excited Delirium' and Deaths."

48. Donna Gehrke, "Both Sides Rest in Williams' Rape Trial," *Miami Herald*, April 27, 1990.

49. Gehrke, "How Investigation of 32 Deaths Kept Going Astray."

50. John Donnelly, "Suspect in Murder of Prostitutes Speaks Out," *Miami Herald*, May 9, 1993.

51. Donnelly, "Suspect in Murder."

52. "Rapist, Murder Suspect Dies of AIDS," *Tampa Bay Times*, September 26, 1994, https://www.tampabay.com/archive/1994/09/26/rapist-murder-suspect-dies-of-aids/.

53. Gamsakhurdia and Kurdiani, "Jezebel Stereotype," 88.

54. McEntire, "Cozbi, Achan, and Jezebel."

55. McEntire, "Cozbi, Achan, and Jezebel."

56. Owens, *Medical Bondage*, 40.

57. H. Washington, *Medical Apartheid*, 61.

58. H. Washington, *Medical Apartheid*, 63.

59. H. Washington, *Medical Apartheid*, 63.

60. H. Washington, *Medical Apartheid*, 63.

61. Williamson, "Why Did They Die?"

62. Willoughby-Herard, "(Political) Anesthesia or (Political) Memory," 264.

63. Taylor, *How We Get Free*, 49.

64. Combahee River Collective, "Six Black Women."

65. Combahee River Collective, "Six Black Women," 45.

66. Combahee River Collective, "Six Black Women," 47.

67. Williamson, "Why Did They Die?," 331.

68. Combahee River Collective, "Six Black Women," 46.

69. Williamson, "Why Did They Die?," 333.

70. Williamson, "Why Did They Die?," 333.

71. Williamson, "Why Did They Die?," 332.

72. Williamson, "Why Did They Die?," 333.

Chapter Four. Manic

1. Miriam Fauzia, "Fact Check: Fentanyl Present in George Floyd's System but Not Enough to Cause His Death, Experts Say," *USA Today*, April 16, 2021, https://www.usatoday.com/story/news/factcheck/2021/04/16/fact-check-fentanyl-george-floyd-not-enough-to-cause-death/7239448002/.

2. Rod Dreher, "Why George Floyd Died," *American Conservative*, August 5, 2020, https://www.theamericanconservative.com/why-george-floyd-died-bodycam/.

3. Steve Karnowski, "Explainer: 'Excited Delirium' and George Floyd," *AP News*, January 26, 2022, https://apnews.com/article/death-of-george-floyd-health-george -floyd-minneapolis-thomas-lane-1c6776d265e6f3c09e32df7039e80720.

4. Karnowski, "Explainer: 'Excited Delirium.'"

5. Joshua Budhu, Méabh O'Hare, and Altaf Saadi, "How 'Excited Delirium' Is Misused to Justify Police Brutality," *Brookings Institute* (blog), August 10, 2020, https:// www.brookings.edu/blog/how-we-rise/2020/08/10/how-excited-delirium-is-misused -to-justify-police-brutality/.

6. See John Elder, "Investigative Update on Critical Incident," Minneapolis Police, May 26, 2020, https://web.archive.org/web/20210331182901/https://www.insidempd .com/2020/05/26/man-dies-after-medical-incident-during-police-interaction/.

7. See Appelbaum, "Excited Delirium, Ketamine, and Deaths in Police Custody"; Kathryn Quinlan, Jess Palan, Sarah Murtada, and Christiane Dos Santos, "Excited Delirium: The Connection between George Floyd and Elijah McClain," *Bloomberg Law*, March 23, 2021, https://news.bloomberglaw.com/us-law-week/excited-delirium -the-connection-between-george-floyd-and-elijah-mcclain.

8. News articles have revealed the truth about excited delirium syndrome. See, for example, CBS Colorado, "'Excited Delirium': Elijah McClain's Mother Talks to *60 Minutes* about Use of Ketamine to Sedate Suspects," *CBS News*, December 14, 2020, https://www.cbsnews.com/colorado/news/excited-delirium-elijah-mcclain-60 -minutes-ketamine-sedate-suspects/.

9. "How a Questionable Syndrome, 'Excited Delirium,' Could Be Protecting Police Officers from Misconduct Charges," *CBS News*, December 13, 2020, https://www.cbsnews .com/video/excited-delirium-police-custody-george-floyd-60-minutes-2020–12–13/.

10. Henderson, "Forgotten Meta-realities of Modernism," 2.

11. David A. Fishbain, a professor of psychiatry and behavioral sciences and an adjunct professor of neurological surgery and anesthesiology at the University of Miami School of Medicine, has also worked at the Rosomoff Comprehensive Pain and Rehabilitation Center in Miami, Florida. Fishbain has published on chronic pain treatments such as opioids and has been the editor of several medical journals. He is listed as the "psychiatric editor" for *Current Pain and Headache Reports* and *Pain Medicine News* and was the chair of the American Pain Society (APS) Scientific Program Committee. In Florida he served on the Pain Management Commission. "Dr. David A. Fishbain, M.D.," *WebMD Care*, accessed January 7, 2023, https://doctor.webmd.com /doctor/david-fishbain-9c9633dc-bc9e-4281-b06a-78b6ad37e6bc-overview.

12. See both articles by David Fishbain and Charles V. Wetli: the first, published in 1981, "Cocaine-Induced Psychosis and Sudden Death in Recreational Cocaine Users"; and the second, published in 1985, "Cocaine Intoxication, Delirium, and Death in a Body Packer."

13. Fishbain and Wetli, "Cocaine-Induced Psychosis and Sudden Death."

14. Gus Garcia-Roberts, "Is Excited Delirium Killing Coked-Up, Stun-Gunned Miamians?," *Miami New Times*, July 15, 2010, https://www.miaminewtimes.com/news /is-excited-delirium-killing-coked-up-stun-gunned-miamians-6367399.

15. Garcia-Roberts, "Is Excited Delirium Killing Coked-Up, Stun-Gunned Miamians?"

16. Garcia-Roberts, "Is Excited Delirium Killing Coked-Up, Stun-Gunned Miamians?"

17. Shields, Rolf, and Hunsaker, "Sudden Death Due to Acute Cocaine Toxicity," 1647.

18. Shortt, "Physicians and Psychics," 342.

19. Shortt, "Physicians and Psychics," 342 (emphasis added).

20. Shortt, "Physicians and Psychics," 349.

21. Shortt, "Physicians and Psychics," 346.

22. Shortt, "Physicians and Psychics," 343.

23. Shortt, "Physicians and Psychics," 343.

24. Shortt, "Physicians and Psychics," 346.

25. Shortt, "Physicians and Psychics," 346.

26. Shortt, "Physicians and Psychics," 349.

27. Dyson, "Spiritualism and Crime," 2–3.

28. Dyson, "Spiritualism and Crime," 2–3.

29. Shott, "Physicians and Psychics," 354.

30. Shott, "Physicians and Psychics," 353–54.

31. Shott, "Physicians and Psychics," 354–55.

32. Ortiz, *El hampa Afro-Cubana*, 241.

33. Ruttenber, McAnally, and Wetli, "Cocaine-Associated Rhabdomyolysis and Excited Delirium." See also, Ruttenber et al., "Fatal Excited Delirium following Cocaine Use." Charles Wetli was one of this article's coauthors.

34. Wetli, Mash, and Karch, "Cocaine-Associated Agitated Delirium," 427.

35. Wetli, Mash, and Karch, "Cocaine-Associated Agitated Delirium," 427.

36. See Jenkins, *Keeping the Peace*.

37. Carstairs, "'Most Dangerous Drug,'" 47.

38. Carstairs, "'Most Dangerous Drug,'" 46.

39. Prohibitionists in the South also "used the image of the drunken 'negro,' violent and lascivious, to promote the banning of alcohol." Carstairs, "'Most Dangerous Drug,'" 47.

40. Edward Huntington Williams, "Negro Cocaine 'Fiends' Are a New Southern Menace; Murder and Insanity Increasing among Lower Class Blacks because They Have Taken to 'Sniffing' since Deprived of Whisky by Prohibition," *New York Times*, February 8, 1914, https://www.nytimes.com/1914/02/08/archives/negro-cocaine -fiends-are-a-new-southern-menace-murder-and-insanity.html (emphasis in original).

41. The article took up a full page, in which the author, Dr. Edward Huntington Williams, whose accompanying image showed him as a stern, "respectable-looking" White male doctor. Catherine Carstairs, "'Most Dangerous Drug,'" 46.

42. Williams, "Negro Cocaine 'Fiends'" (emphasis in original).

43. Williams, "Negro Cocaine 'Fiends'" (emphasis in original).

44. Ida B. Wells, *Southern Horrors: The Ku Klux Klan*, 1892, pamphlet accessed via Encyclopedia.com, August 22, 2023, https://www.encyclopedia.com/politics/energy -government-and-defense-magazines/southern-horrors.

45. Crystal Feimster, "Ida B. Wells and the Lynching of Black Women," *New York Times*, April 28, 2018, https://www.nytimes.com/2018/04/28/opinion/sunday/ida-b -wells-lynching-black-women.html

46. Feimster, "Ida B. Wells."

47. Wells found that only about 30 percent of lynching victims had actually been accused of rape. Even in those cases, we know that the lynchings were not about punishment for any actual crimes, but rather a force of terror that was meant to reverberate across the United States to reaffirm White supremacy.

48. See A. Wood, *Lynching and Spectacle.*

49. A. Wood, *Lynching and Spectacle*, 3–4.

50. Wetli, Mash, and Karch, "Cocaine-Associated Agitated Delirium," 425.

51. Wetli, Mash, and Karch, "Cocaine-Associated Agitated Delirium," 425.

52. Wetli, Mash, and Karch, "Cocaine-Associated Agitated Delirium," 427–28.

53. Wetli, Mash, and Karch, "Cocaine-Associated Agitated Delirium," 425.

54. Wetli, Mash, and Karch, "Cocaine-Associated Agitated Delirium," 425.

55. Wetli, Mash, and Karch, "Cocaine-Associated Agitated Delirium," 425.

56. Wetli, Mash, and Karch, "Cocaine-Associated Agitated Delirium," 427.

57. Wetli, Mash, and Karch, "Cocaine-Associated Agitated Delirium," 427.

58. Metzl, *The Protest Psychosis*, xix.

59. See Dána-Ain Davis's excellent work on racial science research and premature birth as a means to document the "inherent" biological differences between Whites and Black Americans. D.-A. Davis, *Reproductive Injustice*, 38, 106–7.

60. See Erickson, "George Clinton and David Bowie," 13n12.

61. Erickson, "George Clinton and David Bowie," 13n12.

62. Wolff, "Myth of the Actuary," 85.

63. Cooper, "Are Culture-Bound Syndromes as Real as Universally-Occurring Disorders?"

64. Myatt and Roberts, "Preeclampsia."

Chapter Five. Panicked

1. Daniel Burke, "Pope Francis Canonizes Controversial Saint Serra," CNN, September 23, 2015, https://www.cnn.com/2015/09/23/us/pope-junipero-serra -canonization/index.html.

2. Steve Huff, "After 44 Years, DNA Solved the Satanic Murder of Arlis Perry. Was She the Only Victim?," Inside Hook, July 5, 2018, https://www.insidehook.com/article /crime/44-years-dna-solved-satanic-murder-arlis-perry-victim.

3. Joseph A. Taylor, "Memorial Church History Stanford University, Office for Religious and Spiritual Life, accessed August 28, 2023, https://orsl.stanford.edu/who-we-are /memorial-church-companion-spaces/memorial-church-details/memorial-church-history.

4. Huff, "After 44 Years."

5. Robert Salonga, "Stanford Church Slaying Suspect Was Likely Considering Suicide for Two Years," *Mercury News* (San Jose, CA), June 29, 2018, https://www

.mercurynews.com/2018/06/29/stanford-church-slaying-suspect-was-likely-plotting
-suicide-for-two-years/.

6. *Palo Alto Weekly* Staff, "Sheriff: Grisly 1974 Stanford Murder Solved: Family of Arlis Perry Still Question Why 19-Year-Old Woman Was Murdered," *Palo Alto Weekly*, June 29, 2018, https://www.paloaltoonline.com/news/2018/06/28/suspect-in-grisly -stanford-memorial-church-murder-kills-self.

7. *Palo Alto Weekly* Staff, "Sheriff: Grisly 1974 Stanford Murder."

8. *Palo Alto Weekly* Staff, "Sheriff: Grisly 1974 Stanford Murder."

9. *Palo Alto Weekly* Staff, "Sheriff: Grisly 1974 Stanford Murder."

10. *Palo Alto Weekly* Staff, "Sheriff: Grisly 1974 Stanford Murder."

11. Salonga, "Stanford Church Slaying Suspect."

12. *Palo Alto Weekly* Staff, "Sheriff: Grisly 1974 Stanford Murder"; Salonga, "Stanford Church Slaying Suspect"; Huff, "After 44 Years."

13. *Palo Alto Weekly* Staff, "Sheriff: Grisly 1974 Stanford Murder."

14. Salonga, "Stanford Church Slaying Suspect"; Huff, "After 44 Years."

15. Salonga, "Stanford Church Slaying Suspect"; Huff, "After 44 Years."

16. "Sheriff Investigating Whether Stanford Watchman Linked to Other Campus Murders: Three Cases from Early 1970s Remain Unsolved," *Palo Alto Online*, July 3, 2018, https://paloaltoonline.com/news/2018/07/03/sheriff-investigating-whether -stanford-watchman-linked-to-other-campus-murders.

17. Brent Swancer, "A Headless Corpse, Black Magic, and an Unsolved Occult Murder in San Francisco," Mysterious Universe, October 10, 2019, https:// mysteriousuniverse.org/2019/10/a-headless-corpse-black-magic-and-an-unsolved -occult-murder-in-san-francisco/.

18. "'Looking Back': Alvord Lake," *Richmond Review / Sunset Beacon* (San Francisco), August 3, 2022, https://sfrichmondreview.com/2022/08/03/looking-back -alford-lake/.

19. "Decapitated Body Found in SF Park," *Santa Cruz Sentinel*, February 9, 1981.

20. "Beheading Baffles Police," *Journal and Courier* (Lafayette, IN), February 9, 1981.

21. "A Headless Body of a Man, Suspected to be Killed during a Ritual, Is Found." Horror History.net, February 8, 2020. https://horrorhistory.net/2020/02/08/a -headless-body-of-a-man-suspected-to-be-killed-during-a-ritual-is-found/.

22. "A Headless Body of a Man."

23. "A Headless Body of a Man."

24. C. J. Lynch, "The Unsolved: Leroy Carter Jr." Morbid Library, August 16, 2020, https://themorbidlibrary.com/2020/08/16/the-unsolved-leroy-carter-jr/.

25. Lynch, "The Unsolved: Leroy Carter Jr."

26. Lynch, "The Unsolved: Leroy Carter Jr."

27. Lynch, "The Unsolved: Leroy Carter Jr."

28. "The Murders of Arlis Perry, Leslie Perlov and Janet Taylor," *Talk Murder with Me* (blog), February 23, 2022, https://www.talkmurderwithme.com/blog/2022/2/23 /arlis-perry-murder.

29. Cited In Martinez and Wetli, "Tattoos of the Marielitos," 317.

30. White fears about Haiti's successful Black slave revolution (1791–1804) reverberated across the Caribbean (McAlister, *Rara!*). See Kate Ramsey's *The Spirits and the Law* for a discussion of how stories that the Haitian Revolution was born out of a Vodou ceremony brought fear to White rulers and violence to Black religions, which were subsequently punished by the world.

31. Wilkinson, *Detective Fiction*, 87.

32. I. Miller, *Voice of the Leopard*, 25.

33. Pappademos, "Cuban Race War of 1912."

34. I. Miller, *Voice of the Leopard*, 25. Worth noting here is the blood libel legend, used against Jews for the past thousand years, which claimed that they consumed the blood of Christian children as a Passover ritual. These stories justified many massacres of Jews. See Berenson, *The Accusation*.

35. Bronfman, "'En Plena Libertad y Democracia.'"

36. Bronfman, "'En Plena Libertad y Democracia.'"

37. Wilkinson, *Detective Fiction*, 87.

38. Helg, *Our Rightful Share*, 10–11.

39. Pappademos, "Cuban Race War of 1912," 258.

40. Associated Press, "Voodoo Evidence of Cult found in Florida," *Burlington (VT) Daily Times News*, June 25, 1980, 10 (emphasis added).

41. The twenty-five-minute *Roving Report* episodes consisted of a series of documentary-style news reports that were featured on ITN. Wetli was interviewed for the October 1981 episode. The archive of the episode can be found at https://www.youtube.com/watch?v=xTf6QYbrE90.

42. Associated Press, "Voodoo Evidence of Cult found in Florida," 10 (emphasis added).

43. Dianne Klein, "Satan Sleuths: Once Scoffed at by Peers, Police Experts in Occult Crime Now Are Frighteningly in Demand," *Los Angeles Times*, May 25, 1989, https://www.latimes.com/archives/la-xpm-1989-05-25-vw-676-story.html.

44. Klein, "Satan Sleuths."

45. Klein, "Satan Sleuths."

46. Weisenfeld, *New World A-Coming*, 183.

47. Weisenfeld, *New World A-Coming*, 183. Weisenfeld notes that in the 1960s and 1970s, groups such as the Children of God, the Divine Light Mission, the Unification Church, and the International Society of Krishna Consciousness were attracting young, middle-class Whites to a degree that generated a cultural panic and motivated the application of theories of brainwashing (183). This was a panic about the influence of Asian religions in the United States, although the Children of God emerged from the Jesus people movement (65, 75). See also Sean McCloud's work *Making the American Religious Fringe*.

48. Frankfurter, *Evil Incarnate*, 8.

49. Andersen, *Fantasyland*, 330.

50. Andersen, *Fantasyland*, 330.

51. In 1988, *The Courage to Heal: A Guide for Women Survivors of Child Sexual Abuse*, by self-help poet Ellen Bass and Laura Davis, was published and further con-

vinced people that, even if a person had no memories of such abuse but was dealing with mental health issues as an adult, it was likely that the person was the victim of rape or molestation as a child. Much of this literature framed Satanism and "the occult" as a "new police problem" and would espouse conspiracy theories. See Bass and Davis, *The Courage to Heal*.

52. Andersen, *Fantasyland*, 331.

53. Andersen, *Fantasyland*, 327.

54. Andersen, *Fantasyland*, 327.

55. Bucky and Dalenberg, "Relationship between Training."

56. Bucky and Dalenberg, "Relationship between Training," 237.

57. Bucky and Dalenberg, "Relationship between Training," 237.

58. Anderson, *Fantasyland*, 336.

59. Andersen, *Fantasyland*, 336.

60. Hicks, *In Pursuit of Satan*, loc. 111 of 5994, Kindle.

61. Hicks, *In Pursuit of Satan*, loc. 111 of 5994, Kindle.

62. Andersen, *Fantasyland*, 331.

63. Andersen, *Fantasyland*, 331.

64. Ric Leyva, "'Blaming the Devil' Hurts Prosecution of Child Abuse," *AP News*, December 8, 1987, https://apnews.com/article/27f38f89f34f6831b6ddeccfd29bbf60.

65. Andersen, *Fantasyland*, 331.

66. Andersen, *Fantasyland*, 331.

67. Andersen, *Fantasyland*, 331.

68. Andersen, *Fantasyland*, 336.

69. Leyva, "'Blaming the Devil.'"

70. Hicks, *In Pursuit of Satan*, loc. 156–57 of 5994, Kindle.

71. This is based on interviews with police officers who took the courses, as well as on discussions with Rafael Martinez and others who participated in and conducted these trainings.

72. Hicks, *In Pursuit of Satan*, loc. 28 of 5994, Kindle.

73. Hicks, *In Pursuit of Satan*, loc. 161–62 of 5994, Kindle.

74. Hicks, *In Pursuit of Satan*, loc. 106 of 5994, Kindle.

75. Hicks, *In Pursuit of Satan*, loc. 156–57 of 5994, Kindle.

76. Hicks, *In Pursuit of Satan*, loc. 173–74 of 5994, Kindle.

77. Hicks, *In Pursuit of Satan*, loc. 173–74 of 5994, Kindle.

78. Andersen, *Fantasyland*, 336.

79. To fight this perceived menace, "people have banded together to influence the legislative process in Virginia, Idaho, Texas, Illinois, and other states to enact laws or modify criminal codes." Hicks, *In Pursuit of Satan*, loc. 34 of 5994, Kindle.

80. Nephew, "Playing with Power," 144.

81. Gayland W. Hurst and Robert L. Marsh, *Satanic Cult Awareness*, report presented to the National Criminal Justice Reference Service, US Department of Justice, National Institute of Justice, https://pdf4pro.com/amp/view/satanic-cult-awareness -office-of-justice-programs-708f86.html, 8–10. The report's acknowledgments read

as follows: "This training manual is the result of compiling information from several years of occult investigations including volumes of written documentations from several investigators across the nation. We take this opportunity to express our gratitude, and give recognition to the following persons and organizations for the information and documentation they provided. Dale Griffis, Ph.D.—Tiffin, Ohio P.D.; Detective Sandi Gallant Daly—San Francisco P.D.; Lt. Larry Hones—Boise, Idaho P.D.; Sgt. J. Hill—San Diego P.D.; Kurt Jackson—Beaumont, California P.D.; Gary Bradford and Jim Craig—U.S. Defense Investigative Service."

82. Grappo, "'Four Lives Lost,'" 8.

83. Grappo, "'Four Lives Lost,'" 8.

84. Grappo, "'Four Lives Lost,'" 6.

85. Joey Palacios, "'San Antonio Four' Exonerated in Child Sexual Assault Case," Texas Public Radio, December 3, 2018, https://www.tpr.org/san-antonio/2018-12-03/san-antonio-four-exonerated-in-child-sexual-assault-case.

86. Grappo, "'Four Lives Lost,'" 14.

87. See DeYoung, "Another Look at Moral Panics"; Gough, "Another Man's Memories"; Soto-Vásquez and Sánchez-Santos, "El Cabal, Vacunas, y Donald Trump."

88. Brandon, "Sacrificial Practices in Santeria," 136.

Journal Entry. Friday, December 17, 2021, Stanford, California

1. "The warriors" consist of the orisha Elegua, Ogun, Ochosi, and Osun. They are a team of spiritual copresences who protect people on the road of life. The warriors are considered your feet; they guide you, protect you, and keep away enemies.

Chapter Six. Tormented

1. California Office of Criminal Justice Planning and Olson-Raymer, "Occult Crime," 34.

2. Office of Criminal Justice Planning and Olson-Raymer, "Occult Crime," 34.

3. Wetli, Foreword, xiii.

4. Wetli, Foreword, xiii.

5. Wetli, Foreword, xiii.

6. Wetli, Foreword, xiii.

7. Wetli, Foreword, xiii.

8. O'Brien, *Animal Sacrifice*, 34.

9. O'Brien, *Animal Sacrifice*, 34.

10. O'Brien, *Animal Sacrifice*, 34.

11. O'Brien, *Animal Sacrifice*, 43.

12. O'Brien, *Animal Sacrifice*, 44.

13. O'Brien, *Animal Sacrifice*, 44.

14. O'Brien, *Animal Sacrifice*, 44.

15. O'Brien, *Animal Sacrifice*, 44.

16. Holzer, "Contradictions Will Out," 83, 85.

17. Catherine Wilson, "Church Argues for Animal Sacrifices," *Panama City (FL) News Herald*, August 4, 1989.

18. O'Brien, *Animal Sacrifice*, 83.

19. O'Brien, *Animal Sacrifice*, 84.

20. O'Brien, *Animal Sacrifice*, 85.

21. O'Brien, *Animal Sacrifice*, 85.

22. O'Brien, *Animal Sacrifice*, 85.

23. O'Brien, *Animal Sacrifice*, 82.

24. O'Brien, *Animal Sacrifice*, 89.

25. O'Brien, *Animal Sacrifice*, 90.

26. O'Brien, *Animal Sacrifice*, 92.

27. O'Brien, *Animal Sacrifice*, 93.

28. O'Brien, *Animal Sacrifice*, 93.

29. O'Brien, *Animal Sacrifice*, 93.

30. Wetli, Mash, and Karch, "Cocaine-Associated Agitated Delirium," 427–28.

31. Wetli, Foreword, xii.

32. Through ancestral data, I found that Wetli's grandmother Alberta Carveax Erschens (also spelled Urschens) was also born in Wisconsin; her mother was born in Germany, and her father, Peter Erschens, was born in Wisconsin. Both of Peter Erschens's parents were born in Germany. US Census, Year: 1930; Census Place: Green Bay, Brown County, Wisconsin; Page 2A; Enumeration district: 0026, s.v. "Alberta Carveax Erschens," Ancestry.com.

33. Most of Charles Victor Wetli's family members were buried in the Allouez Catholic Cemetery and Chapel Mausoleum in Green Bay, Wisconsin. "Marie C. Berendson Wetli," Find a Grave, accessed August 29, 20223, https://www.findagrave .com/memorial/169132252/marie-c-wetli.

34. "Earl Park Farmer Dies at Hospital," *Lafayette (IN) Journal and Courier*, October 9, 1926, https://www.newspapers.com/image/261984574.

35. "Mrs. Wetli Dies; Services Friday," *Green Bay (WI) Press-Gazette*, March 3, 1954, 40, https://www.newspapers.com/clip/113431005/obituary-for-marie-c-wetli/.

36. "Mrs. Wetli Dies."

37. "Mrs. Wetli Dies."

38. From the 1962 University of Notre Dame yearbook, in *U.S. School Yearbooks, 1880–2012*.

39. "Wetli, Brother Elred," *Green Bay (WI) Press-Gazette*, August 2, 2009, 10, https://www.newspapers.com/clip/113280272/obituary-for-elred-wetli/.

40. David Dell, "Elred Wetli: Memorial Statue in Volcan," YourPanama.com, accessed August 29, 2023, https://www.yourpanama.com/wetli-statue.html.

41. Dell, "Elred Wetli: Memorial Statue in Volcan."

42. Dell, "Elred Wetli: Memorial Statue in Volcan."

43. Dell, "Elred Wetli: Memorial Statue in Volcan."

44. There are two similar orders of Christian Brothers: one was started in France by the priest Jean Baptiste de la Salle at Rouen in 1684 and has been prominent in educational works of all kinds throughout the world since the eighteenth century; the second was started in the early 1800s in Ireland, by Edmund Rice, a wealthy businessman. See Coldrey, "'Strange Mixture,'" 346.

45. "The Congregation of Christian Brothers: Christian Brothers of Ireland," BBC, February 12, 2009, https://www.bbc.co.uk/religion/religions/christianity/priests/christianbrothers.shtml.

46. Coldrey, "'Strange Mixture,'" 346.

47. Charlotte King, "Celibacy, Order and Obedience: Inside the Christian Brothers," *Earshot*, October 3, 2019, https://www.abc.net.au/news/2019–10–04/life-inside-the-christian-brothers-religious-order/11500746.

48. King, "Celibacy, Order and Obedience."

49. US Department of State, Office of International Religious Freedom, *2021 Report on International Religious Freedom: Cuba.*

50. See "Cuban Santeria Practices," Anywhere Cuba, accessed January 3, 2023, https://www.anywhere.com/cuba/travel-guide/santeria; also José Jasán Nieves, "The Catholic Church in Cuba." *OnCuba News*, October 1, 2015, https://oncubanews.com/en/styles-trends/technologies-of-communication-and-media/the-catholic-church-in-cuba/.

51. Larry Rohter, "Pope Carries Message to the 'Rome' of a Cuban Cult," *New York Times*, January 25, 1998, https://archive.nytimes.com/www.nytimes.com/library/world/012598pope-santeria.html.

52. Rohter, "Pope Carries Message."

53. Sandoval, "Santeria."

54. Lefley, Review of *Santeria* (1977); and Lefley, Review of *Santeria* (reprinted 1979).

55. Lefley, Review of *Santeria* (1979 reprint), 94.

56. Lefley, Review of *Santeria* (1979 reprint), 94.

57. As Lee Baker has noted, however, Boas's push for immigrant assimilation in the United States still had its own entrenched racist undertones. Baker, "The Racist Antiracism of American Anthropology."

58. Shull, "Somos los Abandonados," 2.

59. Shank, "Social Justice."

60. Boullosa and Wallace, "How the Cartels Were Born."

61. Boullosa and Wallace, "How the Cartels Were Born."

62. "Mexican and U.S. Authorities Discover Tunnel That Connected Matamoros and Brownsville," *El Universal*, August 27, 2020, https://www.eluniversal.com.mx/english/mexican-and-us-authorities-discover-tunnel-connected-matamoros-and-brownsville.

63. Marco Margaritoff, "Inside the Gruesome Murder of Mark Kilroy at the Hands of a Satanic Cult," All That's Interesting, July 22, 2021, https://allthatsinteresting.com/mark-kilroy.

64. O'Brien, *Animal Sacrifice*, 20.

65. Nicholas Sammond discusses minstrelsy as the performance of an imagined Blackness, in which White racist fantasies are embodied. Sammond, *Birth of an Industry.*

66. Bergen-Cico, *War and Drugs*.

67. Associated Press, "Leader in Cult Slayings Ordered Own Death, Two Companions Say," *New York Times*, May 8, 1989, https://www.nytimes.com/1989/05/08/us/leader-in-cult-slayings-ordered-own-death-two-companions-say.html.

68. Associated Press, "Leader in Cult Slayings."

69. "What Happened to the Host of *El Show de Cristina*, an Important Icon of Hispanic TV?," *News Glory*, April 20, 2022, https://thenewsglory.com/what-happened-to-the-host-of-el-show-de-cristina-an-important-icon-of-hispanic-tv/.

70. Charles Wetli and Rafael Martinez, *Palo Mayombe*, Division of Criminal Investigation, Investigative Analysis Bureau, Florida Department of Law Enforcement, September 1989, 1.

71. Wetli and Martinez, *Palo Mayombe*, 1.

72. Wetli and Martinez, *Palo Mayombe*, 4.

73. Baartman's body was displayed in France at the Musée de l'Homme until the early 1970s. Youé, "Sara Baartman," 559.

74. Youé, "Sara Baartman," 561.

75. Winburn, Martinez, and Schoff, "Afro-Cuban Ritual Use," 1, 23.

76. Winburn, Martinez, and Schoff, "Afro-Cuban Ritual Use," 23.

77. Winburn, Martinez, and Schoff, "Afro-Cuban Ritual Use," 23 (emphasis added).

78. Beliso-De Jesús and Pierre, "Anthropology of White Supremacy."

Journal Entry. Wednesday, March 16, 2022, Stanford, California

1. Christina Sharpe argues that slave ships "were more than floating tombs. They were floating laboratories, offering researchers a chance to examine the course of diseases in fairly controlled, quarantined environments." Sharpe, *In the Wake*, 50.

2. Park, Konge, and Artino, "Positivism Paradigm of Research."

Chapter Seven. Brutalized

1. Ralph, *Torture Letters*.

2. Franke, "Law," 172.

3. Spillers argues that the depiction of the suffering Black body has itself become a kind of "trope," a figure of sadistic delight that involves the denigration of Black people for White viewing pleasure. Hortense Spillers, as cited in Weheliye, "Pornotropes," 71.

4. "Strange Fruit," composed by Abel Meeropol, is Billie Holiday's 1939 protest song about lynching, describing Black men hanging from trees. See also the work of Nicholas Villanueva, who examines the lynching of Mexicans after the Anglo push to take over the US Southwest following the 1848 Treaty of Guadalupe Hidalgo. Villanueva, *Lynching of Mexicans*; Carrigan and Webb, "Lynching of Persons of Mexican Origin."

5. Alexander Weheliye identifies the sadistic pleasure of viewing slavery films, which display gory scenes of whippings and beatings, as part of this titillating pleasure of witnessing Black suffering. Weheliye, "Pornotropes," 71.

6. Franke, "Law," 172. See also, Laurence Ralph's "Alibi," which argues that neither Abner Louima nor Rodney King's assaults were exceptional. Ralph, "Alibi," 248.

7. Franke, "Law," 172. Policing has been linked to a "cult of masculinity," in which sexual violence and police brutality go hand in hand (Silvestri, "Police Culture and Gender"; and Purvis and Blanco, "Police Sexual Violence"). For example, police are known to display militarized masculinity at home and to engage in domestic violence (Goodmark, "Hands Up at Home"). This is often thought to be part of a "warrior" mentality and to reflect the role of US gun violence (Carlson, "Police Warriors and Police Guardians"). I saw this in my own work, with police trained to embody White supremacy in the force (Beliso-De Jesús, "Jungle Academy").

8. McCarthy Brown, "Making Wanga," 233.

9. Johnnie Cochran and Peter Neufeld, redacted memorandum, November 20, 1997. Cochran and Neufeld were two of Louima's attorneys. They wrote the memo after meeting privately with Officer Tommy Wiese's counsel. In the meeting, Wiese's lawyers provide their client's version of events. Original documents from the case can be found on the Smoking Gun. See "The Abner Louima Torture Case," Smoking Gun, April 6, 1999, https://www.thesmokinggun.com/documents/crime/abner-louima-torture-case-0.

10. Later it was claimed that Louima's cousin may have hit Volpe. This claim was used to justify the purported resemblance.

11. Cochran and Neufeld memorandum, November 20, 1997, 2.

12. Initially it was thought that Volpe assaulted Louima with a plunger handle.

13. Bernard Ryan Jr. And Michael Butgan, "Justin A. Volpe et al. Trials: 1999 and 2000," Encyclopedia.com, https://www.encyclopedia.com/law/law-magazines/justin-volpe-et-al-trials-1999-2000.

14. McCarthy Brown, "Making Wanga," 234.

15. McCarthy Brown, "Making Wanga," 234

16. McCarthy Brown, "Making Wanga," 234.

17. Ryan and Butgan, "Justin A. Volpe et al. Trials."

18. Ryan and Butgan, "Justin A. Volpe et al. Trials."

19. Special Agent Richard J. Defilippo and Michael S. Craft, transcript of interview with Thomas Bruder, November 8, 1997, p. 2, New York Office of the Federal Bureau of Investigation, Brooklyn, NY. The document can be accessed via "The Abner Louima Case," Smoking Gun, https://www.thesmokinggun.com/file/bruder-implicates-volpe-fbi-interview.

20. Defilippo and Craft, transcript of interview with Thomas Bruder, 3, 7. In Bruder's account, a Black off-duty officer identified himself to Officer Volpe at the nightclub, but they began fighting. Officer Bruder allegedly told Volpe to "collar him or let's go," referring to arresting the Black officer, but Volpe was already fighting with the man.

21. McCarthy Brown, "Making Wanga," 237.

22. Peter Noel, "Police Brutality and Voodoo Justice," Village Voice, June 13, 2000, https://www.villagevoice.com/2000/06/13/police-brutality-and-voodoo-justice/.

23. Noel, "Police Brutality."

24. McCarthy Brown, "Making Wanga," 237.

25. James Ridgway de Szigethy, "A Christmas Murder in Hollywood," American Mafia, December 2003, http://www.americanmafia.com/feature_articles_256.html.

26. "Noel, "Police Brutality."

27. "Noel, "Police Brutality."

28. "Noel, "Police Brutality."

29. "Noel, "Police Brutality."

30. De Szigethy, "A Christmas Murder."

31. De Szigethy, "A Christmas Murder."

32. Lipman, "'The Fish Trusts the Water.'"

33. See García Hernández, "Creating Crimmigration," 1457.

34. Stepick and Joubert, "We Don't Want No Goddamn Black Refugees!"

35. O'Brien, *Animal Sacrifice*, 74.

36. US Citizenship and Immigration Services, "Overview of INS History."

37. O'Brien, *Animal Sacrifice*, 75.

38. O'Brien, *Animal Sacrifice*, 75.

39. Lipman, "'The Fish Trusts the Water,'" 133. See also UPI, "Around the World; U.S. Official Finds No Repression in Haiti," *New York Times*, April 3, 1982, https://www.nytimes.com/1982/04/03/world/around-the-world-us-official-finds-no-repression-in-haiti.html.

40. Ramsey, *Spirits and the Law*.

41. During the US occupation of Haiti (1915–34), Marines tried to suppress Vodou through violence and propaganda. See Boaz, *Banning Black Gods*, 4.

42. Farmer, "Anthropology of Structural Violence."

43. Pierre, "Growing Up Haitian," 3.

44. Farmer, "Anthropology of Structural Violence," 316.

45. Ioanide, "Story of Abner Louima," 8.

46. Ioanide, "Story of Abner Louima," 8.

47. Ioanide, "Story of Abner Louima," 8.

48. Nyong'o, "'I've Got You,'" 46.

49. Nyong'o, "'I've Got You,'" 11–12.

50. Franke, "Law," 171.

51. Franke, "Law," 171.

52. See Rosen, *Terror in the Heart of Freedom*; Museus and Truong, "Racism and Sexism in Cyberspace"; Meyer, *Violent Differences*; D. Perkins, "50 Shades of Slavery."

53. Ioanide, "Story of Abner Louima," 7.

54. Ioanide, "Story of Abner Louima," 7.

55. Ioanide, "Story of Abner Louima," 18.

56. In her important book *Lose Your Mother*, Black feminist Saidiya Hartman discusses the "afterlife of slavery," asking when it might be eradicated and what to do with the "future of the ex-slave." Hartman, *Lose Your Mother*, 45. Afro–Puerto Rican scholar Yomaira Figueroa responds with a decolonial feminism, showing us how intergenerational politics and the relationality of women of color "unseat coloniality in its variant iterations." Figueroa, "After the Hurricane," 220. Indigenous scholars

George J. Sefa Dei and Cristina Jaimungal have called for Indigenous spiritualities as a form of decolonial resistance to colonial relations and White supremacy. Sefa Dei and Jaimungal, *Indigeneity and Decolonial Resistance*. And John Márquez and Junaid Rana see the possibility for Black radical potentials in a "decolonial international." Márquez and Rana, "Black Radical Possibility."

57. McCarthy Brown, "Making Wanga," 241–42.

58. For the logic of the slave patrol and the myth of Black predatory violence in the use of police shootings, see Ralph, "Logic of the Slave Patrol." On the justification for White violence, see Coates, "Case for Reparations." Jeremi Duru looked at how this myth operated in the incarceration of the innocent Central Park Five, who were demonized as rapists. Duru, "Central Park Five," 1315.

59. Sherene Razack identifies similar tropes used in police killings of Indigenous people, showing how fear is mobilized in settler colonial narratives of violence. Razack discusses the killing of Loreal Tsingine, a twenty-seven-year-old Navajo woman who was shot and killed by police on March 27, 2014. The officer said he "felt a fear and a threat" that justified the shooting. Razack, "Settler Colonialism," 1.

60. Associated Press, "George Holliday, Who Shot the Video of Officers Beating Rodney King, Has Died," NPR, September 21, 2021, https://www.npr.org/2021/09/21/1039236256/george-holliday-who-shot-the-video-of-officers-beating-rodney-king-has-died.

61. Butler, "Endangered/Endangering Schematic Racism," 140.

62. Butler, "Endangered/Endangering Schematic Racism," 140.

63. Butler, "Endangered/Endangering Schematic Racism," 140.

64. Ralph, "Logic of the Slave Patrol," 7.

65. Ralph, "Logic of the Slave Patrol," 6.

66. Ralph, "Logic of the Slave Patrol," 6.

67. Ralph, "Logic of the Slave Patrol," 8.

68. Editors of Encyclopaedia Britannica, "What Happened to Emmett Till's Killers?," *Britannica*, accessed January 7, 2023, https://www.britannica.com/question/What-happened-to-Emmett-Tills-killers.

69. "The Trial of J. W. Milam and Roy Bryant," *American Experience*, PBS, accessed January 7, 2023, https://www.pbs.org/wgbh/americanexperience/features/emmett-trial-jw-milam-and-roy-bryant/.

70. Ralph, "Logic of the Slave Patrol," 6.

71. Sarah Kuta, "The Murder of Laquan McDonald: Why Was the Chicago Teen Killed by Police?," *A&E: True Crime Blog*, September 2, 2021, https://www.aetv.com/real-crime/laquan-mcdonald.

72. Ralph, "Logic of the Slave Patrol," 6.

73. Thornton, "African Dimensions of the Stono Rebellion," 1101.

74. Littlefield, "Echoes of Liberty," 189.

75. Washington, *Medical Apartheid*, 36.

76. Willoughby, "Running Away from Drapetomania," 579.

77. Geggus, *Impact of the Haitian Revolution*.

78. Geggus, *Impact of the Haitian Revolution*, xi.

79. Trouillot, *Silencing the Past*.

80. Jenson, "Dessalines's American Proclamations of the Haitian Independence," 36.

81. Roberts, *Voodoo and Power*.

82. Ross, "Voodoo, Religious Culture, 117–18.

83. Roberts, *Voodoo and Power*, 1–2.

84. McCarthy Brown, *Mama Lola*.

85. McCarthy Brown, "Making Wanga," 239.

86. McCarthy Brown, "Making Wanga," 239.

87. Ryan and Butgan, "Justin A. Volpe et al. Trials."

Journal Entry. Tuesday, December 2, 2021, Stanford, California

1. At the time, the police claimed that Woods had his arm outstretched, prompting the shooting and "leaving the officers no choice but to use deadly force." The chief of police, Greg Suhr, held a town hall in the predominantly Black Bayview community with blowups of the grainy cell phone footage that he claimed vindicated officers and justified the actions leading to Woods's death. Subsequently, however, another video was released by the family's attorney that showed Woods with his arms to his sides and walking slowly when he was fired on by the five officers. Whereas the San Francisco Police Department claimed that officers had fired fifteen times, the autopsy revealed that Woods's body contained twenty bullet wounds, with several shots to the back of his head and body.

2. This is the cleansing song used by Uncle Tobaji and Iya Wanda to cleanse Woods's death location. See full translation by Óchání Lele, "Aumbá Wá Orí, Song One," *Óchání Lele* (blog), February 8, 2017, https://ochanilele.wordpress.com/2017/02/08/aumba-wa-ori-song-one/#comments.

3. Villepastour, *Ancient Text Messages*.

4. Villepastour, *Ancient Text Messages*.

5. Brad Erickson discusses how in Afrofuturist work, such as Ngozi Onwurah's 1995 film *Welcome II the Terrordome*, "radio appears as the modern equivalent of tribal drums." Erickson, "George Clinton and David Bowie," 566, and note 9.

6. My translation, from "La Santeria en Matanzas, Cuba: An Interview with Alfredo Calvo," interview filmed in 2009, https://www.youtube.com/watch?v=2xq3yxf0HvY.

7. Lukumi song of the dead, translated by Óchání Lele.

Chapter Eight. Excited

1. S. Lewis et al. "'On Our Watch.'"

2. S. Lewis, "Oscar Grant Killing Will Get New Review."

3. Benavides, "Taser Guns."

4. Shrontoria Pratt, "Natasha McKenna (1978–2015)." Black Past, August 30, 2018, https://www.blackpast.org/african-american-history/mckenna-natasha-1978–2015/.

5. Pratt, "Natasha McKenna (1978–2015)."

6. Pratt, "Natasha McKenna (1978–2015)."

7. Tom Jackman, "The Death of Natasha McKenna in the Fairfax Jail: The Rest of the Story," *Washington Post*, April 13, 2015, https://www.washingtonpost.com/news/local/wp/2015/04/13/the-death-of-natasha-mckenna-in-the-fairfax-jail-the-rest-of-the-story/.

8. Jackman, "Death of Natasha McKenna."

9. As part of its investigations into Tasers, Reuters has provided a confidential document produced by Taser International and distributed to police, titled "Advanced Taser M26 Less-Lethal EMD Weapon: Medical Safety Information." Every page of the document is marked "CONFIDENTIAL: DO NOT REPRODUCE OR DISTRIBUTE." The quote is taken from page 10 of the document, which I access online in the Reuters document cloud: Taser International, "Introduction to the M26 Taser," accessed September 6, 2023, https://www.documentcloud.org/documents/3935233-TASER-Medical-Safety-Information.html#document/p4/a370328.

10. Michael Pope, "Death of Natasha McKenna Raises Question: Is Excited Delirium a Real Medical Condition?," WAMU, September 25, 2015, https://wamu.org/story/15/09/25/fairfax_death_raises_question_is_excited_delirium_a_real_medical_condition/.

11. *Say Their Names*, Green Library exhibit supporting the Black Lives Matter Movement, Stanford University, accessed February 15, 2023, https://exhibits.stanford.edu/saytheirnames/feature/natasha-mckenna.

12. Jackman, "Death of Natasha McKenna."

13. Jason Szep, Tim Reid, and Peter Eisler, "How Taser Inserts Itself in Probes Involving Its Stun Guns." Shock Tactics, Part 3, Reuters, August 24, 2017, https://www.reuters.com/investigates/special-report/usa-taser-experts/.

14. Brave et al., "Medical Examiner Collection."

15. Szep, Reid, and Eisler, "How Taser Inserts Itself."

16. Szep, Reid, and Eisler, "How Taser Inserts Itself."

17. Katharine Q. Seelye, "Charles Wetli, Medical Examiner for T.W.A. Flight 800 Crash, Dies at 76," *New York Times*, September 7, 2020.

18. Szep, Reid, and Eisler, "How Taser Inserts Itself."

19. Szep, Reid, and Eisler, "How Taser Inserts Itself."

20. Brave et al., "Medical Examiner Collection."

21. Brave et al., "Medical Examiner Collection."

22. Brave et al., "Medical Examiner Collection."

23. Szep, Reid, and Eisler, "How Taser Inserts Itself."

24. Szep, Reid, and Eisler, "How Taser Inserts Itself."

25. Gau, Mosher, and Pratt, "Inquiry into the Impact of Suspect Race," 41.

26. Vikram Todd, "Black People More Likely to Be Tasered for Longer, Police Watchdog Finds," *Guardian*, August 25, 2021, https://www.theguardian.com/uk-news/2021/aug/25/black-people-more-likely-to-be-tasered-for-longer-police-watchdog-finds.

27. Szep, Reid, and Eisler, "How Taser Inserts Itself."

28. M. Meyer, "Police Call It 'Excited Delirium.'"

29. Szep, Reid, and Eisler, "How Taser Inserts Itself."

30. Szep, Reid, and Eisler, "How Taser Inserts Itself."

31. Jennifer Valentino-DeVries, Mike McIntire, Rebecca R. Ruiz, Julie Tate, and Michael H. Keller, "How Paid Experts Help Exonerate Police after Deaths in Custody," *New York Times*, December 26, 2021, https://www.nytimes.com/2021/12/26/us/police -deaths-in-custody-blame.html.

32. Valentino-DeVries et al., "How Paid Experts Help Exonerate Police."

33. Valentino-DeVries et al. "How Paid Experts Help Exonerate Police."

34. The first IPICD conference was held in Las Vegas, Nevada, in 2005. Since then, each fall, the IPICD conference hosts "researchers, scientists, attorneys, physicians, and criminal justice practitioners who share the latest scientific, legal, medical, and best practices with attendees who come from across the globe. Since its founding, the IPICD has added several programs of instruction, including the hosting of the *first* international symposium on the medical, scientific, and legal constraints on human re- straints." Quoted from the website, Institute for the Prevention of In-Custody Deaths, "About Institute for the Prevention of In-Custody Deaths, Inc. (IPICD)," accessed January 7, 2023, https://ipicdtc.com/ipicd/.

35. Szep, Reid, and Eisler, "How Taser Inserts Itself."

36. Szep, Reid, and Eisler, "How Taser Inserts Itself."

37. My aunt Petra De Jesus, a Latina Democrat and public interest attorney who has provided representation to low-income clients, was known for being a tough critic of the police during her tenure as San Francisco police commissioner. She retired in 2021 after serving fifteen years. See Michael Barba, "Petra DeJesus Departs Police Commis- sion after 15 Years," *San Francisco Examiner*, April 22, 2021, https://www.sfexaminer. com/news/petra-dejesus-departs-police-commission-after-15-years/article_dbaf5328- 8aa9-5257-94dc-7ec4ea94e543.html.

38. Tim Redmond and Sana Saleem, "A Heated Battle over Tasers in San Fran- cisco," 48 hills, May 25, 2016, https://48hills.org/2016/05/san-francisco-public -defenders-justice-summit-tasers/.

39. Valentino-DeVries et al., "How Paid Experts Help Exonerate Police."

40. Stephen Nellis, "Taser Changes Name to Axon in Shift to Software Services," Reuters, April 5, 2017, https://www.reuters.com/article/us-usa-TASER/TASER -changes-name-to-axon-in-shift-to-software-services-idUSKBN177265.

41. In 2016, Axon received $202.6 million of its revenue mostly from Taser replace- ment cartridges. Nellis, "Taser Changes Name to Axon."

42. Szep, Reid, and Eisler, "How Taser Inserts Itself."

43. Szep, Reid, and Eisler, "How Taser Inserts Itself."

44. Szep, Reid, and Eisler, "How Taser Inserts Itself."

45. Szep, Reid, and Eisler, "How Taser Inserts Itself."

46. Pathologists are recruited from across the country and paid to work in the Uni- versity of Miami's Brain Endowment Bank to get brain samples. See the Miller School of Medicine's page on the University of Miami Brain Endowment Bank, https://med .miami.edu/en/programs/brain-endowment-bank/researchers/pathologists.

47. Kelley Uustal Trial Attorneys, "Teen Dies after Getting Tased by Police," *Firm News*, August 25, 2017, https://kelleyuustal.com/18-year-old-israel-hernandez-llach-dies-as-a-res/.

48. Shaila Dewan, "Subduing Suspects Face Down Isn't Fatal, Research Has Said. Now the Research Is on Trial," *New York Times*, October 2, 2021, https://www.nytimes.com/2021/10/02/us/police-restraints-research-george-floyd.html; Valentino-DeVries et al., "How Paid Experts Help Exonerate Police."

49. Valentino-DeVries et al., "How Paid Experts Help Exonerate Police."

50. Valentino-DeVries et al., "How Paid Experts Help Exonerate Police."

51. Valentino-DeVries et al., "How Paid Experts Help Exonerate Police."

52. Seelye, "Charles Wetli, Medical Examiner."

53. Seelye, "Charles Wetli, Medical Examiner."

54. Associated Press, "Relatives of Black Man Shot by White Officer File Lawsuit," *Enterprise-Record* (Chico, CA), September 30, 2016, https://www.chicoer.com/2016/09/30/relatives-of-black-man-shot-by-White-officer-file-lawsuit/.

55. Ko Bragg and Justin Brooks, "Ricky Ball Family Receives Narrow Explanation from Attorney General's Office for Dropped Manslaughter Charge," *Mississippi Today* (Jackson, MS), June 17, 2020, https://mississippitoday.org/2020/06/17/ricky-ball-family-receives-narrow-explanation-from-attorney-generals-office-for-dropped-manslaughter-charge/.

56. It was alleged that Boykin called Ball a "moolie," a racial slur against Black people commonly used by Italians. Boykin's attorney claimed that Boykin had said "bully" and that he "does not know what 'moolie' means." Bragg and Brooks, "Ricky Ball Family."

57. The first report does not mention that Boykin tased Ball. The second version of the report, released in January 2016, added that Boykin had first tased Ball before he shot him. Matt Kessler, "Why Did Mississippi Police Release Two Versions of Fatal Shooting Report?," ACLU Mississippi, February 9, 2016, https://www.aclu-ms.org/en/news/why-did-mississippi-police-release-two-versions-fatal-shooting-report.

58. Kessler, "Why Did Mississippi Police."

59. Justice for Ricky Ball website, http://www.justiceforrickyball.com.

60. Boykin, on the other hand, claims that he immediately tased Ball after stopping him. However, the traffic stop is documented at 10:08 p.m., while the Taser log, which cannot be altered, shows the Taser was deployed at 10:49 p.m., forty-one minutes later.

61. Justice for Ricky Ball website, http://www.justiceforrickyball.com.

62. Bragg and Brooks, "Ricky Ball Family."

63. Matt Kessler, "Mississippi Grand Jury Indicts Ex-Police Officer in Killing of Ricky Ball," *Guardian*, September 9, 2016, https://www.theguardian.com/us-news/2016/sep/09/ricky-ball-shooting-mississippi-jury-indicts-police-officer-canyon-boykin.

64. Kessler, "Why Did Mississippi Police."

65. Alex Holloway, "Ricky Ball Shooting: Ricky Ball's Father Sues Columbus for Wrongful Death," *Dispatch* (Columbus, MS), October 18, 2016, https://cdispatch.com/news/2016-10-18/ricky-ball-shooting-ricky-balls-father-sues-columbus-for-wrongful-death/.

66. Kelly Swanson, "Trump Tells Cops They Should Rough People Up More during Arrests," *Vox*, July 28, 2017, https://www.vox.com/policy-and-politics/2017/7/28/16059536/trump-cops-speech-gang-violence-long-island.

67. Matt Kessler, "White Police Officer Alleges Racial Bias after Being Fired for Shooting Black Man," *Guardian*, February 11, 2017, https://www.theguardian.com/us-news/2016/feb/11/mississippi-police-officer-racial-bias-ricky-ball-shooting.

68. "Boykin Reaches Settlement in Wrongful Termination Lawsuit," *AP News*, September 15, 2017, https://apnews.com/article/545bf82821764d419a4f12648a927432; Associated Press, "Relatives of Black Man"; Jeff Amy, "Call for Grand Jury to Probe Police Shooting in Mississippi," *Midland (MI) Daily News*, July 6, 2016, https://www.ourmidland.com/news/article/Call-for-grand-jury-to-probe-police-shooting-in-8371225.php.

69. "Former Police Officer's Lawsuit against City Reaches Settlement," wcbi, September 13, 2017, https://www.wcbi.com/former-police-officers-lawsuit-city-reaches-settlement/.

70. Bragg and Brooks, "Ricky Ball Family."

71. Bragg and Brooks, "Ricky Ball Family."

72. Ko Bragg and Justin Brooks, "Family of Black Mississippi Man Killed by Police Receives Narrow Explanation for Dropped Manslaughter Case," The Appeal, June 17, 2020, https://theappeal.org/family-of-black-mississippi-man-killed-by-police-receives-narrow-explanation-for-dropped-manslaughter-case/.

73. Seelye, "Charles Wetli, Medical Examiner."

74. Clarke asserts that we must interrogate how power plays into what expertise is recognized by courts, especially when marginalized groups are negotiating their relationships to legal frameworks. Clarke, "Toward Reflexivity," 584.

75. Clarke "Toward Reflexivity," 586.

76. Wynter. "No Humans Involved," 42.

77. Sylvia Wynter. "No Humans Involved."

78. See also Khalil Muhammad's *The Condemnation of Blackness*, on the way statistics were used to link Blackness and criminality.

Chapter Nine. Forced

1. "Stand Your Ground and Castle Doctrine Laws," Bill of Rights Institute, accessed January 3, 2023, https://billofrightsinstitute.org/e-lessons/stand-your-ground-and-castle-doctrine-laws-elesson.

2. *Mother Jones*. "Transcript of George Zimmerman's Call to the Police," Mother Jones, DocumentCloud, accessed June 29, 2022, https://www.documentcloud.org/documents/326700-full-transcript-zimmerman.

3. "Transcript of George Zimmerman's Call to the Police."

4. Chelsea B. Shealy, "Who Was on Top in Zimmerman-Martin Tussle? Witness Testimony in Conflict," *Christian Science Monitor*, June 28, 2013, https://www.csmonitor.com/USA/USA-Update/2013/0628/Who-was-on-top-in-Zimmerman-Martin-tussle-Witness-testimony-in-conflict.

5. According to the *Orlando Sentinel*, neighbor Selma Mora testified that "after she heard what she now believes was a gunshot, she rushed outside and saw the man who survived the fight on his knees straddling Trayvon." Rene Stutzman and Jeff Weiner, "Key Witness Holds Firm that Zimmerman Was the Aggressor," *Orlando Sentinel*, June 27, 2013, https://www.orlandosentinel.com/news/trayvon-martin-george-zimmerman/os-george-zimmerman-trial-day-14–20130627-story.html.

6. V. Di Maio and Franscell, *Morgue*, 21.

7. V. Di Maio and Franscell, *Morgue*, 21.

8. V. Di Maio and Franscell, *Morgue*, 22.

9. V. Di Maio and Franscell, *Morgue*, 22.

10. V. Di Maio and Franscell, *Morgue*, 5.

11. V. Di Maio and Franscell, *Morgue*, 2.

12. V. Di Maio and Franscell, *Morgue*, 5.

13. Greg Botelho and Carma Hassan, "George Zimmerman Arrested on Suspected Domestic Violence," *CNN*, January 13, 2015, https://www.cnn.com/2015/01/10/us/george-zimmerman-arrested/index.html.

14. He had testified for the defense of Drew Peterson, the Illinois police officer accused of murdering his wife, Stacy. In the Peterson case and other high-profile cases, Di Maio was known to make his testimony match the defense's theory. Bloom, *Suspicion Nation*, 105–6.

15. Vincent Di Maio told jurors that it was unequivocally clear based on the gunshot residue analysis that Trayvon Martin was on top, which corroborated George Zimmerman's self-defense story. But that was not what Di Maio told NBC's *Today Show* on May 13, 2012, when he stated that the gunshot residue "around the bullet hole in Trayvon's body showed that 'the range was most likely between two and four inches.'" He did not say that this meant unequivocally that Trayvon was on top, as he had testified in court. Bloom, *Suspicion Nation*, 111.

16. Bloom, *Suspicion Nation*, 107.

17. Bloom, *Suspicion Nation*, 111–12.

18. Bloom, *Suspicion Nation*, 111–12.

19. Bloom, *Suspicion Nation*, 122.

20. Bloom, *Suspicion Nation*, 122.

21. "The Trial of J. W. Milam and Roy Bryant," *American Experience*, PBS, accessed January 7, 2023, https://www.pbs.org/wgbh/americanexperience/features/emmett-trial-jw-milam-and-roy-bryant/.

22. Adam Taylor and Brett LoGiurato, "Obama Releases Statement on George Zimmerman Verdict," *Insider*, July 14, 2013, https://www.businessinsider.com/obamas-statement-on-george-zimmerman-verdict-2013-7.

23. See the dedication, in T. Di Maio and V. Di Maio, *Excited Delirium Syndrome*, v.

24. Sherwin, "Why 'Excited Delirium.'" A copy of the Di Maios' book, *Excited Delirium*, costs $165 but contains only about 130 pages of text.

25. V. Di Maio and Franscell, *Morgue*, 20.

26. V. Di Maio and Franscell, *Morgue*, 1.

27. V. Di Maio and Franscell, *Morgue*, 21.

28. "New Mexico Officer Testifies at Ex-partner's Murder Trial," *AP News*, July 12, 2022, https://apnews.com/article/new-mexico-las-cruces-44289399875e5feb14432c9 9c3a87057.

29. "New Mexico Officer Testifies."

30. "New Mexico Officer Testifies."

31. Erika Esquivel, "Former Las Cruces Officer Now Faces Murder Charge after Use of Chokehold," *KFOX 14 News*, July 16, 2020, https://kfoxtv.com/news/local/former -las-cruces-officer-now-faces-murder-charge-after-use-of-chokehold?src=link.

32. Martinez and Flores, "Resurrecting Brown Bodies."

33. Esquivel, "Former Las Cruces Officer."

34. T. Di Maio and V. Di Maio, *Excited Delirium Syndrome*, 2–3.

35. T. Di Maio and V. Di Maio, *Excited Delirium Syndrome*, 4.

36. T. Di Maio and V. Di Maio, *Excited Delirium Syndrome*, 97.

37. T. Di Maio and V. Di Maio, *Excited Delirium Syndrome*, 42.

38. T. Di Maio and V. Di Maio, *Excited Delirium Syndrome*, 2.

39. T. Di Maio and V. Di Maio, *Excited Delirium Syndrome*, 2–3.

40. Memorandum from Deputy Attorney General Lisa Monaco, "Chokeholds and Carotid Restraints; Knock and Announce Requirement," US Department of Justice, September 13, 2001, 2, https://www.justice.gov/d9/pages/attachments/2021/09/14 /2021.09.13_chokehold_carotid_restraint_knock_and_announce_policy_final_0.pdf.

41. Memorandum from Deputy Attorney General Lisa Monaco, "Chokeholds and Carotid Restraints; Knock and Announce Requirement," US Department of Justice, September 13, 2001, 2, https://www.justice.gov/d9/pages/attachments/2021/09/14 /2021.09.13_chokehold_carotid_restraint_knock_and_announce_policy_final_0.pdf.

42. T. Di Maio and V. Di Maio, *Excited Delirium Syndrome*, 20.

43. T. Di Maio and V. Di Maio, *Excited Delirium Syndrome*, 42.

44. T. Di Maio and V. Di Maio, *Excited Delirium Syndrome*, 42–43.

45. T. Di Maio and V. Di Maio, *Excited Delirium Syndrome*, 42–43.

46. T. Di Maio and V. Di Maio, *Excited Delirium Syndrome*, 42–43.

47. Joseph Neff and Emily Siegel, "'He Died Like an Animal': Some Police Departments Hogtie People Despite Knowing the Risks," Marshall Project, May 24, 2021, https://www.themarshallproject.org/2021/05/24/he-died-like-an-animal-some-police -departments-hogtie-people-despite-knowing-the-risks.

48. T. Di Maio and V. Di Maio, *Excited Delirium Syndrome,* 27.

49. O'Halloran and Frank, "Asphyxial Death."

50. O'Halloran and Frank, "Asphyxial Death," 45–46.

51. O'Halloran and Frank, "Asphyxial Death," 45–46.

52. O'Halloran and Frank, "Asphyxial Death," 50.

53. O'Halloran and Frank, "Asphyxial Death," 50.

54. O'Halloran and Frank, "Asphyxial Death," 49–50.

55. A few examples include Carlos Mata in San Antonio, Texas, who died on August 7, 2015; Juan Carlos Reyes-Gallardo in Dallas, Texas, who died on July 26,

2009; and Manuel Delacruz in Port Arthur, Texas, who died on August 1, 2016, among many others. Many of these cases—such as that of Rodolfo Cisneros Jr. in Brownsville, Texas, who died on June 7, 2008—are considered to involve excited delirium, but that is not listed as cause of death. All these people died in the course of questionable uses of police force and prone restraint. For Cisneros, the cause of death remains listed as "pending." "Restraint Death Detail: Rodolfo Cisneros Jr.," A Question of Restraint, accessed January 3, 2023, https://apps.statesman.com/question-of-restraint/data/400 /rodolfo-cisneros-jr/.

56. Jordan Foster, "Jesse Aguirre's Family Hoping for Justice for Loved One Who Died in Police Custody in 2013," *KENS5 News*, April 28, 2021, https://www .kens5.com/article/news/local/law-enforcement/jesse-aguirres-family-hoping-for -justice-for-loved-one-who-died-in-police-custody-in-2013/273-81de5ea8-4020-433b -a890-38304daf8fb2; also, Iris Dimmick, "San Antonio Pays $466,300 Settlement to Family of Unarmed Man Killed in Police Custody," *San Antonio Report*, June 9, 2022, https://sanantonioreport.org/san-antonio-pays-settlement-family-unarmed-man -killed-police-custody/.

57. Simon Romero, Giulia McDonnell Nieto del Rio, and Nicholas Bogel-Burroughs, "Another Nightmare Video and the Police on the Defensive in Tucson," *New York Times*, June 25, 2020, https://www.nytimes.com/2020/06/25/us/carlos -ingram-lopez-death-tucson-police.html.

58. Simon Romero, "Tucson Police in Turmoil after Death of Latino Man in Custody," *New York Times*, June 24, 2020, https://www.nytimes.com/2020/06/24/us /tucson-police-carlos-ingram-lopez-death.html.

59. Romero, "Tucson Police in Turmoil."

60. T. and V. Di Maio claim that excited delirium is a syndrome despite lack of medical evidence. They divided the deaths into four categories: "those occurring (1) during arrest and transport, (2) within 24 hours of arrest, (3) after 24 hours but before trial, and (4) after trial." Di Maio and Di Maio, *Excited Delirium Syndrome*, 3.

61. T. Di Maio and V. Di Maio, *Excited Delirium Syndrome*, 101.

62. T. Di Maio and V. Di Maio, *Excited Delirium Syndrome*, 102.

63. The "behavioral" indicators that the Di Maios claim police should look out for are extreme agitation and restlessness, incoherent and rambling speech, hallucinations or delusions with paranoid features, disorganized thought content, bizarre behavior, combativeness, and violence. T. Di Maio and V. Di Maio, *Excited Delirium Syndrome*, 102–3.

64. T. Di Maio and V. Di Maio, *Excited Delirium Syndrome*, 102.

65. T. Di Maio and V. Di Maio, *Excited Delirium Syndrome*, 102.

66. T. Di Maio and V. Di Maio, *Excited Delirium Syndrome*, v.

67. T. Di Maio and V. Di Maio, *Excited Delirium Syndrome*, 98.

68. Although I looked into both Vincent Di Maio and his wife and *Excited Delirium Syndrome* coauthor, Theresa Di Maio, I found limited records and information about her, making it challenging to gain insight into her professional background, contributions, or motivations. In contrast, Vincent Di Maio was a prolific author and a well-known figure in the field of forensic pathology. His extensive body of work, along

with his involvement in high-profile cases as an expert witness, drew more attention and yielded a wealth of publicly accessible information. This made it possible for me to delve deeper into his career, beliefs, and impact, ultimately leading to a more comprehensive exploration of his role in shaping the discourse around excited delirium syndrome.

69. Vincent Di Maio was involved in a number of high-profile cases, such as the exhumation of Lee Harvey Oswald and the cases of Genene Jones, Phil Spector, Michael Morton, Claus Von Bülow, Bob Crane, George Zimmerman, the West Memphis Three, the Smolensk airplane bombing, the siege at Ruby Ridge (Idaho), and many others. See Bloom, *Suspicion Nation*, 108; see also Steve Schmadeke, Matthew Walberg, and Stacy St. Clair, "Drew Peterson Trial Updates: Testimony Done for the Day," *Chicago Tribune*, August 28, 2012, https://www.chicagotribune.com/news/breaking/chi -drew-peterson-trial-updates-defense-will-call-son-20120828-story.html; Paul Venema, "Doctor Plays Role in Important Court Cases," *KSAT News*, July 28, 2016, https://www .ksat.com/news/2016/07/28/doctor-plays-role-in-important-court-cases/.

70. Edward Kirkman, "Patience Paid for New City ME [Medical Examiner]," *Daily News* (New York), September 7, 1976.

71. In cross-examination, defense attorney Peter O'Malley "asked [Dominick] Di Maio why he had resigned from his top post in the medical examiner's office shortly after his appointment. The lawyer speculated the physician had been forced out because of his frequent consultations around the country in which he would testify 'for a price.'" See "Testimony of New York City Medical Examiner on Death Attacked at Genovese Hearing," *Times-Tribune* (Scranton, PA), August 18, 1978.

72. Kirkman, "Patience Paid."

73. Kirkman, "Patience Paid."

74. Dennis Duggan, "Morgue Revelry Probed," *Newsday* (Suffolk ed.; Melville, NY), June 11, 1976.

75. Kirkman, "Patience Paid."

76. Kirkman, "Patience Paid."

77. Alex Michelini, Marcia Kramer, and Ruth Landa, "City, State to Probe Gross: The Mayor Will Appoint Special Counsel," *Daily News* (New York), January 29, 1985.

78. Michelini, Kramer, and Landa, "City, State to Probe Gross."

79. "This Day in History: December 22, 1984—Bernhard Goetz Shoots Four Youths on the Subway," History.com, accessed January 5, 2023, https://www.history .com/this-day-in-history/the-bernhard-goetz-subway-shooting.

80. "This Day in History: December 22, 1984—Bernhard Goetz Shoots Four Youths on the Subway," History.com, accessed January 5, 2023, https://www.history .com/this-day-in-history/the-bernhard-goetz-subway-shooting.

81. "Prosecutor Aims at Goetz Witness," *Daily Record* (Morristown, NJ), June 8, 1987.

82. "Prosecutor Aims at Goetz Witness."

83. D. Di Maio and V. Di Maio, *Forensic Pathology*, 4.

84. D. Di Maio and V. Di Maio, *Forensic Pathology*, 5.

85. Dwyer, "Artifacts of Restraint and Enslaved African Women of the Eighteenth Century Transatlantic Slave Trade," 65–69.

86. Dwyer, "Artifacts of Restraint and Enslaved African Women of the Eighteenth Century Transatlantic Slave Trade," 69.

87. Dwyer, "Artifacts of Restraint and Enslaved African Women of the Eighteenth Century Transatlantic Slave Trade," 69.

88. Mullings, "Necropolitics of Reproduction."

89. Burton, "Captivity, Kinship," 622.

90. Burton, "Captivity, Kinship," 622.

91. Hejtmanek, "Caring through Restraint."

92. Sussman, "Mechanical Restraints," 109, 110.

93. Hejtmanek, "Caring through Restraint."

94. See Saks, "The Use of Mechanical Restraints," 1836; Saks, "Putting Patients at the Center of Restraints," 1; Klein, "Theory of Punishment"; Scurich and John, "Constraints on Restraints."

95. "Coroner Classifies Death of Mario Gonzalez during Alameda Police Confrontation as Homicide." CBS Bay Area, December 10, 2021, www.cbsnews.com /sanfrancisco/news/mario-gonzalez-death-alameda-police-homicide/.

96. As cited in Martinez and Flores, "Resurrecting Brown Bodies," 260.

97. Martinez and Flores, "Resurrecting Brown Bodies," 261.

98. Burton, "Captivity, Kinship," 623.

99. Alves, *Anti-Black City*, 122.

100. Alves, *Anti-Black City*, 155.

Journal Entry. Tuesday, March 22, 2022, Stanford, California

1. Nagel, "Hands of Albert Einstein."

2. Mesmerism, hypnotism, trance, and the uncanny were all popular modalities of healing that were widely utilized. Grimes, *Late Victorian Gothic*, 9.

3. Henderson, "Forgotten Meta-realities," 2.

4. The Scottish mathematician and scientist James Clerk Maxwell described ether as "infinite continuity." In the 1898 Presidential Address for the British Association for the Advancement of Science, British chemist and physicist Sir William Cookes stated, "Ether vibrations have powers and attributes equal to any demand—even to the transmission of thought." Henderson, "Forgotten Meta-realities," 2.

5. Einstein was known to have met with at least six psychics: Wolf Messing in 1913, a "thought reading lady" in 1920, Otto Reimann in 1930, a "metagraphologist" around 1930, Roman Ostoja in 1931, and Mrs. Akkeringa between 1914 and 1933. The "metagraphologist" was also the psychic Gene Dennis. Nagel, "Hands of Albert Einstein," 74.

6. See Alap Naik Desai, "Did Albert Einstein Believe in Psychic Abilities?" Inquisitr, September 9, 2014; George Pendle, "Einstein's Close Encounter," *Guardian*, July 14, 2005; New Republic Staff, "Albert Einstein Endorsed a Popular Psychic in 1932," *New Republic*, March 9, 1932, https://newrepublic.com/article/119292/ controversy-einsteins-endorsement-psychic-upton-sinclair-defends.

7. Einstein "cherished" Madame Blavatsky's work, having read her books *Isis Unveiled* (1877) and *The Secret Doctrine* (1888); Yoko Chiba, "W. B. Yeats's Occultism," 241.

8. Nagel, "Hands of Albert Einstein," 74.

Chapter Ten. Delirious

1. Petition, "Justice for Elijah McClain," Change.org, https://www.change.org/p/adams-county-district-attorney-justice-for-elijah-mcclain-9df9e907–117b-4a48–8889–81182ea92250.

2. "Elijah McClain Killing 911 Call and Police Body Cam Footage Transcript," Rev, August 25, 2019, https://www.rev.com/blog/transcripts/elijah-mcclain-killing-911-call-police-body-cam-footage-transcript.

3. Lucy Tompkins, "Here's What You Need to Know about Elijah McClain's Death," *New York Times*, January 28, 2022, https://www.nytimes.com/article/who-was-elijah-mcclain.html.

4. Quinlan, Palan, Murtada, and Dos Santos, "Excited Delirium."

5. "Elijah McClain Killing 911 Call."

6. Petition, "Justice for Elijah McClain."

7. See "Ketamine Dose for Elijah McClain 'Too Much,' Says Anesthesiologist," *CBS Colorado*, July 7, 2020, https://denver.cbslocal.com/2020/07/07/elijah-mcclain-ketamine-aurora-police-anesthesiologist/. Researchers have found consistent evidence that non-Black people overestimate "young Black men as taller, heavier, stronger, more muscular, and more capable of causing physical harm than young White men." Wilson, Hugenberg, and Rule, "Racial Bias in Judgments of Physical Size," 74. The researchers found that participants' "associations between race and physical size were strong enough to bias their judgments of the size of *identical* bodies simply because they were led to believe that [the subjects] were Black or White" (74). These perceptions of Black people as more threatening have been found to impact judgments about the force necessary to restrain Black suspects.

8. "Ketamine Dose for Elijah McClain."

9. "Ketamine Dose for Elijah McClain."

10. "Ketamine Dose for Elijah McClain."

11. Andrea Fox, "What to Know about Ketamine, a Common Date Rape Drug," Gov1, March 30, 2018, https://www.gov1.com/public-safety/articles/what-to-know-about-ketamine-a-common-date-rape-drug-8DxnS7OteEhx7UmX/.

12. Ketamine is a close chemical cousin to PCP or "angel dust." In 1956, in Detroit, Michigan, two scientists at the Parke-Davis (now a subsidiary of Pfizer) synthesized PCP as a promising anesthetic. Although both are dissociative anesthetics, ketamine has a lower incidence of side effects than PCP. Hevers et al., "Ketamine, but Not Phencyclidine."

13. Denomme, "Domino Effect," 300.

14. Given its relatively short half-life, there are reports of repeated ketamine binges, in which people get high and then re-up when they start to crash. There is even experimentation with ketamine microdosing to relieve schizophrenia. As a numbing agent,

ketamine is celebrated as a magic drug that desensitizes people and elicits a pleasurable delirium. Patients who use it for depression describe feelings of numbing and a relief from the stress of modern life. For its uses for fibromyalgia, see Pastrak et al., "Systematic Review of the Use of Intravenous Ketamine." For its use in treating depression, see Mandal, Sinha, and Goyal, "Efficacy of Ketamine Therapy."

15. Ketamine can cause confusion, muscle spasms, and hallucinations. If it is injected, sedation ensues in most cases in less than five minutes. If the drug is snorted or ingested, its effects can begin in five minutes and last about an hour. If ketamine is smoked, the effect is immediate and can last several hours. "Ketamine: Modern Drug of Abuse?" Drugs.com, accessed January 30, 2024, https://www.drugs.com/illicit/ketamine.html.

16. MPD Involvement in Pre-Hospital Sedation, Office of Police Conduct Review (OPCR), Minneapolis, July 26, 2018, 64–66, https://lims.minneapolismn .gov/Download/File/1389/Office%20of%20Police%20Conduct%20Review%20 (OPCR)%20Pre-Hosptial%20Sedation%20Study%20Final%20Report.pdf.

17. Josiah Hesse, "'Weaponization of Medicine': Police Use of Ketamine Draws Scrutiny after Elijah McClain's Death," Guardian, December 17, 2021, https://www .theguardian.com/us-news/2021/dec/17/ketamine-law-enforcement-deaths-custody -elijah-mcclain.

18. Deon J. Hampton, "Mom of 5 Died after Ketamine Injection by a Paramedic, Family Alleges in Wrongful Death Suit," NBC News, November 4, 2022, https://www .nbcnews.com/news/us-news/family-mom-5-died-ketamine-injection-paramedic-files -wrongful-death-la-rcna55509.

19. Hampton, "Mom of 5 Died after Ketamine Injection."

20. Elise Schmelzer, "Family of Colorado Woman Who Died after Paramedic Injected Her with Ketamine Sues Ambulance Company," Lamar (CO) Ledger, October 28, 2022, https://www.lamarledger.com/2022/10/28/colorado-ketamine-jerica -lacour-lawsuit/.

21. Hampton, "Mom of 5 Died after Ketamine Injection."

22. In 1859, Albert Nieman, a German chemist, isolated the active ingredient, hydrochloride, and named it cocaine. Jason Ferris, Barbara Wood, and Stephanie Cook, "Weekly Dose: Cocaine, the Glamour Drug of the '70s, Is Making a Comeback," The Conversation, March 8, 2018, https://theconversation.com/weekly-dose-cocaine-the -glamour-drug-of-the-70s-is-making-a-comeback-88639.

23. Sigmund Freud praised cocaine in the 1880s as useful in treating depression. Redman, "Cocaine."

24. Carstairs, "'Most Dangerous Drug,'" 47.

25. "The Truth about Crack Cocaine," Foundation for a Drug-Free World, accessed January 5, 2023, https://www.drugfreeworld.org/drugfacts/crackcocaine/a-short -history.html.

26. Adrienne Santos-Longhurst, "Everything You Need to Know about Freebasing," Healthline, February 20, 2020, https://www.healthline.com/health /freebasing#freebase-vs-crack.

27. Marisa Crane, "Slang and Nicknames for Cocaine," American Addiction Centers, December 16, 2022, https://americanaddictioncenters.org/cocaine-treatment /slang-names.

28. Hinton, *From the War on Poverty to the War on Crime*.

29. Finamore, "Geeking and Freaking," 60.

30. Editors of the Encyclopaedia Britannica, s.v. "John D. Ehrlichman," *Britannica*, accessed January 5, 2023, https://www.britannica.com/biography/John-D-Ehrlichman.

31. Editors of the Encyclopaedia Britannica, s.v. "John D. Ehrlichman."

32. Levy-Pounds, "Beaten by the System," 462, 480.

33. "Hillary Clinton on 'Superpredators,'" C-SPAN, January 28, 1996, https://www .c-span.org/video/?c4582473/user-clip-hillary-clinton-superpredators-1996.

34. Quoted in Elizabeth Becker, "As Ex-Theorist on Young 'Superpredators,' Bush Aide Has Regrets," *New York Times*, February 9, 2001.

35. Quoted in Becker, "Ex-Theorist on Young 'Superpredators.'"

36. Quoted in Becker, "Ex-Theorist on Young 'Superpredators.'"

37. Carroll Bogert and LynNell Hancock, "Analysis: How the Media Created a 'Superpredator' Myth That Harmed a Generation of Black Youth," NBC News, November 20, 2020, https://www.nbcnews.com/news/us-news/analysis-how-media-created -superpredator-myth-harmed-generation-black-youth-n1248101.

38. M. Alexander, "New Jim Crow," 7; Hinton, *From the War on Poverty to the War on Crime*.

39. Ralph, "Logic of the Slave Patrol," 7.

40. Annie Reneau, "Elijah Mcclain Played Violin for Lonely Kittens. His Last Words to Police Are Devastating," *Upworthy*, June 29, 2020, https://www.upworthy .com/elijah-mcclain-police-investigation-death.

41. Matory, *Fetish Revisited*, 110–12.

42. Matory, *Fetish Revisited*, 110.

43. Matory argues that both Karl Marx and Sigmund Freud's notions of "the fetish" were modalities through which two assimilated Jewish men could Whiten themselves and displace their own internalized anti-Semitism onto Black and Brown people. Like the antithesis of the properly treated European worker that Marx identified in the "negro slave," Freud's "savage" was a pedestal lifting up racially and class-ambiguous men, such as Marx and Freud, at the undeserved expense of the ostensible "savage," especially the African. See, Matory, *Fetish Revisited*, 20, 114.

44. Fanon, *Wretched of the Earth*, 41.

45. In *Black Skin, White Masks*, Frantz Fanon discusses the internalized assimilation that leads to embodied moments of disequilibrium for colonial subjects, experienced somatically. Fanon interrogates how these colonial tropes of the White gaze of African religions are experienced on his own body as a Black person when he is racialized as "savage." Fanon, *Black Skin, White Masks*, 112.

46. Elise Schmelzer, "Aurora Bans Emergency Responders' Use of Ketamine until Elijah McClain Investigation Complete," *Denver Post*, September 14, 2020, https:// www.denverpost.com/2020/09/14/elijah-mcclain-ketamine-ban-aurora/.

47. MPD *Involvement in Pre-Hospital Sedation.*

48. Andy Mannix and Rochelle Olson, "Mpls. Police Trained to Ignore City Report on Ketamine, Testimony Says," *Star Tribune* (Minneapolis), January 31, 2022, https://news.yahoo.com/mpls-police-trained-ignore-city-190900637.html.

49. Andy Mannix, "Minneapolis Police Oversight Office Calls for Stronger Policy in Ketamine Report," *Star Tribune* (Minneapolis), July 27, 2018, https://www .startribune.com/minneapolis-police-oversight-office-calls-for-stronger-policy-in -ketamine-report/489292511/.

50. Mannix, "Minneapolis Police Oversight Office."

51. Mannix, "Minneapolis Police Oversight Office."

52. American Medical Association, "New AMA Policy Opposes 'Excited Delirium' Diagnosis," press release, June 14, 2021, https://www.ama-assn.org/press-center/press -releases/new-ama-policy-opposes-excited-delirium-diagnosis.

53. American Medical Association, "New AMA Policy Opposes 'Excited Delirium' Diagnosis."

Journal Entry. Sunday, April 10, 2022, Emerald Hills, California

1. Baclawski, "Observer Effect."

Chapter Eleven. Conjured

1. Afro-Latiné people from the United States, Cuba, Puerto Rico, the Dominican Republic, and elsewhere in Latin America and the Caribbean have found solidarity in the United States through our traditions and countermobilizations. See Garcia Peña, *Translating Blackness*, 61–66.

2. Román and Flores, *The Afro-Latin@ Reader*, 2.

3. Pastrana, "Black Identity Constructions."

4. Notable here is the work of Jose Muñoz, which aims toward a queer utopia. Muñoz, "Cruising Utopia." Also crucially important is Audre Lorde's work on anger and the erotic as Black women's power. Lorde, *Sister Outsider*. In addition, see Anzaldúa's powerful poetic treatise of unity and liberation, *Borderlands*, as well as Anzaldúa and Moraga's *This Bridge Called My Back*. See also Cathy Cohen's critiques of sex and gender binary, in Cohen, "Punks, Bulldaggers, and Welfare Queens." Also important is the spiritual and political project of M. Jacqui Alexander's use of "the sacred," as well as Jafari Allen's reimagining of life by queer Cubans. J. Alexander, *Pedagogies of Crossing*, 281; Allen, *¡Venceremos?*

5. Alexander, *Pedagogies of Crossing*, 281.

6. Alexander, *Pedagogies of Crossing*, 286.

7. Hartley, "Curandera of Conquest."

8. Garza, foreword to *Who Do You Serve, Who Do You Protect?*, ix.

9. Taylor, *From #BlackLivesMatter*, 164.

10. Taylor, *From #BlackLivesMatter*, 164.

11. Taylor, *From #BlackLivesMatter*, 164.

12. Ralph, *Torture Letters*.

13. Ritchie, *Invisible No More*, 319.

14. Ritchie, *Invisible No More*, 320–22.

15. Andrea J. Ritchie, a Black immigrant and police misconduct attorney, created the Invisible No More database to document police violence against Black women and other women of color. See https://invisiblenomorebook.com/database/.

16. AP News, "Taser Victim Died of 'Excited Delirium,'" *Sun Journal* (Lewiston, ME), June 24, 2007, https://www.sunjournal.com/2007/06/24/taser-victim-died -excited-delirium/.

17. Ken Raymond, "Report Says 'Excited Delirium' Is to Blame in Woman's Death," *Oklahoman*, June 23, 2007, https://www.oklahoman.com/story/news/2007/06/23 /report-says-excited-delirium-is-to-blame-in-womans-death/61766010007/.

18. Molly Hennessy-Fiske, Michael Muskal, and Christine Mai-Duc, "Mystery Clouds Details of Sandra Bland's Volatile Arrest and Jail Death in Texas," *Los Angeles Times*, July 21, 2015, https://www.latimes.com/nation/la-na-sandra-bland-20150722 -story.html.

19. WFAA-TV, Brian Collister, and Eva Ruth Moravec, "New Cellphone Video Shows What Sandra Bland Saw during Arrest by Texas Trooper," *Texas Tribune* (Austin), https://www.texastribune.org/2019/05/06/sandra-bland-shot-cell-phone-video -texas-trooper-arrest/.

20. Molly Hennessy-Fiske, "Answers Sought in Jail Cell Death," *Los Angeles Times*, July 21, 2015.

21. See M. Brown et al., "#SayHerName"; see also Ritchie, "Say Her Name."

22. M. Brown et al., "#SayHerName," 1833.

23. M. Brown et al., "#SayHerName," 1833.

24. Ritchie, "Say Her Name," 81.

25. Wesley Lowery, "Korryn Gaines, Cradling Child and Shotgun, Is Fatally Shot by Police," *Washington Post*, August 2, 2016, https://www.washingtonpost.com/news /post-nation/wp/2016/08/02/korryn-gaines-is-the-ninth-black-woman-shot-and -killed-by-police-this-year/.

26. *Insider* created a database to document the story. See "50 Black Women Have Been Killed by US Police Since 2015: Not One of the Officers Has Been Convicted," *Insider*, accessed January 7, 2023, https://www.insider.com/black-women-killed-by -police-database-2021-6.

27. Crenshaw et al., "Say Her Name," 1.

28. Brittney Cooper, "I Could Have Been Sandra Bland: Black America's Terrifying Truth," *Salon*, July 23, 2015, https://www.salon.com/2015/07/23/black_americas _terrifying_truth_any_of_us_could_have_been_sandra_bland/.

29. D.-A. Davis, *Reproductive Injustice*, 106–7.

30. In September 2020, the YWCA compiled a report that addresses the violence against women and girls of color. Polanco's case is addressed as part of these numerous accounts of violence (11–12). YWCA, *We Still Deserve Safety: Renewing the Call to End*

the Criminalization of Women and Girls of Color, September 2020, https://www.ywca
.org/wp-content/uploads/20200909-WeStillDeserveSafety-FINALREPORT.pdf.

31. Madison Feller, Savannah Walsh and Hilary Weaver, "Activists Demand Justice and Cash Bail Reform for Layleen Polanco a Year after Her Death in Solitary," *Elle*, August 12, 2020, https://www.elle.com/culture/career-politics/a27921290/who-is
-layleen-polanco-transgender-woman-died-solitary-confinement/.

32. Taylor, *From #BlackLivesMatter*, 40.

33. Massey and Sampson, "Moynihan Redux," 14.

34. Greenbaum, *Blaming the Poor*, 54.

35. Crenshaw, "Demarginalizing the Intersection of Race and Sex," 139.

36. Geary, *Beyond Civil Rights*, 1.

37. Shamoo, "Unethical Medical Treatment," 5.

38. Volscho, "Sterilization Racism," 17.

39. Committee for Puerto Rican Decolonization, "35% of Puerto Rican Women Sterilized," *Herstory Project*, Chicago Women's Liberation Union, n.d. (probably late 1970s), accessed January 3, 2023, https://www.cwluherstory.org/health/35-of-puerto
-rican-women-sterilized.

40. Shamoo, "Unethical Medical Treatment."

41. Shamoo, "Unethical Medical Treatment."

42. Richard A. Oppel, "Here's What You Need to Know about Breonna Taylor's Death," *New York Times*, May 30, 2020, https://www.nytimes.com/article/breonna
-taylor-police.html.

43. Courier Journal Staff, "Louisville Police Has Pattern of Violating Constitutional Rights, DOJ Finds," *Courier-Journal*, March 9, 2023, https://www.courier
-journal.com/story/news/local/breonna-taylor/2023/03/08/federal-investigation
-louisville-metro-police-breonna-taylor-announced-live-updates/69983642007/.

44. Courier Journal Staff, "Louisville Police Has Pattern."

45. Oppel, "Here's What You Need to Know about Breonna Taylor's Death."

46. Oppel, "Here's What You Need to Know about Breonna Taylor's Death."

47. T. Washington, *Architects of Existence*, 8.

48. T. Washington, *Architects of Existence*, 85.

49. T. Washington, *Architects of Existence*, 85.

50. T. Washington, *Architects of Existence*, 90.

51. T. Washington, *Architects of Existence*, 90–91.

52. Morales, *Medicine Stories*, 49.

53. Sam Levin, "Four Oakland Police Officers Fired, Seven Suspended, in Sexual Misconduct Case," *Guardian*, September 8, 2016, https://www.theguardian.com/
us-news/2016/sep/07/oakland-police-officers-fired-sexual-misconduct-scandal.

54. The persistence of colonial arrangements has been described aptly as a "coloniality of power," a term coined by the Peruvian sociologist Anibal Quijano. Coloniality recognizes that European systems of classification and forms of global domination are built into the world's structures and permeate all areas of social existence. Coloniality is about the residual and lasting mechanisms of dominance and control of racial

colonial relations. Ongoing "colonial situations," as Puerto Rican sociologist Ramon Grosfoguel shows, are key relations of empires that link Black, Indigenous, and Latiné underdevelopment and debility. Martinez-San Miguel has described these mechanisms as an "extended colonialism," referring to the persistence of sixteenth-century colonialism in the Philippines and the Caribbean into the present. She shows how we can see the "coloniality of diaspora" through "coerced, voluntary, and massive displacements," which have produced circuits of resettlement often neglected in migration studies. Quijano, "Coloniality of Power"; Grosfoguel and Georas, "'Coloniality of Power' and Racial Dynamics," 90; Martínez-San Miguel, *Coloniality of Diasporas*, 6–8.

Journal Entry. Wednesday, May 25, 2022, Antioch, California

1. Ryan J. Reilly, "Postal Service Sued for Seizing Black Lives Matter Masks during 2020 Protests," NBC *News*, June 2, 2022, https://www.nbcnews.com/politics/politics -news/postal-service-sued-seizing-black-lives-matter-masks-2020-protests-rcna31287.

2. In my article "Brujx: An Afro-Latinx Queer Gesture," I discuss how groups of priests began to mobilize through collective spiritual hexings against White supremacy. See Beliso-De Jesús, "Brujx."

Chapter Twelve. Empower

1. Minyvonne Burke, "Black Lives Matter Co-founder's Cousin Dies after LA Police Blasted Him with Taser," NBC *News*, January 12, 2023, https://www.nbcnews.com/news /us-news/bodycam-video-released-black-man-died-tased-los-angeles-police-rcna65524.

2. "Tyre Nichols: 5 Fired Memphis Cops Charged with Nichols' Death," Yahoo!, January 26, 2023, https://www.yahoo.com/now/tyre-nichols-5-fired-memphis -203405500.html.

3. See the following articles for these descriptions: Minyvonne Burke, "Memphis Police Scorpion Unit Is Permanently Deactivated after Tyre Nichols' Death," NBC *News*, January 29, 2023, https://www.nbcnews.com/news/us-news/memphis-polices -scorpion-unit-permanently-deactivated-tyre-nichols-dea-rcna68029; Mitchell S. Jackson, "Here We Are Again: But This Killing of a Black Man Is Different," *Esquire*, January 30, 2023, https://www.esquire.com/news-politics/a42698149/tyre-nichols -police-killing-why-its-different/; "Tyre Nichols: 5 Fired Memphis Cops Charged with Nichols' Death"; and Michael Nabors, "Rev. Michael Nabors: Responding to the Unacceptable Murder of Tyre Nichols," Evanston RoundTable, January 30, 2023, https://evanstonroundtable.com/2023/01/29/rev-michael-nabors-responding-to-the -unacceptable-murder-of-tyre-nichols/.

4. See also Ralph, "Alibi," 6.

5. Deena Zaru and Deborah Roberts, "Trayvon Martin's Mother, Sybrina Fulton, Reflects on Her Son's Legacy a Decade after His Death," ABC *News*, February 1, 2022, https://abcnews.go.com/GMA/News/trayvon-martins-mother-sybrina-fulton -reflects-sons-legacy/story?id=82581087.

6. Du Bois, *Souls of Black Folk*.

7. Cauls are considered sacred and are preserved, used in talismans for protection and placed under the pillow of dying persons to ease their transition to the afterworld. Perkinson, "The Gift/Curse of 'Second Sight,'" 19.

8. Du Bois, *Souls of Black Folk*.

9. Edith Turner described how White anthropologists, in a form of "intellectual imperialism," dismiss Indigenous societies' truths as "magical beliefs." Even as many different societies, including Western society, have experiences with spirits, the hold of scientific positivism creates "a kind of force field between the anthropologist and her or his subject matter making it impossible for her or him to come close to it, a kind of religious frigidity." Turner calls for training that would allow scholars to really see what Indigenous communities are talking about. When they say spirits are present, scholars need to stop trying to interpret this away as something different, but instead attempt to shift their consciousness so that they might be able to actually *see* the spirits—so that anthropologists can actually *feel* the energies being activated. Turner, "Reality of Spirits," 11.

10. Larcenia Floyd died on May 30, 2018.

11. Samuel and Olorunnipa, *His Name Is George Floyd*, viii.

12. Samuel and Olorunnipa. *His Name Is George Floyd*, 284.

13. Derek Chauvin's defense attorney tried to claim that Floyd was calling for his girlfriend and not his mother. But I disagree with that assumption. His brother and family all attest to how close he was with his mother, who had just passed away the year before. End-of-life experiences across the world attest to the spirits of loved ones coming to a person as they die. See A. Smith, "Galvanizing Grief," 347.

14. Apata, "'I Can't Breathe.'"

15. Police also countermobilized after Eric Garner's death with their slogan "#WeCantBreathe" to describe how police conceived themselves as "suffocating." K. Pérez, "Embodying 'I Can't Breathe,'" 84.

16. Crawley, "Breath"; Houdek, "In the Aftertimes, Breathe."

17. Oya's power over death breaks captivity. She harnesses the illusive qualities of air and wields them against enemies. In the divination story *(odu) osá melli*, ruled by Oya, enslaved Black people revolt against White slave masters to begin a new society.

18. Heinrich Pas, "Why More Physicists Are Starting to Think Space and Time Are 'Illusions,'" *Daily Beast*, January 30, 2023, https://www.thedailybeast.com /why-more-physicists-are-starting-to-think-space-and-time-are-illusions?source =articles&via=rss.

19. C. Smith, "Facing the Dragon," 31.

20. Collins, "Meaning of Motherhood," 3.

21. C. Smith, "Facing the Dragon."

22. D.-A. Davis, *Reproductive Injustice*, 77.

23. C. Rodriguez, "Mothering While Black."

24. Brittney Cooper, "I Could Have Been Sandra Bland: Black America's Terrifying Truth," *Salon*, July 23, 2015, https://www.salon.com/2015/07/23/black_americas _terrifying_truth_any_of_us_could_have_been_sandra_bland/.

25. R. Williams, "Toward a Theorization of Black Maternal Grief."

26. Schenwar, Macaré, and Price, *Who Do You Serve, Who Do You Protect?*, 11.

27. Zaru and Roberts, "Trayvon Martin's Mother, Sybrina Fulton."

28. You can find the web archive of the original posting online. See John Elder, "Investigative Update on Critical Incident," Inside Minneapolis Police, May 26, 2020, https://web.archive.org/web/20210331182901/https://www.insidempd.com/2020/05/26/man-dies-after-medical-incident-during-police-interaction/.

29. Karnowski, "Explainer: 'Excited Delirium.'"

30. Claire Sanford, "Defense Closing Argument Transcript: Derek Chauvin Trial for Murder of George Floyd," *Rev Blog*, accessed January 30, 2024, https://www.rev.com/blog/transcripts/defense-closing-argument-transcript-derek-chauvin-trial-for-murder-of-george-floyd.

31. Jay Senter and Shaila Dewan, "Killer of George Floyd Sentenced to 21 Years for Violating Civil Rights," *New York Times*, July 7, 2022, https://www.nytimes.com/2022/07/07/us/derek-chauvin-george-floyd-sentence.html.

32. Larry Buchanan, Quoctrung Bui, and Jugal K. Patel, "Black Lives Matter May Be the Largest Movement in U.S. History," *New York Times*, July 3, 2020, https://www.nytimes.com/interactive/2020/07/03/us/george-floyd-protests-crowd-size.html.

33. Sam Levins, "These US Cities Defunded Police: 'We're Transferring Money to the Community,'" *Guardian*, March 11, 2021, https://www.theguardian.com/us-news/2021/mar/07/us-cities-defund-police-transferring-money-community.

34. Levins, "These US Cities Defunded Police."

35. Levins, "These US Cities Defunded Police."

36. McDowell and Fernandez, "'Disband, Disempower, and Disarm,'" 376.

37. Du Bois, *Souls of Black Folk*.

38. A. Davis, *Political Prisoners, Prisons, and Black Liberation*, 75.

39. Faye Harrison first argued for abolition in anthropology. Harrison, "Everyday Neoliberalism," 13. See also Keisha-Khan Perry, who addresses abolition in the struggles of Afro-Brazilian women and African American women. Perry, "Groundings with My Sisters." Savannah Shange describes abolition as "an ethic and a scholarly mode that attends to the interface between the multisided anti-Black state and those who seek to survive it." Shange, "#OurLivesMatter," 10. Sociologist Matt Desmond argues that America should abolish poverty. Desmond, *Poverty, by America*.

40. Iwai, Khan, and DasGupta, "Abolition Medicine," 159.

41. Iwai, Khan, and DasGupta, "Abolition Medicine," 159.

42. Seigel, "Dilemma of 'Racial Profiling.'"

43. Wall, "Police Invention of Humanity."

44. Wall, "Police Invention of Humanity," 322.

45. Wall, "Police Invention of Humanity," 321.

46. Akbar, "An Abolitionist Horizon for (Police) Reform," 1782.

47. Gilmore, *Abolition Geography*, 48.

48. Gilmore, *Abolition Geography*, 185.

49. Walcott, *On Property*.

50. See Joy James, "The Architects of Abolitionism: George Jackson, Angela Davis, and the Deradicalization of Prison Struggles," Center for the Study of Slavery and Justice's Carceral State Reading Group at Brown University, April 8, 2019, https://www.youtube.com/watch?v=cE3xI9T6OGs

51. James, "The Architects of Abolitionism."

52. James, "The Architects of Abolitionism."

53. Mariame Kaba, "Yes, We Mean Literally Abolish the Police," *New York Times*, June 12, 2020, https://www.nytimes.com/2020/06/12/opinion/sunday/floyd-abolish-defund-police.html.

54. See the 2018 opinion by Judge William H. Orrick in *Woods v. City of S.F.*, Case No. 3:15-cv-05666-WHO (N.D. Cal. October 9, 2018), https://casetext.com/case/woods-v-city-of-sf.

55. Arwa Mahdawi, "No Charges for San Francisco Police over Mario Woods and Luis Gongora Deaths," *Guardian*, May 24, 2018, https://www.theguardian.com/us-news/2018/may/24/san-francisco-police-shooting-mario-woods-luis-gongora-no-charges; Bay City News, "Judge Rules Lawsuit against Officers in Mario Woods Shooting Can Go to Trial," *San Francisco Examiner*, October 10, 2018, https://www.sfexaminer.com/news/judge-rules-lawsuit-against-officers-in-mario-woods-shooting-can-go-to-trial/article_9d5f5da5-a036-59d9-9abc-b450fc8b2e15.html.

56. Michael Barba, "SF to Pay 400k Settlement to Mother of Mario Woods over Fatal Police Shooting," *San Francisco Examiner*, June 3, 2019, https://www.sfexaminer.com/archives/sf-to-pay-400k-settlement-to-mother-of-mario-woods-over-fatal-police-shooting/article_d5703213-d1ed-5685-8724-cb1d0e3abaea.html

57. In October 2019, after Colorado governor Jared Polis announced an independent investigation into Elijah McClain's death, pictures surfaced of officers posing at the site where McClain had been detained, reenacting the choke hold restraint that had been used on him.

58. Jonathan Smith, Melissa Costello, and Roberto Villasenor were commissioned by the City Council of Aurora, Colorado, to produce a report and recommendations. Their report, *Investigation Report and Recommendations*, February 22, 2021, can be downloaded from a link on the city's website. See "Independent Report Released in Elijah McClain Case," Aurora Colorado, March 16, 2021, https://www.auroragov.org/news/whats_new/independent_report_released_in_mc_clain_case.

59. A *Terry stop* is a stop-and-frisk stop permitted by the 1968 US Supreme Court ruling in *Terry v. Ohio*, which requires police to have a reasonable suspicion that the person being stopped is armed and involved in a crime "Terry Stop / Stop and Frisk," Legal Information Institute, Cornell Law School, accessed February 12, 2023, https://www.law.cornell.edu/wex/terry_stop/stop_and_frisk.

60. Smith, Costello, and Villasenor, *Investigation Report and Recommendations*, 6.

61. Smith, Costello, and Villasenor, *Investigation Report and Recommendations*, 134.

62. Martin Kaste, "California Bans 'Excited Delirium' Term as a Cause of Death," NPR, October 15, 2023, www.npr.org/2023/10/15/1206041620/california-bans-excited-delirium-term-as-a-cause-of-death.

63. Kevin Short, "Emergency Medicine Association Finally Withdraws Its Approval of Policy Paper Endorsing 'Excited Delirium' as Cause of Death." PHR, October 13, 2023, phr.org/news/emergency-medicine-association-finally-withdraws-its -approval-of-policy-paper-endorsing-excited-delirium-as-cause-of-death/.

64. David K. Li and Phil Helsel, "Colorado Paramedics Convicted in the Death of Elijah Mcclain," NBCNews.com, December 23, 2023, https://www.nbcnews.com/ news/us-news/colorado-paramedics-convicted-death-elijah-mcclain-rcna130920.

65. Li and Helsel, "Colorado Paramedics Convicted in the Death of Elijah Mcclain."

66. This was the second acquittal in the trials of officers who detained and forefully restrained Elijah McClain. Former officer Randy Roedema was the only officer convicted. The two paramedics were convicted in December 2023. Audra D. S. Burch and Kelley Manley, "Second Police Officer Acquitted in Elijah McClain Death," *New York Times*, November 6, 2023, https://www.nytimes.com/2023/11/06/us/elijah-mcclain -death-police-verdict.html.

67. Burch and Manley, "Second Police Officer Acquitted in Elijah McClain Death."

68. Otero similarly shows how poetry is ritual and creates embodied transformations that are resonant with spiritual mediumship. Otero, *Archives of Conjure*, 6.

69. Craig and Blount-Hill, *Justice and Legitimacy in Policing*, 267.

70. Gilmore, *Abolition Geography*, 338.

Afterword

1. Richard Seymour, "The Murder of Hélène Rytman," *Verso* (blog), July 24, 2017, https://www.versobooks.com/blogs/3324-the-murder-of-helene-rytman.

2. See Gordon, *Ghostly Matters*, 8; Derrida, *Specters of Marx*.

3. See the powerful work of Black, Chicanx, and Latiné queer scholars who have theorized radical spiritual academia, such as Gloria Anzaldúa's *Borderlands,* a poetic treatise that uses academia as spiritual activism. See also Anzaldúa and Moraga, *This Bridge Called My Back*, which conjures women of color feminist solidarity through activist scholarship. The work of Irene Lara is also powerful alchemy toward liberation. Lara, "Healing Sueños for Academia"; and Lara, "Bruja Positionalities." Laura Pérez, in *Chicana Art*, shows how Chicana art is its own form of spiritual work. adrienne maree brown, in *Emergent Strategies*, has taken up spiritual activism through Octavia Butler's writings in what Taisia Kitaiskaia has called a kind of "literary witchcraft." See Kitaiskaia, *Literary Witches*.

4. Historians have discussed how they feel haunted by their archives. Solimar Otero has talked about the conjuring potential of archives in what she describes as the "residual transcripts" that link copresences to human actors. Otero, *Archives of Conjure*, 4.

5. Otero, *Archives of Conjure*, 6–7.

Bibliography

Aber, Shaina, and Mary Small. "Citizen or Subordinate: Permutations of Belonging in the United States and the Dominican Republic." *Journal on Migration and Human Security* 1, no. 3 (2013): 76–96.

Akbar, Amna A. "An Abolitionist Horizon for (Police) Reform." *California Law Review* 108, no. 6 (2020): 1781–1846.

Alexander, Michelle. "The New Jim Crow." *Ohio State Journal of Criminal Law* 9 (2011): 7–26.

Alexander, M. Jacqui. *Pedagogies of Crossing: Meditations on Feminism, Sexual Politics, Memory, and the Sacred.* Durham, NC: Duke University Press, 2006.

Allen, Jafari S. *¡Venceremos? The Erotics of Black Self-Making in Cuba.* Durham, NC: Duke University Press, 2011.

Alves, Jaime Amparo. *The Anti-Black City: Police Terror and Black Urban Life in Brazil.* Minneapolis: University of Minnesota Press, 2018.

Andersen, Kurt. *Fantasyland: How America Went Haywire: A 500-Year History.* New York: Random House, 2018.

Anderson, Elijah. *Streetwise: Race, Class, and Change in an Urban Community.* Chicago: University of Chicago Press, 2013.

Anderson, Norman B., Maya McNeilly, and Hector Myers. "Autonomic Reactivity and Hypertension in Blacks: A Review and Proposed Model." *Ethnicity and Disease* 1, no. 2 (1991): 154–70.

Anderson, Norman B., Maya McNeilly, and Hector Myers. "Hypertension in Blacks: Psychosocial and Biological Perspectives." *Journal of Hypertension* 7, no. 3 (1989): 161–72.

Anzaldúa, Gloria. *Borderlands/La Frontera: The New Mestiza.* San Francisco: Aunt Lute, 1987.

Anzaldúa, Gloria, and Cherríe Moraga, eds. *This Bridge Called My Back.* New York: Kitchen Table Press, 1981.

Apata, Gabriel O. "I Can't Breathe: The Suffocating Nature of Racism." *Theory, Culture and Society* 37, nos. 7–8 (2020): 241–54.

Appelbaum, Paul S. "Excited Delirium, Ketamine, and Deaths in Police Custody." *Psychiatric Services* 73, no. 7 (2022): 827–29.

Baclawski, K. "The Observer Effect." Paper presented at the IEEE conference on Cognitive and Computational Aspects of Situation Management (CogSIMA), Boston, MA, 2018. https://ieeexplore.ieee.org/document/8423983.

Baker, Lee D. "The Racist Anti-racism of American Anthropology." *Transform Anthropology* 29 (2021): 127–42.

Beliso-De Jesús, Aisha. "Brujx: An Afro-Latinx Queer Gesture." In *Critical Dialogues in Latinx Studies*, edited by Ana Ramos Zayas and Merida Rúa, 528–38. New York: New York University Press, 2021.

Beliso-De Jesús, Aisha. *Electric Santería: Racial and Sexual Assemblages of Transnational Religion*. New York: Columbia University Press, 2015.

Beliso-De Jesús, Aisha. "A Hieroglyphics of Zora Neale Hurston." *Journal of Africana Religions* 4, no. 2 (2016): 290–303.

Beliso-De Jesús, Aisha. "The Jungle Academy: Molding White Supremacy in American Police Recruits." *American Anthropologist* 122, no. 1 (2020): 143–56.

Beliso-De Jesús, Aisha. "Santería Copresence and the Making of African Diaspora Bodies." *Cultural Anthropology* 29, no. 3 (2014): 503–26.

Beliso-De Jesús, Aisha M., and Jemima Pierre. "Anthropology of White Supremacy." *American Anthropologist* 122, no. 1 (2020): 65–75.

Benavides, Michael D. "Taser Guns: Less-Than Lethal Weapons for Law Enforcement." Research paper, Galveston County Sheriff's Office, April 22, 2004. https://shsu-ir.tdl.org/bitstream/handle/20.500.11875/1364/0963.pdf?sequence=1.

Berenson, Edward. *The Accusation: Blood Libel in an American Town*. New York: W. W. Norton, 2019.

Bergen-Cico, Dessa K. *War and Drugs: The Role of Military Conflict in the Development of Substance Abuse*. New York: Routledge, 2015.

Blanco, María del Pilar, and Esther Peeren, eds. *The Spectralities Reader: Ghosts and Haunting in Contemporary Cultural Theory*. New York: Bloomsbury, 2013.

Bloom, Lisa. *Suspicion Nation: The Inside Story of the Trayvon Martin Injustice and Why We Continue to Repeat It*. New York: Counterpoint Press, 2014.

Boaz, Danielle N. *Banning Black Gods: Law and Religions of the African Diaspora*. University Park: Pennsylvania State University Press, 2021.

Bonilla, Yarimar. "Ordinary Sovereignty." *Small Axe: A Caribbean Journal of Criticism* 17, no. 3 (2013): 152–65.

Bonilla, Yarimar, and Marisol LeBrón, eds. *Aftershocks of Disaster: Puerto Rico before and after the Storm*. Chicago: Haymarket Books, 2019.

Boullosa, Carmen, and Mike Wallace. "How the Cartels Were Born." *Jacobin*, accessed January 3, 2023. https://jacobin.com/2015/03/mexico-drug-cartel-neoliberalism/.

Bradford, Anita Casavantes. "Operation Pedro Pan: The Migration of Unaccompanied Cuban Children to the United States, 1960–1962." *Oxford Research*

Encyclopedia of Latin American History, August 22, 2017. https://doi.org/10.1093 /acrefore/9780199366439.013.334.

Brandon, George. "Sacrificial Practices in Santeria, an African-Cuban Religion in the United States." In *Africanisms in American Culture*, edited by Joseph E. Holloway, 119–47. Bloomington: Indiana University Press, 2005.

Brave, Michael A., Steven B. Karch, Mark W. Kroll, Michael A. Graham, and Charles V. Wetli. "Medical Examiner Collection of Comprehensive, Objective Medical Evidence for Conducted Electrical Weapons and Their Temporal Relationship to Sudden Arrest." U.S. Department of Commerce, National Institutes of Standards and Technology presentation. Accessed January 7, 2023. https://www.nist.gov/system/files/documents/director/med_exam_collection _of_comprehensive_objec_med_evid_for_conducted_electrical_weapons_and _their_temporal_relationship_to_sudden_arrest-brave-death.pdf.

Bronfman, Alejandra. "En Plena Libertad y Democracia: Negros Brujos and the Social Question, 1904–1919." *Hispanic American Historical Review* 82, no. 3 (2002): 549–87.

brown, adrian maree. *Emergent Strategies: Shaping Change, Changing Worlds*. Chico, CA: AK Press, 2017.

Brown, David H. *Santería Enthroned: Art, Ritual, and Innovation in an Afro-Cuban Religion*. New York: Routledge, 2021.

Brown, Melissa, Rashawn Ray, Ed Summers, and Neil Fraistat. "#SayHerName: A Case Study of Intersectional Social Media Activism." *Ethnic and Racial Studies* 40, no. 11 (2017): 1831–46.

Buchanan, Ian. *Deleuze and Guattari's "Anti-Oedipus": A Reader's Guide*. London: Bloomsbury, 2008.

Bucky, Steven F., and Constance Dalenberg. "The Relationship between Training of Mental Health Professionals and the Reporting of Ritual Abuse and Multiple Personality Disorder Symptomatology." *Journal of Psychology and Theology* 20, no. 3 (1992): 233–38.

Burton, Orisanmi. "Captivity, Kinship, and Black Masculine Care Work under Domestic Warfare." *American Anthropologist* 123, no. 3 (2021): 621–32.

Butler, Judith. "Endangered/Endangering Schematic Racism and White Paranoia." In *Reading Rodney King / Reading Urban Uprising*, edited by Robert Gooding-Williams, 15–22. New York: Routledge, 2013.

Byrd, Jodi A. *The Transit of Empire: Indigenous Critiques of Colonialism*. Minneapolis: University of Minnesota Press, 2011.

California Office of Criminal Justice Planning, and Gayle Olson-Raymer. "Occult Crime: A Law Enforcement Primer." *Research Update: Special Edition* 1, no. 6 (Winter 1989–1990): 1–65. https://www.ojp.gov/pdffiles1/Digitization /124094NCJRS.pdf.

Capo, Julio, Jr. "Queering Mariel: Mediating Cold War Foreign Policy and US Citizenship among Cuba's Homosexual Exile Community, 1978–1994." *Journal of American Ethnic History* 29, no. 4 (2010): 78–106.

Carlson, Jennifer, "Police Warriors and Police Guardians: Race, Masculinity, and the Construction of Gun Violence." *Social Problems* 67, no. 3 (2020): 399–417.

Carrigan, William D., and Clive Webb. "The Lynching of Persons of Mexican Origin or Descent in the United States, 1848 to 1928." *Journal of Social History* 37, no. 2 (Winter 2003): 411–38. https://www.jstor.org/stable/3790404.

Carstairs, Catherine. "'The Most Dangerous Drug': Images of African-Americans and Cocaine Use in the Progressive Era." *Left History: An Interdisciplinary Journal of Historical Inquiry and Debate* 7, no. 1 (2000): 46–61.

Carter, Michele M., Tracy Sbrocco, and Clifford Carter. "African Americans and Anxiety Disorders Research: Development of a Testable Theoretical Framework." *Psychotherapy* 33, no. 3 (1996): 449–63. https://doi.org/10.1037/0033-3204.33.3 .449.

Carter, Terrance S., and R. Johanna Blom. "Update on Christian Brothers." *Charity Law Bulletin* 24 (2003): 1–6.

Castellanos, Israel. *La brujería y el ñañiguismo en Cuba desde el punto de vista médico-legal: Lema: Kulturkampf.* Havana: Imp. de Lloredo, 1916.

Chiba, Yoko. "W. B. Yeats's Occultism as a Symbolic Link to Other Cultures." *HJEAS: Hungarian Journal of English and American Studies* 10, nos. 1/2 (2004): 237–46.

Clarke, Kamari M. "Beyond Genealogies: Expertise and Religious Knowledge in Legal Cases Involving African Diasporic Publics." *Transforming Anthropology* 25, no. 2 (2017): 130–55.

Clarke, Kamari M. "Toward Reflexivity in the Anthropology of Expertise and Law." *American Anthropologist* 122, no. 3 (2020): 584–87.

Coates, Ta-Nehisi. "The Case for Reparations." In *The Best American Magazine Writing 2015*, edited by Sid Holt, 1–50. New York: Columbia University Press, 2015.

Cohen, Cathy J. "Punks, Bulldaggers, and Welfare Queens: Sexual Identities, Queer Politics." *GLQ: Journal of Gay and Lesbian Studies* 3, no. 4 (1997): 437–65. https://doi.org/10.1215/10642684-3-4-437.

Coldrey, Barry. "A Strange Mixture of Caring and Corruption: Residential Care in Christian Brothers Orphanages and Industrial Schools during Their Last Phase, 1940s to 1960s." *History of Education* 29, no. 4 (2000): 343–55.

Collins, Patricia Hill. "The Meaning of Motherhood in Black Culture and Black Mother-Daughter Relationships." *Sage* 4, no. 2 (1987): 325–40.

Combahee River Collective. "Six Black Women: Why Did They Die?" *Radical America* 13 (1979): 44–46.

Cooper, Rachel. "Are Culture-Bound Syndromes as Real as Universally Occurring Disorders?" *Studies in History and Philosophy of Science* 41, no. 4 (2010): 325–32.

Cortez, Julio García. *El Santo (la Ocha): Secretos de la religión Lucumí.* Self-published, Librería & Distribuidora Universal, 1971.

Craig, Miltonette Olivia, and Kwan-Lamar Blount-Hill, eds. *Justice and Legitimacy in Policing.* London: Taylor and Francis, 2023.

Crawley, Ashon T. "Breath." In *Blackpentecostal Breath: The Aesthetics of Possibility*, 32–85. New York: Fordham University Press, 2017.

Crenshaw, Kimberlé. "Demarginalizing the Intersection of Race and Sex: A Black Feminist Critique of Antidiscrimination Doctrine, Feminist Theory and Antiracist Politics." *University of Chicago Legal Forum* (1989): Article 8. https:// chicagounbound.uchicago.edu/uclf/vol1989/iss1/8.

Crenshaw, Kimberlé, Andrea Ritchie, Rachel Anspach, Rachel Gilmer, and Luke Harris. *Say Her Name: Resisting Police Brutality against Black Women.* African American Policy Forum, July 2015. https://scholarship.law.columbia.edu/cgi /viewcontent.cgi?article=4235&context=faculty_scholarship.

Davis, Angela Yvonne. *Political Prisoners, Prisons, and Black Liberation.* Boston: Boston Anarchist Black Cross, 2005.

Davis, Dána-Ain. *Reproductive Injustice: Racism, Pregnancy, and Premature Birth.* New York: NYU Press, 2019.

Deleuze, Gilles, and Félix Guattari. *Anti-Oedipus: Capitalism and Schizophrenia.* New York: Penguin, 2009.

De Moya, Maria. "Protesting the Homeland: Diaspora Dissent Public Relations Efforts to Oppose the Dominican Republic's Citizenship Policies." In *Protest Public Relations: Communicating Dissent and Activism,* edited by Ana Adi, 106–27. New York: Routledge, 2019.

Denomme, Nicholas. "The Domino Effect: Ed Domino's Early Studies of Psychoactive Drugs." *Journal of Psychoactive Drugs* 50, no. 4 (2018): 298–305.

Derrida, Jacques. *Specters of Marx: The State of the Debt, the Work of Mourning, and the New International.* New York: Routledge, 2012.

Desmond, Matthew. *Poverty, by America.* New York: Crown, 2023.

DeYoung, Mary. "Another Look at Moral Panics: The Case of Satanic Day Care Centers." *Deviant Behavior* 19, no. 3 (1998): 257–78.

Di Maio, Dominick, and Vincent J. Di Maio. *Forensic Pathology.* Boca Raton, FL: CRC Press, 2001.

Di Maio, Theresa C., and Vincent J. Di Maio. *Excited Delirium Syndrome: Cause of Death and Prevention.* London: Taylor and Francis, 2006.

Di Maio, Vincent J., and Ron Franscell. *Morgue: A Life in Death.* New York: St. Martin's Press, 2016.

Duany, Jorge. "Nation on the Move: The Construction of Cultural Identities in Puerto Rico and the Diaspora." *American Ethnologist* 27, no. 1 (2000): 5–30.

Du Bois, W. E. B. *Souls of Black Folk.* Introduction by Manning Marable. 1903. New York: Routledge, 2015.

Duru, Jeremi. "The Central Park Five, the Scottsboro Boys, and the Myth of the Bestial Black Man." *Cardozo Law Review* 25, no. 4 (2003): 1315–65. https:// digitalcommons.wcl.american.edu/cgi/viewcontent.cgi?article=2556&context =facsch_lawrev.

Dwyer, Kelsey K. "Artifacts of Restraint and Enslaved African Women of the Eighteenth Century Transatlantic Slave Trade." In *Excavating the Histories of Slave-Trade and Pirate Ships: Property, Plunder and Loss,* edited by Lynn Brenda Harris and Valerie Ann Johnson, 61–82. Cham, Switzerland: Springer International, 2022.

Dyson, Erika White. "Spiritualism and Crime: Negotiating Prophecy and Police Power at the Turn of the Twentieth Century." PhD diss., Columbia University, 2010.

Edwards, Erica Johnson. "Christianity's Role in Colonial and Revolutionary Haiti (Article Commentary)." *Studies in Religion and the Enlightenment* 2, no. 2 (2021): 1–4. https://dr.ntu.edu.sg/bitstream/10356/148563/2/Edwards%20Final%202021.2.2.1.pdf.

Erickson, Brad. "George Clinton and David Bowie: The Space Race in Black and White." *Popular Music and Society* 39, no. 5 (2016): 563–78.

Estrella, Amarilys. "Muertos Civiles: Mourning the Casualties of Racism in the Dominican Republic." *Transforming Anthropology* 28, no. 1 (2020): 41–57.

Fanon, Frantz. *Black Skin, White Masks.* 1952. New York: Grove Press, 2008.

Fanon, Frantz. *The Wretched of the Earth.* 1961. New York: Grove Press, 2004.

Farmer, Paul. "An Anthropology of Structural Violence." *Current Anthropology* 45, no. 3 (2004): 305–25.

Fassin, D. *Writing the World of Policing: The Difference Ethnography Makes.* Chicago: University of Chicago Press, 2017.

Fernandez, Nadine T. *Revolutionizing Romance: Interracial Couples in Contemporary Cuba.* New Brunswick, NJ: Rutgers University Press, 2010.

Ferrer, Ada. "Speaking of Haiti: Slavery, Revolution, and Freedom in Cuban Slave Testimony." In *The World of the Haitian Revolution,* edited by David Patrick Geggus and Norman Fiering, 223–47. Bloomington: Indiana University Press, 2009.

Figueroa, Yomaira. "After the Hurricane: Afro-Latina Decolonial Feminisms and Destierro." *Hypatia* 35, no. 1 (2020): 220–29.

Finamore, Adrianna. "Geeking and Freaking: Black Women and the 1980s Crack Epidemic." *California History* 99, no. 2 (2022): 59–80.

Finch, Aisha K. *Rethinking Slave Rebellion in Cuba: La Escalera and the Insurgencies of 1841–1844.* Chapel Hill: University of North Carolina Press, 2015.

Fishbain, David A., and Charles V. Wetli. "Cocaine-Induced Psychosis and Sudden Death in Recreational Cocaine Users." *Journal of Forensic Sciences* 30, no. 3 (1985): 873–80.

Fishbain, David A., and Charles V. Wetli. "Cocaine Intoxication, Delirium, and Death in a Body Packer." *Annals of Emergency Medicine* 10, no. 10 (1981): 531–32.

Font, Mauricio A., and Alfonso W. Quiro. *Cuban Counterpoints: The Legacy of Fernando Ortiz.* Washington, DC: Lexington Books, 2004.

Franke, Katherine. "Law." In *A Companion to Gender Studies,* edited by Philomena Essed, David Theo Goldberg, and Audrey Kobayashi, 160–80. Hoboken, NJ: Wiley, 2009.

Frankfurter, David. *Evil Incarnate: Rumors of Demonic Conspiracy and Ritual Abuse in History.* Princeton, NJ: Princeton University Press, 2006.

Freimuth, Vicki S., Sandra Crouse Quinn, Stephen B. Thomas, Galen Cole, Eric Zook, and Ted Duncan. "African Americans' Views on Research and the Tuskegee Syphilis Study." *Social Science and Medicine* 52, no. 5 (2001): 797–808.

Gamsakhurdia, Nino, and Ana Kurdiani. "The Jezebel Stereotype." *Journal in Humanities* 10, no. 2 (2021): 88–93.

Garcia, Alyssa. "Situating Race, Navigating Belongings: Mapping Afro-Cuban Identities in the United States." *Latino(a) Research Review* 7, no. 1 (2008): 59–90.

García Hernández, César Cuauhtémoc. "Creating Crimmigration." *Brigham Young University Law Review* no. 6 (2013): Article 4. https://digitalcommons.law.byu .edu/cgi/viewcontent.cgi?article=2903&context=lawreview.

García Peña, Lorgia. *Translating Blackness: Latinx Colonialities in Global Perspective.* Durham, NC: Duke University Press, 2022.

Garza, Alicia. Foreword to *Who Do You Serve, Who Do You Protect? Police Violence and Resistance in the United States,* edited by Maya Schenwar, Joe Macaré, and Alana Yu-lan Price, vii–x. Chicago: Haymarket Books, 2016.

Gau, Jacinta M., Clayton Mosher, and Travis C. Pratt. "An Inquiry into the Impact of Suspect Race on Police Use of Tasers." *Police Quarterly* 13, no. 1 (2010): 27–48, 41.

Geary, Daniel. *Beyond Civil Rights: The Moynihan Report and Its legacy.* Philadelphia: University of Pennsylvania Press, 2015.

Geggus, David P., ed. *The Impact of the Haitian Revolution in the Atlantic World.* Columbia: University of South Carolina Press, 2020.

George, Paul S. "Colored Town: Miami's Black Community, 1896–1930." *Florida Historical Quarterly* 56, no. 4 (1978): 432–47. http://www.jstor.org/stable /30150329.

Gilmore, Ruth Wilson. *Abolition Geography: Essays towards Liberation.* New York: Verso Books, 2022.

Goodmark, Leigh. "Hands Up at Home: Militarized Masculinity and Police Officers Who Commit Intimate Partner Abuse." *Brigham Young University Law Review* no. 5 (2015): Article 5. https://digitalcommons.law.byu.edu/lawreview/vol2015 /iss5/5/.

Gordon, Avery F. *Ghostly Matters: Haunting and the Sociological Imagination.* Minneapolis: University of Minnesota Press, 2008.

Gough, Charlotte. "Another Man's Memories: Masculine Trauma and Satanic Panic in *The Believers* (1987) and *Angel Heart* (1987)." *Horror Studies* 13, no. 2 (2022): 193–208.

Grappo, Laura Ramos. "'Four Lives Lost': Criminalization and Innocence in the Case of the San Antonio Four." *Latino Studies* 18, no. 1 (2020): 3–26.

Greenbaum, Susan D. *Blaming the Poor: The Long Shadow of the Moynihan Report on Cruel Images about Poverty.* New Brunswick, NJ: Rutgers University Press, 2015.

Grimes, Hilary. *The Late Victorian Gothic: Mental Science, the Uncanny, and Scenes of Writing.* New York: Routledge, 2016.

Grosfoguel, Ramon. "Race and Ethnicity or Racialized Ethnicities? Identities within Global Coloniality." *Ethnicities* 4, no. 3 (2004): 315–36.

Grosfoguel, Ramon, and Chloe S. Georas. "Coloniality of Power and Racial Dynamics: Notes toward a Reinterpretation of Latino Caribbeans in New York City." *American Journal of Sociology* 98, no. 6 (2000): 85–125.

Guridy, Frank Andre. *Forging Diaspora: Afro-Cubans and African Americans in a World of Empire and Jim Crow*. Chapel Hill: University of North Carolina Press, 2010.

Gutiérrez, Elena R., and Liza Fuentes. "Population Control by Sterilization: The Cases of Puerto Rican and Mexican-Origin Women in the United States." *Latino(a) Research Review* 7, no. 3 (2009): 85–100.

Hamm, Mark S. *The Abandoned Ones: The Imprisonment and Uprising of the Mariel Boat People*. Boston: Northeastern University Press, 1995.

Hanna, Philippe, and Frank Vanclay. "Human Rights, Indigenous Peoples and the Concept of Free, Prior and Informed Consent." *Impact Assessment and Project Appraisal* 31, no. 2 (2013): 146–57.

Harrison, Faye V. "Everyday Neoliberalism, Diminishing Subsistence Security, and the Criminalization of Survival: Gendered Urban Poverty in Three African Diaspora Contexts." *IUAES Inter Congress on Mega-urbanization, Multi-ethnic Society, Human Rights, and Development*, edited by Buddhadeb Chaudhuri and Sumita Chaudhuri, 82–103. New Delhi: Inter-India Publications, 2007.

Hartley, George. "The Curandera of Conquest: Gloria Anzaldúa's Decolonial Remedy." *Aztlán: A Journal of Chicano Studies* 35, no. 1 (2010): 135–61.

Hartman, Saidiya. *Lose Your Mother: A Journey along the Atlantic Slave Route*. New York: Macmillan, 2008.

Harvey, David L., and Michael H. Reed. "The Culture of Poverty: An Ideological Analysis." *Sociological Perspectives* 39, no. 4 (1996): 465–95.

Hazel, Yadira Perez. "Sensing Difference: Whiteness, National Identity, and Belonging in the Dominican Republic." *Transforming Anthropology* 22, no. 2 (2014): 78–91.

Hejtmanek, K. "Caring through Restraint: Violence, Intimacy and Identity in Mental Health Practice." *Culture, Medicine, and Psychiatry* 34, no. 4 (2010): 668–74.

Helg, Aline. *Our Rightful Share: The Afro-Cuban Struggle for Equality, 1886–1912*. Chapel Hill: University of North Carolina Press, 1995.

Hemenway, E. *Zora Neale Hurston: A Literary Biography*. Champaign: University of Illinois Press, 1980.

Henderson, Linda. "The Forgotten Meta-realities of Modernism: Die Uebersinnliche Welt and the International Cultures of Science and Occultism." *Glass Bead Journal* (2016). https://www.glass-bead.org/article/the-forgotten-meta-realities-of-modernism/?lang=enview.

Hevers, Wulf, Stephen H. Hadley, Hartmut Lüddens, and Jahanshah Amin. "Ketamine, but Not Phencyclidine, Selectively Modulates Cerebellar $GABA_A$ Receptors Containing α6 and δ Subunits." *Journal of Neuroscience* 28, no. 20 (2008): 5383–89. https://doi.org/10.1523/JNEUROSCI.5443-07.2008.

Hicks, Robert D. *In Pursuit of Satan: The Police and the Occult*. Amherst, NY: Prometheus Books, 2010. Kindle.

Hinton, Elizabeth. *From the War on Poverty to the War on Crime: The Making of Mass Incarceration in America*. Cambridge, MA: Harvard University Press, 2016.

Holzer, Henry Mark. "Contradictions Will Out: Animal Rights vs. Animal Sacrifice in the Supreme Court." *Animal Law* 1 (1995): 83–107. https://law.lclark.edu/live /files/26630-01f-holzer.

Houdek, Matthew. "In the Aftertimes, Breathe: Rhetorical Technologies of Suffocation and an Abolitionist Praxis of (Breathing in) Relation." *Quarterly Journal of Speech* 108, no. 1 (2022): 48–74.

Hurston, Zora Neale. *Dust Tracks on a Road: Autobiography.* 1942. Toronto: McClelland and Stewart, 2018.

Hurston, Zora Neale, Ruby Dee, and Ann C. Villet. *Mules and Men.* New York: Perennial Library, 1935.

Ioanide, Paula. "The Story of Abner Louima: Cultural Fantasies, Gendered Racial Violence, and the Ethical Witness." *Journal of Haitian Studies* 13, no. 1 (2007): 4–26.

Iwai, Yoshiko, Zahra H. Khan, and Sayantani DasGupta. "Abolition Medicine." *Lancet* 396, no. 10245 (2020): 158–59.

Jenkins, Herbert. *Keeping the Peace: A Police Chief Looks at His Job.* New York: Harper and Row, 1970.

Jenson, Deborah. "Dessalines's American Proclamations of the Haitian Independence." *Journal of Haitian Studies* 15, no. 1/2 (2009): 72–102.

Johnson, E. Patrick, and Ramón H. Rivera-Servera. eds. *Blacktino Queer Performance.* Durham, NC: Duke University Press, 2016.

Jones, Branwen Gruffydd. "Definitions and Categories: Epistemologies of Race and Critique." *Postcolonial Studies* 19, no. 2 (2016): 173–84.

Joseph, Fiona. "The Treatment of Haitian Bahamians in Bahamian Society." *International Journal of Bahamian Studies* 20, no. 1 (2014): 63–69.

Kelley, Robin D. G. "'We Are Not What We Seem': Rethinking Black Working-Class Opposition in the Jim Crow South." *Journal of American History* 80, no. 1 (1993): 75–112.

Kitaiskaia, Taisia. *Literary Witches: A Celebration of Magical Women Writers.* New York: Basic Books, 2017.

Klein, Jacqueline. "A Theory of Punishment: The Use of Mechanical Restraints in Psychiatric Care." *Southern California Review of Law and Social Justice* 21, no. 1. (2011): 47–74.

Lara, Irene. "Bruja Positionalities: Toward a Chicana/Latina Spiritual Activism." *Chicana/Latina Studies* 4, no. 2 (2005): 10–45.

Lara, Irene. "Healing Sueños for Academia." In *This Bridge We Call Home,* edited by Gloria Anzaldúa and Analouise Keating, 447–52. New York: Routledge, 2002.

Lee, Erika. "The 'Yellow Peril' and Asian Exclusion in the Americas." *Pacific Historical Review* 76, no. 4 (2007): 537–62.

Lefley, H. P. Review of *Santeria: Afrocuban Concepts of Disease and Its Treatment in Miami,* by Mercedes C. Sandoval. *Journal of Operational Psychiatry* 8 (1977): 52–63.

Lefley, H. P. Review of *Santeria: Afrocuban Concepts of Disease and Its Treatment in Miami,* by Mercedes C. Sandoval. *Transcultural Psychiatric Research Review* 16, no. 1 (1979): 90–94.

Lennox, Malissia. "Refugees, Racism, and Reparations: A Critique of the United States' Haitian Immigration Policy." *Stanford Law Review* 45, no. 3 (1993): 687–724.

Levy-Pounds, Nekima. "Beaten by the System and Down for the Count: Why Poor Women of Color and Children Don't Stand a Chance against US Drug-Sentencing Policy." *University of St. Thomas Law Journal* 3 (2006): 464–98. https://papers.ssrn.com/sol3/papers.cfm?abstract_id=917410.

Lewis, Oscar. "The Culture of Poverty." *Society* 35, no. 2 (1998): 7–9.

Lipman, Jana K. "'The Fish Trusts the Water, and It Is in the Water That It Is Cooked': The Caribbean Origins of the Krome Detention Center." *Radical History Review* 2013, no. 115 (2013): 115–41.

Littlefield, Daniel C. "Echoes of Liberty: Historians, the Stono Rebellion, and the Atlantic World." *South Carolina Historical Magazine* (2019): 186–203.

López, Antonio. *Unbecoming Blackness: The Diaspora Cultures of Afro-Cuban America.* New York: NYU Press, 2012.

López, Iris, and David Forbes. "Borinki Identity in Hawai'i: Present and Future in Spanish." *Centro Journal* 13, no. 1 (2001): 110–27.

Lorde, Audre. *Sister Outsider: Essays and Speeches.* Berkeley, CA: Crossing Press, 2012.

MacLachlan, Colin M. Review of *Afro-Latin America 1800–2000*, by George Reid Andrews. *Hispanic American Historical Review* 87, no. 1 (2007): 576–77.

Maguire, Emily. *Racial Experiments in Cuban Literature and Ethnography.* Gainesville: University Press of Florida, 2011.

Mandal, S., V. K. Sinha, and N. Goyal. "Efficacy of Ketamine Therapy in the Treatment of Depression." *Indian Journal of Psychiatry* 61, no. 5 (2019): 480–85.

Marchetti, Gina. *Romance and the Yellow Peril: Race, Sex, and Discursive Strategies in Hollywood Fiction.* Berkeley: University of California Press, 1994.

Márquez, John D., and Junaid Rana. "Black Radical Possibility and the Decolonial International." *South Atlantic Quarterly* 116, no. 3 (2017): 505–28.

Martinez, Amy Andrea, and Humberto Flores. "Resurrecting Brown Bodies to Advance the Theory and Praxis of Police Abolition in the United States." In *Justice and Legitimacy in Policing*, edited by Miltonette Olivia Craig and Kwan-Lamar Blount-Hill, 256–77. London: Taylor and Francis, 2023.

Martinez, Rafael. "Afro-Cuban Santería among the Cuban-Americans in Dade County Florida: A Psycho-Cultural Approach." Master's thesis, University of Florida, 1979.

Martinez, Rafael, and Charles V. Wetli. "Tattoos of the Marielitos." *American Journal of Forensic Medicine and Pathology* 10, no. 4 (1989): 315–25.

Martínez-San Miguel, Yolanda. *Coloniality of Diasporas: Rethinking Intra-colonial Migrations in a Pan-Caribbean Context.* New York: Springer, 2014.

Massey, Douglas S., and Robert J. Sampson. "Moynihan Redux: Legacies and Lessons." *Annals of the American Academy of Political and Social Science* 621, no. 1 (2009): 6–27.

Matory, J. Lorand. *Black Atlantic Religion.* Princeton, NJ: Princeton University Press, 2009.

Matory, J. Lorand. *The Fetish Revisited: Marx, Freud, and the Gods Black People Make.* Durham, NC: Duke University Press, 2018.

McAlister, Elizabeth. *Rara! Vodou, Power, and Performance in Haiti and Its Diaspora.* Berkeley: University of California Press, 2002.

McCarthy Brown, Karen. "Making Wanga: Reality Constructions and the Magical Manipulation of Power." In *Transparency and Conspiracy: Ethnographies of Suspicion in the New World Order*, edited by Harry G. West and Todd Sanders, 233–57. Durham, NC: Duke University Press, 2003.

McCarthy Brown, Karen. *Mama Lola: A Vodou Priestess in Brooklyn.* Berkeley: University of California Press, 2001.

McCloud, Sean. *Making the American Religious Fringe: Exotics, Subversives, and Journalists, 1955–1993.* Chapel Hill: University of North Carolina Press, 2005.

McDowell, Meghan G., and Luis A. Fernandez. "'Disband, Disempower, and Disarm': Amplifying the Theory and Practice of Police Abolition." *Critical Criminology* 26 (2018): 373–91.

McEntire, Mark M. "Cozbi, Achan, and Jezebel: Executions in the Hebrew Bible and Modern Lynching." *Review and Expositor* 118, no. 1 (2021): 21–31.

Meyer, Doug. *Violent Differences: The Importance of Race in Sexual Assault against Queer Men.* Berkeley: University of California Press, 2022.

Meyer, Matthew. "Police Call It 'Excited Delirium.' Civil Rights Groups Call It a Sham." *Harvard Civil Rights–Civil Liberties Law Review*, November 15, 2019, https://journals.law.harvard.edu/crcl/police-call-it-excited-delirium-civil-rights-groups-call-it-a-sham/.

Michalowski, Raymond I. *Crime and Justice in Socialist Cuba: What Can Left Realists Learn?* Toronto: University of Toronto Press, 1992.

Milian, Claudia. *Latining America: Black-Brown Passages and the Coloring of Latino/a Studies.* Athens: University of Georgia Press, 2013.

Miller, Abraham H., and Nicholas A. Damask. "The Dual Myths of 'Narco-Terrorism': How Myths Drive Policy." *Terrorism and Political Violence* 8, no. 1 (1996): 114–31.

Miller, Ivor. "Cuban Abakuá Chants: Examining New Linguistic and Historical Evidence for the African Diaspora." *African Studies Review* 48, no. 1 (2005): 23–58.

Miller, Ivor. *Voice of the Leopard: African Secret Societies and Cuba.* Jackson: University Press of Mississippi, 2010.

Moore, Robin D. *Nationalizing Blackness: Afrocubanismo and Artistic Revolution in Havana, 1920–1940.* Pittsburgh: University of Pittsburgh Press, 1997.

Morales, Aurora Levins. *Medicine Stories: History, Culture, and the Politics of Integrity.* Boston: South End Press, 1998.

Morgan, Jennifer L. *Laboring Women: Reproduction and Gender in New World Slavery.* Philadelphia: University of Pennsylvania Press, 2004.

Mosby, Ian. "Administering Colonial Science: Nutrition Research and Human Biomedical Experimentation in Aboriginal Communities and Residential Schools, 1942–1952." *Histoire sociale / Social History* 46, no. 1 (2013): 145–72.

Muhammad, Khalil Gibran. *The Condemnation of Blackness: Race, Crime, and the Making of Modern Urban America*. Cambridge, MA: Harvard University Press, 2019.

Mullings, Leith. "The Necropolitics of Reproduction: Racism, Resistance, and the Sojourner Syndrome in the Age of the Movement for Black Lives." In *The Routledge Handbook of Anthropology and Reproduction*, edited by Sallie Han and Cecilia Tomori, 106–22. New York: Routledge, 2021.

Muñoz, José Esteban. *Cruising Utopia: The Then and There of Queer Futurity*. 10th anniversary ed. New York: New York University Press, 2019.

Museus, Samuel D., and Kimberly A. Truong. "Racism and Sexism in Cyberspace: Engaging Stereotypes of Asian American Women and Men to Facilitate Student Learning and Development." *About Campus* 18, no. 4 (2013): 14–21.

Myatt, Leslie, and James M. Roberts. "Preeclampsia: Syndrome or Disease?" *Current Hypertension Reports* 17, no. 11 (2015): 1–8.

Nagel, Alexandra. "The Hands of Albert Einstein: Einstein's Involvement with Hand Readers and a Dutch Psychic." *Correspondences* 9, no. 1 (2021): 49–87.

Neal, Angela M., and Samuel M. Turner. "Anxiety Disorders Research with African Americans: Current Status." *Psychological Bulletin* 109, no. 3 (1991): 400–410.

Nephew, Michelle Andromeda Brown. "Playing with Power: The Authorial Consequences of Roleplaying Games." PhD diss., University of Wisconsin–Milwaukee, 2003.

Nyong'o, Tavia. "I've Got You Under My Skin: Queer Assemblages, Lyrical Nostalgia and the African Diaspora." *Performance Research* 12, no. 3 (2007): 42–54.

O'Brien, David M. *Animal Sacrifice and Religious Freedom: Church of the Lukumi Babalu Aye v. City of Hialeah*. Lawrence: University Press of Kansas, 2004.

Ochoa, Todd Ramón. *Society of the Dead: Quita Manaquita and Palo Praise in Cuba*. Berkeley: University of California Press, 2010.

O'Halloran, R. L., and J. G. Frank. "Asphyxial Death during Prone Restraint Position Revisited: A Report of 21 Cases." *American Journal of Forensic Medicine and Pathology* 21, no. 1 (2000): 39–52.

Ortiz, Fernando. "Del fenómeno social de la transculturación y de su importancia en Cuba." *Revista Bimestre Cubana* 46, no. 2 (1940).

Ortiz, Fernando. *El hampa Afro-Cubana: Los Negros brujos*. Madrid: Editoria-America, 1906.

Otero, Solimar. *Archives of Conjure: Stories of the Dead in Afrolatinx Cultures*. New York: Columbia University Press, 2020.

Owens, Deirdre Cooper. *Medical Bondage: Race, Gender, and the Origins of American Gynecology*. Athens: University of Georgia Press, 2017.

Owens, Deirdre Cooper. Review of *The Politics of Reproduction: Race, Medicine, and Fertility in the Age of Abolition*, by Katherine Paugh. *Bulletin of the History of Medicine* 92, no. 4 (2018): 704–5.

Pappademos, Melina. "The Cuban Race War of 1912 and the Uses and Transgressions of Blackness." In *Breaking the Chains, Forging the Nation: The Afro-Cuban Fight* for *Freedom and Equality, 1812–1912*, edited by Aisha Finch, 248–71. Baton Rouge: Louisiana State University Press, 2019.

Paradis, Cheryl M., and Steven Friedman. "Panic Disorder in African-Americans: Symptomatology and Isolated Sleep Paralysis." *Culture, Medicine and Psychiatry* 26, no. 2 (2002): 179–98.

Paradis, Cheryl M., and Steven Friedman. "Sleep Paralysis in African Americans with Panic Disorder." *Transcultural Psychiatry* 42, no. 1 (2005): 123–34.

Park, Yoon Soo, Lars Konge, and Anthony R. Artino. "The Positivism Paradigm of Research." *Academic Medicine* 95, no. 5 (2020): 690–94.

Pastrak, Mila, Alaa Abd-Elsayed, Frederick Ma, Bruce Vrooman, and Ognjen Visnje-vac. "Systematic Review of the Use of Intravenous Ketamine for Fibromyalgia." *Ochsner Journal* 21, no. 4 (Winter 2021): 387–94.

Pastrana, Antonio. "Black Identity Constructions: Inserting Intersectionality, Bisexu-ality, and (Afro-)Latinidad into Black Studies." *Journal of African American Studies* 8, no. 1 (2004): 74–89.

Peña, Susana. "'Obvious Gays' and the State Gaze: Cuban Gay Visibility and US Immigration Policy during the 1980 Mariel Boatlift." *Journal of the History of Sexuality* 16, no. 3 (2007): 482–514.

Pérez, Kimberlee. "Embodying 'I Can't Breathe': Tensions and Possibilities between Appropriation and Coalition." In *Precarious Rhetorics*, edited by Wendy Hesford, Adela Licona, and Christa Teston, 82–102. Columbus: Ohio State University Press, 2018.

Pérez, Laura E. *Chicana Art: The Politics of Spiritual and Aesthetic Alterities*. Durham, NC: Duke University Press, 2007.

Pérez, Louis A., Jr. "Cubans in Tampa: From Exiles to Immigrants, 1892–1901." *Florida Historical Quarterly* 57, no. 2 (1978): 129–40.

Perkins, Dedrick K. "50 Shades of Slavery: Sexual Assault of Black Male Slaves in Antebellum America." Undergraduate paper, Department of History, University of Oklahoma, April 24, 2017.

Perkinson, Jim. "The Gift/Curse of Second Sight: Is Blackness a Shamanic Category in the Myth of America?" *History of Religions* 42, no. 1 (2002): 19–58.

Perry, Keisha-Khan Y. "The Groundings with My Sisters: Toward a Black Diasporic Feminist Agenda in the Americas." *Scholar and Feminist Online* 7, no. 2 (2009). http://sfonline.barnard.edu/africana/perry_01.htm.

Pierre, Jemima. "Growing Up Haitian in Black Miami: A Narrative in Three Acts." *Anthurium* 16, no. 1 (2020): 1–15.

Pierre, Jemima. "The Racial Vernaculars of Development: A View from West Africa." *American Anthropologist* 122, no. 1 (2020): 86–98.

Pinto, Andrew D. "Denaturalizing 'Natural' Disasters: Haiti's Earthquake and the Hu-manitarian Impulse." *Open Medicine* 4, no. 4 (2010): e193–e196. https://www.ncbi.nlm.nih.gov/pmc/articles/PMC3090106/.

Pistol, Rachel. "The Historical Presidency: From Truman to Trump—Presidents' Use and Abuse of the Incarceration of Japanese Americans." *Presidential Studies*

Quarterly 51, no. 2 (2021): 385–403. https://onlinelibrary.wiley.com/doi/full/10 .1111/psq.12695.

Portes, Alejandro, and Aaron Puhrmann. "A Bifurcated Enclave: The Economic Evolution of the Cuban and Cuban American Population of Metropolitan Miami." *Cuban Studies* 43 (2015): 40–63.

Portes, Alejandro, and Alex Stepick. *City on the Edge: The Transformation of Miami.* Berkeley: University of California Press, 1993.

Purvis, Dara E., and Melissa Blanco. "Police Sexual Violence: Police Brutality, #MeToo, and Masculinities." *California Law Review* 108 (2020). https://www .californialawreview.org/print/police-sexual-violence-police-brutality-metoo -and-masculinities.

Quijano, Anibal. "Coloniality of Power and Eurocentrism in Latin America." *International Sociology* 15, no. 2 (2000): 215–32.

Quinlan, Kathryn, Jess Palan, Sarah Murtada, and Christiane Dos Santos. "Excited Delirium: The Connection between George Floyd and Elijah McClain." *Bloomberg Law*, March 23, 2021. https://news.bloomberglaw.com/us-law-week /excited-delirium-the-connection-between-george-floyd-and-elijah-mcclain.

Rae, Khalisa. *Ghost in a Black Girl's Throat: Poems.* Pasadena, CA: Red Hen Press, 2021.

Ralph, Laurence. "Alibi: The Extralegal Force Embedded in the Law (United States)." In *Writing the World of Policing: The Difference Ethnography Makes*, edited by Didier Fassin, 248–68. Chicago: University of Chicago Press, 2017.

Ralph, Laurence. "The Logic of the Slave Patrol: The Fantasy of Black Predatory Violence and the Use of Force by the Police." *Palgrave Communications* 5 (2019): Article 130. https://www.nature.com/articles/s41599-019-0333-7.

Ralph, Laurence. *The Torture Letters: Reckoning with Police Violence.* Chicago: University of Chicago Press, 2020.

Ramsey, Kate. *The Spirits and the Law: Vodou and Power in Haiti.* Chicago: University of Chicago Press, 2011.

Razack, Sherene H. "Settler Colonialism, Policing and Racial Terror: The Police Shooting of Loreal Tsingine." *Feminist Legal Studies* 28, no. 1 (2020): 1–20.

Reardon, Jenny, and Kim TallBear, "'Your DNA Is Our History': Genomics, Anthropology, and the Construction of Whiteness as Property." *Current Anthropology* 53, no. S5 (2012): S233–45. https://www.journals.uchicago.edu/doi/10.1086/662629.

Redman, Melody. "Cocaine: What Is the Crack? A Brief History of the Use of Cocaine as an Anesthetic." *Anesthesia and Pain Medicine* 1, no. 2 (Fall 2011): 95–97.

Ritchie, Andrea J. *Invisible No More: Police Violence against Black Women and Women of Color.* Boston: Beacon, 2017.

Ritchie, Andrea J. "Say Her Name: What It Means to Center Black Women's Experiences of Police Violence." In *Who Do You Serve, Who Do You Protect? Police Violence and Resistance in the United States*, edited by Maya Schenwar, Joe Macaré, and Alana Yu-lan Price, 79–90. Chicago: Haymarket Books, 2016.

Roberts, Kodi A., ed. *Voodoo and Power: The Politics of Religion in New Orleans, 1881–1940.* Baton Rouge: Louisiana State University Press, 2015.

Rodriguez, Cheryl. "Mothering While Black: Feminist Thought on Maternal Loss, Mourning and Agency in the African Diaspora." *Transforming Anthropology* 24, no. 1 (2016): 61–69.

Rodríguez, Dylan. "Abolition as Praxis of Human Being: A Foreword." *Harvard Law Review* 132, no. 6 (2019): 1575–612.

Rodríguez, Dylan. "The Terms of Engagement: Warfare, White Locality, and Abolition." *Critical Sociology* 36, no. 1 (2010): 151–73.

Román, Miriam Jiménez, and Juan Flores, eds. *The Afro-Latin@ Reader: History and Culture in the United States*. Durham, NC: Duke University Press, 2010.

Román, Reinaldo L. "Ritual, Discourse, and Community in Cuban Santería: Speaking a Sacred World." *Caribbean Studies* 38, no. 2 (2010): 223–25.

Rosen, Hannah. *Terror in the Heart of Freedom: Citizenship, Sexual Violence, and the Meaning of Race in the Post-emancipation South*. Chapel Hill: University of North Carolina Press, 2009.

Ross, Michael A. "Voodoo, Religious Culture, and Racial Politics in Jim Crow New Orleans." Review of *Voodoo and Power: The Politics of Religion in New Orleans 1881–1940*, by Kodi A. Roberts. *Journal of the Gilded Age and Progressive Era* 16, no. 1 (2017): 117–18. https://doi.org/10.1017/S1537781416000621.

Ruttenber, A. James, Janet Lawler-Heavner, Ming Yin, Charles V. Wetli, W. Lee Hearn, and Deborah C. Mash. "Fatal Excited Delirium following Cocaine Use: Epidemiologic Findings Provide New Evidence for Mechanisms of Cocaine Toxicity." *Journal of Forensic Sciences* 42, no. 1 (1997): 25–31.

Ruttenber, A. James, Heath B. McAnally, and Charles V. Wetli. "Cocaine-Associated Rhabdomyolysis and Excited Delirium: Different Stages of the Same Syndrome." *American Journal of Forensic Medicine and Pathology* 20, no. 2 (1999): 120–27.

Saks, Elyn R. "Putting Patients at the Center of Restraints." *Southern California Review of Law and Social Justice* 21, no. 1 (Fall 2011): 1–17. https://gould.usc.edu/students/journals/rlsj/issues/assets/docs/volume21/Fall2011/1.Saks.pdf.

Saks, Elyn R. "The Use of Mechanical Restraints in Psychiatric Hospitals." *Yale Law Journal* 95 (1985): 1836–56. https://openyls.law.yale.edu/bitstream/handle/20.500.13051/16430/94_95YaleLJ1836_1985_1986_.pdf?sequence=2&isAllowed=y.

Sammond, Nicholas. *Birth of an Industry: Blackface Minstrelsy and the Rise of American Animation*. Durham, NC: Duke University Press, 2015.

Samuel, Robert, and Toluse Olorunnipa. *His Name Is George Floyd: One Man's Life and the Struggle for Racial Justice*. New York: Penguin, 2022.

Sandín, Lyn Di Iorio, and Richard Perez, eds. *Contemporary U.S. Latino/a Literary Criticism*. London: Palgrave Macmillan, 2007.

Sandoval, Mercedes Cros. "Santeria: Afro-Cuban Concepts of Disease and Its Treatment in Miami." *Journal of Operational Psychiatry* 8 (1977): 52–63.

Santa Ana, Otto. *Brown Tide Rising: Metaphors of Latinos in Contemporary American Public Discourse*. University of Texas Press, 2002.

Santos-Febres, Mayra. *Boat People*. Translated by Vanessa Pérez-Rosario. Phoenix, AZ: Cardboard House Press, 2021.

Sarma, Shohinee, Lisa Richardson, and John Neary. "One Hundred Years of Solitude: Underrepresentation of Indigenous and Minority Groups in Diabetes Trials." *Lancet Global Health* 10, no. 10 (2022). https://www.thelancet.com/journals/langlo/article/PIIS2214-109X(22)00356-4/fulltext.

Schenwar, Maya, Joe Macaré, and Alana Yu-lan Price, eds. *Who Do You Serve, Who Do You Protect? Police Violence and Resistance in the United States.* Chicago: Haymarket Books, 2016.

Scurich, Nicholas, and Richard S. John. "Constraints on Restraints: A Signal Detection Analysis of the Use of Mechanical Restraints on Adult Psychiatric Inpatients." *Southern California Review of Law and Social Justice* 21, no. 1 (Fall 2011): 75–108.

Sefa Dei, George J., and Cristina Jaimungal, eds. *Indigeneity and Decolonial Resistance: Alternatives to Colonial Thinking and Practice.* Gorham, ME: Myers Education Press, 2018.

Seigel, Micol. "The Dilemma of 'Racial Profiling': An Abolitionist Police History." *Contemporary Justice Review* 20, no. 4 (2017): 474–90.

Shamoo, Adil E. "Unethical Medical Treatment and Research in US Territories." *Accountability in Research* 30, no. 7 (2022): 516–29. https://doi.org/10.1080/08989621.2022.2030720.

Shange, Savannah. "#OurLivesMatter: Mapping an Abolitionist Anthropology." In *Progressive Dystopia: Abolition, Antiblackness, and Schooling in San Francisco,* 1–21. Durham, NC: Duke University Press, 2019. https://doi.org/10.1215/9781478007401-001.

Shank, Gregory. "Social Justice." *Peace Review* 26, no. 4 (2014): 520–24.

Sharpe, Christina. *In the Wake: On Blackness and Being.* Durham, NC: Duke University Press, 2016.

Shields, Lisa B. E., Cristin M. Rolf, and John C. Hunsaker III. "Sudden Death Due to Acute Cocaine Toxicity: Excited Delirium in a Body Packer." *Journal of Forensic Sciences* 60, no. 6 (2015): 1647–51.

Shortt, S. E. D. "Physicians and Psychics: The Anglo-American Medical Response to Spiritualism, 1870–1890." *Journal of the History of Medicine and Allied Sciences* 39, no. 3 (July 1984): 339–55.

Shull, Kristina. "Somos los Abandonados: Mariel Cuban Stories from Detention and Resisting the Carceral State." *Anthurium* 17, no. 2 (2021). https://anthurium.miami.edu/articles/10.33596/anth.445/.

Silvestri, Marisa. "Police Culture and Gender: Revisiting the 'Cult of Masculinity.'" *Policing: A Journal of Policy and Practice* 11, no. 3 (2017): 289–300.

Smith, Aidan. "Galvanizing Grief: Black Maternal Politics, Respectability, and the Pursuit of Elected Office." *Journal of Women, Politics and Policy* 43, no. 3 (2022): 347–62.

Smith, Christen A. "Facing the Dragon: Black Mothering, Sequelae, and Gendered Necropolitics in the Americas." *Transforming Anthropology* 24, no. 1 (2016): 31–48.

Soto-Vásquez, Arthur D., and Mariana Sánchez-Santos. "El Cabal, Vacunas, y Donald Trump: An Analysis of Spanish-Language Disinformation Leading Up to the

US Capitol Insurrection." *Cultural Studies—Critical Methodologies* 22, no. 5 (2022): 454–65.

Stepick, Alex, and Tareena Joubert. "We Don't Want No Goddamn Black Refugees! The Politics of Haitian Refugees in Florida." In *Immigrant Entrepreneurs and Immigrant Absorption in the United States and Israel*, edited by Ivan Light and Richard E. Isralowitz, 167–84. New York: Routledge, 2019.

Stuesse, Angela, and Mathew Coleman. "Automobility, Immobility, Altermobility: Surviving and Resisting the Intensification of Immigrant Policing." *City and Society* 26, no. 1 (2014): 51–72. https://anthrosource.onlinelibrary.wiley.com/doi /10.1111/ciso.12034.

Stumpf, Juliet. "The Crimmigration Crisis: Immigrants, Crime, and Sovereign Power." *American University Law Review* 56, no. 2 (2006): 367–419. https:// digitalcommons.wcl.american.edu/cgi/viewcontent.cgi?article=1274&context =aulr.

Sussman, Zoe. "Mechanical Restraints: Is This Your Idea of Therapy?" *Southern California Review of Law and Social Justice* 21, no. 1 (Fall 2011): 109–34. https:// weblaw.usc.edu/students/journals/rlsj/issues/assets/docs/volume21/Fall2011/5 .Sussman.pdf.

Taylor, Keeanga-Yamahtta. *From #BlackLivesMatter to Black Liberation*. Chicago: Haymarket Books, 2016.

Taylor, Keeanga-Yamahtta, ed. *How We Get Free: Black Feminism and the Combahee River Collective*. Chicago: Haymarket Books, 2017.

Terry, Karen J. "Child Sexual Abuse within the Catholic Church: A Review of Global Perspectives." *International Journal of Comparative and Applied Criminal Justice* 39, no. 2 (2015): 139–54.

Tetsuden, Kashima. *Judgment without Trial: Japanese American Imprisonment during World War II*. Seattle: University of Washington Press, 2011.

Thornton, John K. "African Dimensions of the Stono Rebellion." *American Historical Review* 96, no. 4 (1991): 1101–13.

Trouillot, Michel-Rolph. *Haiti: State against Nation*. New York: NYU Press, 1990.

Trouillot, Michel-Rolph. *Silencing the Past: Power and the Production of History*. Boston: Beacon, 2015.

Turner, Edith B. "The Reality of Spirits: A Tabooed or Permitted Field of Study?" *Anthropology of Consciousness* 4, no. 1 (1993): 9–12.

US Citizenship and Immigration Services. "Overview of INS History." USCIS History Office and Library, 2012. https://www.uscis.gov/sites/default/files/document /fact-sheets/INSHistory.pdf.

US Department of State, Office of International Religious Freedom. *2021 Report on International Religious Freedom: Cuba*. June 2, 2022. https://www.state.gov /reports/2021-report-on-international-religious-freedom/cuba/.

U.S. School Yearbooks, 1880–2012. Provo, UT: Ancestry.com Operations, Inc., 2010.

Villanueva, Nicholas, Jr. *The Lynching of Mexicans in the Texas Borderlands*. Albuquerque: University of New Mexico Press, 2017.

Villepastour, Amanda. *Ancient Text Messages of the Yorùbá Bàtá Drum: Cracking the Code.* Farnham, UK: Ashgate Publishing, 2010.

Volscho, Thomas W. "Sterilization Racism and Pan-ethnic Disparities of the Past Decade: The Continued Encroachment on Reproductive Rights." *Wicazo Sa Review* 25, no. 1 (2010): 17–31.

Walcott, Rinaldo. *On Property: Policing, Prisons, and the Call for Abolition.* Windsor, Ontario: Biblioasis, 2021.

Wall, Tyler. "The Police Invention of Humanity: Notes on the 'Thin Blue Line.'" *Crime, Media, Culture* 16, no. 3 (2020): 319–36.

Washington, Harriet A. *Medical Apartheid: The Dark History of Medical Experimentation on Black Americans from Colonial Times to the Present.* New York: Doubleday Books, 2006.

Washington, Teresa N. *The Architects of Existence: Àjé in Yorùbá Cosmology, Ontology, and Orature.* N.p.: Oya's Tornado, 2014.

Weheliye, Alexander G. "Pornotropes." *Journal of Visual Culture* 7, no. 1 (2008): 65–81.

Weisenfeld, Judith. *New World A-Coming: Black Religion and Racial Identity during the Great Migration.* New York: NYU Press, 2018.

Wetli, Charles V. Foreword to *Santería, the Religion: Faith, Rites, Magic,* edited by Migene González-Wippler, xi–xiv. 1989. Woodbury, MN: Llewellyn, 1994.

Wetli, Charles V., and Rafael Martinez. "Brujeria: Manifestations of Palo Mayombe in South Florida." *Journal of the Florida Medical Association* 70, no. 8 (1983): 629–34.

Wetli, Charles V., and Rafael Martinez. *Palo Mayome.* Report for the Division of Criminal Investigation, Investigative Analysis Bureau, Florida Department of Law Enforcement, September 1989.

Wetli, Charles V., and Rafael Martinez. "Tattoos among Cuban (Mariel) Criminals: A Cultural Analysis." Report submitted to the Dade/Miami Criminal Justice Council Office, 1986.

Wetli, Charles V., Deborah Mash, and Steven B. Karch. "Cocaine-Associated Agitated Delirium and the Neuroleptic Malignant Syndrome." *American Journal of Emergency Medicine* 14, no. 4 (1996): 425–28.

Wilkinson, Stephen. *Detective Fiction in Cuban Society and Culture.* Oxford: Peter Lang, 2006.

Williams, Patricia J. *The Alchemy of Race and Rights.* Cambridge, MA: Harvard University Press, 1991.

Williams, Rhaisa Kameela. "Toward a Theorization of Black Maternal Grief as Analytic." *Transforming Anthropology* 24, no. 1 (2016): 17–30.

Williamson, Terrion L. "Why Did They Die? On Combahee and the Serialization of Black Death." *Souls* 19, no. 3 (2017): 328–41.

Willoughby, Christopher D. E. "Running Away from Drapetomania: Samuel A. Cartwright, Medicine, and Race in the Antebellum South." *Journal of Southern History* 84, no. 3 (2018): 579–614.

Willoughby-Herard, Tiffany. "(Political) Anesthesia or (Political) Memory: The Combahee River Collective and the Death of Black Women in Custody." *Theory and Event* 21, no. 1 (2018): 259–81.

Wilson, John Paul, Kurt Hugenberg, and Nicholas O. Rule. "Racial Bias in Judgments of Physical Size and Formidability: From Size to Threat." *Journal of Personality and Social Psychology* 113, no. 1 (2017): 59–80.

Winburn, Allysha Powanda, Rafael Martinez, and Sarah Kiley Schoff. "Afro-Cuban Ritual Use of Human Remains: Medicolegal Considerations." *Journal of Forensic Identification* 67, no. 1 (2017): 1–30. https://ircommons.uwf.edu/esploro /outputs/99380090343306600.

Wirtz, Kristina. "Hazardous Waste: The Semiotics of Ritual Hygiene in Cuban Popular Religion." *Journal of the Royal Anthropological Institute* 15, no. 3 (2009): 476–501.

Wolff, Megan J. "The Myth of the Actuary: Life Insurance and Frederick L. Hoffman's Race Traits and Tendencies of the American Negro." Public Health Report 121, no. 1 (2006): 84–91. https://doi.org/10.1177/003335490612100115.

Wood, Amy Louise. *Lynching and Spectacle: Witnessing Racial Violence in America, 1890–1940*. Chapel Hill: University of North Carolina Press, 2011.

Wynter, Sylvia. "'No Humans Involved': An Open Letter to My Colleagues." In "Forum N.H.I. Knowledge for the 21st Century." Special issue, *Knowledge on Trial* 1, no. 1 (Fall 1994): 42–73. https://files.libcom.org/files/Wynter5.pdf.

Youé, Chris. "Sara Baartman: Inspection/Dissection/Resurrection." *Canadian Journal of African Studies* 41, no. 3 (2007): 559–67.

Index

Abakuá brotherhood, 36, 38, 85
abolition, 202–4, 269n39; "abolition democracy," 198; decolonial, 209; in medicine, 202–3
activism: Black feminist mobilizations, 55–56; spiritual, 4, 8, 185–86, 192, 228n6, 272n3
African American Policy Forum, 189
African religions: anti-African stereotypes about, 7, 36–38, 41–49, 115, 179; used to justify underdevelopment, 37, 234n26. *See also* Afro-Latiné religions
afrocubanismo movement, 40
Afro-Cuban refugees (Marielitos), 14–25; "boat people," as political category, 22, 24, 25, 125, 126; detention of in prisons, 19–23, 230n14; Haitians conflated with, 22, 24–25, 125; Mariel boatlift, 14–17, 22–23, 125, 182; news media criminalization of, 22, 35, 125, 231n30; prison siege by, 23, 231nn30–31; sponsorship required, 19, 22; "streetwise philosophy" attributed to, 35, 49, 51; and White Cuban exceptionalism, 19, 21–22, 24, 40, 230n21. *See also* Black and Brown people; tattoos
"Afro-Cuban Ritual Use" (Martinez), 114–15
"Afro-Cuban Santería among the Cuban-Americans in Dade County Florida: A Psycho-Cultural Approach" (Martinez), 17–18
Afro-Cuban Underworld: The Black Witches (*El hampa Afro-Cubana: Los Negros brujos*) (Ortiz), 67

Afro-Latiné, as term, 5, 228–29n10
Afro-Latiné religions: Abakuá brotherhood, 36, 38, 85; backlash against after Haitian Revolution, 126, 243n30; ceremonies held on behalf of Black men killed by police, 134–36, 137; Christian lumping together of, 92; healing process through, 4, 9–11, 44–45, 95–96, 115–16, 119, 134–36, 185–86, 192–93, 204–5; legal justice suits, 94, 98, 101; mental illness and pathologizing of, 67, 179; misinformation about spread by Wetli, 13, 14, 31, 82–86, 87, 112; origin of in survival mobilizations, 7; practitioners depicted as "Black witches," 67, 84–85, 110–11; primitiveness attributed to, 36–37, 86; spiritual mass (misa spiritual), 43–45; spiritual pathways (caminos), 209; systems of, 125–26; targeted by Satanic Panic, 91–94. *See also* African religions; criminalization of Afro-Latiné religions; orishas; Palo Monte; sacred objects; Santeria; spirits; vibrations
Aguirre, Jesse, 159
AIDS/HIV pandemic, 126–27
Àjé flying abilities, 193
Albizu Miranda, Carlos, 17
Alexander, Michelle, 176
Alexander, M. Jacqui, 185
All Souls Day (Dia de los Muertos), 58
Althusser, Helene, 212
Althusser, Louis, 211–12
Alves, Jaime Amparo, 165

American Civil Liberties Union (ACLU), 61, 103, 141

American Journal of Emergency Medicine, 68

American Medical Association (AMA), 180–81

Amnesty International, 140

ancestral interactivity, 18, 32; Palo Monte veneration of ancestors, 113–14; and possession, 186; proper deaths and burials, 135; through spiritual masses, 43–45. *See also* spirits

Anderson, Elijah, 49

Anderson, Keenan Darnell, 197, 203

animal rights groups, 100–102, 108–9

animal slaughter: "animal sacrifice" as legal category, 101; sensationalized, 98–101

anti-African stereotypes: of Afro-Latiné religions, 7, 36–37, 115, 179; central to White supremacy, 35–36, 38

antillanos (African diasporic networks), 185

Antioch, California, 3

Antoine, Patrick, 122

Anzaldúa, Gloria, 185–86, 228n6

Arará Dahomey peoples, 95

Arizona Republic, 158

Armed Forces Institute of Pathology, 160

arrivants, 233n7

Asians, 40, 149, 165, 174; Afro-Asian influences in Cuba, 37; Japanese internment in United States, 29–30; religious influences in United States, 89; as "yellow peril," 23, 231n35

asphyxia: in Florida serial murders, 48, 53; "positional," 71, 143, 158–59, 208; "restraint," 159, 199

Association of American College of Emergency Physicians (ACEP), 208

The Audacity of Hope (Obama), 191

A umba wa ori (Lukumi song of the dead), 134, 135–36, 207

Aurora, Colorado, City Council of, 180, 207

awan (cleaning ritual), 95–97

Axon: *See* Taser International

Azaka (spirit/lwa), 132

Baartman, Saartjie, 113

BADD (Bothered About Dungeons and Dragons), 92

Bakersfield, California, Satanic Panic wave, 90–91

Ball, Ricky, 145–48, 255nn56–57, 255n60

Bao, Shiping, 155

Barbara, Saint, 36, 37, 86

Bass, Ellen, 243n51

Bay Area Rapid Transit (BART), 137

Bayview district (San Francisco), 134

"beasts," Black people portrayed as, 38, 49, 70, 203

Beaty, Robert, 52

The Believers (horror film), 110

Bell, Luther, 65–66

"Bell's mania" ("excited catatonia"), 66, 67, 72

Berendson, Bernardus "Bernard" Martinus, 103

Beyoncé, 207

Bias, Leonard Kevin, 47–48, 68

Biden administration, 205

The Birth of a Nation (film), 129

Black, Barbara Ann, 48, 71

Black and Latiné communities, 4–7, 185–86, 193, 216; driving as high-risk activity in, 164; Latiné community in "the Mission," 1–2, 26–28; LGBTQ+ communities targeted, 93

Blackening, 179–80

"Black extinction hypothesis," 72

Black Feminist Statement (Combahee River Collective), 55

Black Lives Matter, 187, 207

"black magic/witchcraft" (brujería), 85, 86, 110–11, 114, 193–94; blamed for police brutality, 121

Black men: brains of executed Black men preserved, 85, 113, 143; ceremonies held for murder victims, 134–36, 137; "superhuman strength" attributed to cocaine use by, 68–70; "youths," Black and Brown men transformed into, 33–34. *See also* Black people; lynching; *individual Black and Brown people*

Black Panther Party for Self-Defense, 206–7

Black people: African "germ" of criminality theory, 71, 115; Black predator myth, 128–88; Colombians, 39–40; criminalized by racial science, 67; dehumanization of, 31, 148–49, 190; "Great Migration" (1910–70), 68; identified as "Negro" in Cuba, 38; Indigeneity mobilized against Blackness, 115; kept "in their place" by White violence, 129–30; medical experimentation on, 54–55, 113, 235–36n51; portrayed as "beasts," 38, 49, 70, 203; as "savage," 264n43, 264n45; discourse on windpipes, 148–49. *See also* classification systems, White; racism, institutionalized

Black Power movement, 206–7

Black women: Black feminist mobilizations, 55–56; blamed for own deaths, 46–55,

190–92; cased closed after medical examiner's report, 51–52; demands for accountability, 189; denial of trauma on victims' bodies, 48; hanging, 188–89; higher pain tolerance attributed to, 54–55; medical experimentation on, 54–55; as "medical superbodies," 48–49; not believed, 52–53, 187; as not capable of being raped, 47; obvious homicides, 48; not permitted to testify, 53–54; in police custody, 138–39, 187–90; racist tropes of as hypersexual, 46–47; reproductive policies aimed at, 191; #SayHerName campaign, 188–89; "serial killings" used to focus away from structural oppression, 56; "superhuman strength" attributed to, 48–49, 187, 236–37n18; trans, 4–5, 187, 190; used to reinforce White expertise, 55; Wetli's "sex-cocaine deaths" theory, 46–55, 65, 71, 75, 87. *See also* charges of murder; *individual Black and Brown people*

Bland, Sandra, 187–90
Blavatsky, Madame, 166
Boas, Franz, 106–7, 247n57
"boat people," 22, 24, 25, 125, 127
bodies, Black and Brown: breath denied to, 60, 138–39, 158–59, 164, 170–71, 173–74, 199–200; criminal sculpting of by medical examiners, 31–34, 37–38; of dead immigrants, used to categorize and criminalize, 19, 25, 31; as exhibition of for Whites, 113, 248n3; human remains, historical context of, 113; sterilization of, 191, 235–36n51; violation of by medical examiners, 32–34, 37–38; White doctors' gynecological experimentation on Black women, 54–55, 113; White spectatorship of violence against, 70, 121–22
body cameras: footage from, 60, 81, 146, 170–71, 188; Taser/Axon weapons software industry, 141
"boogeyman-type" tropes, 84–87, 111
"boosting" (theft), 63
Boucourt, Lucumi Domingo, 85
Boykin, Canyon, 146–47, 255nn56–57, 255n60
Brain Endowment Bank (University of Miami), 143, 254n46
Brazil, 165, 229n11
breath: in Afro-Latiné practices, 96, 200; denied to Black and Brown people, 60, 139, 158–59, 164, 170–71, 174, 199–200
Brown people: as "beasts," 38, 203; broad spectrum of skin colors, 40; dark Brown, 7, 22, 23, 25, 29, 33, 125; harassed by police, 2, 164; incarceration of entire generation of Black and Brown youth, 176; Latiné groups characterized as "Brown tides," 23; and Latino White supremacy, 7, 229n15; light brown, 7, 41; war on drugs and portrayals of, 39–40; Whiteness approximated by some Cubans, 41; "youths," Black and Brown men transformed into, 33–34. *See also* Afro-Cuban refugees (Marielitos); Asians; Black and Latiné communities; bodies, Black and Brown; classification systems, White; Indigenous people; Latiné communities; Latiné people
Brownsville, Texas, 109–10
Bruder, Thomas, 123, 127–28, 132, 249n20
brujería ("Black witchcraft"), 85, 110–11, 114; White alarmism about, 85
Bryant, Roy, 129–30
Burlington (VT) Daily Times, 86
Burns, Antoinette, 53, 71
Burton, Orisanmi, 163–64
Bush, George H. W., 109
Byrd, Jodi, 233n7

Cabey, Darrell, 162
Cabrera, Pedro Ortiz, 15
California Office of Criminal Justice Planning, 98
Candomblé, 229n11
cannibalism, Western, 113
Cardoso, Silvio, 101
Carlos Albizu University (Miami and San Juan), 16–17
Carlton, Sidney, 130
Carter, Jimmy, 15–16, 19–20
Carter, Leroy, Jr., 78, 82–84
Carter administration, 230n23
Cartwright, Samuel A., 130–31
Casar, Gregorio, 202
Castellanos, Israel, 38
Castro, Fidel, 15
Catholic Church, 104–7
caul, 198, 269n7
cause-of-death classifications, xi, 2–3, 162–63, 258–59n55; deceased not able to testify to, 72–73; excited delirium syndrome banned by state of California, 207–8; heart failure, attributions of, 47–48, 61, 64–65, 68, 71, 138–39, 142–43, 159, 162–63, 172; "unclassified," 64–65; "up and died," 2–3, 6, 61, 65. *See also* death; excited delirium syndrome

Center for Advanced Study in the Behavioral Sciences (CASBS, Stanford University), 77–78, 81–82, 117
Center for Intersectionality and Social Policy Studies, 189
Centers for Disease Control and Prevention (CDC), 51, 127
Changó (Alaàfin, deity), 36
Chapman, Kindra, 189
charges of murder, 3–4, 157; acquittals, 129–30, 154–55, 162, 208–9, 272n66; Black police, 197–98; convictions, 3, 201, 272n66; dismissal of case, 147; guilty verdicts, 3, 132; indictments, 147, 197–98. *See also* defenses; police violence
Chauvin, Derek, 60–61, 75, 142, 195, 269n13; Axon board member in defense of, 143–44; conviction of, 3, 201
CHIC (Cuban-Haitian Intake and Case-Management) Program, 20–21, 230n17
Child Protective Service (CPS), 90–91, 93–94
children: and "animal sacrifice," 100, 102; Black and Latiné in danger from police, 150; interrogated by CPS, 90–91; Lukumi "Sunday School," 150; used by enslavers to capture mothers, 236–37n18; witnesses to killings, 74, 134, 189
Chinese laborers, 37
Christian Brothers, 105, 106, 247n44
Christians, White: opposition to founding of Santeria church, 100; racist misinformation about African religions, 31, 36–37, 91–92; "suffering," notions of, 102
Christian saint "avatars," 36
Church of Lukumi Babalu Aye (Hialeah, Florida), 94, 95, 98–103
Church of Lukumi Babalu Aye v. City of Hialeah, 98–103
Cisneros, Rodolfo, Jr., 258–59n55
"civil death," 24–25
clairvoyance, 198
The Clansman (novel), 129
Clarke, Kamari, 148, 256n74
classification systems, White, 34; Asians as "yellow peril," 23, 231n35; "color lines" brought into being by White supremacy, 7, 40; colors, groups of people classified as, 23–25, 149, 229n13; in Cuba, 38–39; divisions among non-White groups fostered by, 41, 165, 198; Latiné groups characterized as "Brown tides," 23; racial blurring through

immigration policy, 24–25; "streetwise" attributed to Black and Brown people, 35, 49, 51. *See also* eugenics; racial science; racism, institutionalized
Clinton, Bill, 176
Clinton, Hillary, 175
Clinton administration, 24
cocaine, 263nn22–23; criminalization of, 68–69, 174; "negro cocaine 'fiends,'" rhetoric of, 68–72, 176, 240n40; racial history of, 174–75; use of implicated in excited delirium syndrome deaths, 65, 71–82; Wetli's "sex-cocaine deaths" theory, 46–54, 65, 71, 75, 87
"Cocaine-Associated Agitated Delirium and the Neuroleptic Malignant Syndrome" (Wetli et al.), 68
Coldrey, Barry, 105
Cold War, 15, 22, 40, 111
Collins, Joan, 88
Collins, Patricia Hill, 200
"Colombian Cocaine Rings," 39
Colombians, 39–40
colonialism, 77, 233n7, 267–68n54; African religions used as justification for, 36–37; spiritual activism against, 185–86
"color lines," 6–7, 40
colors, groups of people classified as, 23–25, 149, 229n13
Columbus, Mississippi, Police Department, 145
Combahee River Collective (CRC), 55–56, 73
Constanzo, Adolfo de Jesus, 109–13
Consumer Product and Safety Commission, 92
Contras (Nicaragua), 40
Cooper, Brittany, 189–90
Cooper, Jeremy, 171
copresences, 7–8, 9, 45, 74–75, 229n16, 245n1; una prueba (proof) from, 167. *See also* spirits
Cortéz, Julio Garcia, 107
The Courage to Heal (Bass and Davis), 243–44n51
COVID-19 pandemic, 95–96, 116, 195, 199; racist origin stories, 126
Crawford, Stephen, 79–81
Crenshaw, Kimberlé, 189
criminalization: and Black predator myth, 128–30; of cocaine, 68, 174; crimmigration, 231n34; dead Black and Brown bodies used

in, 19, 25, 31; of grieving families, 142, 177,
190; of Marielitos by Wetli, 30–32; of Marielitos in news media, 22, 35, 124–25, 231n30;
mass incarceration as result of, 176; medical
examiners, sculpting by, 31–35, 37–38; of
Puerto Ricans, 29–30; scholarship's role in,
31–32; segregation linked to, 50; of spiritualists, 66–67, 72
criminalization of Afro-Latiné religions, 2, 7,
8–9, 14, 114; in Cuba, 38, 84–85, 234n29;
"ritualistic crimes," 39; tattoos linked with,
31–36, 124–25, 178. *See also* Afro-Latiné
religions
crimmigration, 231n34
Cuba: and Cold War politics, 15; criminalization of Afro-Cuban religions, 38, 84–85,
234n29; homosexuality criminalized by, 35;
lynching in, 84–85. *See also* Afro-Cuban
refugees (Marielitos); Mariel boatlift
Cuban Adjustment Act (CAA, 1966), 22
"Cuban/Haitian Entrant" legal status, 22
"cult craze" of the 1960s and 1970s, 89
cultural relativism, 106–7
"culture of poverty" myth, 49
curanderos (healers), 115–16

Dade County coroner's office, 15
Dade-Miami Criminal Justice Council, 39,
83–84
Daily News (New York), 123
dance and performance rituals, 185
Davis, Angela, 202
Davis, Dána-Ain, 190
Davis, Joseph, 53
Davis, Laura, 243–44n51
"dead lead the way," (Lukumí saying), 198
death: "Black extinction hypothesis," 72; blame
of victim for, 34, 42, 49–55, 88, 154, 190–91;
"civil," 24–25; cocaine use implicated in
excited delirium syndrome, 65, 71–82;
conflated with detention, 32, 35, 38; due to
"positional asphyxia," 71, 143–44, 157–59,
208; guns planted by officers, 147; of homeless people, 75–76; medical defenses used
preemptively by police, 60–61; premature,
56–57, 62; restraint-related, 159; serialization
of Black death, 56–57, 88; "sudden" deaths
during medical experiments, 65–66; by
Taser, 9, 137–49, 156–58, 188; Wetli's "sex-
cocaine deaths" theory, 46–54, 65, 71, 75, 87.
See also cause-of-death classifications

Dechovitz, Susan, 53
decolonial abolition, 209
decolonial approaches, 118–19, 185–86, 205–6,
250–51n56
defenses: excited delirium syndrome used
preemptively as, 60–61, 140, 201; "feared
for their lives," 129, 130, 137, 208–9; medical,
60–61, 69–70. *See also* charges of murder;
Taser International
defunding of police movement, 201–2
dehumanization, 31, 148–49; of Black women,
190; "No Humans Involved" (NHI),
148–49
De Jesus, Petra, 141, 254n37
democracy, linked with Black captivity, 165,
202
Department of Justice, 23, 92–93, 244–45n81
dermatography, 38
de Szigethy, James Ridgway, 124–25
detention, unjust: 32, 35, 38; of Haitians,
24, 125, 230n23, 230–31n25; for HIV-
positive refugees, 127; of Japanese, 29–30;
of Marielitos, 19–23, 230n14. *See also*
incarceration
Dewar, Heather, 50–51
diagnoses: "Bell's mania" ("excited catatonia"),
66, 67, 72; instability of, 61, 72; mania,
medicalization of, 65–67; medio mania, 66,
72, 89; as racially biased conjectures, 73, 194;
and Satanic Panic, 90, 92; "symptoms," 72;
Wetli's "sex-cocaine deaths" theory, 46–54,
65, 71, 75, 87. *See also* excited delirium
syndrome
Diallo, Amadou, 128
diaspora, Black and Latiné, 5, 22, 113–14;
House/Full of Black Women, 185–86,
193–94; Puerto Rican, 27–28; resilience
of, 113–14; targeting of religious practices,
125–26; transnational dynamics; 7, 228n7;
Yorùbá, 36, 109
DiIulio, John J., Jr., 175–76
Di Maio, Dominick, 161–63, 165, 260n69,
259n71
Di Maio, Teresa, 155, 172, 259–60n68
Di Maio, Vincent, 153–63, 165, 172, 257nn14–15;
background of, 160–63; criticism of, 160–61;
*Writings: Excited Delirium Syndrome:
Cause of Death and Prevention*, 155–60, 164,
173, 258n60, 259n63, 259–60n68; *Forensic
Pathology* (Di Maio and Di Maio), 162;
Morgue: A Life in Death, 154, 156

Donham, Carolyn Bryant, 129–30
"Do Not Resuscitate" (DNR) order, 177
double consciousness, 198, 199
drapetomania (resistance to slavery patholo-
gized), 131
drug cartels, 109–11
drug politics: racialization of substances,
174–75; war on drugs, 39–40, 109–11, 175
drums, 134–35; *batá*, 135, 182, 192
Duarte, Jorge, 102–3
Du Bois, W. E. B., 198, 202, 209
Dungeons and Dragons, 92
Dynasty (television soap opera), 88

Edwards, Erica Marie, 50–51, 53–54
Eguardo (Egbado, Ewardo) lineage, 97
Egungun (collective spirits of the dead), 192,
194
Ehrlichman, John, 175
Einstein, Albert, 118–19, 166–67, 261n5,
262n7
Encinia, Brian, 188
Entrant Misdemeanant Placement and Program
Assessment Component (EMPAC), 39
Estrella, Amarilys, 24–25
ether, 166, 261n4
ethnoracial intimacies, 5, 7, 185
eugenics, 67, 70–71, 149; sterilization of Black
and Brown women, 191, 235–36n51
excited delirium syndrome: AMA rejection
of, 180–81; autopsy results show minimal
support for, 159; banned by state of California as cause of death, 207–8; brain tissue
samples used to substantiate, 142–43; as
business venture, 141, 143–44; code words
for, 173, 197; "discovered" by Wetli, 8–9,
34, 48, 65; gendered aspects of, 187; genetic
defect theory of, 68, 70, 103, 145, 176; and
medicalization of mania, 65; not recognized
by psychiatric organizations, 61; questioned
after death of Floyd, 140, 142; reliance on
police and paramedic accounts, 72–73;
roots in slavery, 131; "superhuman strength"
attributed to, 2–3, 60, 70–71; symptoms
attributed to, 127; trainings in, 141; used
preemptively as police defense, 60–61, 140,
201; used to defend Taser deaths, 9, 137–48,
155–58, 188; White supremacy as, 179–81,
198, 203
*Excited Delirium Syndrome: Cause of
Death and Prevention* (Di Maio and Di

Maio), 155–60, 164, 173, 259n60, 259n63,
259–60n68
"expertise": as business venture, 141, 143–44,
154–55, 253n34; experts as negative spirits,
149; industry of, 9, 141–44, 148, 169; used
to cover up deaths, 213
"extinction hypothesis," 72

Falzone, Todd, 143
families: grieving members criminalized by po-
lice, 142, 177, 190; not notified of incidents,
176–77; separation at US-Mexico border,
30; traditions of seen as threat, 28
Fanon, Frantz, 179–80, 264n45
Fatal Force database (*Washington Post*), 164
Federal Bureau of Investigation (FBI), 123,
127–28
Ferguson, Missouri, uprising, 186
"fetish," 179, 264n43
Fishbain, David A., 65
Fitch, Lynn, 147
Florida Department of Law Enforcement
Investigative Analysis Bureau, 112
Floyd, George Perry, 3–4, 59, 60–61, 64–65,
72, 75, 159, 195, 269n13; excited delirium
considered as defense, 140, 201; excited de-
lirium questioned after death of, 140, 142,
163, 207; protests in wake of killing, 195,
201–2, 204; and reexamination of McClain's
death, 180–81
Floyd, Larcenia "Cissy," 199–201, 268n13
Forensic Pathology (Di Maio and Di Maio),
162–63
"Formation" (Beyoncé), 206–7
Fox, Michael, 101–2
Francis, Pope, 77
Frank, Janice, 159
Franke, Katherine, 122, 128
Franscell, Ron, 156
Frazier, Darnella, 61
Freud, Sigmund, 179, 263n23, 264n43
Fruitvale Station (film), 137
Fulton, Sybrina, 201
Funte, Lisa, 147

Gaines, Korryn, 189
Gallant, Sandi, 82–83, 84, 86–89, 91, 93
Garcia, Alyssa, 21–22
Garner, Eric, 199, 269n15
Garza, Alicia, 187
Gates, Darryl, 148–49

generational traumas, 8–9, 75, 182, 186–87; intergenerational cycle of captivity and aggression, 165

gentrification, 26; killings due to, 191

Gibson, Mike, 207–8

Gilmore, Ruth Wilson, 203, 209

Giuliani, Rudolph, 125, 127, 132

Goetz, Bernhard, 161–62

Gongora, Luis, 206

Gonzalez, Mario, 164

González-Wippler, Migene, 99–100, 103, 105

Gordon, Avery, 227n3, 228n5

Gore, Tipper, 92

Grant, Oscar, 137

Gray, Sharminita, 48

Green, Matthew, 170–71

"Grievances and Greens" meeting, 186, 187, 194

Griffith, D. W., 129

Grissom, Leah, 173–74

Gross, Elliott, 161

Gross, Richard, 101

Gulf Cartel, 109–10

Gunder-James, Beverly, 53–54

Haiti, 232n44, 250n41; United States role in, 24, 126, 131

Haitian immigrants, 22, 24–25, 121, 125, 230n23, 230–31n25; AIDS as pretext for mandatory HIV testing, 126–27; conflated with Marielitos, 22, 24–25, 125; flight from Duvalier dictatorship, 125–26; litigation, 125

Haitian Revolution, 24–25, 126, 130, 131, 243n30

Harlem Renaissance, 40

Harvard University, 150–51

haunting, 7–9, 10, 14, 46, 58–59, 62, 227n3; "picking up" spirits, 43–45; and scholarship, 2, 9, 227n3, 272n4; skepticism as defense against, 167–68; by White science, 38. See also spirits

Hawai'i, sugarcane plantations, 29

heart failure, deaths in police presence attributed to, 47, 61, 64, 68, 71, 138–39, 142–43, 159, 162–63, 172

Herbert, Dan, 176

Herhold, Scott, 80

Hernandez-Llach, Israel, 142–43

Hialeah, Florida, City of, 98–103, 125

Hicks, Robert, 91–92

Hines, Laura, 146

Hinton, Elizabeth, 176

Hoffman, Fredrick, 72

Holliday, Billie, 122, 248n4

Holliday, George, 128–29

Holtzclaw, Daniel, 187

homeless people, deaths of, 75–76

homosexuality, stereotypes of, 32, 35, 123–24, 127. See also queer people of color

hospitals: "Do Not Resuscitate" (DNR) order, 177; "Full Code" order, 177; medical procedures violated by police, 177–78

House/Full of Black Women, 185–87, 193

Humane Society of the United States (HSUS), 101–2

Hurricane San Ciriaco, 29

"identity politics," pioneered by Combahee River Collective, 55

ideology, 211–12

Ile EgbadoSito, 205–6

ile (house-temple), 4, 63–64

Immigration and Naturalization Service (INS), 41, 125

immigration enforcement, 164. See also detention, unjust; incarceration

The Impact: Organized Crime Today; Report to the President and the Attorney General, 39

incarceration: crimmigration, 231n34; of entire generation of Black and Brown youth, 176; of Japanese immigrants, 29–30; police violence mirrored in, 163–64; solitary confinement, 190; "stop and frisk" strategy, 127; "Three Strikes and You're Out" law (California), 64. See also Afro-Cuban refugees (Marielitos); detention, unjust

Independent Office for Police Conduct (IOPC, UK), 140

Indigenous people, 269n9; curanderos (healers), 115–16; Indigeneity mobilized against Blackness, 115; murder of, 251n59; opposition to Serra's canonization, 77

Inoue, Miyako, 212

Inside Hook, 78, 79, 80

Institute for the Prevention of In-Custody Deaths (IPICD), 141, 143–44, 254n34

Institute of Police Technology and Management (University of North Florida), 91

International Protection of Assets Consultants Inc., 92

interpellation, 212

"intracolonial migrations," 230n22

Invisible No More Database, 188, 266n15

Ioanide, Paula, 128

McCarthy Brown, Karen, 132

McClain, Elijah, 170–72, 176–81, 201, 207–8, 271n57; reexamination of death of, 180–81, 207–8

McClain, Sheneen, 177, 190, 201, 209

McCoy, Tony, 147

McDonald, Laquan, 130, 176

McKenna, Natasha, 138–40, 187

McLean Asylum for the Insane, 65

Mechoso, Julio, 30–31

"Medical Examiner Collection of Comprehensive, Objective Medical Evidence for Conducted Electrical Weapons and Their Temporal Relationship to Sudden Arrest," 139–40

medical examiners: corruption allegations against, 161, 165; criminal sculpting by, 31–34, 37–38; institutionalized racism, role in, 156, 163–64, 165; intergenerational trauma, role in, 165; police violence and killings defended by, 9, 142–44, 148, 153–54, 164, 192; reliance on police and paramedic accounts, 72–73; Taser International's influence on, 140, 142, 158; White, violation of Black and Brown bodies, 32–34, 37–38. *See also* racial science

medical experiments: brains of executed Black men preserved, 85, 113, 143; historical continuity of brain and spinal cord tissue banks, 143; slave ship as a "floating laboratory," 85, 118, 248n1; "sudden" deaths during, 65–66; Tuskegee syphilis study, 235–36n51; Wetli in lineage of, 55; White doctors' gynecological experimentation on Black women, 54–55, 113. *See also* racial laboratory

medicalization: and eugenics, 67, 70–71, 149; of mania, 65–66; objective facts disregarded, 72; of police violence, 9, 143–44, 148–49, 171–74; "weaponization of medicine," 173

mediums, 43–45

Mehserle, Johannes, 137

mental illness, based on racist stereotypes of African religions, 67, 179

Mental Radio (Sinclair), 166–67

methamphetamine, 64–65

Mexican-American War, 65–66

Mexico, 109–11; drug cartels, 109–11; Indigeneity mobilized against Blackness, 115

Miami, Florida: as cultural "experiment," 21–22; murders of Black women, 46; seg-regated areas, 49–50. *See also* Afro-Cuban refugees (Marielitos)

Miami News, 50–51

Miami Orange Bowl processing facility, 19

Michel, Claude, 124

Michelle Remembers, 89, 90

Milam, J. W., 130

Miller, Ivor, 84–85

Minneapolis, Minnesota, 75

Minneapolis Police Department, 60

Minneapolis Police Department Office of Police Conduct Review (OPCR), 173, 180

minstrelsy, Afro-Latiné, 111

Mitchell, Roger, 208–9

Mittan, Garrett, 146–47

"model minority" status, 21–22

Molina, Victor, 85

Monaco, Lisa, 158

"monstrous races," Africans and Indigenous peoples as, 48–49

Mora, Selma, 153, 257n5

Morgan, Jennifer, 48–49, 236–37n18

Morgue: A Life in Death (Di Maio), 154, 156

mothers: activation of, 199, 200; fears for children, 2, 150–51; held responsible for social issues, 190, 200; litigation by, 206, 207; "radical Black mothering," 200, 209

Mothers of the Movement collective, 201

Movement for Black Lives (M4BL), 195, 203

Movement Ink, 195

Moynihan, Daniel Patrick, 190–91

MPD Involvement in Pre-Hospital Sedation, 173

Mullings, Leith, 163–64

multiple personality disorder (MPD)/dissociative identity disorder, 90, 91–92

National Association for the Advancement of Colored People (NAACP), 61

National Association of Medical Examiners, 61

National Crime Prevention Institute (University of Louisville), 92

National Rifle Association (NRA), 162

National Spiritualists Association (National Spiritualist Association of Churches), 67

neck chains, 163

"NEGRO COCAINE 'FIENDS' ARE A NEW SOUTHERN MENACE: Murder and Insanity Increasing among Lower Class Blacks because They Have Taken to 'Sniffing' Since Deprived of Whisky by Prohibition" (Williams), 68–72, 176

The Negro Family: The Case for National Action (Moynihan), 190–91

Nelson, Cliff, 53

Nelson, Eric, 201

neurological models of the mind, 67

news media: "cocaine-sex deaths" stories, 47, 50–51, 54, 68–69; complicity with police violence, 59, 60, 123–24, 132–33, 152; complicity with racist science, 47, 50, 86–87, 121; criminalization of Black and Brown people, 169, 175; lynching photographs published in, 70, 121–22; Marielitos criminalized by, 22, 35, 125, 231n30; racially charged language used by, 70, 125, 175; Reconstruction era, 131; and Satanic Panic, 86–87; 1900s racist reports in, 68–71; Wetli's campaigns, 47, 50–51, 54, 86–87, 169, 194

New York Police Department (NYPD): fear of protestors, 132; sexual assault and torture of Louima, 121–25, 127; shooting of unarmed man, 128

New York Times, 126–27; "How Paid Experts Help Exonerate Police after Deaths in Custody," 142, 144; racist reports on Black people and cocaine, 68–69

ngangas, prendas (sacred receptacles/spirit homes, for deceased family members), 109–14; bones said to be from sources other than United States, 112–13; confiscation of by police, 114; Constanzo's misinterpretation of, 109–10; human bones in, 15, 18, 84, 112–13

Nichols, Tyre, 197, 203

Nixon, Richard, 175

"noble savage" trope, 115

"No Humans Involved" (NHI), 148–49

Nyong'o, Tavia, 127

Oakland Police Department (OPD), 193–94

Obama, Barack, 155, 190–91

"observer effect," 183, 193–94, 208–9

"Occult Crime: A Law Enforcement Primer," 98, 103

Ogun, 200

O'Halloran, Ron, 159

On the Reproduction of Capitalism: Ideology and Ideological State Apparatuses (Althusser), 211–12

opium, administered during medical experiments, 65–66

orishas: Aganyu, 182; Babalu Aye (Azojuano), 94, 95–97; Changó (king Alaàfin), 36; genders of, 62, 97; Obatala, 62, 97; Ochun, 196; Olokun, 97; Oya, 200, 269n17; Yemaya, 184. spirits

Ortega, Jaime, 106

Ortiz, Fernando, 36, 67, 71, 115

Otero, Solimar, 212–13

Oyo Kingdom (West Africa), 36–37

paleros (Palo Monte priests), 84, 112

Palo Mayombe (Wetli and Martinez), 112

Palo Monte: Constanzo's misinterpretation of, 110, 113; historical and cultural truths of, 113–14; inherent criminality assumed, 114–15; nfumbe (spiritual essence), 114; paleros (priests), 84, 112; practiced by Marielitos, 36; prendas (sacred receptacles), 18; religious spirit-home (nganga), 15, 18, 84

Paoletti, Antonio, 78–79

paramedics, 160, 169, 170–74; "code words" as signals to, 173; collusion with police, 173, 180

Pazder, Lawrence, 89

Pearl Harbor attack, 29–30

People's Temple, 88, 112

Perry, Arlis, 78–81, 82–83

Perry, Bruce, 79

Peruvian Embassy (Havana), 15

PETA (People for the Ethical Treatment of Animals), 108–9

Peterson, Drew, 257n14

physics, 166–67, 183, 200

Pichardo, Ernesto, 94, 102, 108–9

Pierre, Jemima, 36–37, 126, 234n26

Polanco, Layleen Xtravaganza Cubilette, 190

police: ceremonies held on behalf of Black men killed by, 134–36, 137; "confused by their own gunfire," 191; Cuban detainees acting as during siege, 23; "cult cops," 86, 87–88, 124; "cult of masculinity," 248n7; defunding movement, 201–2; as embodiment of White supremacy, 198, 249n7; M4BL masks seized by, 195; medical procedures violated by, 177–78; Mexican, fear of Constanzo's compound, 111; misunderstandings of Afro-Caribbean religions, 85–86; paramedic collusion with, 173, 180; as possible killers, 83, 124; as practitioners of Santeria, 17, 83, 103, 109, 152; racial profiling by, 31–32, 140, 189; removed from schools, 202; sadistic pleasure derived from brutality, 122, 128; said to be bystanders in excited delirium syndrome deaths, 2–3; Santeria trainings for, 14, 17, 18–19, 108–9; sex trafficking involvement, 193–94

police violence: African religions used as justification for, 121; "black magic" blamed for, 121; bonding through violence, 128; coverups by police, 123–24, 127–28, 142; defense of by Wetli, 71–72, 142, 145–46; justified by tattoo research, 38; medical examiners' role in whitewashing, 9, 142–43, 148, 192; medicalization of, 9, 143–44, 148–49; medical term to exonerate sought, 143–44; news media's complicity with, 59, 60, 123–24, 132–33; pandemic of, 197; profit to Axon/Taser from, 141; and sexual arousal, 122, 127; types of, 3–4, 9, 71, 121, 144, 158; video recordings of, 61, 128–29, 130, 134, 138–39, 141–42, 159; "voodoo" spells as justification for, 124, 133. See also charges of murder

political pronouncements, as storytelling, 40–41

Portes, Alejandro, 22

"positional asphyxia," 71, 143–44, 157–59, 208

positivism, 118, 156, 167, 269n9; alternatives to, 193, 198

possession, spiritual, 186

Poulson, Jason, 173–74

primitiveness, attributed to Afro-Latiné religions, 36–37, 86

probable cause, 170

Proby, Michelle, 89

psychoanalysis, 179

psychologists: medicalization of, 67; surge in practitioners, 90

Puerto Ricans, 26–27, 233n2, 233n4; on "Big Five" sugarcane plantations, 29; sterilization of, 191, 235n51

queer people of color, 4, 55–56, 185, 205–6; wrongly convicted of "satanic related" sexual abuse, 93. See also homosexuality, stereotypes of

Quinto, Angelo, 3

The Race Traits and Tendencies of the American Negro (Hoffman), 72

racial laboratory, 115, 133, 148, 190, 209; excited delirium as White gaze of, 181; slave ship as "floating laboratory," 118. See also medical experiments

racial profiling, 31–32, 189; "stop and frisk" strategy, 127, 271n59; Taser use as, 140

racial science, 32–34, 37–39, 53, 72, 110; criminalization of Black people, 67; infantilization by, 33–34; news media's complicity with, 47, 50, 87, 121; and positivism, 118, 156; social evolutionism, 38–39; as Western cannibalism, 113; White racial fantasy sanitized by, 181. See also medical examiners; scholarship

racism, institutionalized: colors, groups of people classified as, 23–25, 149, 229n13; and "expert witnessing," 148–49; ignored by Moynihan, 190–91; long-term health consequences of, 163–64; role of medical examiners in, 156, 163–64, 165; role of racial laboratory in, 115. See also classification systems, White

Rae, Khalisa, 1

Ralph, Laurence, 129

Rancho Santa Elena murders. See Matamoros, Mexico, (Rancho Santa Elena) murders

Reagan, Ronald, 89–90, 109

Reagan administration, 22; Haitians interdicted by, 125, 230–31n25; use of rumors as data, 39–40

Reconstruction period, 68, 131

A Red Record: Tabulated Statistics and Alleged Causes of Lynchings in the United States, 1892–1893–1894 (Wells), 70

reform agendas, 203

Refugee Act (1980), 22

la Regla de la Ocha (Rule of Ocha). See Santeria

Rent, Tiffany, 188

reparations, 24, 195

reproductive policies, 191

restraints, 159, 170–74; as intimate violence, 164; ketamine, 160, 171–74; restraint asphyxia, 159, 199

Reuters, 140, 253n9

Reyes Borás, Juana "Niti," 28, 58

Rikers Island, 190

Ritchie, Andrea, 188, 266n15

Roche y Monteagudo, Rafael, 38

Rodriguez, Dylan, 40–41

Roedema, Randy, 170–71, 272n66

Roman, Agustin, 231n30

Rosenblatt, Jason, 170

rumors, presented as data, 39–40

trauma: effect of *batá* drums on, 135; gen-
erational, 8–9, 75, 182, 186–87; scholars
affected by, 2, 9; spiritual baths (*baños*) for
grieving Black and Brown people, 196
Trouillot, Michel-Rolph, 131
Trump, Donald, 147
Trump administration, 30, 205
Tsingine, Loreal, 251n59
Turner, Edith, 269n9
Tuton, Andrew, 157
Tuttle, Steve, 141

uncanny sense of connection, 206–7
United States: afrocubanismo movement, 40;
Afro-Cubans excluded from, 40–41; AIDS
as pretext for mandating HIV tests, 126–27;
Asians, attacks against, 126; Blackening
by, 24; colors, groups of people classified
as, 23–25, 149, 229n13; criminalization of
Black and Brown people, 29–30; Haiti,
role in, 24, 126, 131; racialization practices,
22, 23; transatlantic slave trade, role in, 24;
undocumented people targeted by, 164;
US-Mexico border, 23, 109–10; war on
drugs, 39–40, 109; White Cuban exceptionalism, 19, 21–22, 24, 40–41, 230n21. *See also*
Afro-Cuban refugees (Marielitos); Mariel
boatlift
United States Penitentiary (Atlanta, Georgia),
19–20, 31–32
United States Penitentiary (Lompoc, California), 19–20, 230n14

Valenzuela, Antonio, 156–57, 159
Van Dyke, Jason, 130, 176
Varela Zequiera, Eduardo, 85
Velasquez-Aguilu, Lola, 199
vibrations, 44, 134–35, 166; ether, 166, 261n4;
"observer effect," 183, 193; shifting, 135,
192–94, 200, 209
victims: blamed for own deaths, 10, 34, 42,
46–51, 53, 55, 57, 88, 154, 190–92, 213; White
fears eased by blaming of, 51–52
video games, anti-satanic conspiracies about,
92
video recordings of police violence, 61, 128–29,
130, 134, 138–39, 141–42, 159, 188
violence: restraints as intimate, 164; sexual
assault as form of race-based terror, 127–28;
sexual violence by Whites linked with
lynching, 69–70

Violent Crime Control and Law Enforcement
Act (1994), 176
Vodou religions, 121, 124–27, 243n30, 250n41;
"voodoo," accusations of, 124–25, 131–32, 133
Vodun religion, 126
Volpe, Justin, 122–25, 127–28, 132
Volpe, Robert, 124

Walker, Adrian, 50–51
Walker, Kenneth, 191, 192
Wallace, Alfred Russel, 66
war on drugs, US, 39–40, 109–11, 175
"war on poverty," 176
Washington Post, 164
Weheliye, Alexander, 248n5
Wells, Ida B., 69–70, 240n47
Wesolowski, Sergeant, 53
West, Don, 153–54
Wetli, Charles Joseph, 103–4
Wetli, Charles Victor: animal slaughter
defended by, 100–102; asphyxia rejected by,
48, 71; career trajectory, 16; as chief medical
examiner for Suffolk County, Long Island,
139, 144; "cocaine-sex deaths" manufactured
by, 46–54, 65, 71, 75, 160; collection of bodies and artifacts, 13–15, 19, 31–33, 37–38, 46,
86, 112–13; criminalization of Marielitos by,
30–32; death of, 96–97, 148; defense of police violence, 71–72, 142, 145–46; as deputy
chief medical examiner for Dade County, 15,
65; early 1900s racist news reports cited by,
68, 70–71; eugenicist beliefs of, 71, 103, 145,
176; "excited delirium" "discovered" by, 8–9,
34, 47–48, 65; as "expert" on Afro-Cuban
religions, 10–11, 39, 78, 82–84; as expert
witness for Church of Lukumi Babalu Aye,
98–101; as expert witness for Taser, 139–40;
as expert witness in Boykin case, 147; exposure of faulty theories of, 52–53, 67; "genetic
defect" theory of, 103, 145; German Catholic background of, 103–5, 246n32; haunting
of Martinez by, 96–98; influence in law
enforcement community, 85–86; Jezebel
trope used by, 54; law enforcement trainings
in 1990s, 103, 108; in lineage of medical
experimentation, 55; media campaigns, 47,
50–51, 54, 86–87, 169, 194; misinformation on Afro-Cuban religions spread by,
13–14, 82–87, 112; "negro cocaine 'fiends'"
rhetoric as source of theories, 68–72, 176;
in networks of experts, 9, 91, 143–44, 181;

patterns in racist science of, 42, 87, 144–45, 169; photographs in collection as key to "expertise," 86–87; possible attempts to undo racist stereotypes, 98–100, 110, 139, 148; power dynamic with Martinez, 41–42; and Satanic Panic, 79–80; as self-made "expert," 11, 54–55, 86–87, 99; and TWA Flight 800 case, 144–46, 148; and US-Mexico border issues, 110; *Writings:* "Cocaine-Associated Agitated Delirium and the Neuroleptic Malignant Syndrome," 68; foreword to González-Wippler's book, 99–100, 103, 105; *Palo Mayombe* (with Martinez), 112; "Tattoos among Cuban (Mariel) Criminals: A Cultural Analysis" (with Martinez), 39, 83–84; "Tattoos of the Marielitos" (with Martinez), 31–38, 41

Wetli, Elred Joseph (Brother Elred), 104–5
Wetzel, Bill, 101
Whiteness: approximated by some non-White Cubans, 41; Latinidad conflated with, 7, 229n15; political pronouncements as storytelling, 40–41; and spatial entitlement, 41; White Cuban exceptionalism, 19, 21–22, 24, 40, 230n21

Whites: Black and Brown bodies as exhibition for, 113, 248n3; Constanzo's logics, 109–11; fear of Black people used as justification for violence, 129–32, 162; as in need of protection, 41, 70–71, 85, 89, 128; behavior for based on racist stereotypes, 179; paranoia of, 129; split racial fantasy of, 179–80

White supremacy: Anglo, 7; anti-African stereotypes central to, 35–37, 38; embodied by Black and Brown police, 198; as excited delirium syndrome, 179–81, 198, 203; "exorcising" ether of, 116; and "expert witnessing," 148–49; Latino, 7, 229n15; lynching used to uphold, 70, 129–30; perpetual morphing of, 165; police as embodiment of, 198, 249n7; sexual assault used to reinforce, 127–28; spatial entitlement, 41

Wiese, Thomas, 122, 132, 249n9
Williams, Charles Henry, 52–54, 187
Williams, Edward Huntington, 68–71, 240nn40–41
Williams, Patricia, 227–28n3
Williamson, Terrion L., 56–57
women, White, medicalization of, 66–67
Woods, Amy Louise, 70
Woods, Gwendolyn, 206, 207
Woods, Mario, 134–35, 141, 206–7, 252n1
Woodyard, Nathan, 170, 208
Wunderly, Clint, 51–52
Wynter, Sylvia, 149

"yellow peril," 23, 231n35
Yorùbá practices, 109, 192
"youths," Black and Brown men transformed into, 33–34

Zimmerman, George, 152–56, 162, 257n5, 257n15
Zoila (child murder victim), 85

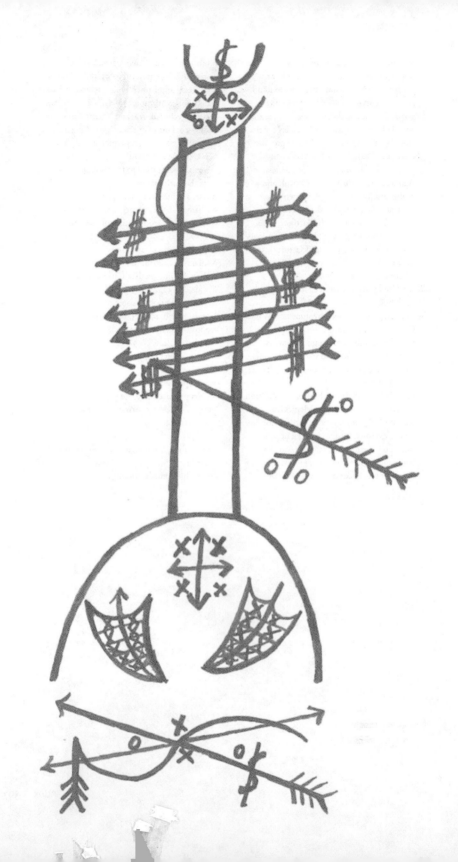